QUARTET ENCOUNTERS

SELECTED LETTERS 1902–1926

'By will-power and concentration, a sense of which is immanent in all his letters, as if some great quiet animal were crouching there, Rilke made himself into a great European genius, probably the last of the breed. And it was a very special breed. The almost mystical cosmopolitanism of those days, the first fated fourteen years of our century, might make us weep for the feeling they still give of a vanished age of culture, now almost inconceivably remote; perhaps not a golden but a silver age, as the Russian poetess Akhmatova herself described it, but an age in which for poets and artists there seemed to be no national or linguistic boundaries.'

From the Introduction by John Bayley

RAINER MARIA RILKE

Rilke is perhaps the most famous of all twentieth-century European poets. He was born in Prague in 1875 but much of his life is characterized by a restless wandering which brought him into contact with some of the greatest figures of the age, among them Lou Andreas-Salomé, Tolstoy, Rodin and Cézanne. He died in Switzerland in 1926.

RAINER MARIA RILKE

Selected Letters 1902–1926

Translated from the German by
R.F.C. HULL
With an Introduction by
JOHN BAYLEY

Quartet Books London New York

Published by Quartet Books Limited 1988
A member of the Namara Group
27/29 Goodge Street, London W1P 1FD

British Library Cataloguing in Publication Data

Rilke, Rainer Maria
Selected letters; and Letters to a young poet.—
(Quartet encounters).
1. Rilke, Rainer Maria—Biography
2. Authors, German—20th century—Biography
I. Title II. Rilke, Rainer Maria. Letters to a young poet III. Ausgewählte Briefe. *English*
831'.912 PT2635.I65Z/

ISBN 0-7043-0041-9

Reproduced, printed and bound in Great Britain
by The Camelot Press plc, Southampton

" Only the very great are artists in that strict sense, which alone is true : that art has become a way of life for them. All the others, all of us who only occupy ourselves with art, meet on the same long road and greet each other in the same silent hope and yearn for the same distant mastery. . . ."

—R. M. Rilke.

" Lo ! here is he whom in childhood I dedicated to my altars. This is he that once I made my darling. Him I led astray, him I beguiled ; and from heaven I stole away his young heart to mine. Through me did he become idolatrous ; and through me it was, by languishing desires, that he worshipped the worm, and prayed to the wormy grave. Holy was the grave to him ; lovely was its darkness ; saintly its corruption. Him, this young idolater, I have seasoned for thee, dear gentle Sister of Sighs ! Do thou take him to *thy* heart, and season him for our dreadful sister. And thou," — turning to the *Mater Tenebrarum*, she said, " wicked sister, that temptest and hatest, do thou take him from *her*. See that thy sceptre lie heavy on his head. Suffer not woman and her tenderness to sit near him in his darkness. Banish the frailties of hope ; wither the relenting of love ; scorch the fountain of tears ; curse him as only *thou* canst curse. So shall he be accomplished in the furnace ; so shall he see things that ought *not* to be seen, sights that are abominable, and secrets that are unutterable. So shall he read elder truths, sad truths, grand truths, fearful truths. So shall he rise again *before* he dies. And so shall our commission be accomplished which from God we had, — to plague his heart until we had unfolded the capacities of his spirit."—Thomas de Quincey, *Suspiria de Profundis*.

CONTENTS

TRANSLATOR'S NOTE

WITH two exceptions [1] this selection is made exclusively from the five volumes of letters published by the *Inselverlag* up to 1935, covering the period 1902 to 1926. Those acquainted with the letters in German will remark, therefore, that of the fifteen miscellaneous volumes published so far only a third has been used, and they may complain that such a limited selectiveness must result more in an anthology than a true selection. My restriction to so narrow a field is due partly to the peculiar nature of the German editions and partly to a personal idiosyncrasy which, I hope, will not be considered unwarrantable. I can best explain it by saying that I wanted the selection to give the impression of something complete, with a definite beginning and end and unbroken continuity between. In order to achieve this chronological unity I had to disregard that other principle of selection on which the German editors sometimes, but by no means consistently, worked — namely, that of grouping according to particular correspondents. There is, however, much to be said for isolating the series of letters to Anton Kippenberg and to Rodin, also the better-known series *An eine junge Frau* and *An einen jungen Dichter* [2]; they are in themselves unities and I have felt that they should be reproduced in their entirety, if at all. As space was limited, it was not possible to include them in the present selection.

This accounts for all but three of the volumes I have left unrepresented. These, published in 1939 and covering the years 1892 to 1914, duplicate the bulk of the material contained in the first four volumes published earlier (which they were intended to supplant), the additions being in the main confined to the period between 1892 and 1899. It is here that my concern for a " definite beginning " has made itself felt. Although it was at this time that Rilke twice visited Russia, these visits,

1 The opening letter, and the "worker-letter" (pp. 337–346) from *Über Gott*.

2 An English translation by Reginald Snell appears as Part Four of the present volume (see p. 405).

which he regarded all his life as of profound significance, do not constitute a "beginning" in the temporal or narrative sense; a crisis they were indeed, but a purely spiritual one, whose effects are shown more worthily and more legitimately in the poetry that stemmed direct from the Russian experience — the *Stundenbuch*, for instance — than in any of the rather juvenile and helpless letters written at the time. Further, Rilke's vision of Russia was almost neurotic in its intense subjectivity; he saw everything through a haze of poetic euphoria, and the "Holy Russia" of his vision has a remoteness from the realities of the Tsarist yesterday — let alone the Soviet today — that must strike us as positively bizarre. To begin a book with a fantasy of this sort would do but scant justice to Rilke's innate good sense. A genuine and more concrete beginning is rather to be found in Rilke's visit to Paris ten years after the first published letters, for a new life was begun with the disciplines he imposed on himself under the influence of Rodin, who more than anything or anybody else taught him to look outwards before looking in.

If, then, my concern for chronological and dramatic unity has impaired the scope of this selection, I must beg indulgence of the reader, asking him to remember that the reduction of some 2000 pages to a bare 400 — generous though this be in war-time conditions — is a task that leads easily to sins of omission.

A word must be said about the mangled and lacunary state of many of the letters. In most instances I have not been responsible for these deletions, which were made by the German editors. In view of the relative scarcity of purely autobiographical data, to which Professor Butler alludes in her introduction, it is logical to suppose that not all the excised passages contained repetitious matter or uninteresting and irrelevant references. To judge by certain "unexpurgated" letters, we must conclude that the editors have seen fit, in the interests of the hagiographical legend which surrounds Rilke, to suppress, chiefly in the early letters, a good deal of information which would have thrown a revealing light on Rilke the man — husband, father and citizen — as distinct from Rilke the poet. A strong suspicion remains that they have straightened out such human quirks and convolutions as would have distorted the "pure line" Rilke's genius was bent on describing. At the same time, his actual life so nearly corresponded with what his ideal of a poet's life should be, that it would be unwise to assume, in the many lacunae, the emergence of a character greatly at odds with the portrait which has survived the scrupulous care of his German editors.

Finally, I would like to thank the many friends who have helped me in this translation. Their influence has been so continuous, so unconscious and so variously compacted that it does not permit in all cases of individual acknowledgement. Faced with such a massive obligation, I can only acknowledge the most signal help, and this came from Major Alan Crick, who devoted his rare leisure and scholarship to the elucidation of doubtful passages and the finding of right words ; from Dr. Leonard Forster, whose sharp insight saved me from many a grammatical calamity ; from the early criticism of Flight-Lieutenant Peter van Rood ; from the encouragement and advice of Professor E. M. Butler, and always, in ways seen and unseen, from the ministering presence of

J,

to whom this book is dedicated.

R. F. C. HULL

SWANBOURNE, *June* 1944

INTRODUCTION

By will-power and concentration, a sense of which is immanent in all his letters, as if some great quiet animal were crouching there, Rilke made himself into a great European genius, probably the last of the breed. And it was a very special breed. The almost mystic cosmopolitanism of those days, the first fated fourteen years of our century, might make us weep for the feeling they still give of a vanished age of culture, now almost inconceivably remote; perhaps not a golden but a silver age, as the Russian poetess Akhmatova herself described it, but an age in which for poets and artists there seemed to be no national or linguistic boundaries. Another Russian poet, Marina Tsvetaeva, a passionate admirer of Rilke, with whom she conducted after the war what was virtually on her side an adoring love correspondence, put the matter like this.

> No language is the mother tongue. Writing poetry is rewriting it. A poet may write in French: he cannot be 'a French poet' – that's ludicrous. The reason one becomes a poet is to avoid being French, Russian, etc. in order to be everything . . . Yet every language has something that belongs to it alone, that *is* it . . .

Tsvetaeva was enthusing about the book of poems in French which Rilke had just published, entitled *Vergers*. She herself was writing to Rilke in German. Before the war he had made two visits to Russia, and had learnt the language so as to be able to write poems in it, poems expressing his reverence for the language and spirit of Russia, and his sense of its landscape and its people. On his second visit, in 1900, he was accompanied and looked after by that remarkable woman Lou Andreas-Salomé, in her youth the friend of Freud and of Nietzsche, to whom he was to write so many eloquent letters, and who was for him, when he was young, both a mother and a mistress figure. Always down to earth, and herself a native speaker, she memorably observed of Rilke's poems in Russian that 'though the grammar is pretty awful they are still somehow mysteriously poetic'. In his poetic memoir, *Safe Conduct*, which he dedicated to the memory of Rilke, Pasternak recalled the moment of meeting him at the railway station in Moscow, and how 'though I knew the language well I had never heard German spoken as he spoke it'. Like Hölderlin before him, Rilke indeed expressed in his poetry the genius of the German language – the something that *is* it – and his letters too have the same inimitable and personal *sprachgefühl*. But at the same time his letters breathe the most complete European spirit, which reaches out to the reader through the medium of any language.

The spirit of that civilization may have had its affected side. In reaction against what he felt to be its preciosity the poet John Berryman wrote that 'Rilke was a jerk'. A philistine today might well feel so, and poets have to react against their predecessors by pretending, if need be, to be philistines. But the more one reads Rilke's letters the less the charge of any kind of affectation seems relevant. Consider what he wrote to his friends Karl and Elisabeth von der Heydt in 1914, just after the war began, at a time when he himself had been conscripted into the reserve.

> The only thing we can work for now is the survival of the soul: distress and disaster are perhaps no more prevalent than before, only more tangible, more active, more visible. For the misery in which mankind has lived daily since the beginning of time cannot really be increased by any contingency.

There is a detachment in that, as well as a kind of unsentimental moral courage, which was almost unheard of at the time. Such a steadfast adherence to the values and the sanctity that could be won by the personal self was to have its own kind of reward. No wonder that Marina Tsvetaeva was to insist with great vehemence that the legendary status accorded to Rilke in the post-war years was owed to him because of the way his poetry had created a world of inner reality and inner values. Revolution had brought its own version of spiritual togetherness, which is still invoked in its context today, though less often by poets and artists. At that time the aspirations of socialism, or fascism, had been greeted by poets like Blok and Pound and Yeats with factitious fervour. Rilke stood alone, a baptist of solitude, and Tsvetaeva was no doubt right in claiming that European culture honoured him all the more for it.

We might well say, in fact, that Rilke is the truest believer in, and exponent of, that totality of culture which was the major aim of the Modernist movement. The young T.S. Eliot wrote poems in French, and he and Ezra Pound filled their work with quotation and sentence in different language, while Joyce and Proust showed how the inner world of the individual could also be shown forth, through a great work's limitlessly demanding medium, as the inner world of everyman.

It is here that Rilke shows his greatest and in a sense most effortless authority. For one thing his works do not quote and, as it were, patch in different languages: they enter into the universal genius of language as into the common essence of different flowers, fruits, landscapes and animals, all the 'blessed things' which his art explores, and which sanctify it even as it confers its blessing on them. The descriptions in his letters have this extraordinary power of conveying, as no other writer does, the sense of being, in natural colours and textures. Writing to Clara Rilke from Meudon-Val-Fleury in 1906, he notes the arrival of spring . . . 'since yesterday (after many, many radiant days warm as summer) rain has been falling, day and night, a mild, still rain, thick, gentle, and full, as though from the rose of a watering-can: *comme tombant d'un arrosoir*, one would like to say, because that sounds and falls darker and fuller.' There is never anything portentous about the raptness of these descriptions: indeed when they include human beings they can be full of a perceptive and benign humour, as when Rilke notes the way in which Mrs Bernard Shaw, 'a good, careful, and gently caring woman', seems to be 'frisking round her husband as the spring breeze frisks round a billy-goat'. The great sculptor Rodin, for whom Rilke was acting as secretary, was modelling Shaw's head at the time.

The sense of place, and Rilke's sensitivity to it, wanders through these letters like an unrestless but ever inquiring spirit. Russia, Paris, Toledo, Vienna, Rome, southern Sweden . . . they enchant us all by seeming to appear in their inner selves, as Rilke saw them, sometimes in simple and often homely guise, sometimes monumental, as in his vision of Paris scourged by the east wind . . . 'To the west, buffeted and thrust asunder, archipelagos of clouds, chains of islands, grey like the neck feathers and the breasts of water-birds in an ocean of cold, imperceptible blueness, remotely serene . . . houses shining in the blasts of sunlight, and far away in the background, in the blue dove-grey haze, more houses, more houses, clamped into planes, with rectilinear, quarry-like surfaces.'

This inscape is composed like a picture, but others cohere from the simplest recollection, like that of the curious calves who came clustering round the poet when he went bathing in a Swedish meadow. It was his Swedish friend, Ernst Norlind, who sent Rilke a poem he had written in German, which Rilke praises and copies out in his letter back . . . 'Have I not tried to write poems in Russian sometimes, in moments when some inner experience could only clarify itself in that form. And from time to time I am still compelled to write certain things in French in order to express them at all.' Even in German, 'how much I still feel myself a beginner'. And throughout the letters, as the war looms closer, there loom too the oncoming figures of the angels of the *Duino Elegies*, those creations of his mind for which the poet had all the time been patiently waiting, and of whose imminence he sometimes writes in prophetic words. *'Ah, when we waited for help from people – angels rose silently, crossed with one stride over the fallen heart.'*

The irreverent modern mind is sometimes exasperated by what seems Rilke's self-dedication, the seriousness with which he took himself. This is typical of the artistic attitudes of the time, and could indeed be highly mannered, but in Rilke it is not so, just as it is not so in Proust or Joyce, or in the art of Cézanne. Each of these geniuses had solved in his own way the old romantic dilemma: their concentration brought into coincidence the world and the self, the outside world and the personal vision as the unified work of art. It is this concentration that Rilke is exploring in his letters about Cézanne, letters which embody Cézanne's own forms and colours, colours which also seem a part of Rilke himself, of the words and the paper (he often wrote his poems on blue paper) and of his wife Clara to whom he was writing.

He remarks once that in an art gallery he usually finds the paintings less real than the people looking at them, but that in the Cézanne room at the *Salon d'Automne*, 'all of reality is on his side',

> . . . in this dense quilted blue of his, in his red and his shadowless green and the reddish black of his wine bottles. And the humbleness of all his objects: the apples are all cooking apples and the wine bottles belong in the roundly bulging pockets of an old coat.

This was the impression that he was afterwards to record in the lines of the *Neue Gedichte*.

> *Doch als du gingst, da brach in diese Bühne*
> *Ein Streifen Wirklichkeit durch jenen Spalt*
> *Durch den du hingingst: Grün wirklicher Grüne,*
> *Wirklicher Sonnenschein, wirklicher Wald.*

> So, and as you walked, there broke forth in this theatre a streak of reality through the cleft through which you went – green of real green, real sunshine, a real forest.

Cézanne's aim of *réalisation* became Rilke's, was Rilke's; and the artist himself was revered by him as a model of exemplary devotion to the ideal, an ideal with nothing fancy about it. The Rilkean ego melts into the colour of Cézanne, so that it does not seem egocentric of him to claim in one letter that the 'raptness' he must achieve in *being,* in his poetry, means that he can only be 'delighted and awed' inside his own work. I must escape from anything that can 'hook' me, Cézanne had said. Rilke must devote himself to the same realization of himself in things.

Reading between the lines of his letters must have been a sobering experience for his wife Clara, for they show how he meant to live, and had to live, in solitude, in the cell of his art. Yet the letters are suffused with an affection and understanding that seem to be mutual and all-embracing, to come as much from her as from him. These letters seem to belong to her in a very deep sense. Rilke used to say, sometimes diplomatically no doubt, and with his faithful retinue of noblewomen in mind, that each of his works belonged to the person who had inspired it. But these letters – some of the most remarkable in the selection – are also quite unaffected, possessed instead with that almost brutally humble instinct for the nature of things which was typical of Cézanne himself. Rilke was struck by the remark of a friend of his, the painter Mathilde Vollmöller, that Cézanne sat in front of nature 'like a dog, just looking' . . . Rilke looked at things too, and in the same way. No wonder W.H. Auden wrote of him in the New Year Letter those moving words:

> Rilke, whom *die Dinge* bless,
> The Santa Claus of loneliness.

John Bayley

INDEX OF RECIPIENTS

(The capitals in brackets refer to the volumes of original German text from which the Selection has been made. Thus (A) denotes Vol. 1902–1906; (B) 1906–1907; (C) 1907–1914; (D) 1914–1921; (E) 1921–1926. These were all published by the *Insel-verlag* between the years 1930 and 1937. The numbers are the same as in the original.)

SELECTED LETTERS 1902–1926

PART ONE

1902-1911

COLLECTED LETTERS : 1902–1906

1. *To Auguste Rodin* [1]

SCHLOSS HASELDORF, HOLSTEIN
ALLEMAGNE, *le* 28 *juin*

HONORÉ MAÎTRE,—I have undertaken to write for the new German series of art monographs published by Professor Richard Muther, the volume dedicated to your work. One of my most fervent wishes has thus been fulfilled, for the opportunity to write about your work satisfies an inner vocation in me and is a joyful and festive occasion as well as a great and noble duty towards which all my love and zeal are turned.

You will believe me when I say, mon Maître, that I shall do everything to accomplish this task as conscientiously and as profoundly as possible. To that end, nothing less than your generous assistance is required. I am coming to Paris this autumn to see you and steep myself in your creations and especially to penetrate into the spirit of your drawings, of which so little is yet known abroad. But as I shall be obliged to settle down at once to the preliminary studies I shall soon be in need of your invaluable advice, to beseech which is the purpose of this letter.

The editor wishes above all to have reproductions of your work in his possession as soon as possible (the volume is to contain some eight or ten of them) ; hence I am taking the liberty of asking you to whom I should address myself in order to obtain them.

My second request is that you should be so kind as to tell me whether there is in existence any approximate estimate of your work, and to give me the titles of the books in which your work is treated ; in particular, any essays containing biographical

1 Freely rendered from Rilke's somewhat equivocal French. Original appears intact in *Briefe und Tagebücher 1899–1902*, p. 197.

details will be indispensable. I should be most grateful, cher Maître, if you could give me your help in this matter.

You must think it an indiscretion on my part to venture to approach you about such trifles, but it is of great importance to me to have the best information and counsel on this point, and these none but you can give.

I consider it a great loss not to have been able to visit your Prague exhibition, to which the Manes Society had invited me; but during the autumn I hope to see in Paris everything that was collected in Prague.

Should any considerable portion of your major works be on exhibition in another town about that time I would earnestly beg you, mon Maître, to warn me, so that I could then go there before travelling to Paris, for I am particularly anxious to see everything you have done before I set to work.

In concluding this letter (I beg you to forgive its style; writing in French is such an effort to me), I feel bound to recall to you my young wife (Clara Westhoff the sculptress, of Worpswede near Bremen), who in 1900 enjoyed the privilege of working quite close to you and to the grandeur that surrounds your presence. She sent you (some two months since) reproductions of her recent work together with a letter into which she put her whole heart, and now she waits — as I have sensed — with anguish and impatience, cher Maître, for a single word from you, for your advice which is so important to her and will decide her future, and in the absence of which she can only grope like one blind.

There remains only for me to beg you, illustre Maître, to forgive all the indiscretions of this formless letter, and to believe that I am very happy to express my admiration and most profound devotion.—RAINER MAR. RILKE.

2. *To Arthur Holitscher*

WESTERWEDE BEI WORPSWEDE
July 31, 1902

I am completely taken up with Rodin who grows and grows upon me the more I see and hear of his work. Is there anyone,

I ask myself, who is as great as he is, yet still living (often it seems to me as though death and greatness were but one word; I remember when I first read *Niels Lyhne*[1] years ago in Munich, how I took it upon myself to seek out the man who had written it . . . later I heard him spoken of as one long since dead . . .) — and Rodin *is* still living. Quite apart from his art I have the feeling that he is a fusion of greatness and strength, a future century, a man without contemporaries. In such circumstances you can imagine how impatiently I am awaiting the first of September, the day I set out for Paris. . . .

4. *To Clara Rilke*

RUE TOULLIER 11, QUARTIER DE LA SORBONNE
le 28 *août* 1902 (vers le soir)

On ne peut pas s'en douter : je suis à Paris, quoique le coin où je demeure est plein de silence. Je suis une seule Attente : que deviendra ? Ma chambre est à la troisième ou quatrième étage (je n'ose pas compter) et ce qui me fait fier c'est qu'il a une cheminée avec un miroir, une pendule et deux chandeliers en argent.

6. *To Clara Rilke*

PARIS, 11 RUE TOULLIER
Tuesday, 2 *September* 1902

. . . Yesterday, Monday afternoon at three o'clock, I was with Rodin for the first time. Studio rue de l'Université 182. Went there on the Seine. He was modelling. A girl — he had a little plaster thing in his hand which he was scratching at. He stopped working, offered me an arm-chair, and we talked. He was kind and mild. And it seemed to me as though I had always known him. As though I were only seeing him again; I found him smaller and yet greater, kindlier and more sublime. The forehead, the way it stands in relation to the nose, which goes out from it like a ship leaving harbour — is very remarkable. There is something sculptural in this brow and nose. And

[1] Novel by the Danish writer, Jens Peter Jacobsen.

the mouth has a speech whose sound is good, friendly and full of youth. His laugh is like that too, the embarrassed and at the same time joyful laugh of a child receiving a fine gift. I like him very much. I knew that at once. We spoke of many things — (as far as my queer French and his time allowed of it). . . . Then he went on with his work and bade me examine all the things standing about in his studio. Which is not a little. The *Hand* is there. " *C'est une main comme ça* " (he said, and made with his own such a powerfully clinging and forming gesture that you fancied you could see things growing out of it). — " *C'est une main comme ça, qui tient un morceau de terre glaise avec des . . .* " And pointing at the two wonderfully deep and mysteriously united figures : " *c'est une création ça, une création* ". . . . Wonderfully he said that. . . . The French word lost its " charm " yet had none of the elaborate heaviness of the German word : " *Schöpfung* " . . . it had detached itself from all languages, gained its freedom . . . was alone in the world : " *création.* "

A bas-relief is there ; he calls it " Morning Star." A young girl's head with a wonderfully youthful brow, clear, sweet, light, and simple, and deep down in the stone a hand emerges, shielding the eyes of a man, waking, from the brightness. These eyes are almost *in* the stone (so marvellously is the unawakenedness expressed here — so plastic) : one sees only the mouth and the beard. A woman's portrait is there. It is more *there* than one can say, and everything small has so much *size* about it that the space of the studio's " H " seems to extend into the immeasurable, so as to embrace everything.

And now today : today I travelled by the nine o'clock train to Meudon (gare Montparnasse, from there a twenty minutes' journey). The villa, which he himself has called *un petit château Louis XIII* — is not beautiful. It has a three-windowed front, red bricks with yellowish window and door frames, a steep grey roof and a high chimney. The whole " picturesque " disorder of the Val Fleury is spread out before you, a narrow valley where the houses are poor and look like those in Italian vineyards (and vineyards are probably here too, for the steep dirty street of the place you go through is called Rue de la

Vigne . . .) ; then you pass over a bridge, another bit of street, past a small, thoroughly Italian-looking osteria. On the left is the gate. First a long avenue of chestnuts strewn with coarse gravel. Then a little wooden trellis-gate. Again a little wooden trellis-gate. Then you come round the corner of a small red-and-yellow house and stand — before a miracle, — before a garden of stones and plaster-casts. His big pavilion, the same that stood on the Pont de l'Alma at the exhibition,[1] has been set up in his garden, which it appears to fill completely, together with some more studios where there are stone-masons and where he himself works. Then there are rooms for clay-firing and for every kind of handwork. It is a tremendously great and strange sight, this vast light hall with all its white dazzling figures looking out from the many high glass-doors like the denizens of an aquarium. The impression is immense, terrific. You see, even before you have entered, that all these hundreds of lives are *one* life, — vibrations of one force and one will. Everything is there, everything. The marble of *la Prière* : plaster-casts of almost everything. Like the labour of a century — an army of work. Some gigantic glass-windows are entirely filled with wonderful fragments from the *Porte de l'Enfer*. It is indescribable. Acres of fragments lie there, one beside the other. Nudes the size of my hand and bigger, but only bits, scarcely one of them whole : often only a piece of arm, a piece of leg just as they go together, and the portion of the body which belongs with them. Here the torso of one figure with the head of another stuck on to it, with the arm of a third . . . as though an unspeakable storm, an unparalleled cataclysm had passed over his work. And yet the closer you look the deeper you feel that it would all be less complete if the separate bodies were complete. Each of these fragments is of such a peculiarly striking unity, so possible by itself, so little in need of completion, that you forget that they are only parts and often parts of different bodies which cling so passionately to one another. You feel suddenly that it is more the concern of the academician to apprehend bodies as wholes—more that of the artist to create new combinations from the parts, new, greater, more legitimate

[1] World Exhibition, 1900.

unities, more eternal. . . . And this wealth, this infinite, everlasting inventiveness, this presence of the spirit in expression, its purity and vehemence, this inexhaustibility, this youthfulness, this having to say always something more and always the best . . . all this is without parallel in the history of mankind. Then there are tables, stools, chests of drawers . . . completely covered with little figures — in gold-brown and ochre-yellow fired clay. Arms no bigger than my little finger, but bursting with a life that makes your heart pound. Hands which you could cover with a farthing piece, and yet filled with an abundance of knowledge, exactly determined and yet not at all trivial. As though a giant had made them immeasurably great — so this man has fashioned them to *his* proportions. He is so huge ; even when he makes them quite small, as small as he can, they are still bigger than people . . . faced with these little things which are everywhere and which you can take in your hand, I felt as I did that time in St. Petersburg when I saw the little Venus from the excavations. . . . There are hundreds and hundreds of them, no piece like any other — each one a conception, each one a fragment of love, devotion, goodness and discovery. I was in Meudon till about three o'clock. Rodin came to me from time to time, questioned me and said something, nothing of importance. The barrier of language is too great. Today I brought him my poems — if only he could read them. . . . I think now that *Das jüngste Gericht* must have meant something to him. He turned over the pages very attentively. The format astonished him, I believe, especially in the *Buch der Bilder*.[1] And there these stupid languages stand helpless as two bridges, spanning the same river side by side but separated by the abyss between. It is only a trifle, an accident, yet it divides. . . .

After twelve Rodin invited me to déjeuner which was taken in the open and was very odd. Madame Rodin (I had seen her before — he did *not* introduce me) looked tired and on edge, nervy and listless. Opposite me sat a French gentleman with a red nose, and I was not introduced to him either. — At my side a very sweet little girl of about ten (nor did I find out who *she*

[1] First edition, 1902.

was . . .) Scarcely had we sat down when Rodin began complaining about the unpunctuality of the meal ; he was already dressed to go to town. Thereupon Madame Rodin got very agitated. *Comment*, she said, *puis-je être partout ? Dites-le à Madeleine* (probably the cook), and now a flood of precipitate and violent words came out of her mouth, they did not sound exactly angry, nor ugly, but as though coming from a person deeply aggrieved whose nerves would snap the next moment. A restlessness possessed her whole body — she began to push all the things about on the table, so that it looked as though the meal were already over. Everything that had been put properly in its place was left lying anywhere as after a meal. This scene was *not* painful, only *sad*. Rodin was quite calm, went on talking very quietly, saying *why* he was complaining, outlined his complaints with precision, spoke at once gently and inflexibly. Finally a rather grubby man came in bringing a few things (which were well-prepared), carried them round and *forced* me, in his good-natured way, to take some, although I did not want any : obviously he thought I was extremely shy. I have scarcely ever partaken of such a queer déjeuner. Rodin was fairly talkative, — spoke sometimes very quickly so that I could not understand, but on the whole quite clearly. I spoke of Worpswede [1] — of the painters (of whom he knew nothing) ; he knew, as far as I could see, only Liebermann and Lenbach — as illustrators ! . . . The conversation was not conventional, but not the reverse, just usual. Sometimes Madame also took part, always talking very jerkily and passionately. She has grey hair, dark, deepset eyes, looks thin, listless, tired and old, tormented by something. After the meal she spoke to me in a very friendly way — for the first time as mistress of the house — invited me, whenever I was in Meudon, to come to lunch, etc. Early tomorrow I shall go out there again and perhaps some other days also : there is an endless amount to see. But it is terribly exhausting — first because of the quantity of things there, second because everything is white ; you go round the many dazzling plaster-casts in the bright pavilion as though in snow. My eyes hurt me, so do my hands. . . .

[1] Colony of painters near Bremen.

7. *To Clara Rilke*

PARIS, 11 RUE TOULLIER
5 September 1902

. . . I believe that in the last few days much has become clear to me concerning Rodin. After a déjeuner which was not less disturbed and strange than the one recently mentioned, I went with Rodin into the garden, and we sat on a bench which had a wonderful view right out over Paris. It was quiet and lovely. The little girl (she must be Rodin's daughter), the little girl had come along with us without Rodin paying any attention to her. The child did not seem to expect it even. She sat down on the path not far from us and looked slowly and sadly for interesting stones in the gravel. Sometimes she came up, looked at Rodin's mouth as he spoke, or mine when I was saying anything. Once she brought a violet. She laid it with her little hand shyly on Rodin's and wanted to insinuate it into his hand somehow, to fasten it there. But the hand was like stone. Rodin gave it only a perfunctory glance, looked out beyond it, beyond the small shy hand, beyond the violet, beyond the child, beyond this little complete instant of love, with eyes that clung to the things which seemed to be continually taking form in him.

He spoke of art, of art-dealers, of his own solitary position and said many very fine things which I felt rather than understood, for he often spoke very indistinctly and very quickly. Always he came back to the beauty which is everywhere for anyone who truly understands and wills it, came back to *things*, to the life of these things — *de regarder une pierre, la torse d'une femme*. . . . And always, again and again, to work. Ever since the physical, the really heavy work of the craftsman has been regarded as something inferior, — he said, work has ceased altogether. I know five, six people in Paris who really work, perhaps a few more. There in the schools, what do they do year in and year out — they " make compositions ". In this way they learn absolutely nothing of the nature of things. *Le modelé* . . . I know what that means : it is the science of planes as distinct from contours, that which fills out all contours. It is the law governing the relationships between these planes. You see, for him there is *only* the *modelé* . . . on all things, on all bodies, he detaches it from them, and after he has learnt it from them he makes of it an independent entity, that is, a work of sculpture, a work of plastic art. For this reason a piece of arm and leg and body is for him a whole, a unity, because he no longer thinks of arm, leg, and body (that would seem to him too thematic, you see, too *literary*, as it were), but only of the *modelé*, which is self-contained, which is in a certain sense ready and rounded. Extraordinarily illuminating in this sense was the following incident. The little girl brought the shell of a small snail she had found in the gravel. He had not noticed the flower, — but this he noticed at once. He took it in his hand, smiled, admired it, examined it and suddenly said : " *Voilà le modelé grec.*" I understood immediately. He continued : " *Vous savez, ce n'est pas la forme de l'objet, mais : le modelé*". . . . Then another snail-shell was found, broken and crushed . . . : " — *c'est le modelé gothique-renaissance,*" said Rodin with his open pleasant smile. . . . And what he meant was something like this : " It is not my business, that is, the business of the sculptor par excellence, to see or study colours or contours, but that of which sculpture consists, surfaces. The nature of these, whether they are rough or smooth, brilliant or dull (not in colour but in essence). Things are infallible there. This little snail reminds one of the greatest works of Greek art : it has the same simplicity, the same smoothness, the same inner brilliance, the same gay and holiday sort of surface. . . . And in that things are infallible ! They contain the laws in their purest state. Even the *fragments* of such a shell will be of the same order, will be once more *modelé grec*. This snail always remains a whole as far as its *modelé* is concerned, and the smallest fragment of snail is always *modelé grec*. . . ." It is only now that one realises what a revolution his sculpture is. What must it have been for him when he felt that hitherto no one had looked for this basic principle of sculpture ! It was his to find : things in their thousands offered it him : above all the naked body. It was his to transpose, that is, to turn it into *his* expression, to accustom himself to saying *everything* through the *modelé* and *not otherwise*. Here, you see, is the second essential fact in this great artist's life. The first was that he had discovered a new basic principle for his art, the second that he desired nothing more of life than to express himself and everything his entirely through this principle. He married, "*parce qu'il faut avoir une femme*", as he told me (in another connection, namely when I was talking of groups of friends who collect together, and suggested that it is only the solitary struggle that produces anything, then he said it, said: "*non, c'est vrai, il n'est pas bien de faire des groupes, les amis s'empêchent. Il est mieux d'être seul. Peut-être avoir une femme,— parce qu'il faut avoir une femme*") . . . something like that. . . . He was silent a while and then said, wonderfully seriously he said it: . . . "*il faut travailler, rien que travailler. Et il faut avoir patience.*" You should not think of wanting to *do* anything, you should only try to build up your own means of expression so as to say everything. You should work and have patience. Look neither to the right nor left. Draw your whole life into this circle, having *nothing* outside this life. As Rodin has done. *J'y ai donné ma jeunesse*, he said. It is certainly true. You must sacrifice all else. Tolstoi's unpleasing household,[1] the uncomfortableness in Rodin's rooms: it all points to the same thing: you must choose — either this or that. Either happiness or art. *On doit trouver le bonheur dans son art. . . .* Rodin said much the same thing too. And in fact it is all so obvious, so obvious. All the great men have let their lives get overgrown like an old path and have carried everything into their art. Their life is stunted like an organ they no longer use. . . .

Rodin has lived nothing that is not in his work. Thus it grew about him. Thus he did not lose himself even in the years when lack of money drove him to unworthy work; he did not lose himself from having no plan to fulfil, for he realised immediately in the evening what he had willed during the day. Thus everything was always real. This is the essential, that you should not stop at dreams, at intentions, at being in the mood, but that you should transpose everything into *things* with all your strength. As Rodin has done. Why has he won through? Not because he found applause. Friends of his are few, and he stands, as he says, on the blacklist. But his work was there, an

[1] In May 1900 Rilke stayed with Tolstoi in Yasnaya Polyana.

enormous imposing reality which cannot be ignored. Thereby he achieved his place and his right. You could easily imagine a man who had felt and willed all this in himself, waiting for better times in order to accomplish it. Who would be paying attention to him *now*? He would be an old dotard with nothing more to hope for. But doing, doing, that's the thing. And when all at once something is there, ten, twelve things there, sixty, seventy little nudes about you, all of which you have made from this or that impulse, then you have won a scrap of land to stand upright on. Then you lose yourself no more. When Rodin walks round among his things you feel how youth, certainty and new work are continually streaming into him from them. He cannot go wrong. His work stands like a great angel at his side and protects him . . . his great work! . . .

13. *To Clara Rilke*

PARIS, 11 RUE TOULLIER
27 September 1902, *morning*

. . . Here you can, I believe, learn a lot, but you must have a certain maturity, otherwise you see nothing, firstly because there is too much here, and secondly because so many different things speak all at once. From all sides. — I have already told you that I try to feel myself near to the world of Antiquity and that I now and then succeed in finding a new and profound joy in its objects. Rodin has a little plaster-cast, a tiger [1] (antique),

[1] From the *Neue Gedichte*:

THE PANTHER

(Jardin des Plantes)

So weary from the passing bars his eyes
that nothing more can crowd into his mind.
He feels as though a thousand bars gave rise
to other thousands with no world behind.

The padded walk whose strong and supple pace
turns in the smallest circle round and round
is like a dance of power about a place
in which a mighty will stands stunned and bound.

But now and then a picture enters him
as, soundlessly, the pupil-curtains part;
goes through the rigid stillness of each limb
and perishes when it has reached his heart.

in his studio in the rue de l'Université which he prizes very highly: *c'est beau, c'est tout*, he says of it. And from this little plaster-cast I have seen what he means, what Antiquity is and what relates him to it. There is in this animal the same vigorous sensitiveness of modelling, this little thing (it is no higher than my hand is broad, and no longer) has a hundred thousand places like a really big thing, a hundred thousand places all alive, alert and different. And this in plaster! Besides that the representation of the prowling tread is intensified to the utmost, the mighty downward beat of the broad paws and at the same time a cautiousness in which all its strength is wrapped, a noiselessness . . . You will see this little thing, and we will not omit to visit the original (a little bronze), in the Cabinet de Médailles in the Bibliothèque Nationale. — When you turn from such things to the sculpture of the 12th and 13th centuries you often miss in the latter this tranquil moulding and vitalising of the surfaces and only find a sort of stark expressionism and something different, meticulous and painstaking, which seeks for types and stylises the subject. Nevertheless the surface in these things has become, under the influence of time, wind and rain, the sun and night of centuries, just as animated, just as plastic and without the least emptiness.

The Trocadero Museum is very interesting; it contains some tolerably good plaster-casts and replicas of old doorways from the provinces, from Chartres, from Rouen and other towns, fragments, details, columns from which you can see how the whole of life together with all its things and forms passed through the hand of the sculptor into the stone, as though it belonged there. You feel, more even than in the Renaissance, how people's eyes were opened, how suddenly they saw everything and applied themselves to everything. And with them Rodin has many affinities. For instance I am convinced that the flowers on the pedestal of the *Bust of a Woman* in the Luxembourg entered his sculpture just as they did the work of the masters of the twelfth century. Like a thing that was an experience for him, that surged along with the great river which flows everlastingly into his art.

Today I will try again to see him. As a rule I go by the little steamer on the Seine as far as the Pont d'Iéna (opposite the

Trocadero), which is the quickest route wherever I may happen to be. — These days the afternoons are often very beautiful and just a little overcast and subdued ; and then it has such a gentle way of becoming evening. One might say that there is a moment when the hours stop passing, one feels their tread no more, they mount some sort of animal which carries them on its broad back. They keep so still, and only beneath them is there something large and dark, that moves, passes, and takes them with it. — Until five I am generally in the Bibliothèque Nationale, then they close and, standing somewhere on a bridge or a quay of the Seine, I go and drink in this fall of evening ; sometimes I walk as far as the Luxembourg Gardens which are beginning to be filled with twilight, gently resisting the darkness with their many red flowers. Suddenly a roll of drums starts up somewhere, rolls loud and soft, a soldier all in red goes through the avenues. Then from everywhere people pop out, happy, laughing, high-spirited people, grave, sad, quiet and lonely people, people of all kinds, of today, of yesterday and the day before. Such as have sat many hours on a remote bench as though waiting for something — and into their ears it is now being drummed that they have nothing to wait for, and then others who live on the benches during the daytime, eat, sleep and read a newspaper : all sorts of people, faces and hands, many hands go past. It is rather like a Last Judgement. And behind those who are departing the gardens get bigger and bigger : huge. And Paris becomes narrow, garish and rowdy and begins one of its hectic nights again, stimulated by spices, wine, music and women's clothes. — Alas, the Dancer of 1793 still stands on the altar of Notre-Dame, on all the altars throughout Paris, on all the better tables even : Alas ! . . .

20. *To Ellen Key*

Paris, 3 rue de l'Abbé de l'Epée
13 *February* 1903

. . . That my book of stories about God (which was written three years ago at a happy period in seven successive nights) would still find me dear and invaluable friends, I knew in my heart ; for this book is very precious to me.

But now for a long, long time no good or harmonious line has sought out a path to me ; very alone and very deserted I go my way ; and that is good : I have never wished it otherwise. But all the fear and worry that came and grew with the happiness and blessings of the past year have made the creative impulse in me weak and wavering and anxious : therefore it was just the right moment for a letter such as yours, with its great affection, sympathy, and appreciation, to radiate a kindness and a warmth which make me brighten a little in the midst of my anxieties. O I thank you, dear, dear lady that you have known how to receive, read and love these *Stories of God* so well. I feel when I hear your cheerful voice that I shall have to create many more things that are as good and simple as this book, with which I have gained you. But I am a very defenceless person (because I was a very nervy, forlorn and defenceless child), and when Fate calls out to me I must stay quite, quite still for a long time and remain so even when I suffer unspeakably, day and night, with hearing no more. Dear, dear Frau Ellen Key, I have made many books already, and do not be impatient nor think it importunate of me if I send you portions of them now and then, even of the earlier ones. The very old ones are unfortunately no longer obtainable (I myself have no copies of them, and you will miss nothing if you do not become acquainted with them !). But, as it is, I am sending you a little play called *Das Tägliche Leben*. It is three years old ; was produced last year in Berlin, and a perhaps too impatient and hasty public choked it with loud laughter, which does not prevent me from still liking this little work. Then in the coming weeks (as soon as my publisher sends me copies) will follow the two books[1] which appeared after the *Stories of God* — a small volume of tales and a book of poems. And finally I will give you, as soon as I have them, my latest works which are to appear in the spring : a monograph on the Worpswede group of painters, and the little book on Auguste Rodin's work. All of which implores your love and indulgence.

. . . Ought we not perhaps to seek refuge in some peaceful

[1] *Buch der Bilder* (1902) ; *Die Letzten*, now included in *Erzählungen und Skizzen aus der Frühzeit.*

handcraft and no longer have any fear for what ripens into fruit deep within us, behind all stir and agitation ? Sometimes I think it might be a way out, because I realise more and more that there is nothing more difficult and dangerous for my nature than wanting to earn money by writing. Like this I cannot bring myself to write at all ; and the consciousness alone that a connection exists between my writing and the day's nourishment and necessaries, is enough to make my work impossible for me. I must wait for the ringing in the silence, and I know that if I force the ringing, then it really won't come. (It has come so seldom during these last two years.) Sometimes it is there and I am the master of my depths, which open out radiant and beautiful and shimmering in the darkness ; but it is not I that have said the magic Word, God says it when it is time, and it is meet for me only to be patient and to wait and suffer my depths trustingly which, when they are sealed, are like a heavy stone many days of the year. But then Life comes and wants to use me somehow, me and my stone. Then I always get helpless and afraid and would often like to use it just as it is, without thinking of its depths. But I cannot do that either ; for on bad days I have only dead words, and they are so corpse-heavy that I cannot write with them, not even a letter. Is that bad, weak ? And yet God wills it so with me. . . .

24. *To Clara Rilke*

Viareggio presso Pisa Italia
Hotel de Florence, 24 *March* 1903

. . . My departure, in spite of all the time I had, was hurried and unrestful. On my way to the station I drove through the quiet streets of a Paris completely unknown to me. The rapid trot of my horse resounded in them as at midnight, and it must have become unbearably silent behind my carriage. The night was not very good, sleepless and really cold, perceptibly cold despite the camel-hair rug whose presence I felt with gratitude. However, through cunning I succeeded in keeping a crack of window open all night behind the drawn curtain, until towards morning an Italian (who may well have wondered at the cold) discovered it and shut the window. But thanks to this the air in the crowded compartment was still bearable. At about ten on Friday we were at the frontier (in Modane), and the train comported itself in true Italian manner with the result that, after an endless wait, we continued our journey an hour late. Towards noon the guard told me that because of this we should not make the connection to Genoa in Turin : so we were obliged to wait till about eight in Turin for another train which was to reach Genoa about half past eleven.

The hours in Turin were not pleasant, the air was heavy, and although the trees in the gardens I visited were in flower, there was no trace of their breath in the air and only dust and sadness over everything. And so I went on at eight o'clock, was in Genoa at midnight where an overcrowded hotel could only offer me a very small room, in which, tired out, I fell asleep towards morning.

Next morning. I come down to breakfast. The waiter takes my order in German. At the next table they are speaking German (it's possible even for *this* to happen), but they speak German at the second, at the third, at the fourth table, in the hall, on the stairs, in the street : I sit in the midst of German, and such German : sometimes I think I hear my cousin Paula, now this, now that " dear " acquaintance : family-German of the worst sort all round you and not as foreigners speak it, no, absolutely shameless, without restraint, as at home. I then had an inkling of what it is that they call the Italian Riviera. But worse was to follow. In the train, *everything* German, German sprouting and crackling in every conversation. I kept behind a big French paper and heard of the overcrowding of all the hotels in Nervi, Rapallo, in Sestri Levanti with German visitors . . . nobody mentioned Santa Margherita — I held fast to that. But I was quite decided, in spite of all the recommendations, not to get out at Nervi, specially when I heard that a great " Battle of Flowers " was to take place the same day : I did not want, having started on one Mi-Carême, to get into the thick of another.

At 12 o'clock noon (Saturday) I reached Santa Margherita Ligure. The hotel with its big garden was really well situated, but was full to the last room, — and, like the other hotels, full of German, of course. At last (I was so tired with travelling and had to gather strength for further decisions) I found a little north-room under the roof of a big hotel. There was no choice. But the hotel had a small (albeit ugly) garden by the sea, a garden with comfortable deck-chairs — there I sat down (with my cold) in the sun (the little walk in front of it was fairly empty), sat down and wondered why I was not enjoying myself, why the sea was so flat, empty and horribly dazzling like some inland lake, and why the whole landscape with its palms, orange-trees and magnolias had something so untrue, exaggerated, artificially southern about it that I (apart from the momentary peace) wished myself far away.

Didn't want to see any more of the mountains which seem so terrible on the journey from Modane, because you are perpetually burrowing through them, a quarter of an hour at a stretch inside the mountains, in the scanty black air, in the cavernous roar of the train which does not appear to advance at all. And, when you live in the middle of them like that waiting for the light, it feels as though the whole weight of the mountains were upon you, the weight of the stone, of the metals and the springs, and above them the heavy, heavy snow and the cold sky they dwell in. . . . I am glad that I am going back through Ventimiglia and thus shall not have to endure the terrors of those thousand tunnels again.

Well, here I am in Sa. Margherita. Some Marchese or other owns an old spacious park by the sea : there I wandered about and reflected that it was best to write to Malfatti in Viareggio early the next day to ask — etc. And till the answer came, which should arrive in three or four days, to stick it in Sa. M., in this park, where there was solitude. Then came the evening. The meal. Fifty German personages. Commercial travellers and honeymoon couples, — old gentlemen who talked loudly of politics, people from offices or in retirement blatantly enjoying themselves, spinsters with bags full of postcards, female painters with pince-nez, and all those nearest me agog with curiosity, greedy to draw me into the conversation, to entice me, to compel me. . . . all very distressing. Afterwards I went out again ; it was empty outside (for most of the others had retired to needlework, card-tables and similar German assiduities), but the sea was quite intimidated, the air bad and tired and sultry, and I walked sadly about in the dark streets which had no life of their own and no silence. — On Sunday I woke up early — wanted to write first thing to Viareggio, but got cold and had to go out for a walk. I went. Took the road by the sea. One carriage after another, excursionists. Germans. Railway alongside the sea, nowhere quiet. The castle Baedeker speaks of as being Böcklin's favourite spot, stuck up and posed with palms like everything else. I turned back, the heat was terribly heavy, all things loaded with sun, without colour, without form, without joy.

I came back into the hotel. . . . And I paid my bill at once and got to the train just in time, which leaves at 1.30 for the south. By 4.22 I was on the station at Viareggio.

Seldom have I felt, as I did during this journey, the relief there is in action, this unspeakable liberation from chance and its dangers, this power that springs from the simplest *doing*. Of course I was not without my misgivings. Perhaps Viareggio had grown different in the last six years, perhaps it too was full up, perhaps it was too cold, perhaps . . . the perhapses multiplied like mad, and I arrived with whole families, with generations of perhapses which, however, nearly all died with the reality that now began. A few eke out a miserable existence, but things are going badly enough for them.

In Viareggio it was Sunday. The girls of my girl-songs [1] went through the long streets in rows, arms linked. Fishermen sat in front of the osterias and sang. And far and wide the sea's murmur was audible, the sublime presence of the great sea was interwoven with the smallest word that was uttered, and blended with the least silence that arose. Disappointments, however, came all the same, in the midst of this revisitation. The cab did not stop at the dear old out-of-the-way house which stands so peacefully in its garden at the end of the town — it stopped, before I could see the house, at a hotel built on to the last row

[1] Rilke visited Viareggio in 1898 and there wrote the *Lieder der Mädchen* which first appeared in the magazine *Pan*. They are now included in *Collected Works*, vol. i.

of houses stretching along the beach (perhaps fifty paces from the sea). This was *now* the Hotel de Florence. Soon Madame Malfatti, as I did not in the least want to get out, came to my aid, recognised me correctly after a while, said by way of explanation that they had sold the first house because it was too damp, and she had already conducted me inside so that I had neither time nor opportunity to ask about the old house, or even to go there and see whether it was still an hotel. I have been there since. It is exactly the same as before, but in other hands, circumspect and quiet in its garden. Only, there is a very conspicuous inscription on the garden-wall near the gate : " Hotel Sirene ". But in the end it was equally important for me to live with the Malfattis. For the time being there is only a room on the ground floor free, but on Wednesday I shall have one on the first floor, very similar to the room I occupied in the old house. A long, narrow, very high room, with a balcony facing the sea. Now a number of difficulties arose, again with the meals. A small dining-room with, unfortunately, round tables ; I was placed next an old Scotch lady who, at all costs, wanted to talk, first in Italian, then in French. It was frightful. Relentlessly I underlined my silence with the thickest strokes ; it was no good, she began again and again and did not leave off. — And round the other two round tables were English people who carried on conversation from table to table, laughed, so that I had to pass my supper-time in the midst of a lively English chattering and perpetually questioned by my old Scotch lady . . . so yesterday evening (Monday) I had my meal laid in my room, where it is not very nice to eat, but at least quiet. The servant is very pleasant and willing. As soon as one of the old horrors from England goes away I shall sit in the dining-room at a special table and turn down all attempts to make my acquaintance.

. . . On the beach there are little huts with straw roofs and straw walls. They contain a closed cabin for undressing in, a little verandah in front with a straw awning stretched out before it. I have rented the last one right at the end and can now sit there the whole day, taking air-baths and bathing, and can lie in the warm sand and lack nothing. Since a table and two chairs (besides a wash-basin, a straw mat and a clothes-hanger) belong to the appurtenances of the cabin, I can also read and write there very well. . . . The sea is beautiful and big, always moving, without distinction between high and low tide. A flat beach with wonderful soft sand. I have been in to my knees already and have felt the waves in my knee-joints. I am longing for a bathe. In the open of course you have to wear a bathing-dress, but I run farther out where I can take it off. The sun is warm, without sultriness, always movement in the air, a freshness, almost a keenness, but wonderfully invigorating and quite southern to feel. — Now I want to get better. The arrangements at meal-times can be changed ; apart from that I am in high spirits and so inwardly glad to be here that I cannot express it. I shall sit in this little hut and go barefoot to the water and run into the sea, and feel sea and air with every part of my weary, thirsty body which has been harmed by the winter. In this way I shall soon grow happy and good and find courage for all the important things. For the time being, however, I shall think of nothing, only draw breath with a hundred mouths.

. . . Already I feel my loneliness a little, and suspect that it will refuse me nothing if I harken to it with new strength. . . .

Postcriptum, a few hours later, in my room. — I have now bathed. It was a thirst in my body, I could wait no longer. It has done me good in spite of the bathing costume, which of course is a hindrance. But next time I shall go still farther along the beach and perhaps find an hour when fewer people come by. A few happened to come today. I ran straight out of my hut into the sunbeams which the sinking sun (it was after four o'clock) cast over the water. It was very nice. On this marvellous pure sand, where there is no unevenness, no sharpness, no mud. . . .

The sun sinks straight into the sea here ; that is why it is so beautiful when the many fishing boats turn home in the evening and all journey towards the harbour, out of the broad, shining and shimmering water into the rich darkness of the land pointed with lights. . . .

The days are marvellous now, and this evening passed with miracles. Now I shall drink a little more tea (the very salty air makes one terribly thirsty) ; then I shall sleep and begin another good day of sun, shall live and decide. . . .

25. *To Clara Rilke*

VIAREGGIO PRESSO PISA, HOTEL FLORENCE
27 *March* 1903

. . . I want and need these days only for rest. When I get it something heavy begins to fall away from me, quite slowly ; but if I stir myself too soon it quickly rises up in me again.

But gently, very gently a sense of well-being begins sometimes such as I have not known for years. . . . When anxious, uneasy and evil thoughts come I go to the sea, and the sea drowns them with its great wide murmurs, purifies me with its syllables and lays a rhythm in me upon all that is bewildered and confused. And so much is. I feel that I must organise my powers anew right from the bottom, but I feel also that this task is possible here if I have patience and faith.

30. *To Clara Rilke*

VIAREGGIO PRESSO PISA, HOTEL FLORENCE
8 *April* 1903, *Wednesday*

. . . Here is yet another day of restlessness and violence. Storm after storm over the sea. Fleeing light. Night in the wood. And an immense din over everything. The whole morning I was in the wood, and after these four or five glaring days the darkness that dwelt there did all one's senses good and the coolness and the almost keen wind. You must imagine this wood with soaring trunks, dim, straight pines and high overhead their opened branches. The ground quite dark with needles and covered with very tall prickly gorse-bushes which are full of yellow blossoms, bloom on bloom. And today this yellow glowed in the cool, nocturnal twilight and dipped and twinkled, and the wood was lit up from below and very lonely. I walked up and down there for hours and thought a lot. . . . I cannot say how it will turn out and whether the Spanish plan [1]

[1] A trip to Spain to collect material for a study of Zuloaga, the Spanish painter.

will come to anything, or some other to which as yet, perhaps, I cannot put a name. It's no use, either, talking of it now, but one day, I think, it will be known and acted on. And knowing and doing will be one. This much is certain, that I shall come back to Paris to start with, perhaps to write the Carrière book; I feel Paris must grant me another spell of work. . . . Each of us must find in his work the central core of his life and from there be able to radiate outwards as far as he can. And during this no second person should look at him . . . not even he himself should do so. There is a sort of purity and virginity in this looking away from the self; it is like when you are drawing, your eyes bound to the object, interwoven with nature, and somewhere down below the hand goes its way alone, goes and goes, becomes anxious, wavers, grows cheerful again, goes and goes deep down under the face which stands above it like a star, seeing nothing, only shining. I feel as though I had always worked like this: my face in the contemplation of distant things, my hands alone. And certainly that is how it should be. In time I shall be like that again. . . .

Today a very nice letter came from Rodin (dictated), very cordial and full of sympathy. . . . I am looking forward so much to seeing his new things: O how he grows and grows! (Hokusai, the great Japanese painter, said somewhere when speaking of the hundred views he had done of Foujiyama: "*C'est à l'âge de soixante-treize ans que j'ai compris à peu près la forme et la nature vraie des oiseaux, des poissons et des plantes*") . . .

35. *To Clara Rilke*

VIAREGGIO PRESSO PISA, HOTEL FLORENCE
24 *April* 1903

. . . It is a good thing that I did not leave on Wednesday, for lately the weather has been so unspeakable, so unruly with storms and torrents of rain which fell half the day and all night thick as a shawl, that I would not have liked to be in a strange city and specially in one [1] which takes its beauty from the sun and which, designed entirely for southern days, ought to stand beside a blue sea, but not beside one that drags all its deepest,

[1] Venice.

oldest, well-nigh forgotten colours out of the abyss, scatters them far and wide, and then with huge bellying waves scornfully tosses over them its tawny sheep-skins of foam. Also it is no good in the train on such days of tumult when, instead of staying put under *one* rain at least, you have to journey through the rains of all these innumerable little stations which stand there mournfully dripping and look twice as dirty as before.

So it was a good thing, although I am a little impatient and would like to have gone off, particularly as it is not agreeable here with this storm, changeable and noisy; not even in the wood today was it quiet, the sea has come much nearer and the wind drives its din into your ears and twists it round the trees, which are themselves full of rustling and turbulence, as though they had had to watch and wail like that all night long.

Yes, it is time to go back.

. . . Here I am always deep in *Niels Lyhne*, or deep in the bible. . . . I find a lot too in my own books; dip into the *Stories of God* and enjoy much of it and forgive what does not seem good to me for the sake of the rest, which is essential and fine and will not be altered. Isn't it just as though no one had ever read the book? I wish it were all as good as the best in it; then it might be discovered later like something old and beautiful. There was not enough patience in me when I made it, hence it has so many muddled and indistinct places; but perhaps I shall soon get down to another such book, and then I will build at it with all the devotion I have in my hands, and will leave no place while it is less than myself, and will make an angel out of each one and let myself be overpowered by him and force him to bend me to his will, although I have created him. . . .

41. *To Lou Andreas-Salomé*

WORPSWEDE BEI BREMEN
18 *July* 1903

I want to tell you, dear Lou, that Paris was the same sort of experience for me as the Military School; [1] just as then a great

[1] Military School in St. Pölten, Austria, which Rilke attended from 1885 to 1890.

fearful astonishment seized me, so once again I was attacked by all the terror of what, in some unspeakable confusion, is called life. Then, as a boy among boys, I was alone among them, and how alone I was now among these people, how continually denied by all that I encountered! The cabs drove clean through me, and those that were in a hurry made no detour about me and raced over me full of contempt as over a bad place in which foul water has collected. And often, before I went to sleep, I read the thirtieth chapter of the Book of Job, and it was all true of me, word for word. And in the night I got up and sought my favourite volume of Baudelaire, the petits poèmes en prose, and read aloud the most beautiful poem of all, which is entitled *A une heure du matin.* Do you know it? It begins: "*Enfin! enfin! seul! on n'entend plus que le roulement de quelques fiacres attardés et éreintés. Pendant quelques heures nous posséderons le silence, sinon le repos. Enfin! la tyrannie de la face humaine a disparu, et je ne souffrirai plus que par moi-même. . . .*" And the end is immense: it rises, stands, and goes forth like a prayer. A prayer of Baudelaire's; a real, simple prayer made with the hands, clumsy and beautiful as the prayer of a Russian. — He had to go a long way till he reached it, did Baudelaire, and he went crawling on his knees. . . . I came to Paris in August last year. It is the time when the trees in the city are sere without autumn, when the burning streets, which the heat has stretched, won't end and you walk through smells as through many sordid rooms. I went past the long hospitals whose doors stand wide open with a gesture of impatient and greedy compassion. The first time I came by the Hôtel Dieu an open carriage was just driving up with a man lolling inside it, swaying with every movement, all askew like a broken marionette, and with a heavy ulcerating tumour on his long, grey, hanging neck. And what people I have met since then, almost every day! Stumps of caryatids upon whom all suffering, the whole structure of suffering, was laid, beneath which they lived slowly like tortoises. And they were passers-by among other passers-by, alone and undisturbed in their fate. You caught them as impressions at most and you regarded them with a quiet objective curiosity like a new kind of animal, for whom misery had fashioned special organs, organs of hunger and dying. And they suffered the drab, desolate sham-life of these hypertrophied cities and endured beneath the foot of each day that trod on them like tough beetles, they dragged on as though waiting for something, twitched like chunks of a great chopped fish, already going rotten but still alive. They lived, lived on nothing, on dust, on soot and on the dirt of their skins, on what the dogs let fall from their mouths, on any senselessly pillaged thing that might yet be bought for some inexplicable purpose. O what a world is this ! Bits, bits of people, parts of animals, remains of perished things, all of them still animate, still fluttering about in a mysterious wind, some carrying, some being carried, falling and overtaking one another in their fall.

Then there were old women who set down a heavy basket beside some buttress in the wall (quite small women whose eyes were like dried-up puddles), and when they reached out for it again a long rusty hook slowly emerged from their sleeve instead of a hand, and went directly and surely towards the handle of the basket. And other old women who wandered up and down with the drawer of an old bedside-table in their hands, and shewed everybody the twenty rusty knitting needles rolling about inside it, which they had to sell. And once, later in the autumn, a little old woman[1] stood beside me one evening in the light of a shop window. She stood quite still, and I thought she was absorbed as I was in looking at the articles on show, and scarcely heeded her. But finally I felt disquieted by her presence, and I do not know why, but I suddenly glanced at her worn, oddly clasped hands. Very very slowly an old pencil, long and thin, pushed its way out of these hands, it grew and grew, and it was a very long time before it was entirely visible, visible in all its wretchedness. I cannot tell what it was that was so frightful about this scene, but I felt as though a whole destiny were being enacted before me, a long-drawn destiny, a catastrophe which fearsomely increased up to the moment when the pencil grew no longer and stuck out softly trembling from the loneliness of those empty hands. I realised at last that I was supposed to buy it. . . .

[1] Cf. *Malte Laurids Brigge*, pp. 50-51 (*Collected Works*, vol. v.).

And then these women who hurry past you in the long velvet coats of the eighties, with paper roses on their antiquated hats beneath which their hair hangs down as though melted together. And all these people, men and women, who are in a sort of transition, perhaps from madness to health, perhaps towards insanity ; all of them with something infinitely delicate in their faces, with a love, with a knowledge, a joy, as though with a light that burns dimly and fitfully, but only the tiniest bit so, and could certainly burn clear again if someone gave heed and helped. . . . But there is nobody to help. Nobody to help those that are the least bit bewildered, frightened, intimidated ; those who begin to read things differently from the way they are meant ; those who are still of this world and only walk a little crookedly and therefore think, sometimes, that things are hanging over them ; those who are not at home in the cities and get lost in them as in an evil forest that has no end : all those to whom suffering is done every day, all those who do not hear their will working in the noise, all those over whom fear has grown — why does no one help them in the great cities ?

Where are they going to, when they come so quickly through the streets ? Where do they sleep, and when they cannot sleep what visions unroll before their melancholy eyes ? What do they think of, when they sit all day in the open gardens, their heads sunk over hands that have come together from a great distance to hide themselves one in the other ? And what are the words they mumble when their lips gather strength and move ? Do they still fashion real words ? . . . Is it still sentences they say, or does it crowd out all confused, as out of a burning theatre, everything that was in them, spectator and player, audience and hero ? Does nobody think that there is a childhood in them that is getting lost, a power that sickens, a love that falls ?

O Lou, I have tormented myself like this for days. For I understood all these people, and although I went round them in a great curve they had no mystery for me. I was wrenched out of myself into their lives, through all their lives, through all their heavy-laden lives. . . . Nothing was so little laughter as the laughter of these solitaries : when they laughed it sounded as though something fell in them, fell and splintered and filled them full of fragments. . . . Once[1] (it was fairly early in the day) I came up the Boulevard St. Michel intending to go to the Bibliothèque Nationale, where I used to spend much of my time. I walked along rejoicing in all the freshness, clarity and good cheer which the morning and the beginning of a new day diffuse abroad even in the city. The red on the wheels of the cabs delighted me, it was moist and cool as on flower petals, and I was happy because somewhere at the end of the street someone was carrying something bright green, without my thinking what it could be. Slowly the water waggons drove uphill, and the water leapt young and clear from the pipes and made the road dark, so that it did not dazzle you any more. Horses came past in gleaming harness, and their hoofs beat like a hundred hammers. The cries of the merchants sounded different : rose up more lightly and echoed high in the air afterwards. And the vegetables on their handcarts stirred like a little field and had a free morning of their own over them, and deep within, darkness, green and dew. And when it was still for a moment you heard above you the sound of windows being opened. . . .

Then I was suddenly struck by the peculiar behaviour of the people coming towards me ; most of them walked for a while with their heads turned back, so that I had to take care not to collide with them ; there were also some who had stopped still, and by following their glance I perceived among the people walking in front of me a tall man dressed in black who, as he strode along, used both hands to turn down the collar of his coat which apparently would keep sticking up in the most irritating way. During this occupation, which cost him a visible effort, he repeatedly forgot to mind the road, tripped or hopped quickly over some small obstacle. When that had happened a few times in close succession he turned his attention to the road, but it was odd that after two or three paces he still stumbled and hopped over something. Involuntarily I had

[1] The passage that follows bears a very close resemblance to the scene described in *Malte Laurids Brigge*, pp. 102–7.

quickened my pace and now I found myself near enough behind the man to see that the movements of his feet had nothing whatever to do with the pavement, which was smooth and even, and that he only wanted to deceive those coming towards him when he turned round after each stumble, as though reprimanding some guilty object. There was in reality nothing to be seen. Meanwhile the clumsiness of his walk gradually abated, and now he hurried along quite rapidly and remained for a time unnoticed. But all at once the commotion began again in his shoulders, twice pulled them up in the air and let them fall so that they hung away from him all awry as he walked. But how amazed I was when suddenly I had to admit having seen his left hand dart up with indescribable speed to his coat-collar, take hold of it almost imperceptibly and turn it up, whereupon he made a very elaborate attempt with both hands to turn it down again, which, like the first time, he seemed to succeed in doing only with difficulty. And now he nodded his head to the front and to the left, stretched out his neck and nodded, nodded, nodded behind his upraised busied hands as though the collar of his shirt too were beginning to distress him, and as though there were enough to do up there for a long time. At last everything appeared to be in order again. He walked some ten paces completely unnoticed, when suddenly the up and down motion of his shoulders started once more ; at the same time a waiter, who was clearing up in front of a café, stopped still and looked with a curious eye at the man passing, who shook himself unexpectedly, stood and then resumed his way in little hops. The waiter laughed and shouted something into the shop, upon which a few more faces became visible behind the panes. But in the meantime the strange man had attached the stick with its round curved handle behind his collar, and now as he walked he held it erect just over his spine ; there was nothing striking about this, and it supported him. The new position eased him a lot, and he went on quite relieved for a moment. Nobody noticed him ; but I, who could not turn my eyes from him for a second, knew how the spasm was gradually coming back again, how it was getting stronger and stronger, how it tried to find expression now here, now there, how it shook his shoulders, how it clove to his head so as to wrench it out of balance, and how it suddenly and unexpectedly attacked his steps and tore them apart. As yet you scarcely saw anything of this ; it passed off softly and almost secretly in little pauses, but it was there and it grew. I felt how the whole man was filling himself with turmoil, how, as this could not be spent, it multiplied, how it mounted up, and I saw his will, his fear and the desperate expression of his convulsive hands pressing the stick against his backbone, as though seeking to make it a part of this helpless body wherein was lodged the tingling of a thousand dances. And I saw how this stick became something, something momentous on which much depended ; all the strength of the man and all his will went into it and made it a mighty force, a being that might help and on which the sick man hung with wild faith. Here a God was born, and a world rose up against it. But while this battle was in progress the man who suffered it tried to go on, and for some seconds he succeeded in looking harmless and ordinary. Now he crossed the Place St. Michel, and although his avoiding of the cabs and pedestrians, which were very numerous, might have given him an excuse for unusual movements, he remained quite quiet, and there was even a strange rigid composure in his whole body as he stepped on to the trottoir of the bridge on the other side. I was now close behind him, drained of all will, dragged along by his fear which could no longer be distinguished from my own. Suddenly the stick gave way, in the middle of the bridge. The man stood ; uncommonly still and stiff he stood there and did not move. Now he was waiting ; but it seemed as though the enemy within him did not yet trust this submission — it hesitated, only for an instant of course. Then it burst forth like a conflagration, from all windows at once. And a dance began. . . . A dense circle of people rapidly formed round him and shoved me gradually back, and I could see no more. My knees trembled, and everything was taken out of me. I stood for a while leaning on the parapet of the bridge and finally went back to my room ; there would no longer have been any sense in going to the Bibliothèque Nationale. Where is the book that would have been strong enough to help me overcome the thing that was in me? I felt used up; as though another's fear had nourished itself on me and exhausted me, that's how I felt. . . .

42. *To Ellen Key*

At Oberneuland bei Bremen
25 *July* 1903

. . . We have come to Oberneuland[1] from Worpswede for a few days to see our little Ruth[2] again. And now we are with her night and day and are learning to know her; she is indulgent with us. In the morning when she wakes up she tells us of herself in her finished and expressive language, and of her own accord initiates us into her small life; and it seems as though memories in her helped to overcome any strangeness that was between us at first. She came to us herself, and suddenly it was natural for her to say "Mother", and me she calls "Man" and sometimes "Good Man" and every morning is glad that I am still here. And the garden round the quiet house is so beautiful, and we know for certain that it is well with her, and we draw great peace and strength from these days. . . .

45. *To Lou Andreas-Salomé*

Oberneuland bei Bremen
8 *August* 1903

When first I came to Rodin and took breakfast at his house out in Meudon with people with whom I did not become acquainted, with strangers at the table, I knew that his house meant nothing to him, a small and wretched requirement perhaps, a roof against rain and for sleep; and that it was no bother to him and no drag on his loneliness and concentration. Deep within him he bore the darkness, peace and shelter of a house, and he himself had become the sky above it and the wood around it and the distance and the great river that always flowed past. O what a solitary is this old man who, sunk in himself, stands fuller of sap than an old tree in autumn. He has grown

[1] Home of Rilke's parents-in-law.

[2] Rilke's daughter.

deep ; he has dug a deep hole for his heart, and its beating comes from a distance as from the middle of a mountain. His thoughts course round in him and fill him with heaviness and sweetness and do not expend themselves at the surface. He has grown blunt and hard against everything irrelevant, and as though surrounded by old bark he stands there among men. But to everything important he bares his breast, and he is all open when he is with *things*, or when animals and humans touch him quietly, like things. Here he is a learner and beginner and spectator and imitator of the Beautiful that has always been lost among those who sleep, among those who dream and take no part. Here he is the watcher whom nothing escapes, the lover who perpetually conceives, the patient heart that takes no count of time and has no thought of desiring the next thing. Always the thing he sees and surrounds with seeing is the only one for him, the world in which everything happens. When he forms a hand it is alone in space and there is nothing but a hand ; and in six days God made only a hand and poured the waters round it and arched the skies above it ; and he rested when all was finished, and it was a marvel and a hand.

And this way of looking and living is rooted so firmly in him because he acquired it as a craftsman : at the same time that he discovered this infinite, non-thematic, simple principle for his art, he won this great justice for himself, this equilibrium in face of the world which no name could disturb. Since it was given to him to see *things* in everything, he acquired the power to make them ; for in this lies the greatness of his art. No longer does any movement mislead him, as he knows that there is movement even in the contour of a still plane, and only sees planes and systems of planes, which determine forms exactly and distinctly. There is nothing indefinite for him about an object that serves him as a model ; thousands of little planes have here been fitted into space, and when he makes a work of art accordingly, his task is to implant the thing into the surrounding space more passionately, more firmly, and a thousand times better than before, so that it does not move when you shake it. The *thing* is definite, the *art-thing* must be still more definite ; removed from all accident, reft away from all obscurity, withdrawn from time and given over to space, it has become enduring, capable of eternity. The model *seems*, the art-thing *is*. Thus the latter is an indescribable advance on the former, the calm and cumulative realisation of the desire-to-be which proceeds from everything in Nature. Hence the error that would see art as the vainest and most arbitrary of avocations, falls to the ground ; art is the humblest service and is founded absolutely upon law. But all artists and all the arts are full of that error, and it was time for a very powerful personality to rise up against it ; also, he had to be one who *did* things, who did not talk, who created without cease. From the very beginning his art had to be an actualisation (and as such diametrically opposed to music, which transforms the apparent realities of the daily world and still further de-actualises them into insubstantial, ephemeral appearances. Which is just the reason why this direct antithesis of art, this failure to condense, this temptation *towards diffuseness*, has so many friends and sympathisers and slaves, so many who are not free, chained to pleasure, who feel no inner intensity but only a stimulation from outside . . .). Rodin, born in poverty and in a bad social position, saw better than anybody that the beauty of men and animals and things is endangered by time and circumstance, that it is but one instant, a youthfulness that comes and goes in all ages but does not last. What disquieted him was the *appearance* of that which he regards as necessary, indispensable and good : the appearance of beauty. He wanted it to *be*, and saw his task in adapting things (for things lasted) to the less imperilled, quieter and more eternal world of space ; and he unconsciously applied all the laws of adaptation to his work so that it developed organically and became capable of living. Quite early he had tried to make nothing " from its appearance " ; there was no going back for him, rather a perpetual approximation and devotion to the growing thing. And today this peculiarity in him has become so strong that one might almost say the appearance of his things does not concern him : so much does he experience their *being*, their reality, their detachment on all sides from any uncertainty, their completeness and rightness, their self-sufficiency ; they do not stand on the earth, they circle round it.

And since his great work sprang from handcraft, from the *unpurposing* and humble desire continually to make *better* things, he stands today, devoid of all conscious purpose and themes, untouched by them, as one of the simplest among his matured things. The great thoughts, the sublime meanings came to him like laws, fulfilling themselves in perfection and rightness ; he did not invoke them. He did not desire them ; bowed deep as a slave he has gone his way and made an earth, a hundred earths. Yet each of these living earths shines like a heaven and casts starry nights far into eternity. The fact that he laid no plans for anything gives his work this gripping directness and purity. The groups of figures, the larger combinations of forms he did not bring together while they were still ideas (for the idea is one thing — and almost nothing ; but the realisation, another, — and everything). He made things straight away, many things, and from these alone he fashioned the new unity or permitted it to grow, and thus his configurations became intense and legitimate, because not ideas, but *things* allied themselves. — And this work could only come from a workman, and he who accomplished it can easily dispense with inspiration ; inspiration does not descend upon him, because it is *in* him, day and night, occasioned by every glance, a warmth that is generated by every movement of his hand. And the more his things grew about him the less frequent were the disturbances to reach him ; for all noises were consumed upon the realities that surrounded him. His very work protected him ; he lived in it as in a wood, and his life will have to last a very long time, for what he himself planted has become a tall forest. And when you go about among the things with which he dwells, which he sees every day and daily completes, you realise that his house and the noises of it are something unspeakably trivial and irrelevant, and you only see it as in a dream, curiously distorted and filled with a sifting of pallid memories. His daily life and the people who belong to it, lie there like an empty river-bed that he no longer flows through ; but there is nothing sad in that : for near by you can hear the vast murmur and the mighty course of the river that refuses to divide into two branches. . . .

And I think, Lou, that it must be so. . . .

. . . O Lou, in any successful poem of mine there is so much more reality than in any mood or tendency I may feel. Where I create I am true, and I should like to find the strength to base my whole life on this truth, on this boundless simplicity and joy which are sometimes given me. When I first went to Rodin I was seeking this ; for I had known bodingly for years about the measureless example and model of his work. Now that I have come from him I know that I too can demand and seek no other realisations than those of my work. . . . But how shall I begin to tread this path — where is the handcraft of my art, its least and deepest place where I could begin to be diligent ? I will take every path back to that beginning, and all that I have done shall have been as nothing, less than the sweeping of a threshold to which the next visitor will bring the dust of the road again. I have patience for centuries in me and will live as though my time were very great. I will collect myself from everything that distracts me and out of my too facile proficiencies I will win back and husband the things that are mine. But I hear voices that mean well, steps that come nearer, and my doors open. . . . And when I seek people they give me no counsel and do not know what I mean. And with books I am just the same (just as helpless) ; they do not help me either, as though even they were too human. . . . Only *things* speak to me. Rodin's things, the things of the Gothic cathedrals, the things of Antiquity, all things that are perfect things. They point the way to the great archetypes : to the moving and living world, seen simply and without interpretation as a pure occasion for things. I begin to see anew : already flowers mean so infinitely much to me, and from animals have come strange intimations and promptings. And sometimes I perceive even people so, hands live somewhere, mouths speak, and I see everything more quietly and with greater justice.

But I still lack discipline, the ability and the necessity to work for which I have longed for years. Do I lack the strength ? Is my will sick ? Is it the dream in me that inhibits all action ? The days pass, and sometimes I hear the passing of life. And as yet nothing has happened, as yet nothing is real about me ; I keep on dividing myself and flow apart, — I who want to run in *one* river-bed and become great. For it should be like that, shouldn't it, Lou : we should be like a river and not branch off into canals and bring water to the fields ? We should, should we not, keep a grip on ourselves and storm ahead ? Perhaps, when we get very old, once right at the end, we can let go, spread out and pour into a great delta. . . .

46. *To Lou Andreas-Salomé*

OBERNEULAND BEI BREMEN
10 *August* 1903

. . . My letter of Saturday tried to shew you what an event Rodin was for me. He is one of the most significant of men, a signal shining beyond our times, an unparalleled example, a marvel visible from afar — and yet nothing but an unutterably lonely old man, lonely in his great age. You see, he has lost nothing, he has amassed and assembled things about him his whole life long ; he has left nothing in uncertainty and has realised everything ; out of the flight of some fugitive sensation, out of the *débris* of a dream or the first spark of a premonition he has fashioned things and set them about him, thing after thing ; thus a reality grew round him, a large, calm communion with things which united him with the things of another, older age, until he himself seemed descended from a dynasty that knew only greatness : his tranquillity and his patience come from there, his fearless, continuing old age, his pre-eminence above men who are too active, too unstable, meddlers with the balances in which, almost unconsciously, he rests. You are so marvellously right, dear Lou : I was suffering from the too great example which my own art provided me with no means of following directly ; the inability to create *physically* turned to pain in my own body, and my fears also (whose material content was the excessive proximity of something too hard, too stony, too tremendous) arose from the irreconcilable nature of the two worlds of art. . . .

But directly you gave me this explanation, this indescribably helpful and receptive understanding, it became clear to me that I must follow him, Rodin : not by any conversion of my work into sculpture, but by an inward ordering of the creative process ; it is not *forming* that I must learn from him, but profound concentration for forming's sake. I must learn to work, Lou, to work, that's where I fail so badly ! Il faut toujours travailler, toujours — he told me once when I spoke to him about the fearful abysms that open out between my good days ; he could hardly understand it, he, who has become all work (so much so that all his gestures are simple movements taken over from his handcraft). Perhaps it is only a sort of clumsiness that prevents me from working, that is, to glean from everything that happens. . . . For weeks I sat in the Bibliothèque Nationale in Paris and read the books that I had long desired to read ; but the notes I made did not help me to do anything ; for while I read it all seemed to me extraordinarily new and important, and I was tempted to copy out the whole book since I could not take it with me ; inexperienced in books I roam about in them in continual witless peasant-astonishment and emerge confused, laden with the utmost superfluities. And I am equally helpless in face of events that come and go, without the gift of selection, without the ease of acceptance, a mirror turned now here, now there, out of which all images fall . . . hence it is so terribly necessary for me to find the tools of my art, the hammer, *my* hammer, so that it shall become master and grow above all other sounds. There must be a handcraft in this art also ; a faithful, daily labour that uses everything — surely it is possible here as well !

Somehow I too must get down to the making of things ; not plastic, written things, but *realities* springing from some handcraft. Somehow I too must discover the smallest element, the core of my art, the tangible yet insubstantial technique for expressing all things ; then the clear and firm recognition of the mighty task that lay ahead of me would compel and drive me towards it : then I would have so infinitely much to do that one work-day would resemble another, and I would have work which would always succeed because it would start with the littlest and most achievable things and yet be already great. Then all the disturbances and voices would suddenly be far from me, and even what was hostile would merge into my work as sounds enter into dreams, guiding them gently towards the unexpected. My subject-matter would lose still more in importance and weight and become wholly a pretext for work ; but just this apparent indifference towards them would enable me to portray all themes, to fashion and find with the rightful, unpurposing means such pretexts for everything.

Does this handcraft lie perhaps in language itself, in a better awareness of its inner life and desires, its development and its past ? (The huge dictionary of Grimm which I once saw in Paris led me to this possibility. . . .) Does it lie in any special study, in the more accurate knowledge of anything ? (For many people this is undoubtedly the case without their knowing it, and for them some specialisation is their daily work, their handcraft.) Or does it lie in a certain well-inherited and well-augmented culture ? (Hofmannsthal would testify to that. . . .) But with me it is different ; I am ever at odds with all things inherited, and what I have acquired is so slight ; I am almost without culture. My incessantly renewed attempts to embark upon a definite study come to a miserable end, owing to external causes and the curious feeling that has always overcome me at the start : as though I had to return to some inborn knowledge I had left, by a weary road which after many windings only leads back to it again. Perhaps the sciences I essayed were too abstract, and perhaps new things will be born from others ? . . . But for all that I lack the books and for the books the signposts. . . .

47. *To Lou Andreas-Salomé*

Oberneuland bei Bremen
11 *August* 1903 (*Tuesday*)

. . . I do not want to sunder art from life ; I want them, somehow and somewhere, to be of one meaning. But I am one of life's bunglers, and that is why, when life gathers about me, it so often becomes a resting-place, a delay that causes me to lose so much, as when sometimes in a dream you cannot get done with your dressing and miss something very important, which will never come again, in fumbling with two obstinate shoe-buttons. And it is true that life goes by and leaves you no time for omissions and the many losses ; particularly true for anybody who wants to have an art. For art is something much too big and too heavy and too long for one life, and those who are rich in years are but beginners in it. *C'est à l'âge de soixante-treize ans que j'ai compris à peu près la forme et la nature vraie des oiseaux, des poissons et des plantes* — wrote Hokusai ; and Rodin feels just the same, and one might think also of Leonardo who grew to be very old. And they have lived always in their art and, themselves gathered about one single thing, let all else run to seed. Yet how should they not be afraid who come but seldom into their sacred kingdom, because, out there in the embattled world, they get caught in all the traps and knock themselves numb on all obstacles ? Therefore I want so yearningly and so impatiently to find the work, the work-day, because life, once it becomes work, can become art. . . . Have indulgence with me if I keep you waiting ; you have gone ahead like a guiding sign, but I go as the beasts when the close-season is over. . . .

48. *To Lou Andreas-Salomé*

Oberneuland bei Bremen
15 *August* 1903

. . . Behind the park which surrounds this house there pass the express trains from Hamburg, and their noise is great and drowns all the wind in the trees ; and daily it grows more ominous, for already the little bit of quiet that enclosed us is losing its leaves and through it you can glimpse the impending journey and feel approaching, mingled with the fatigues to come, the promise of distant cities and the spirit of far-away places and new things. Next Friday perhaps or Saturday we are setting out on our journey ; the first rest is Marienbad (where a meeting with my father is arranged), and then we make a halt in Munich to look at a fine canvas by a friend we made in Paris. It is the *Bullfighter's Family* painted by Ignacio Zuloaga, and as a man too the Spanish painter made such a great and immediate impression on us that we are looking forward expectantly to this picture — into which he has put so much of himself — just as though we were seeing him again. In Venice also (which is our next stop) we shall see pictures of his; perhaps they will seem the only real thing in this dreamlike town which, in essence, resembles a scene in a mirror. Then, after a short stay, we go on to Florence, that glowing and lovely land which was the home of so much worship, gaiety and renown. There too only a few days' respite will be given us, for then comes Rome, tremendous Rome with its calling voices, Rome which for us is still but a name. Soon, however, it will be a thing formed of a hundred things, a great shattered vessel out of which the Past seeps into the ground, the Rome of the ruins that we shall build up again. Not as they once might have been — we shall build them rather as seekers of the inner future in this past, in which much that was eternal lay dormant. As successors to these isolated, time-lost things which Science misunderstands when it encumbers them with names and periods, which admiration misjudges when it discerns in them a particular and classifiable sort of beauty; for they have kept their faces in the earth and put aside all denominations and significances; and when they were found they rose, lightly, above the earth and had almost gone among the birds, so much were they creatures of space and like stars stationed over the unsettled times. Herein, I think, lies the incomparable worth of these rediscovered things: that you can consider them as good as unknown; no one knows their purpose and (for the unscientific at least) nothing utilitarian clings to them, no irrelevant voice interrupts the stillness of their closely-garnered existence, and their duration is without retrospect and without fear. The masters from whom they derive are no more, no misunderstood fame sullies their shapes, which are pure, no history overshadows their unrobed brightness: they *are*. That's how I imagine the art of Antiquity. The little tiger which Rodin has is like this, the innumerable fragments and débris in the museums (which you pass by unheeding for a long time until one day one of them tears off the veil, reveals itself, shines like a first star, and suddenly, once you have noticed it, hundreds more come out beside it breathlessly from the depths of the sky) are of this order, and the magnificent *Victory of Samothrace* too, standing on the thrusting ship's prow in the Louvre like a sail full of happy wind ; and much that seems slight to those who still, misled by the pretext of some theme or other, seek there for sculpture, dwells in supreme perfection amid those statues, their limbs broken, merely hinted at. Equally fine are the Gothic things which, although they stand nearer to us in time, are just as remote, just as unutterable, just as self-contained in their loneliness, devoid of origin like the things in Nature. They, and what issued from Rodin's hands, lead us up to the most immemorial art-things, to pre-Grecian art in whose spirit there lies a sculptural temerity, an absolute *quiddity* heavy as lead, mountainous and hard. Affinities such as no one had ever dreamed of were disclosed, groupings bound themselves together and formed currents that flowed through the ages, and beneath the history of mankind could dimly be pre-figured the history of infinite generations of *things*, like a procession of slower, quieter transformations whose progress is more profound, more intense, more unswerving than ours. To this history, Lou, the people of Russia will perhaps one day adapt themselves, for they, like Rodin, work at it creatively ; patient and continuously growing they trace their descent from things and are kin to them, kin by blood. That expectancy in the Russian character (which the German with his high-blown concern for things of no import calls laziness) receives thus a new and definite explanation : perhaps the Russian is made to let mankind's history pass him by, so as later to fall into the harmony of things with his chanting heart. He has only to endure and persevere and, like the violinist to whom no sign has as yet been given, sit in the orchestra holding his instrument cautiously lest anything befall it. . . . Filled with a more and more passionate assent I bear within me my love for this wide, holy land, both as a new foundation for solitude and a high fortress against others.

49. *To Lou Andreas-Salomé*

ROME, VIA DEL CAMPIDOGLIO 5
3 *November* 1903

Can you still remember anything of Rome, dear Lou ? What are your memories of it ? Mine will only be of its waters, these clear, exquisite, leaping waters that play in the squares ; its steps which, built in the likeness of falling water, thrust out their ledges one after another so strangely, like waves ; the stateliness of its gardens and the splendour of its broad terraces ; its nights, which last such a long time, tranquil and full of great constellations.

Of its past which maintains a precarious existence I shall probably learn nothing ; nothing of its museums crammed with meaningless statues, and little of its pictures ; I shall remember the bronze statue of Marcus Aurelius on the Capitoline Square, one beautiful marble piece in the Ludovisi Museum (*The Throne of Aphrodite*), a column in some small, forgotten church, a few quite unknown things, the view over the arid Campagna, a lonely road leading into the evening and all the sadness in which I lived.

In which I live. . . .

54. *To Lou Andreas-Salomé*

ROME, VILLA STROHL-FERN
15 *January* 1904

. . . Outside, where so much rain was, there is now a spring afternoon, hours of a spring which may not be there tomorrow, but which now seems to have been there from all eternity : so balanced is the tender, slender wind stirring the leaves, the shining laurel leaves and the modest leaf-buds of the evergreen oak, so confident are the little red shoots on the newly denuded trees, and so strong is the scent rising from the pale grey-green field of narcissi in my quiet acre of garden which an ancient bridge meditatively spans. I have swept the heavy lees of the rain from my flat roof and cleared the withered oak leaves to one side, and that has warmed me, and now, after this little turn of real work, the blood hums in me as in a tree. And, for the first time in ages, I feel the tiniest bit free, almost festive. . . .

Once, in Paris, during the spring of last year, there was an exhibition of antique paintings at Durand-Ruel's,[1] murals from a villa near Boscoreale which were shown once again undis-

[1] Art salon.

turbed in their ruined state before a chance auction scattered them for ever; they were the first antique paintings I had seen, and I have seen none more beautiful here, and they say that even in the museum at Naples there are no better paintings from that almost vanished age, which must have had such great artists. Of these fragments one was preserved quite whole although it was the largest and perhaps the most breakable; on it was portrayed a woman who with a grave and tranquil mien was listening to a man speaking softly and sunkenly, speaking to himself and to her in that dark voice in which destinies long perished are reflected again like the twilit banks of a river; this man, if I remember rightly, had his hands folded on a staff, clasped on the staff with which he had gone long journeys in distant lands; they were resting while he spoke (as dogs lay themselves down to sleep when their master begins to tell a story and they see that it will last a long time); but although this man was deep in his tale and still had a great stretch of memories before him (memories like plains in which the path often takes unexpected turnings), yet you knew, even at the first glance, that he was the man who had come, come and journeyed to this quiet, hieratic woman, this woman who was the prodigal's majestic native-land; so much was the gesture of homecoming still in him as in the waves by the seashore, always, even when they recoil flattened and gleaming like glass; the hurrying from which even the seasoned traveller is not entirely free, had not quite left him; his feelings were still set for unexpectedness and change, and the blood still coursed in his feet which, more feverish than his hands, could not sleep. Thus were peace and movement placed side by side in this picture, not as contrasts, rather as complements to one another, an infinite unity which closed slowly like a wound that heals; for the movement itself was peace, it settled as the snow settles when it falls quietly; became landscape just as the snow does when it spreads over the shapes in the distance; and the Past now assumed, when it returned, the aspect of the Eternal and resembled those great events which had comprised and transfigured that woman's life.

I shall always remember the way in which this great, simple

picture affected me, how absolutely it was painting because it contained only two figures, and how significant because these two figures were filled with themselves, heavy with themselves and united by some matchless necessity. Just as the content of national legends is immediately apparent in good pictures, so I understood the meaning of this painting at first glance. . . .

57. *To Lou Andreas-Salomé*

VILLA STROHL-FERN
17 *March* 1904

. . . Daily I have to wonder whether the Russian War has not brought terror and danger upon your family : your nephews, your mother and yourself. I suppose this catastrophe had to come, this tribulation, this agony for thousands who all felt the war as Garschin felt it : as an agony inflicted.

O God, had one but strength, stores of strength — did one not live, as I do, a quiet, secluded life, meagre and fearful enough, from the daily bread of my strength, — had one but been a real person (a doctor, which is what one should, ultimately, have been) — there would be no place or calling now for anyone who wanted to find a use for his energies and a task to bend to save in those dressing-stations, where the people of Russia die a hard and dreadful death.

I think of young Smirnoff, one of the workmen we met with Schillchen. Later I received two letters from him ; he was a soldier in Warsaw. Perhaps he too is among the chosen out there, suffers and thinks, thinks, tries to understand. . . .

What is happening in the hearts of all these people who have been sent so suddenly towards the east from their quiet snow-covered villages and suburbs ?

Here, the Roman spring is beginning ; the city is filling up with the conventionally enchanted tourists ; every now and then a party of sightseers comes through our park. . . . Then I creep deeper into my little red house which I hardly ever leave. I am reading Soeren Kierkegaard. And this summer I shall learn Danish so as to read him and Jacobsen in the original.

The СПОВО [1] translation is finished. Then in February I

1 " The Song of Igors Heer " (old Russian legend).

am beginning a larger work, a sort of second part to the *Stories of God* ; at the moment I am stuck in the middle of it without knowing if and when it will go on, and whither it will lead. . . .

59. *To Lou Andreas-Salomé*

ROME, VILLA STROHL-FERN
15 *April* 1904

. . . There have been continual interruptions these last few days, and that interruptions would come by the hundred I suspected when I began my new work [1] on the eighth of February ; it was apparent then that my technique of work (and equally my much more comprehensive vision) had altered, so that I shall never again be able to write a book in ten days (or evenings), but shall need for each a long and uncounted time ; that is good, it tends towards the *perpetual work* which I want to achieve at all costs ; perhaps it is the first step. But there is also a new danger in this alteration ; to ward off all external interruptions for eight or ten days is quite possible — but for weeks, for months ? This fear oppresses me, and perhaps it alone is to blame that my work wavered and broke off with the beginning of March. And what I took for a little gap and a pause has now, in despite of myself, become a difficult holiday that is still continuing.

. . . What has been happening here for the last three or four days is, God knows, spring no longer ; it is a sultry young summer. In my little bed the hyacinths, which have long hesitated, are opening their blossomy eyes like someone shrilled at by an alarm-clock and stand there long and erect. The elms and oaks near my house are full, the Judas-tree has ceased blooming and its leaves are all out over-night ; and a syringa which but three days ago was putting forth its first clusters is already fading and withering. The nights now are barely cool and the agitated din of frogs is their voice. The owls call more seldom, and the nightingale has not yet begun. Will she sing now, when it is summer ?

It is beautiful here in the garden, even when nothing much

[1] Portions of *Malte Laurids Brigge* were written in Rome.

blooms in it and the atmosphere of Rome is rather too loud, too obtrusive to be called spring. Even the fields of anemones and daisies are too dense, too heavy, too close-meshed, and in the sky there are none of those grey days behind the empty trees, none of those wide transfiguring winds or softly falling rain which for me are the essence of spring. It is a spring for foreigners who have but little time to spare, loud, blatant, and exaggerated. There is, however, one tree in the garden that might well stand in Tuscany, in an old monastery: a lofty, ancient cypress, completely overgrown with wistaria which everywhere, right to the very top, lifts and dips its pale mauve hangings out of the tree's darkness — it is a joy. That and the glorious fig-trees which stand there with raised, curving boughs like the altar-candlesticks of the Old Testament and slowly open their light-green leaves.

And the fact that I can now peacefully and patiently observe and learn all this is, I feel, a kind of progress and preparation; but you know, all the progress I make is rather like the soft steps of a convalescent, singularly weightless, faltering and boundlessly in need of help. And the help is absent. . . .

62. *To Lou Andreas-Salomé*

ROME, VILLA STROHL-FERN
12 *May* 1904

That I now feel everything so changed is due perhaps to my being in Rome and not in Tuscany, which, with Botticelli and the Robbias, with the white marble and the blue sky, with gardens, villas, roses, bells and foreign girls, spoke to me so intimately; but it did *speak* (and Rome speaks too), it was neither silent nor did it shout: it spoke. It spoke till my cheeks glowed (and I sometimes wonder whether that was not what was really good and important for me, and whether my first trip to Viareggio which, for all my efforts, ended in nothing, like a firework, was not a proof that the Italian influence does not belong to the things that genuinely help me). However that may be, the fact remains that more northerly and graver lands have inured my mind since then to the gentle and the simple, so that it now perceives the forceful glare, the schematic rigidity of Italian things as a relapse into a writing lesson. Quite spontaneously it has come about that I was able to observe and study this loud and ostentatious spring botanically, with the quiet and objective attention which my vision more and more assumes; its motions and voices and the flight and passage of its birds interested me quite dispassionately, without my once coming to feel it as something whole, alive, and mysterious, a soul bordering vitally on my own. I noted details and, as I hitherto have observed so little and am a beginner in simple looking as in so much else — such occupation delighted me and I made progress. But if ever I expected or needed anything from the *whole*, I opened and closed again empty and was inwardly starved. Like a lung in a spent room my soul gasped in an exhausted world, into which nothing new enters with the spring, nothing large and limitless. I felt the great poverty that lies in riches: how, with us, a flower, a small first flower that struggles and comes, is a world, a joy, to share which does you an infinite amount of good — and how here herds of flowers come without anything ever stirring in any of them, without anything bearing part and feeling related and divining its own beginning in another. Here everything is resolved towards lightness, towards the lightest side of lightness. Flowers come, and blossoms, anemones bloom and wistaria, and you say this to yourself and say it again and again, as to a deaf person. But it is all so blank and fair-seeming, like a mask; colours are there, true; yet they subordinate themselves lazily to a cheap colour-scheme and never develop out of themselves. The Judas-tree flowered, flowered and flowered, even from its trunk gushed the coagulated tripes of its bursting unfruitful blossom, and in a few weeks everything, anemones and clover and syringa and wind-flower, everything was drenched with the mauve of its mauve, God knows why — from laziness, from adaptation to circumstance, from lack of original ideas. And even now the red roses, dying, take on this corpse-like mauve, and the strawberries have it if they lie for a day, and the sunsets belch it up, and it spreads over the clouds morning and evening. And the skies in which such cheap tints come and go, are sick and as though silted up;

they are not everywhere, they do not, as the skies of the moor, the sea, and the plains do, play *round* things, they are not an endless beginning of the distance, they are finish, curtain, end, — and behind the last trees, which stand flat as stage-scenery against the indifferent photo-background, — everything stops. They are so rightly the skies above the Past ; skies empty, deserted, sapped dry, sky-husks from which the last sweetness has long been drained. And as the sky is, so are the nights, and as the nights are, so is the voice of the nightingales. Where the nights are wide their note is deep, and they draw it from an infinite distance and carry it to an end. Here the nightingale is really only a lewd little bird with a frivolous song and an easily satisfied longing. In two nights you have grown accustomed to her call and you remark it with an inward reserve, as though you were afraid of injuring your own memories by any greater response, memories of nightingale-nights which are quite, quite different.

The showroom atmosphere, which is so typical of city-life, is also the most obvious characteristic of the Roman spring : it is a showman's spring that takes place here, not Spring. Of course the tourists love it and feel honoured like little princes for whose sake everything has been swept and garnished ; for these respectable Germans Italy must always be a sort of monarchic journey with triumphal gateways, flowers and fireworks. And in a certain sense they are right : they come down, tired of winter, central-heating and darkness, and find sun and comfort ready prepared for them. They do not demand more. And the effects that I used to feel from a stay in Arco or Florence were of this nature, and the benefit that resulted. But once you have seen, as a native, the whole winter here (full of the dogged pertinacity of what *cannot* die), the miracle that then ought to appear fails to materialise. You know that it isn't a spring at all, for you have seen no spring evolving ; these blossoms had as little difficulty in coming to their appointed places as decorations have in being put up anywhere. And you can understand so thoroughly the sham-life of this vanished people, the vapidity of their conventionalized art, the garden-border beauty of D'Annunzio's verses.

It is a good thing that I have experienced all this so slowly and physically ; for Italy has always been a call for me and an unfinished episode. Now, however, I can leave it with a satisfied heart, for the end has come.

Of course it will be hard, because this little house is on the spot and cannot be taken away and set up again in some other, more northerly garden. . . .

Art is a long long life-road, and when I think how slight and rudimentary is all that I have accomplished hitherto, it does not surprise me that this achievement (which is like a hand's-breadth of half-cultivated field) yields me no sustenance. Plans bear nothing, and corn prematurely sown does not burgeon. But patience and work are real and may change into bread at any moment. " Il faut toujours travailler ", Rodin told me every time I tried to complain about the dichotomy of daily life ; he knew of no other solution, and indeed it had been his own. For years they repudiated him, and if he had lived only with his plans and waited for better times, everything would have passed over him as over nothing ; but since his world sprang up among people it forced them to halt and was an obstacle that compelled their attention. — To remain with my work and to put my trust in it alone, this I am learning from his great and greatly given example, just as I am learning patience from him ; my experience, of course, tells me again and again that I cannot count on large reserves of strength, and for this reason I shall, in so far as is feasible, not do two things at once, not separate livelihood from work, but try to find both in the same concentrated struggle ; only in this way can my life grow into something good and necessary, and from its hereditary and immature dismemberment heal into one fertile stem.

Hence I want to fix on my next abode, all other considerations apart, with a view to my work and nothing else. I want that all the more as I now feel myself in the midst of developments and transitions (changes that concern vision and creation in the same degree) which may slowly lead to the possibility of a *toujours travailler*, when all internal and external difficulties, dangers and confusions would, in a certain sense, really be overcome . . . for whoever is always working can live too, *must* be able to.

So it is time to speak of what are my immediate intentions.

The work I am undertaking, to engage my attention by turns, is as follows :

1. The *Prayers*,[1] which I want to go on with.
2. My new book [2] (whose firm, close-grained prose is like a school and an advance that had to come so as to enable me, sometime later, to write all the others — including the novel about the Military Academy).
3. An experiment in drama.[3]
4. Two monographs on : [3]
   The writer : Jens Peter Jacobsen.
   The painter : Ignacio Zuloaga.

Both these necessitate travel. The first a journey to Tistedt and a stay in Copenhagen, the second a journey through Spain. (Zuloaga was, besides Rodin, the only person during my Paris sojourn who profoundly affected me and whose importance and worth I can feel and express. Or rather, shall be able to express. Sometime I will tell you about him.)

The travel and the books, however, are not pressing ; probably I shall get down to the Jacobsen first. You cannot think how necessary he has become for me . . . so much so, even, that when you journey anywhere among things of importance you can be certain of coming out at a point where he also is (if you go far enough) ; and it is curious to find that his and Rodin's words often agree to the letter : here you have that crystal-clear feeling which the moment in mathematical proofs gives you when two parallel straight lines meet at infinity, or when two great complicated numbers which do not look alike can be simultaneously resolved into one simple integer common to both. A curiously inviolable joy comes from such an experience.

Beside this work, accompanying and supplementing it, I plan to take up some studies. I have started to learn Danish, so as to be able, first of all, to read Jacobsen and some of Kierkegaard in the original.

Further I began something in Paris which I would like to

[1] *I.e.* the *Stundenbuch*. [2] *Malte Laurids Brigge*.
[3] Nothing came of either of these projects.

continue : the reading of the great German dictionary by the brothers Grimm, from which a writer can, I think, gain much nourishment and instruction. For one really ought to know and be able to apply everything that is in a language or has ever entered into it, instead of just making do with a fortuitous vocabulary, which is small enough in all conscience and without range. It would be a good thing if such an occupation led me occasionally to read some of the mediaeval poets ; ought not Gothic art which, architecturally, had so much that is unforgettable and majestic to offer, ought it not to have possessed and created a plastic language as well, words like statues and periods like rows of columns ? I know nothing, absolutely nothing about it. Nothing, I feel, of all I would like to know. — There are so many things an old man can tell you of so long as you are small ; for when you grow up you would know them simply as a matter of course. There are the starry heavens, and I do not know what mankind has learned about them, I do not even know the disposition of the stars. And so it is with flowers, with animals, with the simplest laws that are operative everywhere and traverse the world with a few steps from beginning to end. How life arises, how it functions in the minutest beings, how it branches and spreads, how life flourishes, how it bears fruit : I need to learn all that. By taking part in these processes to bind myself firmly to the reality which so often eludes me — to be there, not only in feeling, but also in knowledge, always and always — that's what I need, I think, to become more assured and less homeless. I do not want the sciences, for a lifetime is required for each one, and no life is enough even for its beginning ; but I want to stop being an outsider, one who cannot read the deeper journals of his age which point forward and hark back far beyond its frontiers ; a prisoner who guesses at everything but lacks that little certainty which knows whether it is day or evening, spring or winter. Somewhere, where it is possible, I want to learn what I probably should have known had I been allowed to grow up in the country and with more real people, what an impersonal and hurried schooling omitted to tell me, and all the other things that have been found and recognised since then and belong to it. I don't want to learn the history of art or any other histories, nor the essence of philosophical systems — I only want to obtain and earn for myself one or two of the large and simple certainties that are there for everybody : I want to ask one or two questions, as children ask them, disconnected for those who stand outside, but full of a family likeness for me, who know their birth and pedigree to the tenth generation.

13 *May* 1904

Up to the present universities have given me so little ; there is too much opposition in my nature to their kind. But my own incompetence, which never and nowhere understands how to take, is to blame for my not having had the acuity to recognise what I need, and of course I did not then have the most important thing of all : patience. Perhaps it has got better now, of patience at least I shall have no lack in the future. And if I no longer try, as I once did, to hear various doctrines propounded about which you can hold this opinion or that — words about words, theories about theories — but try to hear new, real truths to which everything imaginative in me assents, so I shall come simply not to notice the particular vexations of circumstance or shall endure them for the sake of what is important. But this kind of learning-period I lack more than anything else, not only because I know so little of the simple and essential, but also because I have always believed that such must be the road by which I should ultimately attain what I happened to need. The fact that I cannot do this, that left alone among books I am helpless, a child that has to be led out again, continually holds me up, makes me perplexed, miserable, confounded. If any application to science gradually resulted in my learning to survey my subject as a whole, to glimpse and even read the titles of the existing bibliography (not to speak of finding it) ; if I acquired the ability to study old books and manuscripts — in short, if I could appropriate to myself a little of the historian's technique and the patience of the delver into archives, and could hear one or two real truths and judgements, — then any place that had so much to offer would be the right one for me. I feel that without some such appropriation I cannot take my next steps ; after the monograph on Rodin I thought of one on Carpaccio,[1] and later another on Leonardo : what fails me here is not a knowledge of the history of art (which precisely I want to avoid), but rather the simple instruments of the research-worker and the technical assurance and practice for which I must often envy quite young people ; I lack the key to the great libraries here and in Paris, the inner directions for use (to put it crudely), and all my reading was a fortuitous reading because, owing to inadequate preparation, it could not become work. What with my education, which was presided over by no plan, and the timidity in which I grew up (everywhere encountering laughter and patronage and driven back by everybody into my own ineptitude), it so happened that I never got to learn very many of the technical preliminaries of life, which later come effortlessly to everyone ; my feelings are filled to the brim with memories of instances when all the people round me knew how to do something and did it mechanically without thinking, whilst I, in my embarrassment, could do nothing, was not even capable of cribbing it from them. Like someone who has got involved in a game the rules of which he does not know, so, on a thousand occasions, I feel myself a fish out of water. Then I am a nuisance to others and a cause of dislike — but the same deficiencies bar my way and make me confused.

Once I spent the whole summer on the Schoenaich estate alone in the library, the archives of which are crammed full of old correspondence and registers and documents ; I felt in all my nerves the proximity of destinies, the stirring and uprising of figures from whom nothing separated me but the fatuous inability to read and interpret old signs and introduce order among the dusty confusion of those papers. What a good, diligent summer it might have been had I understood the least bit about the management of archives ; something like a *Maria Grubbe*,[2] perhaps, might have been given to me in essentials ; at any rate I could have learned and garnered a great deal from so intimate a contact with those still unchronicled events — whilst as it was I only received a new and daily proof of my incom-

[1] Malte (p. 25) wrote a study of Carpaccio " which is bad ". Rilke's appears to have remained unwritten.

[2] Novel of that name by J. P. Jacobsen.

petence, of that banishment which life always gives me to feel whenever I want to approach her more closely.

And not only for work on the monographs, but for everything that I take up this lack of preparation and comprehensive vision will become increasingly evident; with regard to my plans connected with the Russian things, for instance, it has always been a hindrance and the reason why I make so little progress. But would not such a schooling as I have in mind (without being able to imagine it very clearly) enable me to tackle my work with more confidence, and stick to it; would it not also be a means to attaining that "*toujours travailler*" which is at the heart of the matter?

My plans for study reduce themselves therefore to this:

1. I shall read scientific and biological books and attend lectures which conduce to the perusal and study of such things. (See experiments and preparations, etc.)
2. I shall take up historical studies and archive-reading, in so far as they constitute a technique of work.
3. I shall read the dictionary of the brothers Grimm, together with mediaeval writings.
4. I shall learn Danish.
5. Continue reading Russian and now and then translate something from the original.
6. Translate a book by the writer Francis Jammes from the French.

And read the following books attentively: Michelangelo's scientific studies and his history of France; the 18th century of the Goncourts, and others.

For a time I thought of attempting all this in Copenhagen; going there in the autumn and studying.

Against this, however, militates the fact, firstly, that I shall render my plans for study the more difficult by going to a foreign-speaking country, where there is less point in attending lectures and where the practical side too (the use of libraries, collections and laboratories) would be more complicated.

Secondly, that Copenhagen is a very large city and possibly not very good for my health.

But now the question arises whether everything that I want to do could not, in its initial stages at least, be best and most simply realised in one of the smaller German university towns ? It almost seems to me that it could. I don't want to go to a big one, especially not Berlin, and even Munich (which is the most agreeable, tolerant and advanced of the great cities) repels me in many respects. Though I tell myself that one is left more alone in the great cities, one is also more unbefriended just at those points where I shall need help and advice. And a mass instruction as at the Berlin University would only be a new kind of intimidation for the bewildered child in me, such as I have already experienced ; on the other hand the fact that I am older would, even in a little high school where relations are established more quickly, isolate me and keep me as alone as I want to be, and must be. So I am thinking (quietly, for the moment, and in confidence only to you) of looking for a smaller university town in Germany where you can hear good scientific lectures, attend the historical seminary and use libraries, etc.

By the way do you know that quite recently in Copenhagen (in a student club and before a very full hall) they spoke of my books ? Yes, it has really come about that Ellen Key, complete with large manuscript dealing only with my work, has been travelling to Stockholm, to Copenhagen, and to God knows what other Swedish towns — all for me ! There she told the people about me, and now, she writes, many are beginning to buy my books and read them ; and it was thus that she wanted to help and serve me. But not satisfied with this she wants to publish a long essay developing out of the lectures in a Swedish and, translated, in a German newspaper. She is a kind and efficient person and has little by little become an indispensable friend to both my wife and myself (and little Ruth). I understand truly and with heartfelt gratitude the nature of her work and activities even when I clearly feel that such advocacy on my behalf can in no way be justified ; even now, while it is still happening, I regard its beginning with alarm (to be quite frank) ; for in reality and to less well-wishing eyes nothing is as yet accomplished, nothing demonstrable. A little in the *Stories of God*, in *Mir zur Feier*, and in the *Buch der Bilder* might vouch for me (Ellen does not know of the *Prayers* yet) ; but I am afraid she has represented it all as being much less patchy and given it an appearance of completeness which it doesn't possess and about which people will feel deceived if they buy my books now. Also she said many things (so it appears — I do not know the lecture, only a small extract from it) based on passages from my letters of the last few years and so discovered factors which cannot yet be inferred from my work as published hitherto. And apart from this I feel : if any man stood in need of secrecy, that man is I. (Every line and every perplexity in this letter, but also that in which it is determined, bear witness to this.) All the same I realise that I must accept everything that might support my life and prolong the possibility of my going on with my work. And for this it is certainly good to be so named and noised abroad. Moreover, it has come about through the mouth of a sensitive and careful person, and (premature though it be) it can have no ill results. It has also been proved that here and there in Sweden there were young people who already knew of me, it even happened that they could recite poems from my books by heart ; and it came to light on this occasion that one of the young Swedish literati (independently and without knowledge of Ellen Key's intentions) was actually engaged in collecting material for an essay on my work. . . .

66. *To Clara Rilke*

Borgeby gård (Flaedie) Prov. Skåne
26 *June* 1904

. . . Yesterday, then, I left Copenhagen with the big steamer that crosses the Oeresund. There was a high wind and driving rain. The real heavy storm-rain of the North such as I have not felt for ages. Again I stopped the whole time on deck (an hour and a half) and arrived in Malmö with glowing cheeks and soaked through (the rain cost me my " weather-proof " hat, which now hangs on a peg like an eviscerated doll). Norlind[1] was there. I recognised him from a distance. He looks rather like the German student who used to come and

[1] Swedish painter who was staying with Rilke's hostess.

eat with me at Tre Re.[1] But only a little. The blond reddish beard is broader and longer, the nose set very wide at the base, unsymmetrical, with a markedly sensuous *modelé*, rather snub at the broad tip. It, in conjunction with the sensuous mouth and the head which is completely bald in the middle, bears some resemblance to Verlaine, while the wide structure of the nose separating the two halves of the face is reminiscent of Tolstoi. Thus all sorts of significant qualities appear in his features and would be even more impressive and telling were they not somewhat bloated, partly from disposition, partly from the unwholesome life he has led. Inalienably combined with all that is a powerful streak of monasticism. His smell is a monkish smell, the rather plump neck is monkish, monkish too are his hands — and the quick, suave, pattering speech is of a monkish kind ; also he has from time to time the manner of a doctor speaking soothingly to a sick man. With this is allied much of the Munich painter — movement, attitude, and expression : in his laughter, when it starts, when it ends, in his enjoyment. (E.N. was in Munich and Dachau in 1897 and 1900.) Through all these hereditary characteristics and influences there breaks something very cordial and pleasantly northern, which makes contact with him simple and natural. It is, perhaps, in his eyes most of all that his home country has persisted, in his beard and voice.

In Malmö, rain. I was so soaked through from my promenading on deck that I had to change in a hotel. Norlind was there all the time, asking questions and talking and making me talk a lot until the evening, — although he continually excused himself for doing so. At four o'clock we went on. In the train he suddenly said : " You look awfully tired now ; would you like to put your head on my shoulder and sleep a little ? " I didn't sleep, but as we were now silent he fell into such deep thought that we nearly forgot to alight at Flaedie (pronounced with a divided *i–e*) and only jumped out at the last moment. An old closed cab was waiting at the station, and it was raining so hard I could see neither horse nor driver, but felt that we were travelling well.

The country is flat — fields, lonely farms. Enormous cows

[1] Restaurant in Rome.

browse in the rich pastures. At last come trees, very large trees, — farm buildings, one with a stork's nest in it ! A big farmstead, a bend of the road round some huge trees : we drive through the gateway of the middle tower . . . drive out again on the other side, along an avenue of gigantic chestnuts, see on our left the park with meadows dark and fresh from the rain, with long, well-kept paths and trees, trees. To the left of the tower, which contains the actual living-rooms, a small flight of brick steps has been built — there we drove up. An entrance-hall. Fräulein Larsson comes in quickly, with firm step, resolute and awkward at the same time. A solid little body with dark hair, a long brown face, simple like a house-keeper or a farmer's wife, a person rather than a woman, kindly and unquestioningly dutiful. She stumps up to me with somewhat heavy tread, but swift and sure, says simply, quickly, with impulsive heartiness : welcome. Then she asks Norlind to tell me that she is very glad I have arrived. I get my thanks interpreted. Then I am allowed to see my room, that is to say the room in which Norlind has been sleeping and which has been cleared for me. It is a very plain medium-sized room with one window ; at first it seems very dark, owing to its dark carpet and the vines that thrust from all sides in front of the window. But the window is large, — plenty of light and air come in. (I don't know about sun, because none is shining today and I have not yet orientated myself to this part of the world. I am sure, however, that it is not a north room.) The lie of it and the accident of its simple furnishings remind me of the lower rooms in Oberneuland. It so happens that the windows in Oberneuland are placed at the same height, and also the view out on to the trees, bushes, paths between fields and plantations is just the same as in Oberneuland. So from the first moment I felt it as a dear and familiar friend. I shall live in it and probably work in it too. For the " salons " are large rooms in one of which you eat, the other is a sort of drawing-room . . . there is no quiet there, coming and going, and the life of the others is quite close. Whilst I, even when I cross the great hall, am still separated from everything by a little landing of my own. Sitting by my window I hear only the sounds from the garden — the fowls, the little birds and above all the experimental cawings of the young ravens that dwell in tribes in the tops of the trees. — Only that and nothing from the house.

It seems a pity at first that you find no old rooms here. In the three front rooms I now know, everything is freshly furnished. Only in the first room is there a dresser with an old grandfather clock inlaid with light wood (examined more closely it is peasant-style of the last century. And as a matter of fact it came from Frl. Larsson's father, — and was as Norlind said the first bit of furniture he purchased "because of its beauty") — and the materials, curtains and covers and some of the carpets, are good; bright-coloured, strong and firm peasant-fabrics, many of them worked by Frl. Larsson herself. The furniture, which was also made according to her directions, has, despite its efforts to utilise obviously northern and old-fashioned patterns, something at once sham-antique and immature about it, so that you cannot take much pleasure in it, and cannot somehow feel the rooms. It's a pity. Frl. Larsson, who comes from an old peasant family, bought the manor only two years back, presumably without the old stock of furniture, and as she herself is inexperienced and uncertain in her tastes and could only devote herself incidentally to the arrangement of the house (which runs quite simply with the help of one little maid), nothing whole or very remarkable resulted from it. The drawing-room, which has a red-brick fireplace, white furniture with heavy red-gold covers, and the lovely dresser with the clock, is the most effective and the most strongly nordic in its large brightness: like sun and snow-light.

But the main thing is not the house, the main thing is the farm. Frl. Larsson runs this almost entirely alone with the aid of one steward. Yesterday evening I was in the cowsheds, we have two hundred cows, twenty-four horses, bulls, calves, hens of all kinds, two dogs, cats and all sorts of beasts — *two hundred cows!* And while I was there yesterday I saw a long, long stall where they stood by sixes behind one another, about a hundred of them. It was filled with a grey gentle light, and far and wide you could only see backs, warm backs and living breaths. Backs everywhere — standing up, lying down. And soft chewing and rumination and contentment.

Then in a smaller stall a bull that was never untied. A mountain with thunder inside. Full of " primeval worldliness ",[1] as Norlind said. Then the horses : greys, many greys, sorrels, roans. Of the dogs I know but one and not him whose voice I heard this morning.

After all this you can well believe that there is wonderful milk here, and quantities of fruit. A stretch of orchard with strawberry plantations and borders of big gooseberry-bushes. Marvellous strawberries and beautifully prepared gooseberry-compote and a sort of gooseberry fool with cold milk which tastes good. Yes, I think it will be all right with the food too.

Frl. Larsson had waited with the meal yesterday ; so we ate at about five. There was a very nice asparagus soup ; a joint, of which I only tasted a little, for there were potatoes and cauliflower with it, and I kept to those. After that, wonderful fresh strawberries with milk. In the evening the aforementioned gooseberry fool. Before every meal you take bread and butter with cheese or some kind of condiment, of which there are always several to hand. Many varieties of bread, including little round cakes baked of unground corn which taste and smell like a field in summer.

(Interruption : the chief dog, led by Norlind, has just been to visit me. He sniffed attentively at everything new and personal, pressed his head against me, went round enquiringly once more for a little while and then said something deep, approving. He is an enormous beast, a sort of mastiff, with light-pink eyes and a delicate red muzzle, like the inside of a shell.)

In the mornings this is what happens : a large jug of milk is brought up to your room (I have asked for it at seven-thirty), warm milk with two odd little peasant cakes flavoured with cinnamon. The actual family breakfast is rather late, at about half-past nine, and is a proper meal. Today we started with bread, then came a sort of asparagus omelette, very good, eaten with cold milk, and afterwards you drank, as you wished, either a cup of coffee or chocolate. (I had a small cup of coffee.) Lunch, it seems, is not definitely fixed — but appears to be taken somewhere between two and two-thirty. Supper at half-past seven or eight. —

[1] Lit. *Urweltlichkeit.*

This way of living is not bad, — for the time I shall follow it without demur, see how it turns out, and find how I can best arrange my working hours.

We have just eaten : (for breakfast and lunch the steward, greatly rejoicing over the heavy and still continuing rain, sits with us at table). Today there was an excellent barley-milk soup with plums in it, — a joint with butter sauce, rice and asparagus (the latter two in great abundance, so that I again took but a scrappet of meat). Then strawberries with milk. Afterwards a little coffee. (Just a tiny cup.) Everything very good, — I see that I shall like it, and am glad.

Monday, June 27th

. . . Yesterday after lunch I was alone in the park, which lies in the plain like a huge edifice of chestnuts and limes. A big wind rustled in all the trees. I examined everything on my own ; was glad when I recognised something you had pointed out to me. Naturally the great trees confused me a little, I can't recognise all of them, — but that will come in time.

At any rate it was grand to wander about in the big wind-swept garden quite alone and undisturbed. Afterwards the three of us unpacked Norlind's pictures which had come back from an exhibition in Stettin. Then N. and I sat down to a long talk in the yellow room ; he told me a lot about many northern people, about a simple Swedish philosopher, Hans Larsson, whom he described perfectly, eloquent with word and gesture. I listened eagerly, but talked rather too much myself as I was very tired by the evening. That, however, will only be so for the first few days, when N. is all expansive and convivial. He talks, as I said, perfectly, and while he is doing so he has quite another face, young and reflective, with clear shining eyes and an altogether different appearance. Not at all monkish. Even his hands are different.

For supper we had, besides the little introductory dishes, some marvellous porridge cooked with milk, similar to the oatmeal or groats that we know, only much stronger because of the warm aromatic taste of corn. It was a good supper. Afterwards we went, Norlind and I, to the strawberry beds and sought out a few fresh ones for a sweet. And before going to sleep the three of us stood for a while in the square in front of the farm buildings, where there was dancing round the may-tree (June-tree ?). We watched for some moments from a distance and then Norlind suddenly said something to Frl. Larsson, threw his coat into the bushes, leapt into the dance with great strides (like a peasant) and for a good ten minutes turned round and round to the strains of an accordion with one of the girls (I imagine it was our little maid). *Pett wi eens aff !* — In the mornings there is no one to be seen before half-past nine. . . . When I have drunk my milk at seven-thirty I go barefoot on the beautiful lawn behind the house, afterwards taking a long walk through the park. On one side it slopes down to a little flat stream on which there is a boat lying ready. Across this are pastures with calves, cows and powerful horses, manes and tails blowing. Out beyond you see meadows, undulating a little, and then the horizon comes rather soon with a slight rise, behind which is visible to one side the church tower of a village belonging to the estate, to the other the chimney of a brick-kiln. To the north-east the park is bordered by the Borgeby church-yard, on the edge of which stands the old castle church, its steep gabled tower-face opposite our great orchard and rising very strangely into the grey, ever-scudding sky. On this side also is the sea, and soon we shall be going there. . . .

My French won't come back to me at all and is so fragmentary that I can only speak very little with Frl. Larsson. Often I regret it, — for I feel that she is a good, healthy, pleasant sort of person whom you could really talk with. I don't think I shall learn Swedish very quickly (Danish sounds much more mysterious and delicate !) — it is extraordinarily foreign to my ears, — but my French is sure to improve again. Even in Milan I could speak it better — but here, probably because I am hearing an entirely new language, it has been side-tracked and I lack even the rudiments, — for which reason I often prefer to get Norlind to translate for me.

A nice little letter of greeting was awaiting me from Ellen Key. From Borgeby to Oby Alfvesta is seven to eight hours' journey by rail and coach ! (By rail to Stockholm.) Despite that, says N., it is not impossible for her to take us by surprise here one of these days, and I also think she will come. — The article[1] for *Wort und Bild* is being printed here (coming out in the July number) ; the proofs arrived today (it is very long) and N. is translating it.

In her letter of greeting Ellen Key wrote concerning this essay just what we ourselves have often uttered with fear and alarm : " I have said very little about you, mostly let you say it, leading people to you through your own words. I find it too much of a responsibility to say anything about a living and growing writer. By doing so you may exercise a sort of compulsion over him : ' He is like that.' Who knows ? He may be hundreds of things, and perhaps you compel him in one direction by an overhasty utterance : ' He is like *this*. . . .' " Odd, isn't it ? As though she had felt everything we had said. She once wrote that there must be an overseas transmission between us. So it might really have happened ! Anyway she has somehow got hold of the second edition of the *Stories of God* and is very pleased with the dedication. It would be nice if I could see her. In this letter she writes again of two possibilities which she has arranged for me later. . . .

It was a very good thing that we wrote about the room. The lower room where Norlind now sleeps is really sad and dark, a kind of cellar or dungeon buried deep among the foundations of the house, having, high up over a step, only one little window whose lower edge abuts on to the ground. There are sunflowers in front of it, not yet in bloom. The room itself is remarkable, with strong walls, dome-like ceiling and quite nicely furnished ; but for me it would have been too cold, oppressive and mournful. Whereas mine I shall like, I think. (Our stork has just flown past my window, looking huge.) The chestnuts are over, the last gold is dropping from the great hanging laburnums. But the mallows are already in bud, and the dahlias are growing. Cherries and blackcurrants are still green, but present in immense quantities. And in the vegetable garden I discovered ten lovely big carciofi plants with little fruits. . . .

1 *En Oesterikisk Diktare*, first published 1904 in *Ord och Bild*, now entitled *A God-Seeker* in Ellen Key's essays.

70. *To Clara Rilke*

BORGEBY GÅRD, FLAEDIE, SWEDEN
9 *July* 1904

. . . A high wind is blowing across from the Sund, the garden froths, and when you look up you see little bright patches of distant fields coming and vanishing behind the flickering leaves of the bushes. The roses are flowering in their beds, roses that are a trifle shabby, nobody has time for them, and they flower and fade very quickly, it seems to me. Today's storm has scattered many that were not there yesterday, and now they lie in the grass like torn letters. Among the stocks one spray has been open for days, but masses of mallows, dahlias and other flowers are still waiting. In the many-branched, dipping laburnum hang the grey-violet clusters of pods, and their pallor permeates the whole tree and puts a distance between it and the others, thrusts it back, almost veiling it. The little rose-bouquets of the round, turret-like hawthorn bushes have become brown, but behind them the snowy jasmin is still in flower, its single, dead-white blossoms visible from a distance, grouped together like constellations of stars, but quite far apart when seen from close to. And the great flattened sprays of lilac lie like the beginnings of yellowish Brussels lace among the dull taffeta foliage. In the still mornings their perfume (when it is not diffused and can collect and concentrate) is like the strong scent of the sweat of young girls who have been chasing one another and run over the fields and now arrive hot and straggling, with a strained, almost angry seriousness in their faces and wild, exhausted laughter. — But today, in the wind, all the scents are thin, fluid, sail past, come back weak and mixed with the distance and go past again. Walnuts and chestnuts, wrenched from the great loaded trees, fall down with a hard, frightening thud, and the little stream below is all combed up on the surface and battles with the Sund, which shoves it back into the estuary. The bulls, far off in the westerly meadows, are calm, coloured, massive things, but over there the calves are gay and frolicsome, and they drag the horses along with them, and suddenly these give a leap, turn round, trot and gather together with long strides. And overhead, sky in a transparent, remote, vaporous whiteness that has been exhaled by slowly mounting clouds, while the sun continually breaks through and disappears again, so that the day seems very long.

This morning Frl. Larsson went off to Lund, and I sit under the great walnut-tree (while the rain holds off) and am quite alone in Borgeby gård, of whose history and inhabitants I now know a great deal : some of it read toilsomely in Swedish from old descriptions, some that I guessed and some that I only suspect. In front of me stands Bishop Birger's tower, quite spoilt by the restorations of the owner before last, but still *his* tower, a thing people know and talk about throughout all Skåne. In the church, under the belfry, a painted triptych has been preserved (carelessly enough) portraying one Hans Spegel, knight and chamberlain to Frederick II, and his two very different spouses. And in the narrow, prison-like crypt beneath the nave lie three skulls and a number of strong bones of a man, scattered among the crumbling fragments of a coffin and belonging, perhaps, to the picture under the bell. And on the western gable of the house, cut on a steel plate, are the signatures of Hans Spegel's heirs : Otto Lindenow and his wife Elsa Juel, 1638. Then came owner after owner, many of them from Sweden's greatest families, the Counts of Trolle, Bonde, Freiherrn von Ramel, von Hastfer, Counts de Greer and von Wachtmeister (from whom Anna Larsson acquired the manor). It passed from name to name, because it always went as an inheritance on the mother's side from daughter to daughter and received with their husbands a new master. Yet the women were always the actual owners, maybe because they were more diligent and domiciliary than the strangers to whom they gave themselves, maybe because (as generally happened) they outlived them and long survived them : for they all came of upright, solid houses that could stand old age. Of all these no sign or witness has remained ; it is to be supposed that the last of the counts related by marriage to those old families, took everything with them that pertained to their respective women. Only for the one from the House of Hastfer are there two old weatherbeaten stones in the park, which speak gently of a life gone gently by. One of these stones was put up by Colonel

Carl Bergenstrahle for Brita Sophie Hastfer, who, after a long maidenhood, became his wife at forty-three years of age, and it also records her death which took place thirteen years later. The other stone (without date) comes from the nephew of Brita Sophie (who was childless) and only states yet again that she was dear and good and that one cannot forget her.

So it was always a woman's fate that was passed in Borgeby gård, flowing or lingering like a stream. And it is strange: once again (after Frl. Larsson's father bought it) it has come into a daughter's hand; once again, as it was five and six hundred years ago, a strong, circumspect woman reigns in Borgeby, of old peasant stock, hard-working and good and capable, to outlive, perhaps, many suitors.

And in the tops of the old beech-trees dwell the families of crows, hundreds and hundreds of them; and when they fly home of an evening in flocks, screaming, the tree-tops grow smaller under them; and when swarm after swarm sallies forth again and rises and circles, there is a noise as of many dresses and fans, only much greater. And certainly there is one among them, a veteran with a good memory for tradition, who still ponders the chronicles of Borgeby and compares Hanna Larsson (foreshortened in time as he sees her) with Brita Sophie, with Vivika Bonde, and with Elsa Maltesdotter Juel! . . .

We have bread of various sorts here for every meal, each one very good and full of perfume. White bread, home-baked, similar to that which we sometimes had in Westerwede, a sort of "*schrotbrot*", and some excellent, strongly-spiced black bread, not to speak of little discs of baked corn. . . .

The strawberries, which yielded an inexhaustible harvest, are gradually coming to an end, but the currants are already reddening, and the cherries too have the first tinge of red like the reflection of a red frock on them. So there will be hardly any pause at all.

N.'s departure has changed nothing — save that I cannot talk very much and, till about mealtimes, am always quite alone. Conversation in French with Frl. Larsson has, of course, somewhat increased in scope since she has been by herself, but the language sets its own limits and continually puts an end to our discourse. In one way it is a pity, because I should like to talk of this and that with Frl. Larsson and ask her a number of things, but then again the obligatory use of a third language is itself annoying in the midst of the Swedish that is spoken here and to which I want very much to get accustomed. Sometimes the steward and a young assistant of his eat with us at table, and sometimes the housekeeper as well, and then a lot of Swedish is spoken, without my making any progress in the understanding of the talk. When you listen to it, a broad pause is made during every phrase on the vowels, on the *a* and *u*, and if you knew Platt well and spoke out courageously you would get along all right. It is easy to read, easier than Danish almost, but the pronunciation of the latter is infinitely more complicated, more muted and more refined, with a marked difference between the written word and its phonetic value.

But there is a very great deal in these literatures which we don't know the least thing about. Hermann Bang, a neurotic and exhausted morphia-addict, has written twenty-five powerful books; besides *The White House* a *Grey House* and many others including a volume of poetry. Helge Rode is highly esteemed by the Danes and, in addition to four or five plays, has published verse and novels. We know little of Edith Nebelong. The Swedes call Gustaf Froeding (none of whose work has been translated) their greatest poet and they have quantities of good writers: from Strindberg and Selma Lagerloef to the young writers of Skåne. And in the capital of Skåne, Lund, lives also their great, quiet, little-known poet-philosopher Hans Larsson. . . . He has written many little middling-strong books under hard necessity (as he had to); in these he discusses the problems of art — says among other things that no artist can make use of the existing "laws" because they are all too loose, slack and indefinite, whilst in his own work each line must be exact and no point should be passed over. . . . Or he discusses Ibsen's *Peer Gynt*, penetrates deep into it and comes out again from the depths right past gloomy old Ibsen into clarity. Or he emerges unexpectedly from a philosophical controversy into living waters and draws near to you full of the vital and the necessary. Nietzsche, with whom we have all become slightly intoxicated, he has taken as a medicine and has grown healthier from it. In many cases his thought has anticipated Maeterlinck, but from his own experience and, when he read him later, he concurred here and there cautiously and with unconscious superiority (but also not without a certain unconscious mistrust). But he goes far beyond him: his sureness in living is such that he would never be in danger of accepting an easy solution. He knows that by bearing the heavy we make it light (because fundamentally we have gigantic powers), but that to wish to bear the light is a betrayal, a withdrawal from life, a retreat before it. He is firm and reliable, and his words seem, of all those I have ever read (in so far as they came from philosophers) to be the most plausible. On the last day before Norlind departed he read me some more passages from one of Hans Larsson's books. There was one bit I remember approximately as follows: *When you feel the emptiness in and about you, what ought you to do? Society and other distractions are only apparent aids. You must go into yourself. You must concentrate, be alone. You must feel your emptiness round you like an empty room, like an arch. . . .*

With him it always comes down to such large, *created* images in which everything is immeasurably strengthened and exalted. You pass gently from liberation to liberation. Norlind has translated a little of Hans Larsson's work (the MS. is with Larsson) and proposes to translate still more in Russia; then you can read it too, and we might perhaps get it printed by Axel Juncker! — On the 15th of this month Hans Larsson is giving a series of lectures on education (he is professor of philosophy in Lund); I may go over with Frl. Larsson to see him and hear him speak, and she may possibly invite him here later, when Norlind is back. He never goes anywhere, but once he came to Borgeby because he thinks highly of Norlind, who was his pupil, and takes great pleasure in his thought and way of life. . . .

71. *To Clara Rilke*

BORGEBY GÅRD, FLAEDIE, PROV. SKÅNE
SWEDEN, 12 *July* 1904

. . . Torsten Holmstroem, student of zoology at Lund, friend of Ernst Norlind but much younger than he, came over yesterday evening to shoot ducks.

This short notice, read in the light of our German notions, does not sound anything unusual. But a new experience confirms me in the suspicion that " being a student " here means something quite, quite different from what it means in Germany, — the experience, namely, that there was after all something unusual about meeting this student. He was simply a young person, observant, quiet, youthful, delighting in everything he saw, confident, strong, knowledgeable — it is difficult to say *what* he was like, maybe merely typical of the people here, just young and full of life, maybe with many other things brewing in him — who can tell. At any rate he was alive and actively living his experiences, undistracted and good. How well he knew nature, every blade of grass, every stalk, had lived it, felt it, loved it. How attentively he went about outside, with that far-flung hunter-attentiveness which Turgenieff loved. And what enchanted, vivid memories he had in him : the flight of a wild swan, a bird of prey sailing over the autumnal trees, a line of ducks wending across the heavy October skies. How he still observed all this, had never ceased observing it for a moment ! It was fine. And he had the same concentration and strength for other memories : for books, for pictures (of which he knew a great many from reproductions, trying with touching fervour to build them up into realities from this inadequate and equivocal background). How pleased he was when I showed him the Zuloaga volume, and what good and acute comments he made : for instance he drew my attention straight away to the hands with the fan in the portrait of Consuelo, thought it splendid. And as we went through the fields in the evening he turned to the glowing, many-hued landscape and said : " This is much more beautiful " (than the garish dazzle, he meant, which Frl. Larsson always pointed out to us). He was only over for one day to shoot ducks and as you can imagine he would not have much baggage with him. But just think, among the little he did have there was a small book and this book was called *Niels Lyhne* (in the same Danish edition as ours), so you can believe me when I tell you that he must have been a nice person. Today he went out at six, and I only saw him towards eleven when he returned with five ducks at his belt and said as he greeted me : " Nice morning to go out ! " Then he came back again (I was sitting reading in my seat in the garden) and gave me a small, strong-smelling flower (a sort of mint) which had got caught under the strap of his hunting-bag. — This afternoon he journeyed back to Lund, or rather near Lund, where he lives with his parents and brothers and sisters. That was Torsten Holmstroem, student of zoology, whom I wanted to introduce to you. . . .

72. *To Clara Rilke*

BORGEBY GÅRD, FLAEDIE, PROV. SKÅNE
SWEDEN, 19 *July* 1904

. . . On Sunday about eight we drove out by coach to Bjerred (station for the train to Lund), which is at the same time a little sea resort, and, from a wooden jetty built far out into the quiet sea, watched the evening going down in a wash of cloudy and watery greys. Yesterday, Monday, I was in Lund and on the way home alone spent another evening-hour on the jetty. It was the evening of a very windy day, and the broad gale flung an immense, night-grey continent of clouds across the sky and set the sun free, which sank at once, — so that two seas lay there separated by a strip of dazzling light : the one all shadowy-grey, veiled over and ponderous, the other burnished, shining, full of motion, that trembled and glittered to the very ends of the earth.

After two days of great heat we now have a fine rushing wind ; unfortunately we cannot feel it through the windows, because the house stands behind its walls of trees and thickets as in a room. But outside, on the road that forms the edge of the park towards the fields, it is tremendous, and the roaring and buffeting in the trees is full of passion.

Today about morning a little foal was born in the fields. I think I was the first to see it on my early morning walk. Small, pale-brown, tousled, with short neck, dizzy little head-movements and slender diminutive body tightly strapped round the ribs, it stood there on four much too long legs quite close to its brown relieved mother, who slowly and cautiously began to graze again. . . .

73. *To Clara Rilke*

BORGEBY GÅRD, FLAEDIE, PROV. SKÅNE
SWEDEN, 19 *July* (*evening*) 1904

. . . Once, on a hot day, I took a quick bathe in the little stream that flows past the park (not very pleasant for bathing — it has mud and a weedy bottom) ; but the " air-bath " I got at the same time was fine in the clear wind. I shall repeat it occasionally, only the place is not particularly suited to it : it can be seen from a distance, there are often men working near by on the other bank, and sometimes the inquisitive calves grazing in the same field come and congregate round in a circle, about thirty in number, and with outstretched warm muzzles stare and stare from quite close. . . .

76. *To Clara Rilke*

BORGEBY GÅRD, FLAEDIE, PROV. SKÅNE
SWEDEN, 27 *July* 1904

. . . For the time being at least, I have asked not to have to take my supper with the others ; coming as close as it does before I go to sleep the meal is too much for me, and then, as generally happens afterwards, we all remain together, go out together, and talk ; all right for anyone whose day's work is over by the evening (although even for him the silence and quiet joy of being alone ought to be more important than the more tedious noise of words), but bad for me, for whom the evening is the day's essence, fruit, fullness. To have to talk in the evening, not to be alone in the evening, to have to laugh in the evening :

for me, that means unravelling the day thread by thread, seam by seam ; the pattern dissolves in long skeins, the whole work pours back into my hands and I begin a hard, reproachful night. — Hence, and in so far as I can use this stay here to satisfy the best hunger of my being, I have reserved the evenings for myself.

. . . It is now Thursday morning, early, and ragged night-clouds are still spread across the clear sky, everywhere stir little bird-sounds ; perhaps it will rain. (They are all longing for it, that is, the people who have to do with the land, all need it. For three weeks there has been a sunny drought and the corn which promised so well is spoiling ; it is ripening and ripening, but without being fully developed within, which is a disaster indeed.)

. . . Thanks for Kappus' letter. It goes hard with him. And this is only the beginning. And he is right when he says that we have expended too much strength in our childhood, too much of the strength of our grown-up selves — enough, perhaps, for a whole generation. Or is it really only enough for individuals ? What is one to say ? That life has infinite possibilities of renewal. Yes, but this too : that in a certain sense any expenditure of strength is always an increase in strength ; for in reality everything reduces itself ultimately to a circle : all the strength we give out comes back to us in the end, changed and intensified. So it is in prayer. And what is there truly done that is not prayer ?

And another thing, this time about thoughts on convalescence. In the midst of the fields there are patches of dark land with ditches dug round them. They are empty, and yet they lie there as though the bright stalks roundabout were there for their sake, rows of bars for their protection. I asked what sort of condition these dark patches of land were in. They said : "*C'est de la terre en repos*". So beautiful, you see, can repose be, and so does it look beside work. Not at all disquieting, but giving you the feeling of a profound confidence and the anticipation of a great time to come. . . .

77. *To Clara Rilke*

BORGEBY GÅRD, FLAEDIE, PROV. SKÅNE
SWEDEN, 29 *July* 1904

. . . It didn't rain yesterday ; towards evening a wind rose ; high up, out of reach and as though destined for another earth, clouds swept along, innumerable clouds, and by nightfall everything far and wide was clear again, almost empty with clarity like a parade-ground after an inspection of troops. Then the moon rose and I went once again through the park above whose immense stillness the colonies of rooks were tracing their last circles . . . went on and only paused at the park's edge facing the dark grazing-grounds from which, through the great silence, came the crunch of chewing and a warm, secretive mastication. And powerful odours and distance and solitariness. Each moment of the day I see something. I have learned a great deal from Hokusai by just glancing through the *Mangwa*. A path of dark earth, strewn with the cusps of twin acorns — that might have been one of his thousand pictures. The laburnum with its seed-pods, hung up like old-fashioned ear-rings ; the jasmin that won't stop flowering and whose stars form Milky Ways in the darkening green ; and the fruit-trees, these above all, with their travailing branches expressive of the whole tree's overloaded existence and the weary summer ; and the fields, across which the shadows pass like players in many costumes. And further off in their beds the flowers, which have nothing to yield and are only like candles lighted for a little while, burning away (I wonder, incidentally, if the moths take lights for flowers ?). And finally the ornate trees, the growth of centuries — chestnuts that have the space of whole rooms under them, and the one old lime opposite the gate all in blossom, whose rounded dome is the last flash of gold when everything else is dark : it is indeed enough to look at, for there is still a lot more. Such is the world, but here and there are painters who seek themes, who detach five little pieces from the great mosaic so as to build them into a harmony. And perhaps not the painters alone are like that (else they would be the most terribly isolated of all beings), perhaps all humankind is like that — have not they also made their lives out of little themes, are not their joys and sorrows, their professions and their riches only themes ? Ah, and real life is like the real world. And it lies there like a grazing-ground from which, in the evenings, come warm breath and scent and solitariness. . . .

78. *To Tora Holmstroem*

BORGEBY GÅRD, 2 *August* 1904

. . . I have no right to say more than this : that I lack the organ necessary to receive anything from Goethe ; more I really do not know. And that I acknowledge with reverence that which life has taught you to call " Goethe ", the largeness and light which, for you, begin with this name. . . .

84. *To Clara Rilke*

BORGEBY GÅRD, 12 *August* 1904

. . . Look ! the wind is so big and wide and does not stop ; it roars the whole night through and only calms down when the rain falls, and the rain grows heavier and roars too. Autumn ? Why not ; everything is ready, the fruit is big and the young storks can no longer be distinguished from the old. And there is a stretch of park by the high-road that is not swept and raked on Saturday evenings ; weeds are there, all withered and drooping, and the half-grown chestnuts have many yellow leaves and part with them one by one ; not while the gale blows, for then they gather their strength together and hold on as tight as they can, but afterwards, when it is so vastly still, then they strow themselves down, leaf by leaf, masses of big, yellow, crumpled leaves. Decaying thistles grow there with little mournful violet heads, thistles that have sprung up without thinking ; there are beech-trees that are all ragged, and perhaps they have been like that the whole summer, but now it looks as though they were deliberately and joyfully so, and the clouds pass behind them, and through them you can see everything that happens in the sky. And in the air there is a pensive faded smell as of flowers which the sun has dried and the wind pressed, and it is the smell of autumn. And this is why I often go there now, up and down, and avoid my seat under the walnut and all my summer ways; for I want the autumn! It almost seems as if autumn were the true creator, more creative than the spring, which is too even-toned, more creative when it comes with its will-to-change and shatters the much too ready-made, self-satisfied and really almost bourgeois-complacent image of summer. This great, splendid wind piling sky upon sky — I would like to go into its country and along its highways.[1] . . .

86. *To Arthur Holitscher*

BORGEBY GÅRD, 17 *August* 1904

. . . You must not upset your plans for Rome on my account, dear friend; they are so good in themselves. I cannot judge of the other one, regarding London. Everything English is distant and foreign to me; I do not know the language of that country, next to nothing of its art, none of its poets; and London I imagine to be something very harrowing. You know my fear of the very big cities; also I shall never again go further west, as everything calls me back to Russia. If ever anything like a home could be given me somewhere, it would be there, in that great, grievous land. . . .

91. *To Tora Holmstroem*

BORGEBY GÅRD, 24 *August* 1904

. . . I have often asked myself whether those days on which we are forced to be indolent are not just the ones we pass in profoundest activity? Whether all our doing, when it comes

[1] Cf. "Herbsttag": *Buch der Bilder* (*Collected Works*, vol. ii, p. 51).

> Lord, it is time: the summer was so great.
> Upon the sundials lay your shadows, and
> leave the large winds to sweep the meadowland.
>
> Command the last fruits to be full and fine.
> Give them two more of more-than-southern days
> towards perfection pressed; and with your rays
> drive the last nectars through the heavy wine.
>
> He now who has no home will build no more.
> He now who is alone will long be so;
> will watch, read, write long letters and will go
> and pace the avenues upon whose floor
> the fallen leaves are whirling to and fro.

later, is not only the last reverberation of a great movement which takes place in us on those days of inaction ?

At any rate it is very important to be inactive with confidence, with surrender, if possible with gladness. The days when our hands do not move are so uncommonly quiet that it is scarcely possible to live through them without hearing a great deal. . . .

104. *To Lou Andreas-Salomé*

CHARLOTTENBUND BEI KOPENHAGEN
VILLA CHARLOTTENBUND, 4 *December* 1904

. . . Now at last I am on my way back after a long, good stay in Furuborg ; long, because I feel I have had summer, autumn and winter there and each of them entire ; the last summer days with which it all began were so permeated with summeriness, and then every autumn day was a festival of autumn, and finally it turned into a proper deep winter with sleigh-rides into the soft countryside where everything had become distance, and along the cold sea towards the strange, darkening-blue mountains. Then there came a whole journey in white, seven hours by train to Småland, a journey which continued as a swift sleigh-run through a soundlessly snowing afternoon and ended up in the dusk at a lonely farmstead. Accompanied by the tinkling of ten little bells we drove down a long avenue of old lime-trees, the sleigh swung round, and there was the forecourt, flanked by the two wings of the building. But yonder, where four steps climbed wearily and toilsomely out of the snow up to the terrace, and where the terrace, bounded by a balustrade decorated with stone urns, made as though to lead into the house, there was nothing, nothing but a few shrubs sunk in snow ; and sky, a grey, tremulous sky from which falling flakes detached themselves into the dusk. You had to tell yourself : No, there is no house there, and you recalled having heard that it had been burned down years ago ; nevertheless, you still felt it was there, somehow you sensed that the air behind this terrace had not yet become one with the rest of the air, that it was still divided up into corridors and rooms, and that it formed a hall in the middle, a high, empty, deserted, twilit hall.

But now the master of the house stepped out of the wing on the left — tall, burly, with a yellow moustache — and checked the shrill yapping of the four elongated Dachshunds with a word. The sleigh drove past him in a curve and up to the little right wing, and from its door emerged the good Ellen Key, dressed modestly in black, but all joy under her white hair. For this was Oby, her brother's estate, and in the right wing there is the old-fashioned room where, sitting on her grandmother's red settee, she writes the second part of her life and answers countless letters to young girls and young women and young men, who all want to find out from her where life begins. . . . That was a week ago, and now, in the great thaw, I am near Copenhagen, but only for a few days; mainly to see Hammershoej. Therese Krieger is staying with the old man in Damgaar — if possible I shall see her on the through-journey to Fredericia. . . .

110. *To Clara Rilke*

GÖTTINGEN, AUF DEM HAINBERG
22 June 1905

. . . Yesterday and the day before passed in worry over the little dog, which everybody in the house loved so much; suddenly he grew ill and yesterday evening he died in great torment. It is sad and hard for Lou and her husband. And once again I felt distinctly that one should not draw into one's life those cares and responsibilities which are not necessary, just as I felt it as a boy when my rabbit died. I have gone for a few lovely walks into the towns near by, they look very south-German; the country is like numerous others, but friendly and peaceful. And what does me good is the higher and less oppressive air, which enables me to get up earlier without exertion and endure even the hottest days with comparative ease.

132. *To Clara Rilke*

MEUDON-VAL-FLEURY, CHEZ RODIN
20 September 1905

. . . What are all periods of tranquillity, all days by wood and sea, all attempts to live a healthy life and the thoughts of all these : what are they beside this wood, this sea, this indescribably soothing repose in his succouring and upholding glance, beside the sight of his good health and certitude ? There is a torrent of strength pouring into you, you are overcome by a joy of living, a capacity to live of which I never had an inkling. His example has no parallel, his greatness mounts up before one like a tower quite close, and his kindness when it comes is like a white bird that shimmeringly circles round you till it alights trustfully on your shoulder. He is everything far and wide. We talk of many, many things. It does him good to talk of this and that, and even if I cannot always keep up with him, impeded by the language, I am adapting myself better and better each day to listening. And just think, for the last three mornings we have got up quite early at 5.30, yesterday at 5 even, and driven out to Versailles ; at the station we take a cab and drive into the park, and in the park we walk about for hours. He shows you everything : a distant view, a movement, a flower, and everything he invokes is so beautiful, so known, so startled and young that the whole world is at one with the youthfulness of the day, which begins in mists, almost in gentle rain and gradually becomes sunned through and through, warm and soft. Then he talks a great deal of Brussels where he spent his best years. The model for the *Age d'Airain* was a soldier and his comings were irregular, sometimes at five in the morning, sometimes at six in the evening, and as Rodin's fellow-worker used ambitiously to elbow him out of his other jobs he had nearly the whole time free. This he spent in the environs of Brussels, always walking with Madame Rodin (who is a good and faithful soul), in the woods, always roaming. At first he set up his easel anywhere and painted. But soon he noticed that by so doing he missed everything vital, the distances, the changes, the rising trees and the sinking mists, all the myriadfold happening and occurrence ; he saw that, in his painting, he was confronting it like a hunter whereas he himself, the observer, was a part of it, was acknowledged by it, was absorbed, dissolved, was the landscape. And this *being* the landscape, for years — getting up with the sun and participating in all the great events, gave him what he needed : a knowledge, a joyousness, the dewy, inviolable youth of his strength, a harmony with the things that matter and a quiet communion with life. His percipience comes from there, his susceptibility to everything beautiful, his conviction that in small things as in great the same illimitable grandeur can be found that dwells in Nature in a million changing shapes. — " And if I came to draw Nature today, I would do her as I do my nudes, with a single contour, rapidly sketched, which I would touch up at home, but otherwise only look and unite myself and be identical with everything round me." And while we talk of these things, Madame Rodin picks flowers and brings them : autumn crocuses or leaves, or she draws our attention to pheasants, partridges, magpies (one day we had to turn home early because she had found a sick partridge and took it with her to care for it), or she collects mushrooms for the coachman, who is sometimes interrogated when it becomes clear that none of us knows the name of a certain tree. That was in one of the avenues of elms that lead round the Versailles park outside the Trianon. We broke off a twig, Rodin examined it for a long time, felt the plastic, powerfully veined leaves and said finally : " Well, now I know it for always, *c'est l'orme* ". Always he is like this, as receptive as a cup, and everything becomes a fountain wherein he is manifest, glittering like a mirror. Yesterday I had breakfast in the town with him and Carrière and a writer called Charles Morice ; but otherwise I see nobody except him. At evening in the twilight, when he returns from the rue de l'Université, we sit on the edge of the artificial water with its three young swans, and watch them and talk seriously of many things, and of you too. It is wonderful how Rodin lives his life, wonderful. Thus we were to meet Carrière in his studio in the rue de l'Université ; we were there punctually at twelve o'clock. Carrière kept us waiting. Rodin glanced once or twice at the clock whilst he was disposing of his post, but when I looked up again I found him deep in work ! So does he pass the times he has to wait. . . . After supper I soon retire and by 8.30 have long been in my little house. Then the wide night is before me, blossoming with stars, and below my window the gravel path leads up to a little hill where a statue of Buddha reposes in fanatical silence, out of his calm aloofness distilling his gesture of unutterable mediation beneath all the skies of day and night. It is the centre of the world, I said to Rodin. And then he looks at you so kindly, so absolutely a friend. It is wonderful, and so much. Do you remember the big dinner-table in the dining-room ? One half is now entirely taken up with pears, delicious great pears crowded together (gathered yesterday from the garden). Then there is a stone vase with an enormous bouquet of little purple autumn asters in it growing in clumps, and surrounded by these blossoms as by a heaven, a little Greek figure of a girl. It is a marvel. And from his chair Rodin is always looking at it and every day invents tender new comparisons with which to give these lovely things their due. . . .

164. *To Clara Rilke*

MEUDON-VAL-FLEURY, VILLA DES BRILLANTS
8 January 1906

. . . Yesterday afternoon, in a free hour before dusk, I read Hofmannsthal's *Kreuzweg im Lande Phokis* ; there are wonderful lines in it, a swelling and subsiding rhythm which sometimes makes me think of the beat of my *Requiem.* And so beautifully woven together, in many instances compact, indivisible :

> . . . like frothing water my life
> spurted ahead — in a flash
> my hands had slain a man :

it comes so unexpected and real, in very truth like some object swept past by those frothing waters ; and the other speech of Oedipus, where he begins :

> Are you proof against the Powers ?
> Do you know the midnights that break over us
> When we reel past one another,
> Unrecognising ?

and leads up to the scene of the fight which the banquet has become when, sinking back into his thoughts, gigantically towering, he cries out : "*All that is in my blood. Were not madmen among my ancestors ?*"

. . . This evening Madame Rodin showed us a doll Josette

once had and which she, Madame Rodin, has kept for four years, ostensibly because Josette breaks everything but actually because she herself would like to have a doll so much. When Rodin, enormously kind, proposed suddenly : " *Sais-tu, ma vieille, tu enverras cette poupée à la petite fille de M. Rilke* ", she was all confused and nearly in tears, so that I had to gainsay her vehemently and resolutely. But what an idea ! To deprive Madame Rodin of her doll which she can shew everybody with so much pride : it has eyes that go to sleep and long, thick, dark lashes. . . .

166. *To Clara Rilke*

MEUDON-VAL-FLEURY, VILLA DES BRILLANTS
26 January 1906

. . . We came home tired, the weather was too much against us ; after crisp cold, rawness and then snow and immediately after that a thaw and east wind and slippery ice ; all in one day, today of all days, and the most impossible weather for our walk to the station. So we arrived tired ; tired also perhaps because it makes you sad to see this decay and bad restoration in all its starkness and harshness and ugliness, which is even more unendurable than the loss of something beautiful. Chartres seems to me much more of a ruin than Notre-Dame in Paris. Much more hopeless ; much more the victim of those who make ruination. There remains only the first impression, how it rises up as in a great cloak, and the first detail, a slender weatherbeaten angel[1] holding forth a sundial, opened to the day's round of hours, and above that you see, infinitely beautiful even in decay, the deep smile on his gladly ministering face like a reflection of heaven. . . . But that is nearly all. And the Master (it seems) is the only one to whom it all comes and speaks. (If it spoke, even only a little, to others, how could they, how *could* they possibly fail to hear it ?) As in Notre-Dame he was quiet, composed, infinitely acknowledged and accepted. Talking gently of his art and confirmed in it by the great laws which revealed themselves to him wherever he looked. And it was very beautiful ; we reached the cathedral about 9.30 from the

1 " L'Ange du Méridien ", *Neue Gedichte* (*Collected Works*, vol. iii. p. 32).

station ; the sun was not out any longer, there was grey frost, but still quiet. As we neared the cathedral, however, a wind, like somebody very large, unexpectedly swept round the corner where the angel is and pierced us through and through, mercilessly sharp and cutting. " Oh," I said, " there's a storm coming up." " *Mais vous ne savez pas,*" said the Master, " *il y a toujours un vent, ce vent-là autour des grandes Cathédrales. Elles sont toujours entourées d'un vent mauvais agité, tourmenté de leur grandeur. C'est l'air qui tombe le long des contreforts, et qui tombe de cette hauteur et erre autour de l'église. . . .*" That was roughly how the Master said it, only more succinctly, less elaborate and more Gothic. But it is the gist of what he meant. And in this " *vent errant* " we stood like the damned in comparison with the angel, who holds out his sundial so blissfully towards the sun he always sees. . . .

171. *To Clara Rilke*

MEUDON-VAL-FLEURY, VILLA DES BRILLANTS
15 *February* 1906

. . . Yesterday we had yet another breakfast with Troubetzkoi[1] (three vegetarian breakfasts one after another), and later (he lives in Boulogne-sur-Seine) we walked through a quieter part of the Bois — from the depths of which a dainty deer-face had long been peering at us when we caught sight of it — and came to the Jardin d'Acclimatation. We got first of all into a sort of exhibition (just as you and I did) alongside which there is a place for monkeys ; the frightful mandrills were raging as always, chawing their hands and flinging themselves against the wall as though driven demented by the unspeakable hideousness in which a cruel nature left them as she went on to her next work. (She had to make all this, always trying new combinations so as to come to *us*, said the Master.) In the same room, facing a cage, were three monkeys about the size of small dogs, with pallid sickly faces and the large dreamy eyes of consumptives. Infinitely forlorn and hopeless, they had crowded together in a pitiful huddle, each seeking comfort from the warmth of the other, the three faces, each separate, each different, superimposed

[1] Russian sculptor.

on the whole mass as sometimes in Minne's woodcuts, or less solidly drawn and melting into the background, as with Carrière. But when we stepped out again under the wintry afternoon sky and into the wind which came from snow, it was almost painful to see the pink and red flamingoes [1] blossoming in this chill air.

Rodin spent most of his time by the exquisite Chinese pheasants ; they seemed made of enamel and were finished with such care that it was surprising to find on some of them a grey and apparently only half-painted head which had not received the final touches. (How often has Nature gone on to something else, spurred forward by ideas and the rapture of beginning the *next* thing !) The last creature we saw was a marabou, venerable but ugly, with wildernesses in his feelings and utterly despondent in his meditations : (first sketch of a hermit, abandoned and only taken up again much later). . . . There is so very much for the Master to do ; we are once more at work on a "*Discours*" ; he sent one off as a letter for the opening of the first exhibition when I came back recently ; now he has to speak in person at his banquet on the 21st and he has all kinds of fine and fruitful ideas of which he wants to give only the best. My business is to see that they like each other's company, I may add nothing, but that precisely is not easy. And masses of letters. . . .

[1] Cf. "Die Flamingos", *Neue Gedichte* (*Collected Works*, vol. iii. p. 126) :

As in the mirror-world of Fragonard
no more is given of their white and red
than would be shewn to you, if any said
of his beloved : how soft her slumbers are.

For while they step in greenness everywhere
on pink stems lightly turning, flower on flower
as in a flower-bed, blossoming in the air,
they play at self-seduction by the hour

like artful Phrynes ; then they sink their necks
down where the downiest blacks and fruit-reds mix,
hiding the pallid circles of their eyes.

A jealous shriek runs through the aviary :
but one by one they stretch and in surprise
stalk off into the Great Imaginary.

172. *To Lou Andreas-Salomé*

MEUDON-VAL-FLEURY, 21 *February* 1906

. . . Rodin went to London yesterday, and I needed that most desperately ; for work has been heavy since I returned, and for me and my aloneness there was hardly any time left but the minutes which my watch sometimes gains me out of pity. And all the time I am longing more than ever for my work. The *Buch der Bilder* is going into a second edition (at last), and I am carefully augmenting it by some new and some old things which you will enjoy. But I need " only time ",[1] and where is it ? . . .

175. *To Auguste Rodin*

PRAGUE, 15 *mars* 1906 (télégramme)

Je plains la perte de mon très bon père ; de cœur.—RILKE.

Prague, Hotel Goldener Engel.

177. *To Clara Rilke*

MEUDON-VAL-FLEURY, *April* 2, 1906

. . . This evening (I was tired and in the middle of unpacking) suddenly there was a voice down below that called ; I looked out, and there he stood, the good, kind old man, and

1 Probable reference to " Der Alchimist ", *Neue Gedichte* (*Collected Works*, vol. iii. p. 150).

The chemist, strangely smiling, pushed aside
the hot retort which smoked, still simmering.
For now he realised what he was denied
if that most precious and illustrious thing

should form. He needed Time. For him and his
alembic, seething low, a century
of ages, in his brain wide galaxies
and in his consciousness at least the sea.

The vastness that he willed he let away
that night. It turned once more, and in its old
proportion, back to God. But he, he lay

above the secret locker in the chest
and, gibbering like a drunkard, craved the gold,
the lump of heavy gold, which he possessed.

as I appeared at the window he said, full of kindly warmth: *Ah, le voilà.* It cannot be written, it cannot be described, but he said it in such a way that it was like open arms. . . .

And yesterday, Sunday, there was time to sleep my fill; no duties, and guests in the afternoon: Zuloaga, Bourdelle and a writer, M. Fagus. . . . On Saturday I spent some three hours with Paula Modersohn; breakfasted with her at Jouven's and went for a walk with her. She is courageous and young and, it seems to me, on a good upward path, alone as she is without help.

I have courage for my task, humility, love and will.

183. *To Karl von der Heydt*

MEUDON-VAL-FLEURY, VILLA DES BRILLANTS
Wednesday after Easter 1906

. . . What I now in my feelings and consciousness most have need of is two years of working only for myself in circumstances such as I had for a time in Rome; alone, with only my wife, who was also working in the neighbourhood, so that we did not even see each other every day but helped each other all the same. Without duties, almost without external communication. (It was then that the *Aufzeichnungen des Malte Laurids Brigge* came into being; I have not gone back to them and more wanted to come, but my stay had to be broken off.) I then went to friends in Sweden, who offered me everything that the most open hospitality could give, but one thing they could not give me: this unconfined solitude which takes every day like a life, this being together with everything — in short, a spaciousness that puts no limits to your vision and in the midst of which you stand surrounded by infinities.

So the time in Sweden was more a period of assimilation than anything else, as it was later in Friedelhausen with all its fairy-tale beauty, and is now, in a different way, in Meudon. But after all this and after certain profound and alarming events which have put a special relation and interpretation on everything, a time *must* now come for me to be alone with my experience, to listen to it, to give it shape: for the mass of untransformed material presses down on me and confuses me; it was as an outlet for this state of mind that I longed more than ever to take this spring, stirring and straining in all directions, like a vocation upon myself: for it might have become in the highest degree an incentive for so much that was only awaiting the impulse to set it in motion. I do not think I am deceiving myself when I fancy that my age (I shall be 31 this year) and all the other circumstances testify to it that if I could now gather strength for my next steps I could bring to fruition a number of works which would be good, would help me inwardly, and outwardly too might initiate a certainty of life such as no books have yet granted me, but which is not absolutely precluded for the future.

But: I cannot possibly leave Rodin at present; this much is equally obvious. My conscience would not be clear enough for my own work if I went away from him unexpectedly like this. Especially as he has been sick all these weeks and still feels tired and run down and needs my assistance, slight as it is, more than ever. I shall have to compromise with my great longing. I am convinced that patience is always good and that nothing that is in the deepest sense authorised to happen can remain unhappened. Those works for which the conditions are now lacking I shall one day take up and shall carry to a conclusion, if they really are as absolutely necessary and as organically demanded of me as I believe. I shall continue this life for a while longer with a good will and with complete readiness to serve, as best I can, and only abandon it when we have considered whether it is possible to do so and in what manner it shall be done. To meditate, to premeditate on this slowly, for next autumn perhaps, is the only thing, dear friend, you can now do for me. . . . Yet it alters my life and my position very much if I can but hope within measurable time to turn back to my own work and tasks. Then I can look forward with joy to the patience which is demanded of me, which is laid upon me by (in a certain sense) hard, but not hostile, circumstances at the behest of this grand old Master, who wills it so. . . .

185. *To S. Fischer*

MEUDON-VAL-FLEURY, SEINE ET OISE
FRANCE, 19 *April* 1906

. . . A few days ago Rodin began the portrait of one of your most remarkable authors, which bids fair to become something quite special. Scarcely ever, though, has a portrait been so supported in its beginnings by the object of its representation as this one of Bernard Shaw. Not only because he stands excellently (keeping still with such energy and abandoning himself so completely to the hands of the sculptor), but because he also knows how to collect and amass himself in that part of his body which, from inside the bust, will have to represent so to speak the *whole* Shaw — he can do this, I say, so powerfully that his entire being leaps into the bust from that spot, feature by feature with astonishing intensity.

Shaw's personality and his whole way of life make me desirous of reading some more of his books, of which I think I know only *The Man of Destiny*. Would I be justified in asking you to send me some of his books when I say that I hope to write a little something about him (without rashly committing myself just yet)? I would, as you know, be heartily grateful to you if you could send me some of his things. I could also impart some of it to Rodin; he wants to get to know Shaw's books, but since there are no French translations extant, what I could tell him of them would be, for the time being, his only source.

Madame Shaw who, unknown to her husband, initiated the making of this portrait in the most charming way, is a good, careful and gently caring woman, full of fire and enthusiasm for beautiful things, frisking round her husband as the spring breeze frisks round a billy-goat. This in appreciation of your remarkable author. . . .

186. *To Clara Rilke*

MEUDON-VAL-FLEURY, SEINE ET OISE
19 *April* 1906

. . . The summer presses forward quickly. Here at least it seems to be coming on with all speed. Can you believe that the Avenue de l'Observatoire is dense with green just as it was when I used to walk up and down there on my return from Viareggio ? And in the Luxembourg there is nothing but shadows on the upper terraces, and the frocks of the girls shimmer more mysteriously and with more of a nuance under the full chestnuts : no longer in their dazzling spring-bright whiteness. And here in the garden a blue iris opened yesterday ; the strawberry plants are out, and I saw some currant bushes in flower. . . . And since yesterday (after many, many radiant days warm as summer) rain has been falling, day and night, a mild, still rain, thick, gentle and full, as though from the rose of a watering-can : *comme tombant d'un arrosoir*, one would like to say, because that sounds and falls much darker and fuller. And the green leaves grow under this rain, swell and thrust, and here and there something opens, quite fresh and new. . . . (And I think of Rome.)

The Tweeds are here, staying in their old place in Fernand's room. Rodin, who is still a bit run down (Madame Rodin has not yet recovered and is in a very bad humour), avoids his trips to Paris as much as possible, and in his great studio in the house (where the books are) has begun a very fine portrait of Bernard Shaw (the English-Irish writer whose *Man of Destiny* we once read). Bernard Shaw comes out every day with his wife, we see each other often and I was present at the first sittings and saw for the first time how Rodin sets about his work. First there is a firmly-kneaded lump of clay which consists of nothing but a globe placed on a shoulder-like support. This globe is prepared for him and contains no armature, only firm kneading keeps it together. He begins his work by standing the model at a very short distance from him, about half a pace from his easel. With big iron calipers he takes the measurement from the top of the head to the tip of the beard and immediately fixes this proportion on the clay lump by the addition of more clay. Then in the course of his work he takes two more measurements : nose to back of head and ear to ear, from behind. After he has made a quick incision for the eyebrows so that something resembling a nose is formed, and has determined the position of the mouth by a slit such as children make in a snowman, he begins, with the model standing quite close, to shape four profiles, then eight, then sixteen, making the model turn after every three minutes. He began with the front view and the two full profiles, as though he were modelling four different sketches in the clay on top of one another, then inserted intermediate profiles between these contours. Yesterday, at the third sitting, he placed Shaw in a cunning little baby-chair (all of which afforded this satirist and really not uncongenial scoffer an exquisite pleasure) and cut off the head of the bust with a wire (Shaw, whom the bust resembled in an almost *supercilious* way, so to speak, witnessed this decapitation with indescribable joy) and began working at the head reclining on two wedge-shaped supports, viewing it from above in roughly the same position as the model sitting at arm's-length below him. Then the head was set upright again, and the work now continues in the same way. To begin with Shaw stood, often quite close to the easel so that he was a little taller than the bust. But now he sits directly beside it at exactly the same height as the clay and parallel with it. At some distance a dark curtain has been hung so that the profiles always stand out sharply. The Master works quickly, compressing hours into minutes, it seems to me, carrying out strokes and touches in short pauses in which he assimilates tremendously, filling himself with form. You feel somehow that his lightning, hawk-like swoops only fashion one of all the faces that pour into him, and you only grasp his technique of work in your memory, long after the sitting is done. . . .

191. *To Clara Rilke*

Meudon-Val-Fleury, Seine et Oise
3 *May* 1906

. . . There is no nightingale in our garden, hardly any birds' voices ; this on account of the huntsmen who come over every Sunday ; but sometimes I wake up in the night with something calling, calling down below in the valley, calling with all its soul. That sweet mounting voice which never ceases to mount, which is like an entire being changed into voice, a being whose figure, gestures, hands and face, everything, have become voice, a great nocturnal, exorcising voice. From far away the silence wafts it up to my window, and my ear catches it and draws it slowly into my room past my bed, and into me. And yesterday I found them all, the nightingales, and walked past them in a warm, sheltered night-wind, nay, walked through the midst of them as through a throng of singing angels who parted only to let me go by, and closed in front of me and closed again behind me. Thus, from quite near, I heard them. (I had been in the town to dine with some friends of the von der Heydts of Elberfeld who were passing through, and came back by train to Val-Fleury about ten.) There I found them, in all these old neglected parks (in the one with the lovely house whose walls are slowly collapsing, as though Time had trained its guns on them, while the park, bisected in the middle by the railway, shews its inside like a burst fruit, withered and mouldy) ; and a little further across in a dense thicket, and high up at the back in the deserted gardens by the orangery. And from the other side the sound came over the wall of the old Mairie and then suddenly close beside me out of a little tangled garden full of hedges and lilac bushes, came so distinct and yet so intertwined with the garden as it lay there tucked away in the semi-darkness, that it was like recognising a bird in a piece of lace, woven out of the same threads that portray flowers and foliage and massy luxuriance. Everything was sound, and it wrapped me about and swamped all thought in me and all blood ; it was a Buddha of voices, so vast and lordly and supreme, brooking no denial, the uttermost boundary of voice where it turns into silence again, pulsing with the same intense fullness and regularity with which silence pulses, when it grows great and we can hear it. . . .

192. *To Clara Rilke*

MEUDON-VAL-FLEURY
Thursday evening, 11 *May* 1906

. . . This will only be a short Sunday letter because I have a big job of work to do, namely this : to pack and move out of my little house into the old freedom with all its cares, all its possibilities, and the great inheritance of all its hours. I am full of expectation and happy. There is not much to say about how it happened and what there is to say I would rather not write. It had to come, and so it came of its own accord. I bore everything, even these last days, with a quiet inward patience, and I could have borne it for another month or two. But the Master must have felt that I suffered. And now the end has come so quickly, quicker than he expected, for he wants to go into the country for a bit and shut up house and garden. So I am thinking of moving into the town on Saturday; I have booked a room in the little hotel in the rue Cassette (No. 29) where we once visited Paula Becker, the room on the ground floor under the one she had, which looks out on to the apparition of the green trees of the convent over the walls opposite and makes you aware of them. I have booked the room by the week without committing myself any further. There I shall be and there I shall take stock of myself and be alone for a while with what is in me. And begin immediately to get the *Cornet* finished and arrange the *Buch der Bilder* (for which I had neither freedom nor aptitude for a single moment). And now and then see the Louvre and the Cluny and in the darkening avenues of the Luxembourg Gardens go towards the grey sun outside. . . .

193. *To Auguste Rodin* [1]

PARIS, *le* 12 *Mai*, 1906

MON MAÎTRE, . . . I understand. I understand that the wise organism of your life must reject immediately what seems harmful to it in order to keep its functions intact; as the eye spurns the object which hampers its sight.

I understand that; and do you also recall how often I have understood you in our happy reveries? I am persuaded that there exists no other man of my own age (in France or elsewhere) equipped like myself — by temperament and through study — to understand you, to understand your great life and to appreciate it so scrupulously.

So now, grand Maître, you have become invisible for me,

[1] Original in French.

as though carried up by an ascension into the heavens which are your home.

I shall not see you again — but, as for the apostles who remained behind, saddened and alone, for me too life is beginning, a life which will celebrate your high example and which will find its solace in you, its justification and its strength.

We were agreed that in life there is an innate justice which is accomplished slowly but surely. In that justice I repose all my hopes; one day it will repair the wrong which you have thought fit to inflict on one who has no longer either the means or the right to reveal his heart to you.—Rilke.

2. *To Ellen Key*

29 rue Cassette, Paris VIe.
19 *May* 1906

. . . I have waited for nothing so much as for this news of your coming, and would have written to you long since had I known your address. So you are coming at last, and I am *very* pleased. Of course — and I say this merely to anticipate your disappointment — you must give up the idea of seeing Rodin, at least with me. I have not been with him any more for six days. At his own wish I left him, rather unexpectedly, serving him up to the last moment with all my strength ; I could not have done it any longer, for there was really no time for me, none whatever. Only it would have been difficult for *me* to say goodbye, firstly because I did not want to leave him in the lurch with all his correspondence, secondly because of my own uncertain position. But since he has taken the first step I need not reproach myself and must assume that it is all for the good. My longing for my own things was great enough in all conscience ; *they* must now have their turn again ; external circumstances and the conditions of life will just have to take shape as best they can. Things must go on somehow as they have hitherto. I am unable to speak about the closer circumstances of my leave-taking from Rodin ; I can only tell you, as you will have to know, that I *cannot* visit him with you and must also ask you, in case you do see him — which I hope and want very much — not to speak of me.

Maybe you'll be going to him with Verhaeren : what a pity ! — all these months I have been looking forward to just this, and to this above all : to lead you round among his works and into my little house ; but now it has all come different.

Do not conclude, however, that I do not feel for Rodin all the love and admiration I have always felt. My inner relationship to him is unchanged ; it is only that for the moment I can give it no outward expression and must leave it to time to bring about an equilibrium which will vindicate my feelings again.

Will all this hold you back from coming to Paris? I hope not. Paris is so beautiful just now, and I would have drawn an unspeakable consolation and encouragement from seeing you and talking with you now. (Let me know when you are arriving and where you are staying.)

5. *To Clara Rilke*

29 rue Cassette, Paris VIe.
29 *May* 1906

. . . I understand your letter as if I had written it myself, and if there was no mention of all this in mine, which you received on Sunday, it is because I think we must still have patience; you, so long as your work continues and rounds itself off, I until the *Cornet* at the very least, and possibly the *Buch der Bilder* as well, go to press, and till I feel an inner decision and am a little more ordered and collected in mind. My departure from Rodin is still too near, there is still a great deal I want to see in Paris, and this seeing and being alone have yet to work in me. . . . Despite the feeling of restiveness, which has become clamorous and insistent in me too, I have thought more than once that, since I for the time being have none, *your* work, which is fine and important, must be the measure for us; if you have any decisions about it let us plan and take immediate action accordingly. Either you come here, spend a few days (my last) in Paris with me, and we go from here to somewhere by the sea, or I come to your nice house, to your summery room, in Worpswede — and we go from there to some small cheap sea-side resort. (Ah, could we but save money, could we but acquire this knack of living on next to nothing, of keeping everything back and only letting the most necessary things go with grim reluctance!) Ellen Key is almost offended if you ask her for money and incredibly suspicious of anyone who takes it. As a skittle-player his ball, so she follows her franc-piece with the whole of her feeling and expects each of them to score nine! She is avaricious, I see, the good Ellen. She probably had to be, it was a sort of protective colouring which enabled her to survive at certain periods in her life. But it is not pretty to look at. Since she has been here I've been living in such indigence as I have never known except with her. We wait at various corners for buses, we eat between-times at a Duval, furtively, as it were, and I can only suppose that she nourishes herself mostly with what she has set before her on her visits. This stinginess is sad, but it results in a freedom which you and I could well do with. You can do a whole lot in this way, and could last out indefinitely.

But dear Ellen, she is good and honest, she has her convictions and is so touchingly untouched by all experience. Practical as she is you cannot discuss practical things with her, because she takes it for granted when any plans are mentioned that you are only talking of those for which the wherewithal lies all ready, exactly counted out. Then of course she says yes and amen to the beautiful plan ! You live inside the money you have, she thinks, and you make your plans within these confines (which would produce nothing but wretched little vegetable gardens). And you can hardly speak of your inner problems with her either, because she still has certain Sunday ideals and sentiments which pass over at once into a warm gush of emotion. And with this so little can be done. But do not infer from this that I am not content to be with her ; I have a sound affection for her and for some things a quite natural and impulsive admiration. She has made happiness out of a not very fortunate life ; she has got in touch with important things and has fallen in love with life and trusted it with the pure spontaneity and careless serenity of the bird which " knows not this care ". She will be here for a fortnight (during which time I shall not, of course, always dedicate myself to her with complete regularity) ; even the first day, Sunday, was mightily " organised ", as might have been expected. First came the Louvre, where she observes and analyses everything in terms of sensation, quite undisturbed in her viewpoint ; this was very strange indeed with the Mona Lisa, who on that particular day was utterly unapproachable in her haughtiness, deep and clear in all her shadows and with the blue light behind her playing on the rills and waterfalls and the blue flames of the leaping mountains. She displayed a comprehension almost Goethean at times, at others highly inadequate, — and of course a thing like the *St. Anne* simply retires before such a familiar approach and exploitation. The Venus de Milo, which we only saw from a distance (in the end I had to go to my breakfast) would have been the choicest object of Ellen's analysings and, down below in front of her curtain, she seemed to be just waiting for such sense-photographs. (For me, of course, this kind of visual approach is fatal : I feel like a young puppy with its nose held into that little heap of the past which should not be done in the room.) Then in the afternoon, on the way back from Jouven, Ellen was in my room for a while (we sent you a card). She spoke of Worpswede and is still amazed about Ruth and indescribably proud of her. At four, by means of a variety of buses, we met Verhaeren, who has to avoid country and trees on account of his annually recurring hay-fever and make the best of it in a little Mansard flat in Batignolles. We passed a very pleasant hour with his wife and him, but unluckily Frau G. R. turned up in the end, the widow of the writer ; one can well understand why she outlived him. But the most remarkable part of this very long day was the evening. We saw Ibsen's *Wild Duck* at the Antoine. Excellently rehearsed, with a great deal of care and shaping — marvellous. Of course, by reason of certain differences in temperament, details were distorted, crooked, misunderstood. But the poetry ! Thanks to the fact that the two female characters (Hjalmar Ekdal's wife and the fourteen-year-old Gina) were simple, without French frippery, all its splendour came from the inside and almost to the surface. There was something great, deep, essential. Last Judgement. A finality. And suddenly the hour was there when Ibsen's majesty deigned to look at me for the first time. A new poet, whom we shall approach by many roads now that I know one of them. And again someone who is misunderstood in the midst of fame. Someone quite different from what one hears. And another experience : the unprecedented laughter of the French public (albeit very low in the pit) at the softest, tenderest, most painful places where even the stirring of a finger would have hurt. Laughter — there ! And once more I understood Malte Laurids

Brigge and his northernness and his downfall in Paris. How he saw and felt and suffered it. Yesterday, Monday, was important — the Faillet private collection where all the best van Goghs and Gauguins are, the ones reproduced and praised by Meier-Graefe. Something of extreme significance is there, an inner compulsion which borders on madness. I don't know what as yet. It was very remarkable. And I could take it very seriously, whereas an exhibition of Gustave Moreau only gave me the feeling that I did not belong. So I am more advanced than I was four years ago. The weather is summer at last and sultry and will end in a thunderstorm, I think. Only this for today. . . .

13. *To Clara Rilke*

Friday morning, 21 *June* 1906

. . . Ellen Key went off on Sunday to Switzerland ; I accompanied her as far as Fontainebleau, and there we passed one or two not altogether profitable hours, chivvied through the castle by servants with a pack of Sunday visitors (as E. K. must always see everything, with her inexhaustible capacity for " impressions "), and spending a few hours in the afternoon in the great forest which, with its immense beeches, ferns and single birch-trees in quiet clearings, almost makes you think of Danish woods. In the end we were completely without any contact, and our mutual assurances of friendship had reduced themselves to mere formalities and were kept going with a few touches, like a machine. On the little station of Fontainebleau-Avon, from which our trains departed in different directions at almost the same time, this situation raised itself of its own accord into a symbol and thus, become real, lost its oppressive quality ; just as in a piece of poetry a crisis, translated into parable, outgrows the momentary, the painful and the untenable and becomes full of significance and inner validity the instant it is absorbed without trace in a complete image ; so life granted us (or rather me, for Ellen Key, an adept at substituting her antiquated " Ideal " for everything actual, probably noticed nothing of it) the amiable satisfaction of relieving us of what was unspoken in our predicament by the fullest expression of it. Just think, it could not have been done better : two people on two opposite platforms separated by a pair of rails on which, in a little while, two trains bound in contrary directions will enter, to bear one this way, one that. My platform a platform with people, bustle, departures, with nothing to stay for. Ellen's almost exaggeratedly peaceful : bang in the sun, with beds of roses, neat benches and a certain pretentious complacency about it, like a garden suburb. And, to cap all, this firmly established divide between us, so that nothing, absolutely nothing, should be left out or forgotten. And now that life had taken everything so literally upon itself, feature by feature, with this studied and subtly developed symbolism, using all the means at hand, I did not find it difficult now and then to glance across in a friendly and open way and respond warmly to the faithful and smitten gaze that surrounded me from over there. With real warmth in my look. Now I understood that this elderly spinster was only one of the many elderly spinsters who hoard memories in a room, memories and memories of memories and all of them memories of one thing : of that love whose vague, initial, upswelling possibility had been so exuberantly taken up by their hearts that the experience had no need of ever returning again. And the jumble of objects they accumulate round them which always mean this one love and are derived from it, born of unlikely parentage, by mistake, by accident perhaps, all have something uncertain in their look and something timid in their behaviour, themselves inclined to cast doubts on their own legitimacy, while the old spinster does nothing but wail about the unimpeachable respectability of their descent. Can it be that certain people are predestined to embroil themselves in certain fates and never to escape from themselves ? And when, as with Ellen, unusual strength is added, determination, perhaps also a desperate resolve to outgrow that doom to which she feels herself darkly committed, does not despite everything only the *same* fate rise up again, as though housed in a bigger room, with disproportionately large memories which merely serve to make the nothingness of that experience still more apparent ? Maybe the fixed characteristics of those lost lives have to be heightened in individual destinies before we can recognise them. Maybe such is their course : to become as tragic on a great and spectacular scale as they often were on a small. But how good is life ! How just, how incorruptible, how never to be deceived : neither by strength, nor by will, not even by courage. How everything remains what it is, and has only this choice : to fulfil or overreach itself. . . .

16. *To Clara Rilke*

29 rue Cassette, Paris VIe.
29 *June* 1906

. . . Already I am wavering in my absolute determination to shut myself up daily, wherever I am and in whatever external circumstances, for so-and-so many hours for my work's sake : I do not know whether it will really come now or whether I am just making the appropriate gestures, but remain unfilled. . . . Have I not known ever since I was in Russia, and with such great conviction, that prayer and its time and its reverent and unstinted gestures were the condition of God and of his return to all those who barely expect it, who only kneel down and stand up and are suddenly filled to the brim ? So will I kneel down and stand up, daily, alone in my room, and will keep holy all that befalls me : even what has *not* come, even disappointment, even desertion. There is no poverty that is not fullness could we but accept it gravely and worthily, and not surrender or yield it up to bitterness. . . .

18. *To Clara Rilke*

6 *July* 1906

. . . Look you, this is what we must in due season have it in our power to do : not wait (as has happened till now) for the strong things and the good days to make something of us, but to forestall them, ourselves to be them — that is what we must do. And then will not everything be work ? For what could be unfruitful in this state ? There is precious black earth in us, and our blood has only to go like the plough and make furrows. Then, while we are at the harvest, the sowing is already proceeding on some other place. . . .

47. *To Ellen Key*

GRUNEWALD BEI BERLIN, HUBERTUSALLEE 16
6 November 1906

. . . I have had good news of you indirectly from time to time so I did not feel entirely separated from you, albeit I did nothing to give you visible sign of all the fond wishes and thoughts that are accustomed to go to you. I have heard now that you are quite well and am very pleased.

There is much I might tell you about myself, but perhaps I shall be able — I hope so anyway — to give you a budget in person of all the various happenings.

For the moment I pass over everything up to the time when we arrived here (a month ago). Clara is going to make an effort (you will have heard of it by now) to find pupils and work here and undertake a trial winter in this (oh so hideous !) city. I helped her a little with the preparations, had myself to visit one or two places and finally undergo an elaborate dental treatment which led to a great deal of pain and so affected me that my whole organism is in a state of miserable exhaustion, from which I am only now hoping to emerge. The summer as a whole was not very good ; neither for my health nor for anything else. If I could follow my innermost needs I would prefer to go back to Paris, where I worked industriously and well until the first of August. But I lack the means, so I am snatching at a friendly invitation which calls me to Capri, where I hope to concentrate on serious work. It is the sister of the Countess Schwerin, who died last year (Frau Alice Faehndrich von Nordeck-Rabenau) ; she thinks of granting me a little place in her Capri villa. With a heavy heart I gave up the idea of Paris, which was so favourable to my work, but it is indeed a great joy that this other possibility is there, and I hope for a good winter. As soon as I feel a little stronger I shall go to Naples (though I have no rooms) so as to get down to my work right away (for these last few months have kept me away from it entirely).

And now let me tell you at once, dear Ellen, that my hostess would be very pleased to receive you in her house in Capri.

Bear this in mind, and also that I shall be expecting you, and arrange your plans so that if you journey farther south in the course of the winter you can stay with us !

Well, I have told you a little of everything, and now comes a request. I have expressed it in similar form once before and repeat it now in all sincerity. Dear Ellen, would you do me the pleasure of NOT having your essay on my books published *in book form* ? I asked you not to some time back. You said then that you had promised Bard something and had nothing else suitable for him. This reason falls to the ground now that the little book has been withdrawn from the publishers, and once more I take occasion to tell you quite honestly that it would be a relief to me if the book did not appear, not yet. Just now I need so fervently not to be advertised and recommended ; peace and seclusion are what I want most of all in order to take my next steps. The essay, built up so much on extracts from letters for which there is as yet no evidence in my books, outdistances me on the one hand, while on the other it fixes my religious development at a stage beyond which it has in part already progressed. At the moment I have nothing published that could hold its own in this sense, in no way is this the moment to draw attention to me, and I am more and more anxious that my books should speak for themselves, kind and valuable as your voice is ; but it has had its effect, and though this was by no means inconsiderable there is no reason to try any more influencing. Added to which, Fischer's[1] is a very conspicuous and exposed place, and in that position the book would inevitably — and quite rightly — call forth a measure of opposition, which is unnecessary. In short I beg you (counting on your not misunderstanding me) not to bring out a book-edition of the essay just yet, perhaps to reserve it till some future work of mine is there to justify the appearance of such a brochure, for which there is no occasion now. It only disturbs me to be in the limelight at this juncture, and after all, you want to aim at just the opposite, don't you ?

So please let us wait, let me work and let time have its way. You will give me the most heartfelt pleasure by taking my

[1] Publisher of *Die Neue Rundschau.*

request into consideration. Can I count on it? . . .

Eleanore Duse is in Berlin; we shall, I hope, see her this evening in *Rosmersholm*.

48. *To Karl von der Heydt*

GRUNEWALD BEI BERLIN, HUBERTUSALLEE 16
10 *November* 1906

. . . Yesterday was the opening of the theatre season in the beautiful Kammerspielhaus, bringing a guest-performance of Ibsen's *Ghosts* in a ruthlessly worked-out and razor-edged performance (Moissi as Oswald, Sorma in the role of the mother). And a few days ago the Duse as Rebekka West. Pages could be written about it, pages. Later. But here is something that has been worrying me for days. Perhaps you can advise me. Will you? Can you? For a long time I have had the desire and, you will feel, not out of curiosity merely, to meet Eleanore Duse. I have the *Weisse Fürstin* with me, which is dedicated to her, and have often thought of delivering this poem to her myself. Many times I was near doing it and also I had occasional introductions to her. But I let them pass unused because each time I felt how much those who love her must unite in keeping away everything superfluous or at least supernumerary from her solitude. As regards this nothing has altered but after that *Rosmersholm* evening I feel an even stronger and clearer need to meet her. God knows what gives it me, how it will help. . . . In short: it seems to me important to make a real attempt.

But how? I hear that the Duse is staying with the Mendelssohns in Grunewald. Am I wrong in surmising that you have connections with the Mendelssohns? At any rate I imagine that she will only wish to receive and see those strangers who are brought near her by her friends. Could you, dear friend, write me by return whether you can do or advise anything in this matter? One day it will certainly prove that I am not embarking on this course foolishly, for which I have still to pluck up courage. . . .

52. *To Clara Rilke*

NAPLES, HOTEL HASSLER
29 November 1906

You will remember that if you stepped out from the Strada Santa Lucia, going a few houses to the left and then, instead of bearing towards the square with the fountain, bore towards the other side, towards the sea, a street opened out on the right winding along the coast, on the left of which was only the sea and the castle jutting out at the bend (Castello del Ovo), while on the right it was bordered by a long row of hotels. One of these hotels stood back a little, pushing out before it a whole construction of terraces: this is the Hassler; and my room with its high door leads straight out on to these terraces which run along the right of the house into a little garden, in which I am now sitting. Although the last flowers — purple asters — are faded, clematis hangs blossoming over a wall, sun lies on the sea, and behind the sun, just opposite me, the outline of Capri can be seen beside the foothills of Sorrento.

The journey was really not too bad; when I arrived I thought it could easily have gone on like this for five days or so, I wished it had almost; for the desire for the strange and the unknown was strong and determined. But already the journey seems a thing of the past, although there is nothing in between except a supper alone in the empty dining-room (there seem to be only a few people here), a warm bath and a night spent in deep sleep, a breakfast with pale yellow-green honey, and finally the time I have been writing here in the terrace-garden. And another five days of travel might well have gone before, so unknown is it here — so pleasantly strange. There is the bay, the occasional silhouette of oarsmen in lovely concentrated movement, and just that something which gives a boat its being; in the distance, sailing ships. Then the curve towards Posilippo, the whole margin looking as though it had just been flung out, and to the left the projecting castle, as if wrapped in a cloak or set in front of the sun like one of Rembrandt's figures. And strange the noises: the rapid trotting of little horses, the clattering of primitive wheels, the little bells on the horses' necks reproducing their trotting in miniature, cries in between, shouts, music, children's voices and cracking whips — everything strange even to the popping of the acorns under my feet in the little garden. If only it could go on, this being known by no-one. They brought me your telegram immediately on my arrival : I was just giving myself a bit of a wash when they came up with it, straight to me, although I had not even spoken my name. It is conceivable that I shall remain here two or three days before going across to the new world out yonder : to this contour which it will be my task to fill. . . . The sea has changed 20 times since I've been writing. Now I will stop and look. . . .

55. *To Clara Rilke*

NAPLES, HOTEL HASSLER
2 *December* 1906

. . . Naples too, like everything Italian, is not so beautiful now as it was that summer when we were here for the first time ; it has given up much of its incomparable character now that, as my barber said today, the bad weather is coming. I tried to tone down his categorical utterance bit by bit, imperceptibly, in my favour ; but no, he would not budge, now it was coming and there was nothing to be done about it. " *Pioggia, scirocco — eeh !* " And he was right to insist. Yesterday, towards evening, the wind changed, or it had already changed (my geography is nothing to boast of !) ; anyway, something had changed after all the sunshine that seemed so certain : the sea rose mightily, dashed whitely against the breakwaters, was green and grey as far as the eye could reach and looked quiet on the surface as if grown suddenly ponderous, but from over it there came a turbulent wind which piled the clouds high above the rearing, dazzlingly lit city, thoughtlessly — clouds that did not fit at all, and left empty spaces in between or patches of bright sky, all jumbled together — piled them up and up, while from the other side the evening continued to cast a glare over everything, so that the dark grew darker and darker and the light more sudden and dazzling, and the red of Pizzofalcone, with its tiers of false-arcades (the first elevation by the sea below the castle), dissolved into still deeper shades of red, in reds that were extreme and scarcely credible, so that you fancied they could only last for an instant. All this done without any contour, only with mass, like those tremendous Goyas where figures and trees and buildings and mountains are slashed out with the same violence. . . . Then came the night and brought huge storms ; Sunday began with scorching sun, passed over into rain, wind, change ; the massive green of the sea-swell sometimes cast a dull duskiness on the white — and what a white ! — of a seagull : pompeian in quality. We should have realised when we were here before that this place would make a painter ; for painters, real painters, are formed through colour, and there is colour here in all its nuances. At the corner of one of the black alley-ways which branch off from the Via Roma (the long narrow main street leading to the Museum) I saw yesterday the stall of a lemonade merchant. Posts, roof and backcloth of his little booth were blue (the thrilling blue of certain Turkish and Persian amulets, shading off into green) ; it was evening, and the lamps placed opposite the back wall of the booth made everything else shew up very distinctly in front of this colour : the burnt sienna of an earthenware jug continually running over with a thin trickle of water, the yellow of single lemons and finally the smooth, glassified, ever-changing scarlet in some big and little goldfish bowls. All this was very powerful, perhaps rather obvious, but nevertheless very remarkable. Van Gogh would have turned back to it. Maybe I can see all these things because I have been reading his letters (in the complete edition I bought in Munich) ; on my long journey they were my most cherished possession and are really beautiful — immature in some respects, but unutterably sincere, unutterably moving, and for painters really like a kind, helpful voice. Title : *Vincent van Gogh, Letters*. . . .

It is warm in the sun, more than necessary. The Brenner when I crossed was full of snow and wonderfully beautiful this time, more solemn, with black woods like a Swedish mountain scene. And now and then I looked out and into Karin Brand's *Dream*. Then an Ave sounded high up and I even saw the tower built into the mountain ; gently it rang out like an Ave of thirty years ago that had been caught in a mountain crevice and was now streaming forth from somewhere. It was rather mournful, like a farewell to everything wintry, which is filched away from you here a little suspiciously. . . .

58. *To Elizabeth and Karl von der Heydt*

CAPRI, VILLA DISCOPOLI
11 *December* 1906

. . . I have been here a week and wanted to wait at least long enough to send you, apart from the greetings I often post you in my thoughts, something of my impressions and not too much that is unfair and cursory. But now I shall try a few impressions after all. To begin with there are my immediate surroundings, and these are most accommodating. My hostess does everything for my comfort in a very friendly way and gives me so much freedom and right to arrange my own affairs that I can fit in a good deal of solitude for myself, half the day and, when necessary, more. (My inner life, I see, has been dislocated for months, and my present solitude is affording me a sort of psychic plaster-bandage in which something is healing.) But nothing is so important as this ; I felt it even on the long journey. There is nothing, perhaps, as jealous as my profession ; and though mine could be no monk's life shut in and shut off in a cloister, I must try gradually to grow a cloister about myself and take up my stand in the world, with walls around me, but with God and the saints in me, with very wonderful images and implements in me, with courtyards and fountains whose source is no more to be found. But to continue with the essentials. My solitude is maintained by the fact that the room I live in is quite separate, in a special little house about fifty paces from the villa itself. For the time being I am the only guest ; on the 22nd the Baroness Rabenau and the young Countess Manon Solms-Laubach are expected ; they will make the household complete without there being any later additions imminent as far as I can see. . . . My room is simple and very agreeable and already it has a natural attachment to me, for which I am grateful. . . .

You alone know what complete solitude, to be unnoticed, unseen, invisible, means to me. For three days in Naples I carried it around like a treasure in that gloriously strange world. . . . And now Capri. Ah, yes. I have nothing much to learn here. Jacobsen says somewhere : " It requires infinite tact to handle enthusiasm ". Well, this place has been stamped by an enthusiasm thoroughly ill-used ; the tourists are for the most part gone, but the marks of their stupid admiration which always falls into the same holes are so blatant and cling so tenaciously that even the tremendous storms that occasionally take the island in their jaws cannot sweep them away. Always I grow really melancholy in such beauty-spots as these, faced with this obvious, praise-ridden, incontestable loveliness. When it is almost too much to pick up a stone by the wayside, a chestnut, a withered leaf ; when even the beauty of some small, modest and commonly trifling thing (once you have known it) makes the heart overflow, what is one to say to such concerts of beauty where everything is a programme-number and tested and planned and selected ? Perhaps we may *begin* with this picture-book kind of beauty, learn to see and love, but I am rather too far advanced to exclaim A and O in front of it. I have long passed the stage of spelling out my delight, and in this, perhaps, consists the whole joy and task of my life, that I, novice though I am, belong to those who hear the Beautiful and can discern its voice even where it barely detaches itself from the surrounding noise ; that I know God has not placed us among the things to *choose*, but to employ our acceptance so fundamentally and so mightily that we can, in the end, receive nothing *but* the Beautiful into our love, into our watchful attention, into our inextinguishable wonder. And this is not the place to add to such a feeling. The name of Paris would necessarily have shaped itself in me under the influence of this longing, even if I had never heard it, I think. . . .

No, what people here have made of a beautiful island is most appalling. But that says nothing against the people ; there were at all events sincere and industrious and significant persons among the thousands who have played their part in making Capri. But have you ever seen, when men acted or let themselves go in the direction of pleasure, relaxation or enjoyment, that they came by any pleasant results ? Neither the bull-fight, nor the fun-fair, nor any other amusement institute from the dance-hall to the beer-garden is beautiful or delightful or ever has been. The heaven I once heard an excited preacher talking about in the church of San Clemente was filled with a very dubious sort of happiness, tasteless and boring. But in all seriousness, is not Dante a proof of this, whose Paradise is stuffed full of beatitudes all hopelessly heaped together, without form, with no gradation of light, full of repetitions, composed, as it were, of simpering, seraphic vacuity, devoid of knowledge and of all possibility of knowledge — a Paradise of sublime ballyhoo. And beside it, the Inferno. What a compendium of Life ! What discernment, invocation, judgement ! What reality, what nice appraisal even of the darkest darkness ; what a re-encounter with the world ! From this it does not follow that suffering is more right than happiness, or the surrender to it, or the expression and allowance of it ; only that till now humanity has not attained the depth, the fervour, the necessity in the realms of bliss which have been made accessible to it in suffering. (And hence Capri is — a monstrosity.)

For the rest, occasionally one sees Diefenbach, the painter, looming up on the horizon, all in grey, the grey that old wood assumes on fences under the influence of sun and rain. And Gorki has settled here, fêted by the Socialists and scattering money away in all directions. I close now, dear people, in the knowledge of having passed an evening hour with you which I badly needed.

63. *To Clara Rilke*

Capri, Villa Discopoli
17 *December* 1906

I could read your (fifth) letter over and over again. Each time with a new listening in my heart. If Lou only knew how many such letters I write to myself in thought. Long letters full of such objections. They are all familiar to me. I know their faces, I have gazed into them for hours, I know how they come closer and closer, straight at me, blindly. And yet there is something new in the way they come this time, something that made me more attentive, perhaps, than I have ever been towards them. I thank you for passing on to me those words which must have been work and exertion enough for you even to accept, arrange, and, where you thought it good, reject. . . . So this, too, belongs to the many, many things in which you are implicated. It came and needed you, needed all your strength, your memories of words, facts, sadnesses, of all the ruthless, almost desperate exaggerations by means of which I sometimes try to plumb the depths of sincerity, only causing pain both to myself and you. You saw all this rising up before you, with all the menace, hardness and momentary hopelessness that come with it, and you had to find the resolve to set yourself above it, superbly clear-headed, and face Lou, defending what had so often attacked you when you were without defence.

This is how it is with me : I am passionately determined not to miss any of the voices that may come. I will hear each one of them, I will take out my heart and hold it in the midst of these condemning and chiding words so that it shall not be touched by them on *one* side only and from a distance. But at the same time I will not give up my perilous and often irresponsible standpoint and exchange it for a more comprehensible and renunciatory one before the last, uttermost and final voice has spoken to me ; for only on this spot am I accessible and open to them all, only on this spot can I be reached by the fate, the encouragement, the powers that want to reach me ; only from here can I one day obey as absolutely as I now resist. By means of premature alliances with what would overwhelm me in the form of " duty " and put me to some use I might, indeed, exclude a number of uncertainties and the appearance of continual evasion from my life, but I feel that the great and wonderful helps which set to work in me in almost rhythmical sequence would also be excluded from such a limited order, established on energy and the consciousness of duty, to which they would not belong any more. Lou is of the opinion that one has no right to choose one's duties and withdraw from those that are the most immediate and natural ; but my most immediate and natural duties have always been, even in my boyhood, these ones here on whose side I always try to stand, and if I have wished to undertake others I saw them not as new tasks superadded to the primary, already excessively great work of my life ; it is rather that in certain duties I thought I could find a point of support, something that would form a solid core in my shifting homelessness, something rooted, durable, real. I did not plan to do anything definite for the inception of this reality ; I thought it would come as everything miraculous comes, out of the depths of our union, out of its immense necessity and purity. I could not with a good conscience undertake new work, a new profession, and if I have any responsibility in me I mean and desire it to be responsibility for the deepest and innermost essence of a loved reality to which I am inseparably bound. And have I shirked this responsibility ? Do I not try, in so far as I can, to bear it, and on the other hand has not my longing been fulfilled, on the whole, measurelessly ? How can any blunders in small matters prove the contrary ; how can the fact that we still have to postpone our life together, with its mutual offers of practical support, confute me, when my world with you has now, more than ever before, grown into something so completely inexpressible ? It began to grow out from that little snow-covered house where Ruth was born and has gone on growing and growing ever since from that centre, to which I cannot limit my attention while the periphery expands on all sides into the Infinite. But is it not only since *then* that a centre has been there, something immovable, a luminary according to whose position I can determine the movement of my heavens and name the constellations which till now were but a chaos ? Are you not the one tree in the unutterably vast desert of my going, to which I sometimes look back to find out where I am and whither I must bend my steps ? And if we thus, separated from one another by days' journeys, live and try to do what our hearts demand of us day and night . . . tell me, is there *still* not a house about us, a real house for which only the visible sign is lacking, so that the others cannot see it ? But do not we ourselves see it then most clearly, this house of our heart, in which we have been together from the beginning and from which we shall one day step out only to enter the garden. . . . ?

Ah, you understand how much I want to nurture my powers and my measures on greatness ; even as a boy I had the feeling, when I attached myself to great and mature people, that they were elder brothers and sisters, for I never believed that one made oneself worthy of their companionship merely by excelling in mediocrity. It might therefore appear as if I lived life back to front ; most of us do, of course, set about it the other way round and we manage to bring our everyday lives up to the beginning of the uncommon, even right into it. For such people that may be the right way. But for me the ascent from this side was an impossibility. Prematurely exhausted in spirit and body as I was, I would have got stuck in the beginnings of this dailiness and perished. But then for the first time those powers set to work which, lifting me over the most immediate obstacles, placed me at the beginning of greater and less time-bound tasks for which in some remarkable way I was ripe and not yet discouraged. There, in this Beyond, so to speak, I began my work (and Lou was the first person to help me towards it), not transported beyond life's heaviness but only beyond its difficulties. There I was taken from my anxieties and put in a state of mind to which I should never have found a way down below : a love of life sprung from the so necessary experience that it is not Life that is inimical, but I, I myself, and everything connected with me ; and there, from indescribably knowing hands, I received the right to that surrender which would have been annihilation for me down below, whilst yonder, among the great powers, it became my beauty, my growth, a thing on which I could boundlessly rely. And, if I persevere on this summit where I have spent the greater part of my mature life, am I not in the real, in the heavy, still among duties ? And if only I go far enough, must there not come a point at which the Above and the Below imperceptibly converge, just as must one day befall those who have gone the other, lower road honestly and faithfully to the end ? I feel rather like the Russian people of whom distant or mistrustful observers declare that they must eventually be deflected from what has been their line of development hitherto and set on the normal road of evolution and look reality in the face, if they want to achieve anything. And then something would be achieved, doubtless. Just as the western peoples have achieved things, this and that, one after another. But would the Russians achieve that one thing for which alone, above all else, their souls crave? I think they would then be sundered from it completely and for ever. Yet should no one be allowed to strive towards this one thing for which, even in their resignation, the resigned still long?

For the Russians the chances appear to have ceased. I still have one. I know that I have not always used the chances I had as I should, perhaps I have even squandered one or two of them, but I accept them each time as very great tasks and commitments; and if God gives me *so* many and always one more — they cannot be too many as long as he deems them necessary: perhaps he does not desist because I understand him better and better and make gradual progress in the taking of these chances, holding out my little books to him whenever he demands proof. . . .

72. *To Clara Rilke*

CAPRI, VILLA DISCOPOLI
1 *January* 1907

. . . This morning began so gloriously, now it is turning grey; but the first part shone like a new year that had never been used. And the night was clear and large, seeming to hang above much more than the mere earth; you felt that it hung above seas and above the ethereal wastes far beyond them, above its own self, and above stars which looked into its stars from an infinite depth. All this was reflected in it and held by it high above the earth, and only just held, too: for it was like a continual overflowing of the heavens.

I thought there would probably be a midnight mass, and went out soon after eleven o'clock; the streets and the steep ascents between the walls were stretched out like pennons taken down and outspread, black and white, one streak of wall-shadow beside a streak of light; for it was the first night after the full moon and it stood high in the heavens and sharply outshone all the stars, so that only here and there did there twinkle a star huge and remote enough to body forth a surrounding darkness. The tops of the walls were dazzlingly illuminated, the leaves of the olives seemed made entirely of night, as though cut out of sky, an ancient night-sky that was no longer used. And the mountain slopes had the appearance of dilapidated lunar landscapes and towered above the houses like something unconquered. And the houses were dark, and where the wooden shutters were not drawn, the windows had the livid, luminous glaze of blind eyes. At last in the little Piazza under the clock-tower a group of young Capriots stood in converse. From the little red-curtained café that was let into the darkest corner came the occasional impatient jangling of a tambourine. An archway spanning a narrow street that led upwards framed a patch of sky with its curve and clung round it. Somebody in clogs tapped along the houses, the clock started to strike the last quarter before midnight. But the church was closed, as though it had been shut for centuries. And the singing that came remotely and yet with singular distinctness from beyond the olive-trees and vineyards was no Christian singing. Heavy voices, full of ancient, rocking lamentations, long-drawn-out, without beginning, not sounding as though they had suddenly started but as though the ear had been unexpectedly ushered into an everlastingly held note ; voices as though disinterred from the hearing of far-distant mountain-faces ; voices that arose of themselves, or like night-wind caught in the soul of some animal ; long, ponderous, swaying voices, calls and call-sequences proper to some immemorial bacchanalia, dull, mindless, more suffered than willed, and in between, laughter breaking forth like flames and as quickly consumed, brief, lively and warm as on a summer's night — and then, again the shining of the moon. Paths, walls, houses, an earth made of moonlight, of moon-shadows, remaining motionless while the midnight of the New Year is struck, strangely significant, stroke slowly following stroke, each one smooth, widespread, foldless, as though being laid away in store.

I had gone back to my little house again and stood on the roof and wanted to see in all this a good end and find a good beginning in myself. And now let us have faith in the long new year which is given us, new, untouched, full of things that have never been, full of work never before done, full of tasks, demands and encouragement, and let us try to receive it without letting fall the gifts it has to bestow on those who ask the necessary things, the grave and great things. . . . A happy New Year. . . .

76. *To Clara Rilke*

CAPRI, VILLA DISCOPOLI
20 January 1907

. . . It is Sunday once more, and I am still so much in the holiday-mood of our meeting that I feel that in a little while I am going to fetch you down there at the Villa Pagano. But when I look up my eyes fall on the opened atlas, always on the same, now quite familiar picture which has the appearance of a family tree shewing the immensely long life of some old ancestor, ramifying and spreading out in all directions at the bottom. Again and again I look at this wonder-working river, and more and more does it seem to embody the history of the gods of that land ; the mysterious, unknown source of Godhead rising in the inexhaustible reservoirs of high-lying lakes ; the long, mighty swell of its journey during which it always does exactly the same things to whatever it encounters, and finally its division into arms and branches, into the many lesser gods through which every culture reaches its sea, terminates, fades into the Unknown. I have procured for myself the big Andrée Atlas and am deep in this strangely uniform page ; I marvel at the course of this river which, swelling like a Rodin contour, holds within itself a wealth of multifarious energy, detours and side-twistings like sutures on a skull, making millions of tiny gestures as it swings to the left or right like someone who goes through a crowd distributing something and sees somebody here and somebody there who needs him, and makes but slow headway. This is the first time I have felt a river so livingly, real even to the point of personification, as though it had a destiny, a dark birth and a great, wide-spreading death, and between the two a life, an immensely long princely life which gave everybody in its neighbourhood something to do for thousands of years ; so huge was it, so exacting, so little to be overmastered. (How impersonal, on the other hand, is the Volga, only like a colossal road through that other sublime country whose God is still everywhere evolving.) But while I follow the sacred miracle-worker in his tracks, past names heavy with the sediment of ancient meaning, there rises, in contrast to the Nile's clarity and confidence, the desert, uncertain, without end or beginning, like something uncreated ; expanses that come up all of a sudden and are everywhere, shattering the heavens with their nothingness, a network of ancient trade-routes which cancel each other out, an ocean whose ebb plumbs the bottom of the world and whose flow climbs to the stars and mounts like anger, incalculable, incomprehensible, irresistible. When you have seen the sea and accustomed yourself to the endless presence of the sky which reflects the flat earth and against which the earth thrusts the buttresses of its mountain-ranges — when you have understood the beginnings of all this, still the desert remains outside your comprehension. You will see it. Will see the head of the great Sphinx lifting itself wearily out of the continual silt of sand, the head and the face which men proportioned to the size and form of their own, but whose expression and looking and knowing were completed unspeakably slowly and so became quite different from our face. We project images out of ourselves, we make use of every impulse that might serve us as world-builders, we erect one thing after another round our innermost spirit ; but here was a reality that cast itself into these features from outside, and they were nothing but stone. Mornings of centuries, nations of winds, the waxing and waning of countless stars, the vast presence of the constellations, the heats and immensities of the firmament, all these were there and everlastingly there, working on this face and not letting go of its profound indifference until it seemed to look, to display all the tokens of a contemplation of these very images, till it rose up like the countenance of some inner world wherein all these things were contained and the urge and the longing and the need for them. And the moment it was replete with confrontation, wholly a creature of its environment, its *expression* grew out beyond these bounds. Now it was as if the universe had a face, and the face sent forth images far beyond it, beyond the furthest stars to where no images had ever been. . . . Tell me, is it not so ? I think it must be : space, unending space that continues behind the very stars — this is what must, I think, have come into being round the image of the Sphinx.[1] . . .

81. *To Paula Modersohn-Becker*

CAPRI, VILLA DISCOPOLI
5 February 1907

. . . The reproductions of some antique paintings, which probably reached you before this letter, carried with them many greetings — not mine alone but Clara's as well. We chose the photographs for you with special regard to your work, of which we spoke a great deal in the few days Clara spent here on her way to Egypt. We both agreed that it would give you much pleasure to see these paintings, whose purely artistic values have become all the clearer with age and decay. It was probably under the influence of their colouring that we saw the landscape of the South, which so completely nonplussed us three years ago when we were working together, full as it was of tasks for some future artist. Van Gogh, who liked Arles so much, would have gained here an understanding of that grandeur, the continual growth (and transcending) of which makes his simple, objective letters so valuable. How much we saw in Naples! A table with fish on it, that alone was immense, so much so that I would like to tell you about it in more detail: you above all. But this will be done, not told; and if ever it lies in me to do it you shall read it. In the meantime Clara has sent me occasional budgets of news from Egypt, and it is growing evident that this experience will become more hers than almost any other — since that first contact with Rodin she has not reached out for anything with so much need and real hunger as now for these immeasurable things, which she could not have

[1] See Tenth Elegy:

But with the nighing of night they wander more softly
and soon like a moon it soars upward, the world-watching
tomb. Twin-brother to that by the Nile, the transcendent Sphinx,
the countenance of the mysterious chamber within.
And they marvel before that crown-bearing head, whose silence
has set like a symbol for ever
Man's face in the scales of the stars.

mastered at all had not our great Master in Meudon been a preparation for everything immeasurable. Approving and confirming his life and work this tremendous past rises up before Clara and becomes accessible to her — comprehensible, no, but sufficiently so to enable her to persevere with it — through him.

Naturally my thoughts often wander over into that fabulous land of which I am now receiving authentic accounts. But even more do they wander to Paris, for I cannot get over the loss of having left it in the summer, I feel that everything, my work above all, depends upon how soon I can go back to it. I envy you, dear friend, but in this instance my envy is not dangerous. For Paris has enough for everybody (so there is no reason for not being there) — ah ! it has too much for each one of us.

The hundred paintings presented by M. Moreau-Nelaton have been accepted by the Louvre, and you can see the *Déjeuner sur l'herbe* and many others over and over again, as often as you need. I have this need. Need of the Jardin des Plantes, the Luxembourg. They can't be counted. I need everything that Paris is.

May you, who are there, feel the same, and may you be able to use it lavishly for your work, your courage and your future. . . .

84. *To Clara Rilke*

CAPRI, VILLA DISCOPOLI
11 *February* 1907

. . . There is little to see here just now ; the weather has recurrent relapses into imprudence ; the more lonely roads are impassable with mud, the others with tourists who blindly increase and multiply despite the cold and rain. And indoors the curse of summer is combined with the curse of winter : cold feet and midges. (But all this does not excuse the fact that I still haven't done much.) On Thursday evening after I had written to you we went to a local wedding : it was extraordinary, very foreign, notwithstanding the uniformity of all customs nowadays, and in the narrow space between the spectators I saw the tarantella danced three times. What a dance ! as if devised by satyrs and nymphs, old and somehow rediscovered and rearing up all behung with primordial memories : cunning and wildness and wine, men with goats' hoofs again and girls from the clan of Artemis. (Some time we must see it together, in Naples ; perhaps.)

But now some good news which came two days ago — the *Stundenbuch* is sold out (five hundred copies in little over a year — who would have thought it !), and a new impression is to be prepared (like the first, only unnumbered, on different paper and, as I suggested, with an index of first lines) — 1100 copies this time. Joy reigns with the publishers, and astonishment and joy, as you can imagine, with me. . . .

87. *To Clara Rilke*

CAPRI, VILLA DISCOPOLI
18 *February* 1907

. . . Evening has fallen and I am tired, because the day that preceded this evening was very lovely, an endlessly shining, blue, vibrant day, the first of its kind ; one of those that surprised and overpowered us — how well I remember it — in Rome about this time : you intend doing this and that, something quite definite, quite ordinary and nameable, something that is a continuation of yesterday ; but then a day begins that has no yesterday (still less a tomorrow), a sort of *leap-day*, and you notice it as soon as you wake up, even before you've looked out of the window, as though it has entered your sleep. And on top of this Antonio came in with an " *è splendida la giornata* " (and at the " *splen...* " his face lit up with a smile, splitting like a fruit over the south-Italian teeth). I knew then that I would have to go for a walk, a long walk ; and to disperse my sense of guilt and my bad conscience a little (guilt and conscience over a decision wantonly to abandon my writing-desk) I begged to have the Countess for myself, and we climbed the Monte Solaro and viewed the island like birds, feeling that the next moment we would be high above the sea ; for at its extreme tip the Monte Solaro hardly pushed at all against the soles of our feet, and what sustained us and surrounded us was primarily the property of the birds : a deep, shimmering blueness which was warm and rich and mild on the *front*, so to speak, but seemed lined with the sea-wind, like silk, whenever it turned round and brushed gently against us with its underside. I am beginning to discover Anacapri, that ultimate Anacapri which lies beyond the furthest point we reached together. There it grows really lonely and wild and runs on for a long time like that all by itself, and it is something to see even a shepherd. And the houses fall behind, and where the few stony paths stop there is the sea once more, or rather another sea, a sea through which Odysseus might come again, at any moment; an old Grecian sea beginning deep, deep down below you and without end. And it really is here, I read recently, that Odysseus sailed past, and today, from Monte Solaro, we saw the three Isles of the Sirens lying in the Salernian Gulf (three queer rocks blocking the fairway, looking as though they had once been gilded). These were the islands past which he drifted, bound to his mast and only by reason of this constraint safe from the irresistible magic that came chiming across, dissolved in the light wind — drifting, drifting, much too slowly for safety, infinitely slowly he must have thought. And on such days as these, removed from the inquisitiveness and pettiness of the tourist centre, up there among the mountain scenery of a shepherd's world, there grows upon you slowly, yet ever again to be blotted out, a faint idea of the South of Antiquity of which Uexkuell wrote not long ago. When you come we must often go up there ; you will talk, and I will listen. . . .

88. *To Clara Rilke*

CAPRI, 22 *February* 1907

. . . I am thanking you with only a few words for your letter, the fifth ; I can understand it everywhere and enter with you into your sadness, this sadness I know so profoundly and for which one can, of course, discover no reasons. . . . And yet it is nothing more than a sensitive spot in us, always the same, one of those spots which, when they pain us, cannot be located, so that we do not know how to recognise or treat them in our dumb hurtfulness. I know it all. And there is a joy that is similar — and maybe we ought to get beyond both of them, somehow. I was thinking of that only lately when I had climbed for several days in succession into the lonely escarpments of Anacapri and was so happy up there, so wearisomely happy even in soul. We let both of them, equally, fall away from us, time after time: this happiness, that sadness. We possess neither. And what *are* we when we stand there, and a wind outside, or a gleaming, or a fragment of bird-song in the air can take us and have its will of us! It is good to hear and see and accept all this, not be numb to it, but on the contrary to feel it more and more multitudinously in all its gradations without getting lost in it. Once I said to Rodin on an April day full of spring: "How it disintegrates you, how you have to join in the work with all your juices and struggle till you're tired. Don't you feel it too?" And he, who certainly knew in his heart how to take the spring, answered with a quick glance: "*Ah—je n'y ai jamais fait attention.*" This is what we've got to learn — not to pay attention to certain things; to be too concentrated to touch with any sensitive side of ourselves those things which we can never reach with our total being. To feel everything only with the *whole* of our lives — then much indeed (of what is too narrow for us) remains outside, but all the important things are there. . . .

91. *To Clara Rilke*

Capri, Villa Discopoli
25 February 1907

. . . You wish me "spring at last", and your wish has been truly and speedily fulfilled: already last week I was able to tell you of the walks I am taking and my joy at discovering them. These out-of-the-way walks among the heights of Anacapri, these views over the old Grecian sea, this being alone with the little secluded church and the broad mountain slopes which, on one spot, encompass you about like an amphitheatre, with Vesuvius peering in at the open end and, a little withdrawn, the snow-capped peaks standing on either side: all this I have sought out many times in the past week, the first few days of which fully realised your wish. So completely was the spring all at once *there*, and so significant, it seemed, was my penetration into its depths that my conscience remained easy although I used up very many hours, nearly all my mornings. But being in the sun and breathing the spring-sky and listening to the birds' voices — which are so perfectly distributed that you feel there is one in every tract of air that can carry — and the sense of belonging that all these things reinforce in you, — surely this can lead to no loss or omission. And however many reasons I may have to constrain myself to my writing-desk, I always sally forth again when the morning suddenly calls outside, making you surmise the presence of another morning, a great morning, the morning of seagulls and island-birds, the morning of hills and unattainable flowers, that unchanging, eternal morning which need take no account as yet of the people who blink at it dubiously and surlily and critically before breakfast. And you have only to walk for half an hour with those light, rapid steps that carry you so inconceivably far, in order to have it really environing you, the sea-morning, which is confident that everything is for it and nothing against it, which reiterates its gesture of opening a thousand thousand times until it gradually slows down in the smallest flowers and is wholly comprised there. Then I feel the truth of what you wrote recently : that such spring mornings belong to some foreign springtime, and that my particular spring is much more circumspect and hesitant and less obvious. Do you remember how mightily I came to miss in Rome the spring that keeps pace with our hearts ? How bewildered I was by the frenzied simultaneity of the blossom, by its prodigality, its impatience, its effortless achievement that has no counterweights ? How we scorned the swiftly satisfied nightingale, in whose slipshod song it was impossible to recognise the longing we knew so well. Yes, I understood then, and I know now so absolutely what you mean, and how right you are. It may perhaps be that our nature really does revenge itself for all the foreign, disproportionate things we wreak upon it, and that between ourselves and our environment there arise fissures which do not remain wholly on the surface. But why then did our forefathers read of the glamour of far countries — for, by allowing it to proliferate into dreams, into yearnings, into vague fantasies ; by permitting their heart to change its gait, urged on by a certain adventurousness ; by standing at windows, their minds bursting with antipodes, with a look that turned its back almost contemptuously on the courtyard and garden without — they succeeded in conjuring up the very thing that we now have to cope with and, in a sense, put to rights. Together with their immediate surroundings, which they no longer even saw, they lost sight of the whole of reality ; the Near seemed tedious and quotidian to them and the Far depended on their mood and fancy. So Near and Far alike passed into oblivion. Hence it has fallen to us not to differentiate between them, to take both of them on ourselves and to reconstitute them as the one reality which, in actual fact, is nowhere divided and compartmented and not commonplace where we are and romantic a bit further off and not boring here and over there full of modulation. In those days they distinguished so rigorously between the exotic and the familiar ; they did not remark how the two are everywhere in closest interfusion. They saw only that the Near did not belong to them, wherefore they thought that anything they could really possess and value would be far off, and longed for it. And they took their unbridled and fanciful longing as evidence of its beauty and grandeur. For they still supposed that we have the power to appropriate things into ourselves, to absorb them, devour them ; whereas from the very outset we are so brimful that not even the littlest thing can be added. Yet all things can work on us. And all work on us from out of the distance, the near as well as the far, not one of them touches us, all commune with us over and across great divides, and as little as the uttermost stars can pass into us, so little can the ring on my hand ; only as though with their radiance can things reach us, and just as the magnet rouses and organises the forces in something susceptible to it, so they, through their influence, create within us a new ordering. And do not both nearness and farness vanish before such an inward vision ? And is it not *our* vision ? This only by way of a cursory answer to your lovely letter. . . .

95. *To Clara Rilke*

CAPRI, VILLA DISCOPOLI
1 *March* 1907

. . . It is strange how those very things we dreamed of and planned to do on one of our walks together in Friedelhausen, when we needed comforting, are now being fulfilled : that I should see Greece. For no landscape could be more Greek, no sea more brimming with ancient horizons than the land and the sea spread out for my contemplation and experience on these walks in Anacapri. This *is* Greece, without the art-objects of the Grecian world but almost as though before their creation. As though all *that* were still to come the stony slopes lie there ; as though even the gods had still to be born who called forth the torrent of ecstasy and beauty that was Greece. And you ought to hear the language the people speak up there. Never have I heard such an ancient tongue in any human mouth. You ask what the name is of the landscape in which you are standing and they say something huge, mighty, something that sounds like the name of a king, an early, primitive, legendary monarch, and you fancy that you once had an inkling of his name in the storm-winds and in the muted swell of the heavy sea. . . .

96. *To Clara Rilke*

CAPRI, VILLA DISCOPOLI
8 *March* 1907

. . . My letter crossed with your beautiful description of the drives in the evening, and I received more from your sensitive words than you may have hoped to compass in your rapid notes. Your sketches are always very good, sure and decisive, and when you read them through again here, with me, you will be surprised to see how much is contained in them. Then many other things that amplify and complete the rest will be added, and out of the whole we may be able to put together an " Egyptian Journey " such as nobody has had the wit to make or tell before. Go on collecting impressions ; don't think of letters which have to be informative and comprehensible ; take in this and that with quick snatching-gestures : passing thoughts, ideas, fancies that suddenly flare up in you and last only a second under the influence of some occurrence ; all those unimportant things that often become significant through a fleeting intensity of vision or because they take place on a spot where they are absolute in their irrelevance, unceasingly valid and profoundly meaningful for any personal insight which, rising up in us at the same moment, coincides pregnantly with that image. Looking is such a marvellous thing, of which we know but little ; through it, we are turned absolutely towards the Outside, but when we are most of all so, things happen in us that have waited longingly to be observed, and while they reach completion in us, intact and curiously anonymous, *without our aid*, — their significance grows up in the object outside : a powerful, persuasive name, the only name these inner events could possibly have, a name in which we joyfully and reverently recognise the happenings within us, a name we ourselves do not touch, only apprehending it very gently, from a distance, under the similitude of a thing that, a moment ago, was strange to us, and the next moment will be estranged anew. It quite often happens now that some face affects me in this way ; in the mornings, for instance, which generally start off with a lot of sun quite early, a mass of brightness — suddenly, in the shadow of a street, a face is held out to you and you see, under the influence of the contrast, its essence with such clarity (clarity of nuance) that the momentary impression involuntarily assumes the proportions of a symbol. More than ever I wish there were someone here who could paint ; seriously paint. Only just recently, imagine : a green rectangular field running evenly towards the sloping, dark-blue sea, set beside it in such a way that you were unable to see the perpendicular drop of some old terrace which alone separated them. Sitting in this field a woman in rhubarb-red and orange, another passing to and fro in faded green beneath some white sheets and table-cloths hung up to dry on lines, animated in the most varied ways by the wind, now all hollow and drawn in, full of luminous shadows, now dazzlingly blown out, and ever again interspersed with the distinct blue of the sea and overarched by the perpetually descending sky. . . . I wonder if Paula

Becker would have liked it? But it's a sin to write it down in ink. Why does no painter come and drive the money-changers out of the temple and do what is so needful and so obvious? Well then, once again, make many notes, don't even read them through (for in the revision one is often unfair and much that is strictly necessary appears impossible), and if you can, make such sketches as the above with the sheer immediacy of the instantaneous stroke. All of it only as material which we can view here, discuss and piece together at the natural breaks. You will see how it all fits. Only, there must be a lot of it, so that you can really shake it out before you and plunge your hands in. The more the better. Write little, and be greedy of your notes and sketches. (Looking into the interior of a house as into the flesh of a fruit is an experience I have had somewhere. In Rome?) Look, look, look all you can. . . .

99. *To Clara Rilke*

CAPRI, VILLA DISCOPOLI
11 *March* 1907

. . . Always on Monday I write it, the "Oceana"[1] letter, and it is with you the Sunday after at 11.30: so your cards tell me, which I count as a good letter (the tenth). How beautiful these cards are, and on the other hand how fine, as these now prove, have been your descriptions! You conjured up in my mind the avenue leading to the pyramids just as it is in reality, using only what the cards cannot give — light and its movement. Yet the arrangement and distribution of the whole grouped themselves in me at your behest exactly as the cards show them. You wish "to be more and more alone", you say. Yes, how much and how implacably I too would wish the same had I returned from such journeys and such things to the dull, stupefying boredom of social tittle-tattle. . . . It is the fault of our upbringing that we find it so difficult to make an end of these social accessories. The people you know in Heluan, in so far as they are not professional idlers, have learnt from childhood to regard a surfeit of social inconvenience as something inevitable.

[1] Ship plying between Naples and Egypt.

It is the canvas on which they have made the same stitches over and over again. Whereas I, I lived so truly in the little corner of the graveyard in the Institute garden [1] where I was safe from my fellows, and in the extremely unsociable surroundings of their cruelty, that I have become cut out as with a pair of scissors sharp and clear from the mass-image of the unlovely herd. . . . Before people learnt what real work was they devised distractions as the opposite of false work and as a relaxation from it. Had they waited, ah, and been patient, real work would have become a little more accessible to them, and they would have realised that it can as little have an opposite as the world can, or God, or any living soul. For it is *everything*, and what it is not, nowhere exists. Renan wrote once : " *Travailler, ça repose* ". I shall use it as a motto for the new Rodin book (which I shall not begin before we have discussed Egypt). . . .

108. *To Tora Holmstroem*

CAPRI, VILLA DISCOPOLI
29 *March* 1907

. . . From the bottom of my heart I am glad that you are going to Paris and are thinking of resuming your work there. I am only worried lest you should set about it with too much energy and violence simultaneously with the immensity that is Paris : for this you only know later — that Paris is itself a work, a huge, wearing work which you accomplish without noticing it. The demands that this city makes upon you are measureless and unceasing. (I have it to thank for the best work I have done so far.) Hence Paris does not help you immediately and directly with your artistic activities, it does not affect the work you actually do, but it changes, intensifies and develops you continually, it takes the tools you have used hitherto gently from your hands and replaces them with other, infinitely more delicate and precise ones, and does a thousand unexpected things to you like a fairy who delights in seeing somebody assume all the shapes whose possibilities lie hidden in him. When you have

[1] Garden of the Military School in St. Pölten ?

it about you for the first time you must let Paris act like a bath without yourself wanting to do too much : only feeling it and letting it happen.

Therefore, my dear Tora, I would ask you to be careful, for I am afraid of your overtaxing yourself and injuring your health. But here I reach the second, the egotistical part of my joy : soon I shall be in Paris and shall see you. For I am planning to return there in a little while (the beginning of May at the latest, I think) because I need its great solitude more than ever and want to shut myself up there and work, conscious of all its depths and things and destinies. And now this pleasant prospect, which has been my help and my hope the whole winter through, is enriched by you whom, so often in these last years, I have wished cordially to meet again. Our acquaintance in Borgeby and our talks were like a beginning in my memory and not like anything complete. So you can understand why I am glad, and that there is much in me that echoes and answers to the words I now say to you : Auf Wiedersehen. . . .

III. *To Ernest Norlind*

CAPRI, 1907

MY DEAR FRIEND,—The poem I have written out above[1] is faultless as it stands, without my having had to alter anything except a trifle here and there. But it is not quite clear and also the language is not quite German in feeling. Nevertheless it is astonishing that you, in a moment of inner compulsion evidently, should have been so successful. I can see what it is you are conjuring up, and in many places you have found a strong and convincing expression for your feeling, so that another person who did not know you would certainly understand it. But the thing as a whole is not living and clear if you regard it independently on its artistic merits. I can understand the urge you have better than anybody else. Have I not tried to write poems in Russian sometimes, in moments when some inner experience could only clarify itself in that form. And from time to

[1] Norlind sent Rilke a poem he had written in German.

time I am still compelled to write certain things in French in order to express them at all. But I have also come to the conclusion that one must not give way to this urge too much, rather must one apply all one's powers to finding all things in one's own language, to saying everything with it : for it, the language to which we are bound right into the depths of our sub-consciousness, it and it alone can give us in the end, if we take trouble enough, the possibility of portraying accurately, faithfully and punctiliously, to the echo of the furthest echo, the finality of our experience. The writer's material is no more amenable than that of any other art and no easier to grasp ! You would scarcely believe how much I still feel myself a beginner in German, very far from reaching out surely and decisively for those words which are every time the only right ones. My experience and knowledge in these matters are too obvious and too fundamental for me to withhold them from you now that you write of your hope and intention of expressing yourself one day in German. The attraction a " great cultural language " holds for you also disappears when you consider how readily accessible the great thoughts of all languages are for us and how far Swedish has drawn attention to itself whenever your writers outgrew purely national significance. And it often seems to me that it is sufficient for a great thing to be thought in order to enjoy indestructible existence ! If you feel like this there is no sense in choosing a language merely because it is widespread ; it ought rather to be our task to reach the extremes of clarity only in the one we have. (Incidentally if you only knew how little prospect one has nowadays of finding an understanding audience among readers of German when one tries to write of the great, final things — you would not wish to feel your way into it ! I say this quite without bitterness ; for art in all its manifestations can afford to wait : indeed it does nothing else and does it passionately.) . . .

Apart from your nice letter I have still to thank you for the things you sent me : the lithograph, and the photograph of your new painting. In both I find the landscape and the disposition of space extraordinarily delicate and successful, but the birds are not so convincing at first sight. I have the feeling that you often spoil your real knowledge of their form and movement by a too conscious stylisation. The mood emanating from these works is very powerful, but the effect it involuntarily has on you is always disturbed by a certain strangeness in the shape of the birds which does not evoke their motion simultaneously with their gestures. But I am absolutely amazed at your vigorous mastery of space, obtained with an increasingly simple technique. Thank you for thinking of me so affectionately. (What is the size of the picture ?)

I am very proud that I am to hold a place in the guest-book of Borgeby. If you send me the necessary pages I will post them back to you, filled out, as soon as possible. Clara is returning at the end of the month from Egypt (where she has been for a quarter of a year) and will then stay with me for a while here in Capri ; if you would enclose a page for her she would love to contribute something : for you know how fondly she remembers Borgeby and with what joy. You must have enjoyed spending this winter at home once more, and you are lucky enough to see the dear, northern Spring beginning in the park — the Spring which we lack all the more down here as the southern one is not yet really under way. We shiver and wait.

If you go to Lund again and see Gustav af Geijerstam please convey to him and his wife my friendliest greetings. In the meantime we have got to know one another, or have begun to — but even at this stage I owe him so much and like and honour him sincerely.

But give my especial regards to Hanna Larsson ! I hope she, too, has had a good winter. I can well imagine how pleased she is with your work and growth ; Borgeby is good soil, and you are a tree, bearing its leaves and fruit seriously, firm-rooted. . . . All the best wishes for you. . . .

114. *To the Baroness Gudrun Uexkuell*

CAPRI, VILLA DISCOPOLI
15 *April* 1907

. . . I have a pleasant daily work at my back, a translation of the forty-four wonderful *Sonnets from the Portuguese* of

Elizabeth Barrett Browning, for the tackling of which I have to thank my hostess. One day it will grow into a little book,[1] and I am looking forward particularly to placing it in your hands! These English love-sonnets have such perfection and accuracy of expression: crystals of feeling, so clear, so right, shiningly mysterious and issuing from some deep, unbewildered place in the poet. And it was somehow possible for me to allow the German rendering to take shape at a similar depth, so that I am pleased with the success of the translation. . . .

117. *To Karl von der Heydt*

CAPRI, VILLA DISCOPOLI
3 *May* 1907

. . . It may perhaps amuse you to know that in the meantime I have seen Gorki. One evening I sat with him at a round table. The melancholy lamp-light fell upon everything equally without picking out anybody in particular: him, his present wife and a couple of morose Russian men who took no notice of me. We communicated with one another first in Russian, of which a little came back to me under the stress of the moment. Later I spoke in German and Madame Gorki translated. You know my persuasion that the revolutionary is the diametrical opposite of the Russian: that is, the Russian is supremely qualified to be one, much in the same way as a lace handkerchief is very nice for mopping up ink, taking for granted, of course, a complete misuse and ruthless misconception of its true properties! Add to this my inability to visualise the artist — this patient, obedient, slowly evolving being — anywhere in the rôle of revolutionary, and you will understand that the preconditions for our relationship were not exactly promising. And such, indeed, proved to be the case. As a democrat Gorki speaks of art with dissatisfaction, narrow and hasty in his judgements; judgements in which the mistakes are so deeply dissolved that you are quite unable to fish them out. At the same time he possesses a great and touching kindliness (that kindliness which always makes it impossible for the great Russians to remain

[1] *Collected Works*, vol. vi. pp. 5–50.

artists), and it is very moving to find on his completely unsophisticated face the traces of great thoughts and a smile that breaks through with an effort, as if it had to pierce a hard, unsympathetic surface from deep within. Curious, too, was the atmosphere of indefinable, anonymous egalitarianism which you entered as soon as you took a seat at the round table. It was like a limbo where these exiles lingered, and their eyes seemed to turn back towards the earth which is Russia, and which it appeared so utterly impossible ever to revisit. . . .

120. *To Friedrich von Oppeln-Brownikowski*

ROME, HÔTEL DE RUSSIE
29 May 1907

. . . Please forgive this letter the hastiness due to a journey, and for bearing out your expectations so little.

I admire the poetry of Stefan George, and my meeting with him nine years ago in the Boboli Gardens is one of my most cherished memories. He spoke against premature and over-hasty publication by young people, not without reference to me ; and this voice, counselling patient work which expects nothing from the outside, took its effect with other earlier voices and strengthened me in an attitude to which I must already have possessed the necessary predisposition. If you wish to call that an influence you may regard it as such.

The effect of works of art does not appear to me to be in any way measurable. Their influence is so much dissolved in memory and experience and so interwoven therewith that it does not allow of individual representation. Judging from my own experience I should say that the influence of George's poetry, like that of other serious works of art, consists in developing one's capacity for wonder and for work and in compelling one back to nature. That is all I can say on the matter. . . .

123. *To Clara Rilke*

HÔTEL DU QUAI VOLTAIRE
3 *June* 1907

. . . How distinct seeing and working are anywhere else ; you look and think : work will come later. But here they are practically the same thing. One comes back again : it is not surprising, not remarkable, not striking, it is not even a holiday, for a holiday would be an interruption. But here life takes hold of you and sweeps you along and carries you towards everything, great and small. Everything that has happened arranges itself in a different order, falls into line as though somebody stood there giving commands ; and the present is fervently present, as though it were on its knees praying for you. I have lived a long life since Friday morning, and countless memories. You can imagine. On Saturday (1st June) I took my first Turkish bath with great pleasure and without any discomfort. It was marvellous to sit in the good warmth for which I had been prepared by the warmth down in Italy. I even wished there were some of it outside too ; the green is far advanced, but the air fitful, cold in places when it moves, and when it keeps still, dully stuffy, so that you feel badly treated by it and by the terrible prickly dust thrown up by the sudden gusts of wind ; I have never felt this so oppressively before — perhaps I am particularly sensitive after all the sea-air ? But this is nothing compared with the main facts. Everything is there again, reality down to the smallest particle. You go for a walk and are simply and sheerly happy, full of the joy of living. And your tasks go on ahead of you on delicate winged feet and linger a little and are not at all unattainable, only very proud. . . . .

125. *To Clara Rilke*

29 rue Cassette, Paris VIe.
7 June 1907

. . . I have revisited several places here. Tuesday in the little Bagatelle Château where there is an exhibition of *Portraits of Women* from the years 1870–1900. A wonderful Manet amply repays all the rest. There's a painter for you ; after seeing this portrait and the incredible *Déjeuner sur l'herbe*, which I examined today in the newly-arranged Moreau-Nelaton Collection at the Louvre, he begins to live all over again. A painter who is still right and always will be right and nothing but right. Carrière was wrong, and Van Gogh is something different, something inexorable, obsessed by expression, and this forces his painting. With him, things appear that were never before painted, but with Manet everything is paintable. (This sounds odd, for in painting everything must be paintable ; yes, but it isn't, not yet — and Van Gogh wanted and wanted it to be.) I saw some Van Goghs at Bernheim-Jeune's : a night-café, late, bare, as if you were seeing it with bleary eyes. The way he has done the stale lamplit air by drawing concentric circles round the hanging lanterns which then gradually dissolve into the surrounding space — this is painting no longer, but it is somehow accomplished with colours and it simply overwhelms you : you grow really old, shabby and hopelessly sleepy as you look at it. Some Maillols are also there : very, very lovely ones. A girl's torso still in clay (it's going to be fired), which is indescribable. At the same time a well-known Japanese collection is to be auctioned soon, and it should be seen before it goes !

But the heaviness, the fearfulness is always present, somehow — once more it is everything, as always in Paris.

Thank you for your notes on the journey. Perhaps you are right in many ways. I thought so today when I saw two pictures by Berthe Morisot : they were painted for Manet's sake, and Marie Bashkirtsheff painted for Bastien-Lepage, for his sake. What we do for God's sake, will women always do for a man ? But human things and divine things are equally unattainable : therefore, could not women's work still become far-reaching and personal and something entirely their own ? . . .

126. *To Clara Rilke*

PARIS, 29 RUE CASSETTE
13 *June* 1907

. . . It is the fault of various circumstances (unpleasant neighbours and suchlike) which another person would find it easier to overcome, that I am still not feeling at home here and not taking Paris as lavishly as she offers herself to me ; above all it is the fault of my not working. . . . Yes, my plan of hours breaks down item by item, for what comes *has* to come, and not what we put on the programme ; only, let us take what comes and has a right to come well and diligently in our hands. And may it come soon, so that there shall be no pauses. . . .

And I am really writing to you in Oberneuland. Dear one : kiss our little girl — she will receive you well — and tell her that Father is thinking of her. I can picture her in the Luxembourg so perfectly and must often think, when I see the little ones sitting in front of the Marionette Theatre, every afternoon, how sweet she would look — no longer, of course, in the very smallest seats (on the contrary !) — how sweet she would look from behind in all her attentiveness. I must see her soon. But before that I must have accomplished something and got on a little further. Ah, we ought to work — that's all we can do, in everything else we are tenth-rate. . . . Anyhow, yesterday I spent the whole morning in the Jardin des Plantes looking at the gazelles. *Gazella Dorcas*, Linné. There is a pair and a single one.[1] They lay in the grass a few paces from each other, chewing, resting, looking. As women look out of pictures they, too, gaze out of something with a soundless, final turn of the head. And when a horse whinnied one of them listened, and I saw the coronet of ears and horns round its slender head. Were the ears of the deer in Al Hayat [2] also grey (as pewter is to gold, so is this grey to the colour of the other hair), and with a soft, dark, dendriform drawing inside ? I saw one of the gazelles get up, but only for a second — it lay down again immediately

[1] Cf. " Die Gazelle ", *Neue Gedichte* (*Collected Works*, vol. iii. p. 45) :

Enchanted one, O tell me, how can two
words of our choosing unto rhyme aspire
when at a breath rhyme comes and goes in you ?
Up from your forehead quiver leaves and lyre

and all your being moves in melodies
soft as the love-songs of the troubadour,
which lie like rose-leaves on the closing eyes
of him who reads and now will read no more

to gaze on you, who stand suspended there,
an arrow poised for flight and yet unsped,
your taut neck arched into the listening air ;

as though a bather in a woodland place
had heard some sound and, startled, turned her head
the image of the woodlake in her face.

[2] Sanatorium in Heluan, where Clara Rilke stayed.

after ; yet while it was stretching and testing itself I could see the magnificent workmanship of the legs (they were like barrels of rifles cocked to fire). I couldn't tear myself away, they were so beautiful, and I felt just as I did when I saw that delicate snapshot you took : as though they had just been changed into this shape. Today I was at the exhibition of Chardin and Fragonard. Fragonard has some wonderful nudes reclining in their own light, and Chardin things, things, commonplace things done with a pictorial actuality that is incomparable. Everything is cleared out of your vision and then a bottle placed there, right in the middle, or a bowl or an apple. He painted two shields for the firm of Pinaud, the scent manufacturer ; you ought to see how all sorts of herbs lie there in the darkness, and, in between, crucibles and alembics of glass reflecting everything, their interiors full of bubbling coloured liquids and swirling vapour. And over and over again one should see the little Maillols, where "*ventre*" and "*sein*" are every bit as pretty as with Fragonard.

Already Paris has a keynote, a ground-tone of oppressive heat : but in the forefront there is wind, very cool wind even, and always the likelihood of rain. And sometimes the wind withdraws and goes on blowing in the sky and then you notice once more how large it is, how much sky there is above this city (all the sky, one had almost said) ; and somewhere, shining and bright as in armour, Sacré-Cœur, all in armour beneath the sky. The Luxembourg and the fountains, even the young people and the bizarre, obstinate old men who stick to their rituals : nothing has grown less. Only, one is not worthy of being shewn such things when one does nothing oneself. . . .

129. *To Clara Rilke*

29 RUE CASSETTE, PARIS VIe.
19 *June* 1907

. . . I do not know why I am so slow in getting accustomed to Paris this time and making myself at home. The neighbourhood is not bad, and yet it is still the Paris that consumed Malte. There is a student [1] here who has been studying for his degree

[1] Cf. *Malte Laurids Brigge, Collected Works*, vol. v. p. 208.

for years. Shortly before the exam. a malady sets in : his eyes get blurred over his books, the lines dance and one eyelid shuts up, simply shuts up, like a roller-blind whose string has snapped. This state of affairs has made him nervously miserable and now, about the time I moved in, he began to pace up and down his room, stamping at each turn and, late at night, throwing things on the floor in a sort of dull exasperation, all kinds of tin things that were made expressly for this purpose and went on rolling, only to be snatched up again and flung down, again and again. You know, they could not have provided this young person with a more sensitive neighbour. How it made me hold my breath in suspense during the first nights, before I knew what it was ! Ah, because I at once comprehended the rhythm in this madness, the exhaustion in this fury, the labour and the desperation of it — you can imagine. All this has gnawed at me, and confirmed and absorbed me in my hideous dejection. And a person in this state, when he is at the end of his powers, draws strength through the wall. Instinctively, that's no concern of his. This is all. And now they are operating on his eyelid (the muscular debility of which cannot, of course, be remedied surgically). But it is so in keeping with the wretchedness of it all that the hospital should now poke its nose in, together with the expert young men who will be sure to shew a momentary interest in this recalcitrant eyelid. Today, I believe, he is to be operated on for the second time, and then, they say, he will soon go off somewhere, for home. His mother came when he was at his worst. To hear her step outside — ah, little did she guess how much this step helped me as well ! You had only to listen to it, outside in the passage, as she came and went. You heard : a mother has a sick son — heard it as though you saw it on ten bas-reliefs depicting the various stations of a Via Dolorosa : that's how you heard it. This is only as a P.S. So don't worry. . . .

135. *To Clara Rilke*

Paris VIe., rue Cassette
24 June 1907

. . . Early this morning came your long letter with all your thoughts. Art is always the outcome of one's having been in danger, of having gone right to the end of an experience to where no human being can go further. And the further one goes the more peculiarly personal and unique does an experience become, and the art-object is but the necessary, irrepressible and most conclusive utterance of this uniqueness. Therein consists the immense succour which the art-object gives to the life of him who must create it : it is his integrity, his integration ; the knot in the rosary by which his life murmurs a prayer ; the ever-recurrent proof of his singleness and veracity, revealed only to him, applicable only to him, affecting the outside world anonymously, indefinably, as necessity only, as reality, as existence.

Thus we are surely driven to test and measure ourselves against some kind of extreme, but in all probability also bound not to give voice to this extreme before its entry into the work of art, or to share it, communicate it : for as a peculiarity which no one else could or would understand, as a sort of personal madness, so to speak, it has to enter into the work in order to become valid there and reveal its own law, like an inherent design which only becomes visible in the transparency of Art. Yet there are two forms of sharing open to artists, and to me they appear the only possible ones : that in the face of the completed thing, and that within the framework of their daily lives, in which they shew each other what they have become through their labours, acquiring in this way mutual help and support and (in the humblest sense) admiration. But in the one case as in the other they must shew definite results, and it is not lack of confidence, not indifference to each other and not exclusion when they fail to produce the instruments of their evolution, which have so much that is confusing and painful about them and are only valid for personal usage. I often think how insane it would have been, how perturbing for him, had Van Gogh been obliged to share the uniqueness of his vision, or to consider his subjects, with another person *before* he had fashioned his pictures from them, those entities which now prove him right with all their soul, which stand guarantee for him, which conjure up his realness. In his letters he does sometimes think he needs this sharing (although even there he deals mostly with what he has already done), but hardly was Gauguin with him, the longed-for companion, the soul-mate — when in sheer desperation he sliced off an ear after they had both decided to hate one another and get rid of one another at a favourable opportunity. This is only one instance : artist to artist. Another is the woman and her participation. And a third (but this is only conceivable as a task for higher-grade students !) : the complication of the woman also being an artist. Ah, this is altogether a new problem, and thoughts gnaw at you from all sides if you take but a few steps towards it. For this reason I shall write no more about it today. My relation to my " models " is doubtless still at fault, since I have no use at all for human ones (proof : I am not making any humans yet), and am busied with flowers, animals and landscapes, enough for years. (The opening scene of *Alcestis* is perhaps the first thrust into the world of " figures ".) . . .

144. *To Clara Rilke*

PARIS VIe., RUE CASSETTE
12 *July* 1907

. . . Do not alarm yourself about the wearisomeness of my work : it has a natural dependence on certain peculiar circumstances which do not allow one simply to go out, see, hear. — But I have had more time than anybody else to see, hear, be outside. . . . Only, I have forgotten so much, and all my memories, which were suddenly broken off one day, have a fault in them — it runs through them all. This makes my present occupation rather painful. There would, however, be no point in postponing it ; that would only make matters worse. And I have promised myself to finish all my arrears one after another. It is what has NOT been done that lies with all its weight upon what wants to come up from the earth. So do not worry. Everything that is work is good and has its rights, even the right to be difficult. . . .

164. *To Ernst Schellenberg*

PARIS VIe., 29 RUE CASSETTE
2 *September* 1907

. . . It is very kind of you to meet my silence with such lenience although it must appear to you extremely strange and unfriendly. The main reason lies in a correspondence which far surpasses my powers ; but this is no excuse. Neither does it exonerate me when I sincerely confess to you that the answering of your letter was put off and finally passed into oblivion because everything that my books call up in the way of literary appreciation or discussion is very alien to me.

You display such amiable sentiments towards me that I owe you at least a few words on this head. Here you are up against a purely personal feeling, a weakness, if you will, which, while I admit it, I in no way seek to justify. Maybe I am wrong, but I never read anything that concerns my work. I did so years ago, as a young man, when I didn't know any better and was curious. Now the close relation I bear to my work prevents me from laying hands on any critical examination ever again. *I must be alone with my work* and have need of hearing others speak about it as little as anyone would wish to see printed, and to collect, the judgements of others upon the woman he loves. The just and the unjust remarks any critic is capable of making interpose themselves between me and my work, they are foreign bodies, and were it possible to assimilate them it would still seem to me a bad procedure ; for what is expressed in them would increasingly expel and replace the unconscious elements in this inward and intimate relationship which binds the workman in so recondite and enigmatic a manner to his work, to its past and to the future that awaits it. This unconsciousness in the artist's activity and in the continued pursuance of his own road (which ought not to be lost), is imperilled, I feel, by any and every criticism, and it lies with my nature that I, personally, regard all criticism as a letter to the public which the author under consideration, not being he to whom it was directed, ought not to open and read.

Do not understand me as intending to say anything general here ; what I say concerns only myself, who am perforce the object of discussion, since you have willed it.

Forgive me, therefore, if I make no exception of your little volume and place it unread among my books. That you are disposed very kindly towards me I know from your letter, which I was at liberty to read ; for however foreign and unrelated to myself may seem the criticism that is addressed to the outside world, I know of nothing dearer and more helpful than the expression of an approval directed towards me and destined for me alone. This, when it falls to my lot, I accept with all my heart and hold in honour. And whilst thanking you for this especially, I also thank you for the little book that has grown out of your scrutiny of my works. By going out into the world it will certainly do much for me ; please understand that I am not overlooking or underestimating that fact, on the contrary I know very well how great can be the influence of a convinced voice. I rate criticism very highly ; the restriction is merely that, as a result of some fixed, inner organisation I can have no correspondence whatever with anything that concerns my own work.

I am writing in haste and do not know whether I am intelligible ; but I would wish very much to be sufficiently so for you not to find me captious and ungrateful.

Of the erstwhile book *Leben und Lieder* there exist, in point of fact, no copies — which is in no way to be regretted.

Neither can I fulfil your other wish ; I never give away pictures of myself ; also, there is not one that is really valid.

If ever I manage to catch up on my lecture in Weimar, which was crowded out by the circumstances of last year, I shall try to make amends by coming to greet you. . . .

169. *To Clara Rilke*

PARIS VIe., 29 RUE CASSETTE
13 *September* 1907

. . . Never have I been so affected and well-nigh smitten by heather as I was the other day, when I found these three sprigs in your letter. Since then they have been lying in my *Buch der Bilder* and permeating it with their strong serious smell, which is really only the scent of autumn earth. But how wonderful it is, this scent. Never, it seems to me, does the earth allow itself to be inhaled so much in one single scent, the mellow earth ; in a scent that is no whit smaller than the scent of the sea, bitter where it borders on the sense of taste, and more than honey-sweet where you think it must strike on more solemn tones. Harbouring depths in itself, darkness and sepulture, and yet again the wind ; tar and turpentine and Ceylon tea. Grave and needy like the smell of a mendicant friar, yet resinous and heartening like precious incense. And to look at : like embroidery — marvellous ; like three cypresses woven into a Persian carpet with violet silk : a violet so puissant and dewy as to be the colour-complement of the sun. You ought to see it. I do not think the little sprigs could have been as beautiful when you sent them off : otherwise you would have written something of your astonishment. One of them is now lying, by chance, on the dark-blue velvet of an old writing-casket. It is like a firework : no, just like a Persian carpet. Are they all, all these millions of little branches, of such wonderful workmanship ? Look at the colouring of the green, in which there is a splash of gold, and the sandalwood-brown of the stem and the break with its new, fresh, barely-green interior. — Ah, for days I've been marvelling at the magnificence of these three fragments and am thoroughly ashamed that I was not happy when I had the chance to wander about in all the abundance of it. So badly does one live, because one always comes incomplete into the present, inept and scatter-brained. When I think back there is no period of my life without such, and even greater, reproaches. Only the ten days after Ruth's birth, I think, have I lived without loss ; finding Reality as indescribable, even in its smallest part, as it probably always is. — But I suppose it is the stale city-summer that makes me so susceptible to the glory of little bits of heather springing from the splendours of the northern year. So it is not in vain that one has struggled through the summer, pent up in a room, where one seemed housed in the smallest of those boxes that fit into each other twenty times. And there one is, in the very last of them, crouching. Good heavens, how well off I was a year ago, with seas, parks, woods and fields : my longing for it all is sometimes indescribable. Especially now, when winter threatens. Already those misty mornings and evenings are beginning, when the sun is only like the place where the sun formerly was, when all the summer flowers in the beds, the dahlias and the great gladioli and the long rows of geraniums cry the protest of their red into the fog. This saddens me. It calls up comfortless memories, one knows not why : as if the music of the city-summer were expiring on a discord, in an uproar of notes ; but perhaps it is only because I have already gained such a deep insight here and interpreted it and bound myself up with it, without, however, actually *doing anything* about it. . . .

175. *To Clara Rilke*

PARIS VIe., 29 RUE CASSETTE
20 *September* 1907

. . . In the last letter but one you write of the bright sickle of the moon high up in the evening, familiar also to Ruth [1] — but here it is well on the way to becoming a full moon and waits palely in the pale evening sky for darkness to fall round it, and shines over the little monastery garden to the left so that I can feel it everywhere outside as I go to sleep, without actually seeing it : on the dome of the church, in the empty chestnuts, in the air which remains dark but becomes quite transparent and almost like a mirror in places, like glass over a black picture. It does me good to have a real night opposite me, the night belonging to the little garden ; even a little garden has a big night. (Here I broke off, for, in small, strangely recurrent cadences down below in the quiet rue Cassette, I recognised the voice of an old woman who goes along singing, as though she were singing a child to sleep ; she is blind. Her black poodle drags her forward by her left hand, while the stick in her right goes on regularly tapping. When a coin falls the dog leads her to the place where it has dropped, picks it up and deposits it in a little tin plate which the

[1] See Victor Hugo's *Booz endormi* :

> Tout reposait dans Ur et dans Jérimadeth ;
> Les astres émaillaient le ciel profond et sombre ;
> Le croissant fin et clair parmi ces fleurs de l'ombre
> Brillait à l'occident, et Ruth se demandait,
>
> Immobile, ouvrant l'œil à moitié sous ses voiles,
> Quel dieu, quel moissonneur de l'éternel été,
> Avait, en s'en allant, négligemment jeté
> Cette faucille d'or dans le champ des étoiles.

woman holds out to him. During the search the song stops. Except for a repeated call of thanks ; then the song starts up again as though it had never been interrupted and as though one had only not been listening for a spell.) Now my street is quiet once more with only an occasional single step, now and then a cart, and in a while, I know, the stick of a blind man will sound on the edge of the trottoir : for now is the time he goes home. And all this is for the ear as it is for the eye to gaze into the heavens : everything comes up rightfully, at set distances, and makes pictures and is miles away and yet fully explicable and full of affinities for the lonely heart which interprets it and loves it, as though finding a hold for itself among all the infinitudes that begin so close at hand. . . .

183. *To Clara Rilke*

PARIS VIe., 29 RUE CASSETTE
4 *October* 1907

. . . One still seems to be living in a wringing wet sponge. How strange is the effect of being lifted out of the general order of things ! Usually the yearly seasons are so beautiful and helpful in their relation and contrast, they give you something to hang on to ; but this time everything came unheralded, as though one had turned the pages of an encyclopaedia to another letter and had gone on reading something altogether different under J or Z.

Of course, were one as certain of one's work as one ought to be, all this, even in conjunction with a cold, would not disconcert one in the least : one would merely see and make things in that frame of mind too. (It was in just such a frame of mind that I once, in Schmargendorf, if I remember aright, all unexpectedly wrote the *Blätter aus einer Sturmnacht*[1] in a single evening.) But I am still very far from " the state of perpetual work ". Van Gogh might perhaps lose his bearings, but his work was behind them, and he could no longer go completely astray. And Rodin, when he is not well, is quite close to his work, writes beautiful things on innumerable sheets of paper, reads Plato

[1] *Collected Works*, vol. ii. pp. 139-49.

and meditates on him. I have an idea, though, that it is not a mere discipline and a compulsion to stand to your work in this way, which would be a strain, just as these last few weeks have strained me — it is sheer joy ; it is a natural contentment in this one thing which nothing else touches. Possibly we must comprehend the task we have to do still more clearly, still more tangibly, discernible in a hundred details. I feel what Van Gogh must have felt at certain moments, and feel it with great force : that everything is still to be done — everything. But where I fail is in turning to the most immediate objects, or I succeed only in my best moments, whereas it is precisely in the worst that it is most necessary. Van Gogh could do an *Intérieur d'Hôpital* and paint the most direful objects on his direst days. How else could he have survived ? This is what we must attain to, and, I feel, not from compulsion. From understanding, from joy, from the inability to put it off any longer, in consideration of all that still has to be done. Oh that we had no memories of not having worked, memories still pleasurable ! Memories of lying quiet and letting pleasure come. Memories of hours idled away over the fingering of old illustrations, over the reading of casual novels : multitudes of such memories right back into childhood. Whole tracts of life lost, lost even for the re-telling by reason of the seductive quality that still proceeds from their languorousness. Why ? If we had nothing but work-memories from our earliest days — how firm the ground would be beneath us : we could stand. But as it is we sink in somewhere at every moment. The worst of it is that there are two worlds even in oneself. Sometimes I go past little shops,[1] in the rue de Seine, for example ; antiquarians or petty dealers in old books and engravings with overcrowded windows ; nobody ever enters them, apparently they do no business ; but if you glance inside, there they sit and read without a care (yet they are not rich) ; they take no thought for the morrow, do not worry about success, have a dog that sits contentedly before them, or a cat that makes the silence even greater by gliding along the rows of books as though she were wiping the names off the bindings.

[1] Cf. *Malte Laurids Brigge, Collected Works*, vol. v. pp. 54, 55.

Ah, if that were enough ! many a time I have wished to buy such a crowded shop-window for myself and sit behind it with a dog for twenty years. In the evenings there would be light in the back room ; in front, everything quite dark, and we three would sit at the back and eat ; I have noticed that, from the street, it always looks like a Last Supper, so large and solemn is it when seen through the dark room. (But this is how one should take all one's cares, great and small.) You know what I mean : without complaint. And like this, surely, everything is good and would grow better and better. . . .

189. *To Clara Rilke*

PARIS VIe., 29 RUE CASSETTE
8 *October*, 1907

. . . Contemporaneously with Guardi and Tiepolo there lived a woman painter, a Venetian lady, who visited all the courts and whose fame was among the most current of her time. Rosalba Carrièra. Watteau knew of her, and they exchanged a number of water-colours, her own pictures perhaps, and held each other in fond esteem. She travelled largely, painted in Vienna, and in Dresden one hundred and fifty of her works are still preserved. In the Louvre there are three portraits. In one, a young lady, her face lifted high on the straight neck and turned naïvely towards the front, is holding before her low-cut lace dress a little clear-eyed marmoset, which is peering out from the lower edge of the bust-length portrait just as eagerly as she herself is doing, with perhaps a shade more insouciance, on top. With its small treacherous black hand it clutches at her own and pulls it, delicate and abstracted, into the picture by one slender finger. This is so full of a period that it is valid for all periods. And is painted lightly and daintily, but *really* painted. A blue shawl also comes into the picture and a complete spray of lily-white stocks which serves, curiously enough, as a brooch for her bosom. And looking at the blue it occurred to me that this was the distinctive blue of the 18th century, the blue which is everywhere to be found, with La Tour, with Peronnet,[1] and which even with Chardin has not ceased

[1] J. B. Perronneau (1715–1783) is meant !

to be elegant, although in the ribbon of his peculiar cap (in the self-portrait with the horn-rimmed pince-nez) it has been applied with complete ruthlessness. (It is conceivable that somebody should write a monograph on blue ; from the thick waxy-blue of Pompeian murals to Chardin and on to Cézanne : what a history !) For Cézanne's very individual blue is of this origin, it derives from this 18th-century blue which Chardin divests of its sophistication and which now, with Cézanne, is quite without irrelevant overtones. In every way Chardin has been a mediator : his fruits have no further thought of the dish, lie about on kitchen tables and do not give a rap for being nicely eaten. With Cézanne their edibility ceases altogether, so substantially real have they become, so utterly indestructible in their obstinate actuality. When you see Chardin's portraits of his own person you think what a quaint old eccentric he must have been ! How much so, and in how tragic a fashion Cézanne was one, I shall perhaps tell you tomorrow. I know something of his last years, when he was old and shabby and, on his daily walk to the studio, had children at his back who threw things after him as after a mangy dog. But inside, right inside, he was wonderful, and now and then in a fury he shouted something quite marvellous at one of his infrequent visitors. You can imagine what it was like. Goodbye . . . this was today . . .

191. *To Clara Rilke*

PARIS VIe., 29 RUE CASSETTE
9 October 1907

. . . Today I wanted to tell you a little about Cézanne. As regards work, he asserted that up to his fortieth year he had lived as a Bohemian. Only then, in his friendship with Pissarro, did the taste for work dawn upon him. But to such an extent that he did nothing but work for the last thirty years of his life. Without real pleasure, it seems, in continual rage, ever at odds with his every endeavour, none of which appeared to him to achieve what he regarded as the ultimate desideratum. This he called *la réalisation*, and he found it in the Venetian painters whom he had formerly seen in the Louvre, and seen and seen again and unreservedly acknowledged. The incarnation of the world *as a thing carrying conviction*, the portrayal of a reality become imperishable through his experiencing of the object — this appeared the purpose of his inmost labours. Old, ill, wearied every evening to the point of unconsciousness by the regularity of his daily work (so much so that he often went to bed at six o'clock, as soon as it became dark, after a supper mindlessly eaten), surly, mistrustful, laughed at, hooted at, treated with contumely every time he went to his studio, — but celebrating his Sundays, hearing mass and vespers like a child, and very politely requesting of his landlady, Madame Brémond, slightly better food : thus he hoped from day to day still to attain that triumph which he felt was the one essential. At the same time (if one can believe the chronicler [1] of all these facts, a not very sympathetic painter who tagged on to everybody for a while) he had added to the difficulties of his work in the most obstinate way. Taking up his stand conscientiously in front of the object in his landscapes or stills, he set to work only by the most tortuous circumambulations. Starting with the darkest colouring he covered its depths with a layer of colour which he spread out a little beyond it, and so gradually, always extending his colours on top of one another, he reached a second, contrasting factor in his picture which he then, from a new centre, treated in a similar manner. I fancy that these two processes, the sure-eyed transference of objects to his canvas and the complete appropriation and personal treatment of what was transferred, ran counter to one another in him, so that both, possibly because he was too conscious of them, began as it were to speak at once, continually tripping over each other's words and ever at cross purposes. And the old man suffered their dissensions, tore up and down in his room, which had a bad light because the builders did not think it necessary to listen to the old simpleton whom Aix had agreed not to take seriously. He rushed to and fro in his studio, where the green apples lay about, or he went down in despair to the garden and sat. And in front of him was the little town, unsuspecting, with its cathedral ; a town of respectable and modest citizens, whilst he, as his father the hat-maker had fore-

[1] Bernard, *Souvenirs sur Cézanne.*

seen, had turned out different — a Bohemian, in his father's eyes and as he himself believed. Knowing that Bohemians live and die in poverty this father had made up his mind to work for his son, had become a kind of petty banker to whom people brought their money (because he was honest, as Cézanne said), and Cézanne owed it to this providence that he later had enough to paint in peace. Possibly he came to the burial of this father of his; his mother he loved too, but when she was being buried he was not there. He happened to be "*sur le motif*", as he called it. Even in those days his work was so important for him and brooked no exception, not even one which his piety and simplicity must surely have recommended.

In Paris he became known, more so by degrees. But for that sort of "progress" which he himself did NOT make (but which others made with a vengeance!) he had only mistrust; too clearly there stuck in his memory the falsified picture of his fate and aspirations which Zola (his friend from youth and his countryman) had sketched in *L'Œuvre*. Since then he was "not in" for the journalists; "*travailler sans le souci de personne et devenir fort*" — as he bellowed at one of his visitors. But in the middle of a meal he rose up, when this visitor told him of Frenhofer, the painter whom Balzac, with astonishing foreknowledge of coming developments, had created in his novel *Le Chef d'Œuvre inconnu* (which I once mentioned to you), and whom he had caused to die under the impossibility of the task which followed his discovery that there were really no contours at all, only countless vibrating planes merging into one another. Hearing this the old fellow stood up at table, in spite of Madame Brémond who certainly did not approve of such irregular behaviour, and, speechless with excitement, pointed with his forefinger more and more emphatically at himself, into his very soul, — however agonising it must have been for him. It took more than Zola to understand the heart of the matter; Balzac had divined that something colossal could suddenly happen to painting, something no one could ever bring to an end.

But the next day he nevertheless went on with his discipline; was up at six every morning, walked through the town to his studio and stopped there till ten; then he came back by the same way to his meal, ate and was once more on his road, going often half an hour's walk beyond the studio to a valley, "*sur le motif*", in front of which soared the mountains of Saint Victoire with all their thousand tasks, indescribable. There he would si for hours, engaged in finding and absorbing "*les plans*" (of which, curiously enough, he always speaks in exactly the same terms as Rodin). Indeed he often reminds one of Rodin in his sayings. When, for instance, he complains how much they are daily destroying and disfiguring his old town. Only, where Rodin's great, self-confident poise leads to some objective statement, he, the sick, lonely old man, is overcome with wrath. Turning home in the evening he gets furious over some alteration, flares up in a fury and finally, when he sees how terribly his anger exhausts him, promises himself: I will stay at home; work, nothing but work.

From such changes for the worse in the little town of Aix he deduces with horror how things must be faring in the outside world. Once, when the talk turned to the present state of industry and all that, he burst forth "with terrible eyes": *Ça va mal. . . . C'est effrayant la vie!*

Outside, an indeterminate horror on the increase; a little nearer, indifference and mockery, and then, suddenly, this old man deep in his work, painting nudes only from old drawings done forty years ago in Paris, knowing that no model would be allowed him in Aix. "At my age", he says, "the most I could get is a hag of fifty, and I know that even such a creature is not to be found in Aix." So he paints from his old drawings. And lays his apples on counterpanes, which Madame Brémond is sure to find missing one day, and places his wine-bottles in between and anything he can lay hands on. And (like Van Gogh) makes his "saints" out of such things; forces them, *forces* them to be beautiful, to mean the whole world and all its happiness and splendour, and does not know whether he has really succeeded in making them so. And sits in the garden like an old dog, the dog of this work which calls him again and beats him and lets him go hungry. And clings with all his strength to this incomprehensible master, who only allows him to turn back to God on Sunday, as to his first owner, for a while.

— And outside the people say " Cézanne ", and the gentlemen in Paris write his name with a flourish and are proud of being so well informed.

This was what I wanted to tell you ; it concerns much that goes on around us, and ourselves too in innumerable ways.

Outside it is raining prodigally, as always. Goodbye . . . tomorrow I will tell you of myself. But you will understand how much I have done so today. . . .

194. *To Clara Rilke*

PARIS VIe., 29 RUE CASSETTE
12 *October* 1907

. . . It is less difficult to get about now than it was last week. How much a little moon can do ! [1] There are days when everything is about you, light and ethereal, barely hinted at in the luminous air and yet distinct ; the nearest objects take on the tones of the distance, are ravished away and merely *revealed* to the eye, not just placed there as usual. And everything that has affinity with the distance — the river, the bridges, the long streets and the lavish squares — all this has gathered the distance to itself, clings to it, is painted on it as on silk. You feel just *what* a bright-green carriage on the Pont Neuf can be, or a splash of red that cannot contain itself, or simply a poster on the end-wall of a pearl-grey row of houses. Everything is simplified, brought into a few correct, clear planes, like the face in a Manet portrait. And nothing is trivial or superfluous. The booksellers on the quay open their stalls, and the fresh or faded yellow of the books, the violet-brown of the bindings, the green of an album — it all fits, counts, takes part and tones in with the unity of this bright assemblage.

The other day I asked Mathilde Vollmoeller to go with me through the Salon sometime, so as to see my impressions beside those of another person whom I considered quiet and not sidetracked by literature. Yesterday we went there together. Cézanne did not let us go on to anything else. I realise more and more what an extraordinary thing that was. But imagine

1 Cf. *Malte Laurids Brigge*, *Collected Works*, vol. v. p. 24.

my astonishment when Fräulein V., trained and using her eye wholly as a painter, said : " Like a dog he sat in front of it and simply looked, without any nervousness or irrelevant speculation". And she said something else very good in connection with his technique (which you can see from an unfinished picture). " Here," she said, pointing to the spot, " he knew what he wanted and said it (part of an apple) ; but there it is still open, because he didn't yet know. He only did what he knew, nothing else." " What a good conscience he must have had," I said. " Oh yes, he was happy somewhere right inside him. . . ." And then we compared paintings which might have been done in Paris under the influence of others, with his most personal ones, as regards the colour. In the first the colour was a thing by itself ; later he uses it somehow individually, as nobody had ever used colour before, only to make the thing with. In the realisation of this the colour is completely consumed ; nothing is left over. And Fräulein V. said, very tellingly : " It is like something laid in a balance : the thing here, the colour there ; no more and no less than the balance demands. It may be a lot or a little, that depends ; but it is precisely what corresponds to the object." I should not have thought of this last myself ; but it is eminently right and clarifies the pictures. It also struck me yesterday how *different* they are, yet without being mannered, without caring a rap for originality, sure of not losing themselves in the thousand approaches to Nature, rather of discovering, gravely and conscientiously, in her outer multiplicity the inexhaustibleness within. All this is very beautiful. . . .

195. *To Clara Rilke*

PARIS VIe., 29 RUE CASSETTE
13 *October* 1907

. . . Yet again it is the same rain I have so often described to you ; as if the sky had looked up brightly for an instant only to continue its reading of the regular lines of rain immediately after. But it is not easy to forget that beneath this drab wishy-washiness there are the translucencies and the depths one saw yesterday : one at least *knows* that they are there.

I read your description of the autumn the first thing this morning, and all the colours you introduced into your letter were re-transformed in my feelings and filled my mind to the brim with strength and radiance. Whilst I was marvelling yesterday at the tenuous and aerial autumn here, you were passing through that other one, native to us, which is painted on red wood as this is on silk. And we can feel the one as much as the other, so deeply do we hold in ourselves the principle of all change, we, the most changeable of all, who go about with the desire to comprehend everything and who (even though we do not grasp it) turn anything that's too big for us into the action of our hearts so that it shall not destroy us. If I came to you I should certainly see the magnificence of moorland and heath, the drifting luminous green of meadows and birches in a new and different way ; but although these changes, since I once experienced and shared them wholly, did indeed call forth a part of the *Stundenbuch*, yet in those days Nature was still a sort of general excitation for me, an uprush of feeling, an instrument in whose strings my hands were at home ; I did not sit before her ; I let myself be swept along by the spirit that proceeded from me ; she came upon me with her vastness, with her great exaggerate being as the prophesying came upon Saul ; precisely so. I stepped along and saw, saw not Nature but the visions she gave me. How little I should then have known how to learn from Cézanne, from Van Gogh ! From the many things Cézanne now gives me to do I realise how very different I have become. I am on the road to becoming a worker, on a long road perhaps and probably only at the first milestone ; nevertheless I can already understand the old painter who has gone on so far ahead, somewhere, alone, with only children behind him who threw stones (as I once described in the *Fragment von dem Einsamen* [1]). I was with his pictures again today ; it is extraordinary what an environment they create about themselves. Without studying any single one, and standing between the two great halls, you can feel their presence gathering into a colossal reality. It is as if these colours took away all your indecisions for ever and ever. The good conscience

[1] Probably lost in Paris during the war.

of these reds, these blues — their simple truthfulness teaches you; and if you place yourself among them as receptively as you can they seem to be doing something for you. Also you notice, better and better each time, how necessary it was to get beyond even love; it comes naturally to you to love each one of these things if you have made them yourself: but if you shew it, you make them less well; you judge them instead of *saying* them. You cease being impartial; and love, the best thing of all, remains outside your work, does not enter into it, is left over unresolved beside it: this is how the sentimentalist school of painting came into being (which is no better than the realist school). They painted "I love this" instead of painting "Here it is". In the latter case everybody must look carefully to see whether I loved it or not. It is not shewn at all, and many people would even assert that there was no mention of love in it. So utterly has it been consumed without residue in the act of making. This consuming of love in anonymous work, which gives rise to such pure things, probably no one has succeeded in doing so completely as old Cézanne; he was supported in it by his sullen and mistrustful inner nature. It is certain that he would no longer have revealed his love to anybody had it come to the point; but by means of this predisposition, which was developed to the full by his anchoritic eccentricity, he now turned to Nature and knew how to hide his love for each apple and lodge it in the painted apple for ever. Can you imagine this and how much one can feel it?

I have received the first proofs [1] from the Insel. In the poems there are the instinctive beginnings of a similar objectivity. I am leaving *Die Gazelle* in: it is all right. Goodbye. . . .

197. *To Clara Rilke*

PARIS VIe., 29 RUE CASSETTE
16 *October* 1907

. . . But now, before anything else, you must tell me if you are quite recovered and rested? There was such a tiredness in your writing; also you spoke of a cold. I hope this is no longer so. In those circumstances, of course, the Tivoli was definitely

[1] Of the *Neue Gedichte*.

not the right thing. Isn't it the most harrowing, the most unreal milieu one can possibly imagine? Nay, it passes one's wildest conceits, this sort of variété. The ground slips away from under your feet, air, sky, everything real, and apparently for ever. I felt only a vague memory of it rising up menacingly (for as a child such evenings were pitilessly enjoined upon me) when I sat for half an hour with von der Heydt (the last time he was here) in one of the summer-gardens which lie along the Champs-Elysées. (And that was in the open.) And in all this unreality: animals — the realest of all. How we play with everything, we humans. How blindly we abuse that which has never been contemplated, never experienced; diverting ourselves with things collected together without rhyme or reason, and placed all higgledy-piggledy. It is impossible for an age in which demands for "beauties" of this kind are anywhere gratified, to appreciate Cézanne or understand anything of his devotion and hidden splendour. The dealers just make a noise, that is all; and those who need to keep in touch with such things one can count on two hands, and they are silent and apart.

You have only to see the people going through the two galleries on a Sunday: intrigued, ironic, irritated, indignant. And when it comes to delivering a verdict, there they stand, these Monsieurs, bang in the middle of things with a pathetic despair, and you hear them asserting: *il n'y a absolument rien, rien, rien!* And how beautiful the ladies fancy themselves as they pass by; it occurs to them that they have just seen themselves in the glass doors on their entry with complete satisfaction, and conscious of their reflection they pose for a moment beside one of the touchingly attempted portraits of Madame Cézanne in order to make the frightfulness of this painting serve as an extremely favourable comparison (so they think) for themselves. Somebody once told the old man in Aix that he was "famous". But in his heart he knew better and let him talk. Confronted with his work, however, one again hits on the idea of how all recognition (with a few isolated and unmistakable exceptions) must make one mistrustful of one's own endeavours. In the end, if they are good one never lives to see them recognised: or they are only half good and not ruthless enough. . . .

199. *To Clara Rilke*

PARIS VIe., 29 RUE CASSETTE
17 *October* 1907

. . . Rain and rain, all day yesterday, and now it is beginning afresh. If you look straight ahead you would say : snow is coming. But last night I was wakened by moonlight in a corner above my rows of books ; a patch that did not shine, that only covered with its aluminium whiteness the spot upon which it lay. And the room was full of cold night into the furthest corner ; you knew, even lying down, that it was under the wardrobe, under the chest of drawers and round everything without a break, round the brass chandeliers which looked very cold. But a bright morning. A massive east wind, coming over the city with deployed front, since it finds it so capacious. To the west, buffeted and thrust asunder, archipelagoes of clouds, chains of islands, grey like the neck-feathers and the breasts of water-birds in an ocean of cold, imperceptible blueness, remotely serene. And beneath all this, dwarfed by it, the Place de la Concorde, and the shady trees of the Champs-Elysées, black simplified to green, under the westerly clouds. To the right, houses shining in the blasts of sunlight, and far away in the background, in the blue dove-grey haze, more houses, clamped into planes, with rectilinear, quarry-like surfaces. And suddenly, as you approach the Obelisk (round about the granite of which there still flickers a little of the ancient sandy heat, and in the hollows of the hieroglyphics — the ever recurring owl — preserving the old Egyptian shadowy blue, dried-in as in murex-shells), there the marvellous avenue flows towards you in a scarcely perceptible gradient, rich and rapid as a river which, ages ago, with its own violence had washed the red into the rocky walls of the Arc de Triomphe down by the Etoile. And all this lies there with the generosity of a born landscape and scatters space far and wide. And from the roofs, here and there, the banners hold themselves higher and higher into the tall air, stretch, flap their wings as though taking flight. . . .

200. *To Clara Rilke*

PARIS VIe., 29 RUE CASSETTE
18 *October* 1907

. . . you must have known while you were writing how pleased I would be with that understanding judgement of yours which sprang involuntarily from a comparison of the " blue pages "[1] with my experience of Cézanne. What you now say and set forth so genially I had guessed already, somehow, although I could not have indicated just how far that development has been carried in me which corresponds with the immense advances apparent in Cézanne's paintings. I was only convinced that there were deeply personal reasons for it when I stood more seeingly in front of pictures which, a little while ago, I would have passed by with but momentary sympathy, not turning back to them thrilled and expectant. It is not *painting* that I am studying (for despite everything I continue to be unsure about them and find it difficult to distinguish between the good and the less good, and constantly confuse early with late paintings). It is the crisis in these paintings that I recognised because I had reached it in my own work or at any rate come close to it, having long been prepared, probably, for this very thing on which so much depends. Hence I must be careful in my attempts to write about Cézanne, who now of course holds a great attraction for me. Nobody (I realise this at last) who apprehends pictures from such a private standpoint is justified in writing about them ; only a person able to acknowledge them in their actuality, quietly, without experiencing them otherwise than as plain facts, only such a person, surely, could do them justice. Deep down in my life, however, this unexpected contact that suddenly came and made a place for itself is full of acknowledgement and affinity. Another apostle of poverty. And how greatly poverty has advanced since Verlaine (though Verlaine may well have been a step backwards) who could write in *Mon Testament : Je ne donne rien aux pauvres parce que je suis un pauvre moi-même*, and whose whole work, almost, was vitiated by this closeness, this embittered display of empty hands for which

[1] Manuscript of the *Neue Gedichte*.

Cézanne had absolutely no time the last thirty years of his life. *When* could he have shewn his hands ? True enough, whenever he went out spiteful looks met them and lewdly laid bare their nakedness ; but from the labour of these hands we only know how massively and truly the work lay upon them at the end. This work, which had no more preferences, no more inclinations and no fastidious indulgences, whose least ingredient had been weighed in the balance of an infinitely susceptible conscience, concentrated so much incorruptible actuality into the constitution of its colours that it began a new life on the *further side* of colour, devoid of all earlier memories. It is this limitless objectivity, refusing any adulteration that would bring about a unity foreign to it, that makes people find Cézanne's portraits so repellent and comical. They put up with, but do not appreciate, the fact that he rendered his apples, onions and oranges in sheer colour (which they always think of as a subordinate instrument in painting) ; but even with the landscapes they miss interpretation, judgement, reflection, — and as regards the portraits the notion of " the intellectual approach " has been bruited abroad, even among the dyed-in-the-wool bourgeois, with so much success that you can see that sort of thing in Sunday snapshots of betrothed couples and family-groups. And here of course Cézanne seems wholly inadequate to them and not fit to be discussed. In this Salon he is every bit as alone as he was in real life, and even the painters, the younger ones, go quickly past him because they see the dealers on his side. . . . A good Sunday to you both. . . .

202. *To Clara Rilke*

PARIS VIe., 29 RUE CASSETTE
19 *October* 1907

You will certainly remember the passage in *Malte Laurids Brigge* dealing with Baudelaire and his poem *La Charogne.* I am of the opinion that without this poem the whole trend towards objective expression, which we now think we can discern in Cézanne, could not have begun at all ; first *this* had to be there in all its pitilessness. The vision of the artist had to steel itself so far as to see in terrible and apparently only repulsive things the Existing which, in common with all other being, *has value.* As little as any selection is permissible to him, so little is it permitted to the creator to turn away from any form of existence whatever : a single rejection anywhere on his part forces him out of the state of grace, makes him wholly sinful. Flaubert, when he related the legend of Saint-Julien-l'Hospitalier with so much care and circumspection, gave me this simple faith in the midst of the miraculous, because the artist in him had taken the decisions of the saint and assented to them and acclaimed them joyously. This lying-down with the leper and sharing with him all one's warmth, even to the heart's warmth of love-nights — this must have existed at some time or other in the artist's being as the tribulation attendant on his new serenity. You can imagine how moved I was to read that Cézanne, even in his last years, knew this very poem — Baudelaire's *Charogne* — by heart and could recite it word for word. It is certain that one would find among his earlier works some in which he staged a mighty triumph over himself for the sake of love's extremest possibility. Behind this devotion begins, first with small things, saintliness : the simple life of a love which has passed through the fire, which, without ever praising itself therefor, steps up to all things, unaccompanied, unostentatious, wordless. True work, fullness of task, everything begins beyond this ordeal, and he who has been unable to strive thus far will, when he gets to Heaven, no doubt see the Virgin Mary, a handful of saints and petty prophets, King Saul and Charles le Téméraire : — but of Hokusai and Leonardo, of Li Tai Pe and Villon, of Verhaeren, Rodin, Cézanne, even of the Almighty Himself, they will only be able to bring him travellers' tales.

And all at once (and for the first time) I understand the fate of Malte. Is it not that this ordeal was too much for him, that he could not pass it *in reality* although he was convinced *ideally* of its necessity, so much so that he instinctively sought it and sought it until it clung to him and no longer left him ? The book of Malte, once it is written, will be nothing but the book of this knowledge, exemplified in one for whom it was too tremendous. Possibly he did triumph after all : for he wrote the death of the Chamberlain; but, like a Raskolnikov, he remained behind, consumed by his deed, ceasing to act at the very moment when action had to begin, so that his newly acquired freedom turned against him and destroyed him, the weaponless.

Ah, we count the years and make occasional cuttings of them and stop and begin again and hesitate between both. But actually everything that befalls us is of one piece, in whose correlations one thing is kith and kin with another, fashions its own birth, grows and is educated to its own needs, and we have ultimately only *to be there*, simply, fervently, as the earth is there, in harmony with the seasons, dark and light and absolutely in space, not demanding to be cradled in anything but this web of influences and powers in which the very stars feel safeguarded.

One day the time and the tranquillity and the patience will surely come for me so that I may continue writing the note-books of Malte; I now know much more of him, or rather, I shall know it when it is necessary. . . .

205. *To Clara Rilke*

PARIS VIe., 29 RUE CASSETTE
21 *October* 1907

. . . I wanted to say something else about Cézanne: that never before has it been demonstrated to what an extent painting goes on of its own accord among the colours, how much they must be left entirely alone to explain each other. Their intercourse between themselves: that is the essence of painting. Anyone who interrupts, who arranges, who lets his human notions, his wit, his advocacy, his intellectual agility anywhere enter into the action, disturbs and obscures the function of the colours. The painter ought not to become conscious of his knowledge (and this goes for the artist in general): without taking the roundabout road of his own reflection — each step forward, enigmatic even to himself, must enter so quickly into his work that he is unable to recognise its moment of transition. Ah, those who lie in wait for it there, observe it, detain it, — find that it changes like the gold in the fairy-tale which could not remain gold because some little trifle was out of order. The fact that Van Gogh's letters are so readable, that they contain so much, in the end militates against him personally just as it militates against the painter in him (compared with Cézanne) for having *willed* this and that, known it, discovered it : that blue calls up orange, and green red : for having heard all these things spoken within him, listening secretively to the inside of his eye, like an eavesdropper. Thus he painted his pictures under a fundamental contradiction, thinking at the same time of the Japanese simplification of colour, by which planes are graded according to tone and are summed up as a single totality ; and this in turn leads to the deliberately limned and outspoken (and therefore artificial) contour of Japanese art as a sort of framework for the planes, which are all equiponderant. The result is too calculated, too fanciful, — in a word, it is decoration. A literary painter, a painter, therefore, who was no painter at all, by reason of his letters once caused even Cézanne to expatiate in his replies on matters relative to painting ; but, when you see the old man's few letters, you realise how absolutely jammed he was in the helpless beginnings, distasteful even to himself, of articulate speech ! He could say practically nothing. The sentences in which he makes the attempt grow longer and longer, complicate themselves, refuse to go on, tie themselves up in knots, and finally he leaves them, beside himself with rage. On the other hand he manages to say quite clearly : " I believe the best thing is work ". Or : " I make daily progress, albeit very slowly ". Or : " I am nearly seventy years old ". Or : " I will answer you with pictures ". Or : " *L'humble et colossal Pissarro* " (who taught him to work) ; or, after a few more ramblings (you feel with what relief and how beautifully he wrote it), his signature : " Pictor Paul Cézanne ". And in his last letter (September 21, 1905), after a complaint about his bad health, simply : " *Je continue donc mes études* ". And his wish, which was literally fulfilled : " *Je me suis juré de mourir en peignant* ". As in an old picture of the Danse Macabre, Death seized his hand from behind and painted the last stroke himself, trembling with pleasure ; long had his shadow been lying across the palette and he had had time to choose, in the open, crescent-like sequence of colours the one that pleased him best ; as soon as it got on to the brush he would snatch it up and paint. . . . There ! he grabbed it and did his stroke, the only one he could. . . .

206. *To Clara Rilke*

PARIS VIe., 29 RUE CASSETTE
22 October 1907

. . . Today the Salon closes. And now that I am returning home for the last time I want, even now, to seek out again a violet, a green, or a certain blue tone which has made me think I ought to see it better, more unforgettably. Even though I have so often stood attentively and implacably before it, I could as little reproduce in my memory the great combination of colour which comprises the *Woman in the Red Armchair* as I could a number with a great many figures. And yet I have impressed it upon myself figure by figure. In my feelings the consciousness of its presence has grown into an exaltation which I perceive even in sleep ; my blood describes it in me, but the utterance of it passes by somewhere outside and will not be called in. Have I written you of it ? — In front of an earth-green wall with an infrequently recurring cobalt-blue pattern (a cross with an open centre) a low chair all upholstered in red has been placed ; the plumply padded back rounds itself off and slopes down towards the front into arm-rests (which are closed like the dead sleeve-ends of an armless man's coat). The left arm-rest and the tassel depending from it full of cinnabar, have no more wall behind them, only a broad strip of the skirting beneath in greenish blue, against which they cry a vivid contrast. In this red chair, which is a *personality*, a woman is seated, her hands in the lap of a frock with broad vertical stripes. The frock is done quite lightly in little scattered dabs of greenish yellow and yellowish green up to the edges of the blue-grey jacket, which is held together in front by a blue silk bow shot with emerald. In the brightness of the face the close proximity of all these colours serves as simple modelling ; even the brown of the hair curving round the head and the smooth brown of the eyes have to assert themselves against their surroundings. It seems that each part knows of all the other parts. So much does it participate in them ; so much proceeds from their harmony or discord ; so much does each, in its own way, care for the balance and produce it : just as ultimately the whole picture holds the reality poised. For if you say it is a red armchair (and it is the first and last red armchair of all painting), it is so only because it binds up with itself an aggregate of sensed colours which, whatever else they are, fortify and confirm its red. In order to reach the height of expression this chair is painted quite powerfully round about the delicate portrait, so that something like a coat of wax has arisen ; and yet the colour has no ascendancy over the object, which seems so perfectly translated into its pictorial equivalent that, finely as it is caught and rendered, its bourgeois reality loses all its heaviness in its ultimate picture-essence. Everything, as I have already said, has become an affair of the colours among themselves : one masses itself against the others, emphasises itself with reference to them, broods on itself alone. As in the mouth of a dog at the approach of certain things various fluids form themselves and hold themselves in readiness — affinitive ones which only assimilate and corrective ones which seek to neutralise — so, inside each colour there occur concentrations or dilutions by means of which it overcomes the touch of another. Aside from this glandular action within the colour-intensity reflections and refractions play the greatest rôle. (I have always been surprised at their presence in Nature : finding the red of a sunset in water to be a lasting tint in the crude green of water-lily leaves.) Weaker colours give themselves up entirely and are content to reflect the strongest of those present. The interior of the picture pulsates with this balance of various and reciprocal influence, rises and falls back into itself and has not a single motionless spot. Only this for today. . . . You see how difficult it becomes when you want to get down to facts. . . .

207. *To Clara Rilke*

Paris VIe., 29 rue Cassette
23 *October* 1907

. . . I had to wonder, yesterday evening, whether my attempt to reproduce the *Woman in the Red Armchair* gave you any conception of it ? I am not certain even of having hit off the relation of its values : more than ever words seemed to me precluded, and yet it must be possible to compel them to serve this purpose if only one could contemplate such a picture like a scene in Nature : then, as a thing that had existence, it would *have* to be utterable somehow. For a moment it seemed to me easier to talk of the *Self-Portrait* ; it is sooner revealed, it does not extend through the whole range of the palette, — it appears to poise in the centre of the palette between yellow-red, ochre, crimson-lake and gentian-blue and, in the jacket and hair, to plumb the depths of a wet violet-brown which contrasts with a wall done in grey and pale copper. On closer inspection, however, even in this picture there can be established the internal presence of bright green and puissant blue, which throw up the reddish tones and define the light parts. Meanwhile the subject here is seizable in itself, and the words which feel so uncomfortable in their indication of pictorial facts, would be only too willing, when thus confronted by a representation with which their own territory begins, to recover their faculties and describe what is present. There is a man, his right profile quarter-turned to the front, looking. The thick dark hair is scraped together on the back of the head and clings over the ears in such a way that the whole contour of the skull is laid bare ; this is drawn with notable sureness, hard and yet round, down the forehead all in one stroke, and its firmness still holds even at that point where, resolved into form and plane, it becomes only the most extreme of a thousand outlines. At the corners of the eyebrows the powerful structure of this skull (which is wrought, seemingly, from the *inside*) comes into force once more ; but from there, jutting forwards and downwards and as though vamped on to the stubbly chin like a shoe, hangs the face, hangs as though each feature were hung on separately, with unbelievable intensity and at the same time giving that expression, reduced to its most primitive elements, of crass and gaping astonishment in which children and country yokels sometimes lose themselves, — only that here the unseeing imbecility of their absorption has been replaced by an animal attentiveness which maintains a continuing, objective vigilance in the unwinking eyes. And how great and incorruptible this objectivity of his gaze was, is confirmed in an almost touching manner by the circumstance that, without analysing or in the remotest degree regarding his expression from a superior standpoint, he made a replica of himself with so much humble objectiveness, with the credulity and extrinsic interest and attention of a dog which sees itself in a mirror and thinks : there is another dog.

Goodbye for now ; perhaps you can glimpse a little of him from all this, the old man signalised by the words that he himself laid at the feet of Pissarro : "*humble et colossal*". Today is the anniversary of his death. . . .

208. *To Clara Rilke*

PARIS VIe., 29 RUE CASSETTE
24 *October* 1907

. . . I said "grey" yesterday, when I was indicating the background of the *Self-Portrait*, pale copper traversed by a grey pattern. I should have said a particular metallic *white*, similar to aluminium ; for grey, grey in its literal sense, cannot be pointed out in Cézanne's pictures. To his immense painter's vision it did not exist as a colour : he went to the bottom of it and found it violet or blue or reddish or green. Violet in particular (a colour which has never before been extended in such elaborate modulations) he loved to discern where we only expect and are content with grey ; he does not stop there and draws out the infolded violets just as certain evenings do, specially autumn evenings, which address the greying crepuscule of the house-fronts as violet direct, so that they give answer in all the shades and tints of that colour, from a delicate floating lilac to the heavy purple of Finland granite. When I made this observation that there were really no greys in these pictures (in the landscapes the presence of ochre and sienna and umber is too palpable for any grey to arise), Fräulein Vollmoeller pointed out to me how much, when you stood in the midst of them all, a mild soft grey emanated from them like an atmosphere, and we agreed that the inner balance of Cézanne's colours, which never stand out or push to the front, did indeed call forth this peaceful and as it were velvety air, which certainly does not arise in the inhospitable cavern of the Grand Palais. Although it belongs to his peculiarities to use chrome yellow and flaming scarlet-lake absolutely neat on his lemons and apples, he nevertheless knows how to keep their loudness inside the picture : resonantly, as into an ear, they boom into a listening blue and receive soundless answer, so that nobody outside need feel apostrophised or accosted. His still-lifes are so marvellously absorbed in themselves. Take, for instance, the white cloth he so often employs, which miraculously soaks up the preponderant local colour, and the objects placed upon it, all chiming in with expressions of delight. The use of white as a colour was natural to him from the start : together with black, it formed the two ends of his wide-open palette, and in the very beautiful ensemble of a black stone mantelpiece with the pendulum-clock belonging to it,[1] black and white (the latter on a cloth hanging down which covers part of the mantel) behave just like colour beside the other colours, with equal authority and as though long acclimatised. (It is different with Manet, with whom black acts like a break in the current and still stands in opposition to the colours, as though coming from somewhere else.) Against the white cloth a coffee-cup asserts itself vividly with its border-stripe of dark powerful blue ; also a fresh, mellow lemon, a polished goblet with a cut-glass top and, on the left, a large baroque conch-shell, bizarre and outlandish in appearance, its smooth red mouth lying towards the front. The crimson of its interior, curving palely outwards, challenges the wall behind to a stormy azure, which the gold-framed mirror on the mantelpiece near by gives back again in a roomier and profounder hue. Here, in the reflected scene, it meets with yet another contrast : the milky pink of a glass vase which, standing on the black clock,

[1] *Still Life with Sea-Shell and Black Clock* (" La Pendule Noire ").

brings its shape to bear twice over (real and, somewhat more tenuously, reflected). Space and mirror-space are defined absolutely by this double beat and are differentiated as it were musically ; and the picture contains them just as a basket contains fruit and leaves, — as though it were all equally simple to grasp and give. But there is still another object on the bare slab of the mantelpiece, pushed up against the white cloth ; and for this I would like to examine the picture again. Yet the Salon exists no longer ; in a few days it is to be followed by an exhibition of cars, which, each with its fixed idea of speed, will stand there stupidly for weeks. . . .

2. *To Clara Rilke*

PRAGUE, HOTEL ERZHERZOG STEFAN
1 [?] *November* 1907

. . . When will one come here and be able to see this city, see it and say it, from visit to visit ? When will one have to bear its heaviness no longer, the immense meaning it took on when one was small and *it* was already big and spread out far beyond one ; in those days it needed you in order to feel itself. You were a child, and everything made trial of you, saw itself reflected huge and fantastic in you and was haughty and fateful towards your heart. Now this may no longer be. Diminished in itself, returned like one who has long led a life of violence, somehow it is ashamed before me, laid bare, on the defensive, as though it were now meeting you with justice and reparation. But I can take no delight in seeing harm come to those things which were hard and high-stepping towards me, which never condescended and never explained what the difference was that existed between us, what hostile relationship. It makes me sad to see these houses at the corners, these windows and porticos, squares and church-roofs, to see them all humbled, smaller than they were, abased and completely in the wrong. And it is just as impossible for me to get the upper hand of them in their new guise as it was when they were overweening. Their heaviness as a whole has been transformed into its opposite, yet, taken piecemeal, how much it has remained heaviness ! More than ever I have felt since this morning the presence of this city as something incomprehensible and confusing. Either it must have vanished with my childhood, or else my childhood must have flowed away from it, later, leaving it behind, real beside all other realities, something that could be seen and expressed objectively like a Cézanne thing, inconceivable as far as I am concerned, yet still tangible. In this way it is somehow ghostly, like the people who were part of it and of me long ago and who bring us together and speak of us among themselves. — I have never felt it with such astonishment, my aversion has never been so great as this time (probably because my tendency to see everything with reference to my work has grown so much more marked).

Well then, I have been in Prague since this morning and am just writing you this as the first greeting from the first halt on my journey. Naturally everybody is asking after you and Ruth. But you are just as far from them as I am, and somehow this brings us together and away from this immitigable old town.

Goodbye for today, — Your RAINER MARIA.

3. *To Clara Rilke*

EN ROUTE PRAGUE — BRESLAU
4 *November* 1907

. . . The coach drive through the hard and glassy afternoon was lovely, and the naïve landscape. This was the Bohemia I knew, undulating like light music and suddenly flat again behind its apple trees, flat without much horizon and divided up into fields and rows of trees like stanzas in a folk-song. And all at once (as though passing through a weir in a boat) vou found yourself slipping through a park-gate, and there was a park, an old, old park that came quite close to you with its moist autumn. Until after many turnings, bridges and vistas Janovič castle rose up, separated from you by an old moat, looking very venerable, its upper parts backwards-tilted as with hauteur, sporadically dotted with windows and coats of arms, all hedged about with bays, balconies, balustrades and courtyards as though it were supposed never to get to know anybody. The Baronin, who is widowed, remained (it was All Souls' Day) in retirement ; the beautiful Baronesse (who looks like a miniature painted the year before the Revolution, at the last moment) came to meet me on the drawbridge with her two very agreeable young brothers ; we went through the park and then, as dusk was falling, through this remarkable castle (which has an unforgettable dining-room), while two servitors with massive silver candelabra on their arms lighted us into the deep salons as into courtyards. So we remained by ourselves (which was particularly pleasant because time was short), drank tea (with slices of pineapple) and were very happy together, each enjoying the other. It was rather like a children's tea-party, except that there were no grown-ups present and that the boxes of toys were inner ones and were put away again in yourself. A strange thing came to light in the course of conversation, namely that Kamenitz an der Linde, the castle in Bohemia which belonged to our great-grandfather, had been at another time (perhaps afterwards) the property of an ancestor of these Nadhernys — a direct forebear. Prague itself was a muddle. Everybody wanted me as though I were something to eat, — but as soon as they got me I found that they weren't hungry and had to keep to a diet. My mother untiring in her efforts to do everything possible for me — but . . . The lecture was dreary ; again the frightful old ladies who used to astonish me as a child, still the same and not a whit more diverting now that the astonishment was on their side. A few literati, also the same, growing dustier and shabbier and more decrepit every year, inquisitive and too good-humoured and too comfortable to bother about envy. (Sometime I shall get down to plays. I am beginning to *see* people, already I notice the " beast-faces " Ibsen saw, the snouts and muzzles, but I don't stop there ; for behind them it begins to get really interesting and, removed beyond revulsion and antipathy, somehow right.) . . .

6. *To Clara Rilke*

H. MAYREDERS HOTEL, MATSCHAKERKOF
VIENNA, 11 *November* 1907

. . . That same evening Heller gave me a letter from Rodin : *long and affectionate : everything has come right.* I could scarcely believe it and read it over and over again. But the end of the letter leaves no doubt. It runs : " *Venez, quand vous êtes à Paris, me voir. Des choses, des choses. Nous avons besoin de la vérité, de la poésie tous deux et d'amitié.*" How good and just he is, experiencing things so honestly from his work ! How *just* ! I have always known that he was so, and you knew it too. He thinks fondly of you. He speaks of some drawings of his which tell the story of Psyche. He writes that he thought of me ; that I ought to write this old fairy-tale anew just as he has drawn it — it has lifted him beyond everything he had done hitherto : " *C'est l'histoire si délicieuse de la femme et de son entrée dans la vie* ". Through my mediation over sixty drawings are going to be exhibited here at Heller's. They are already on the way. — He was pleased with the essay in *Kunst und Künstler* : " *votre étude . . . je la trouve très belle de vérité. . . .*"

14. *To the Countess Lili Kanitz-Menar*

PARIS, 17 RUE CAMPAGNE-PREMIÈRE
16 *July* 1908

Thank you, my dear friend, for having written. I have wanted to do so fifty times since your last letter and could not get down to it. There are so many things to overcome these days, in my work, I mean, and I have not the strength I ought to have. And then on top of all came this disproportionate occurrence. What is one to say ? how is one to set it in order ? It is always the same question. I have had to face it many times these last few years. The death of the Countess Schwerin and the death of my father (both of whom gave me to feel their infinite nobility and greatness of spirit) have caused me to fear this question no longer. . . . And now I stand towards death in such a way that it shocks me more in those whom I have neglected, who have remained inexplicable or fateful to me, than in those whom I loved with certainty while they lived, even if they shone for but a single instant in the translucency of that closeness which love can attain to. — With a little simplicity and delight in the Real (as something completely independent of Time) people would have had no need to entertain the notion that they could ever again lose that through which they were truly united : no constellation holds so closely together — nothing that is done is so irrevocable as the human union which, at the moment of its visible termination, continues more powerfully and more mightily in the Invisible, deep, deep down where our being is as enduring as gold in the stone ; more constant than a star.

Therefore I agree with you, dear friend, when you think you must mourn those who " pass away ". Ah, only those whom we have never possessed can pass away. And we cannot even mourn not having truly possessed this person or that — we have neither time, nor strength nor right to do so, for the most fleeting experience of any real possession (or of a companionship, which is only possession twice over) casts us back into ourselves with so much force, gives us so much to do there, demands so much loneliest development from us, that it suffices to absorb our individual attention for ever.

Isn't that so ?

Your last letter but one brought such good news ; I now wish a thousand times that your present abode and your inner courage will again lead to similar tidings and that you will not omit to send them to me. Clara is working and making lovely things. I am seeing her at the end of the week.—Your devoted friend, R. M. RILKE.

17. *To Clara Rilke*

PARIS, 77 RUE DE VARENNE
3 *September* 1908

. . . Rodin really did come as soon as I had settled down, came yesterday morning, spoke from his heart without complaint, objectively. I will not be led astray and will be as good to him as I always was. The richest thing that could now happen would be for him to need people only a thousandth part as much as we once needed him. Maybe you feel differently. By all means ! But for me it would be a miracle if this far-flung track along which I journeyed to the point of erring, where it lost itself in sadness and confusion, is not only to be found again but is also to come full circle through his earnest and affectionate need of me.

We sat in your high room ; he went and poised and handled the mask : again he was delighted with it. I read out to him what Beethoven said to Bettina Arnim : " I have no friend, I must live alone with myself ; but I know well that God is nearer to me than to the others in my art, I bear him company without fear, and each time I have recognised him and understood him ;

neither am I anxious about my music, no evil lot can befall it; he to whom it makes itself understood will be rid of all the misery that the others drag about with them". How he loved it. He knew it already: someone had sent him the whole passage when the *Balzac* was exhibited. He knows it better than anybody else, and what we discovered yesterday has long lived with him, and he has had children by it. And now I understand his fate, which may lie in his nationality. I spoke to him of Northern people, of women who do not want to hold the man fast, of possibilities of loving without deception: he listens and listens and cannot believe there is such a thing, and still wants to experience it. To him it seems a calamity that the woman should be the obstacle, the snare, the man-trap on those roads which are the loneliest and serenest. At the same time he also thinks that the sensual must so expand and change as to be equally strong and sweet and seductive in every spot, in everything. So that each thing shall transcend the sexual and with the whole abundance of its sensuality pass over into the spiritual, with which alone one can lie with God. But for him the woman remains apart, and *beneath* all this. Unlike *things*, she does not resolve herself into greater demands: she wants to be gratified and is gratified. And so she is like nourishment for the man, like a drink which courses through him ever and anon: like wine. He believes in wine. And I name him the Nun [1] and speak to him of all her rapture transformed, and of the woman's will *beyond* gratification; he does not believe it; and unfortunately he has so many female saints in support of his view who bear out the contention that they used Christ as a sort of concubine: as a sweet *ersatz* for virility, as the tenderest paramour that could be had, could still, at long last, be had. Over against that I have my Nun. And I shew how, in her few letters, she has grown out beyond the lover, and I know it is true. And I vow that if ever the Count de Chamilly, surrendering to her last letter, had returned, she would have been unable to perceive him at all, just as you do not see a fly down below from the balcony of a tower. And I am inexorable and will not depart an inch from my Nun.

This is one of the situations we reached in our talks of

[1] Marianna Alcoforado. See also Letter 72, dated January 23rd 1912.

yesterday and today, a stalemate such as you can imagine from this illustration. I am so glad that these stumbling-blocks have been come upon all unexpectedly, they were probably always in the way. The moment was bound to arrive when he had to take note of the error in his huge calculation. And it speaks much for the ordering of the world that just when this insidious, ever-recurrent danger was gripping him as a result of some passing difficulty, there should have been once more at his side the very person who needed above all to understand the difficulty and order it according to his wisest knowledge. He is bound like an old god to those usages which are innate in him, even to those which have no value for us, but which were necessary in the cult of his soul before he could be formed. I shall not alter him. Nevertheless, the voice has spoken beside him. It is in his reality and will no more depart from it. And that is much. . . .

23. *To Rosa Schobloch*

PARIS, 77 RUE DE VARENNE
24 September 1908

LIEBE GNÄDIGSTE FRAU,—Before starting work, I cannot bring myself not to say thank you at least for the words with which you acknowledged my letter.

Your attitude towards the position of the artist is more than merely generous — it is right. You do not know how rare it is. How everything seeks to interrupt the creative worker, to draw him aside and prevent him from entering into himself; how everything condemns him when he yearns to cultivate and perfect his inner world so that it may one day hold all external things, the very stars even, poised in the balance and, as it were, equated. — And even those friends who acquiesce in the care of his inner life, how often do they also, as givers, fall into the error of expecting a spiritual return from the creator *outside* his work. I have had to suffer all the more because there exists in my nature a great, almost passionate propensity for every kind of giving : ever since childhood I have known no more tempestuous joy than that of keeping back nothing and pouring out one's gifts, starting with those one loves best.

I know that this betokens a sort of instability on my part and a sentimental desire for pleasure, almost, and is not goodness at all. For it to become a virtue I must acquire strength enough to concentrate all my giving in one single thing, hard and laborious : in work. And the friends who, through their selflessness and mature understanding, help me towards this course, I must hold my best and most cherished, and thus lay your note with its great and affectionate confession among my weightiest documents.

I thank you for your good wishes for my further progress ; I am not afraid of the hardness of these years of learning : my heart longs to be hammered and polished — if only it be *my* hardness, the hardness which belongs to me and not, as was the case during so many years of my youth, an unprofitable bitterness from which I could learn nothing. (And yet, perhaps, *have* learnt after all — but with how much loss of strength !) . . .

33. *To Clara Rilke*

PARIS, 3 *November* 1909

. . . Last week I was with Rodin ; he is still doing his Americans and now really has a series of good powerful portraits at his side. How good it is for him to have to work on people whose nature keeps him close to facts, so that he has to graze in a tight circle like a goat on a short tether with no chance of straying into the open. He now has a gramophone. The Marquise winds it up and the thing wheezes round. I was apprehensive when I found myself invited to hear it. But it was marvellous ; they have bought records of some old Gregorian chants which nobody likes and which, apart from the dealer, nobody possesses but the Pope. And when a castrato's voice intoned a requiem of the 13th or 14th century, wailing forth like the wind from a crack in the world, then you forgot all the fatuity of the instrument, all the stupid mechanical noises, you forgot even the Marquise who, said Rodin, "*ouvre et ferme le robinet d'harmonie*". He himself was magnificent, quite quiet, quite closed, as though facing a great storm. He could hardly breathe with listening and only snatched a little air when the force of the voice abated for a few bars. I said, when it was over : "*C'est*

large comme le silence". This made him happy. "*Rilke dit, c'est large comme le silence — c'est vrai . . .*" cried out Mme de Choiseul and looked quite solemn and pleased. Then the singing started again, howling out of the great horn. "Those in hell," said Rodin, "are pushing somebody forward, lifting him high above their heads so that he can tell us what it is like down there," and so it was, more or less; always it renewed its clear tone; always there was a fresh cut from which the song issued like sap from a bough. Afterwards you felt, physically, as you do after heavy work, and in spirit as though you had immediately to exert yourself strenuously and to the utmost. And now it transpired why the Marquise is there: to lead Rodin slowly down from the great heights beside some merry watercourse. Perhaps Rodin really does need this now, someone to climb down with him, carefully and a little childishly, from the high peaks he was always straying among. Formerly he used to remain up there, and God knows how or where and in what pitchy blackness he finally made his way back again. Seeing him spent beyond his strength you felt something akin to fear for him, and unwillingly as I suffered it I understood why the Marquise was putting on ever stupider records, so that in the end we came to a caterwauling music-hall waltz; and now all the idiotic noises of the needle were audible, and the whole thing was only fit for the waste-paper basket. Through my uncautiousness, however, another Gregorian chant followed, a tremendous one; only in Russia have I heard anything like it; even the songs of the Armenian church seemed new-fangled and feeble beside this primal, mindless music: I mean, even Beethoven could not have been endured afterwards. But now, stop! I really must use only cards next time, otherwise I write as the good rain falls — without end. Goodbye, my dear. And do you also write briefly, we each have so many other things to do.—
RAINER MARIA.

34. *To Elisabeth Freiin Schenk zu Schweinsberg*

PARIS, 77 RUE DE VARENNE
4 November 1909

DEAR FRÄULEIN VON SCHENK,—Each time it is joy for me to read your letters and my first impulse is always to answer you at once. This time I really will do so.

By disposition you must be a very good painter indeed, for even in your writing you use pure, strong basic colours for everything there is to say and you place each one so clearly and surely beside the other. But, painting apart for the moment: this ability to fix the things of life in the great ground-colours, simple and unadulterated, seems to me a fortunate one in general; one has the impression that every comprehensive experience must, like a crystal lens, bring into your focus the pure sunlight from all the details and set you in the midst of its oneness and warmth.

Your sister's departure, from the effect of which you are still suffering, moves me more strongly than you know. Why do people who love one another go away before it is necessary? Perhaps because this necessity may step out challengingly at any moment. Because it is something so very provisional — this being together and loving one another. Because at the back of all of us — often acknowledged, often denied — there lurks the peculiar certainty that everything that transcends the pleasantly mediocre, the essentially unprogressive must be borne and overcome in complete solitude, just as it is received by those who are infinitely alone (almost unique). The hour of death, which brings this knowledge to each of us, is only one of our hours and no exception: our life continually passes over into changes whose intensity is probably no less than the newness and successions which death brings. And so just as we have to leave one another absolutely at a certain point in that most formidable of all changes, we must, strictly speaking, give one another up every instant, let them go on and not hold them back. Does it dismay you that I can write all this like somebody writing a sentence in a foreign language, without knowing the pain it implies? That is because this terrible truth is at the same time the one that is also our most fruitful and serene. If you bear it frequent company, though it loses nothing of its hard sublimity (and even were you to lay yourself weeping round it, you would not warm or soften it) — yet does your confidence in its heaviness and austerity increase daily and all at once, as through clear tears, you think you can divine the far-off knowledge that you yourself, in your rôle of lover, have need of solitude ; that woe, but not wrong, is done to you when this solitude sweeps over you and cuts you off in the midst of your tumultuous feelings of love : that even this seemingly closest of all fellowships, which is love, you can only develop and perfect alone, separate — for the reason that if you are bound up with powerful desires you give rise to a torrent of pleasure which carries you along and finally casts you ashore somewhere, whereas, if you are enclosed in your own feelings, love becomes a daily work upon your own self and a continual laying of bold and great-hearted demands upon the beloved. Beings who love one another in this way call up infinite dangers around them, but they are safe from the petty perils which have frayed and pared down the beginnings of so many great affections. Since they always desire for, and expect from, one another the utmost, neither can do wrong to the other through limitation ; on the contrary they unceasingly create mutual space and distance and freedom, just as throughout the ages the theophile has thrown out from his heart fullness and dominion for his God and founded them in the depths of the sky. This sublime Beloved has had the cautious wisdom, yes, I shall not be misunderstood if I say it, the supreme cunning never to show himself, so that although the love of God might have led to imaginary moments of pleasure in a few ecstatic souls, it has still, in its essence, remained work, the most strenuous daily labour and the hardest of directions.

But if now by this love, by its majesty and by its fruits through the centuries you measure every attempt at loving that was less lonely, less desperate and, if you will, *more gratified*, you will have to admit (no longer dismayed, nay, rather with indescribable consent, or with happy dismay at most) that even between human beings only this mighty love is right, the only one that deserves the name. Can it be — and here it is, at last, that my circle closes — can it be that the foreshadowing of such a knowledge is the reason why people who love one another, go away?

Forgive me, I also thought it would be a comfortable journey, and now I have suddenly taken you with me into the mountain-tops where it is cold and glittering and without familiar greenery. But you put your question and I had to climb thus far in order to shew you my answer in that context in which alone it does not look desolating, but rather (as you yourself must feel) good, or simply existing beyond all judgement, just as Nature exists, which has no wish to understand us and yet holds us and helps. . . .

40. *To the Countess Manon zu Solms-Laubach*

Rome, Hôtel de Russie
11 *April* 1910

Liebe und werte Gräfin,—This is only to make up for lost time, but you must know how pleased I was with your kind letter of the 23rd January. It reached me in Berlin where (you may remember) I have never liked being; among the various things that occur at such infrequent visits there are always indeed pleasant ones, good ones, even indispensable ones: I don't want to complain. Yet always there are too many of them for me, who attach myself more and more to an apart and solitary life, and Berlin is not in the habit of bringing you things one by one — you get everything thrown in at your doors all at once, you must do everything and see everything without recovering consciousness; you are credited with a freshness, an unbroken efficiency, a prompt presence of mind such as I can only occasionally muster, and then only inwardly for work. Thus in Berlin I am always like the bad schoolboy who lags behind everything and who finally, sitting in his place of punishment, has not the remotest idea of what is happening on the blackboard.

Think, then, of the double joy your letter must have been for me in such times as these; with this I could keep pace and was thoroughly at peace and happy.

For it, also, was happy. I read there and in between the lines of the joy and inner progress you are deriving from your fine work, which draws so deeply on reality, life and the future. I do not believe on the whole that it is a matter of being happy in the way ordinary people expect it, — but I can so utterly understand this arduous happiness that lies in arousing, through your own resolute work, forces which in their turn begin to work on you. And whoever tackles such a task as you have now fulfilled, in such a way that he experiences this happiness, — for him things must grow boundlessly fruitful and joyful.

Apart from this excellent news of yourself it was your interest in *Malte Laurids Brigge* and myself that did me all the good in the world. The " Notebook " is now finished ; on that account I was in Germany ; we are about to print it. Since you last heard of him Malte has grown into a figure completely detached from me and has acquired a being and an individuality which interested me more and more strongly the more they differentiated themselves from their author. I don't know to what an extent a complete being will be deducible from these papers. The things this fictitious young person inwardly went through (in Paris and in the memories Paris revived) stretched everywhere to infinity ; more and more notes could have been added ; the present content of the book is by no means anything complete. It is only as if someone had come upon a heap of disordered papers in a drawer and had found no more for the moment and had had to make do with those. Artistically regarded its unity is poor, but in the human sense it is possible, and what rises up at the back of it is nevertheless the sketch of a real life and a shadowy concourse of mutually touching powers. . . .

46. *To Clara Rilke*

PARIS, 77 RUE DE VARENNE
7 June 1910

. . . Now, at last, I am sending you the first " Malte ". You must take off the jacket at once and have and use the book in its cardboard covers. The way I imagined it would look has been well carried out ; only the outside title is missing, which really can't be dispensed with in this book. Besides this ordinary edition, which follows my intentions pretty well, two others are being planned: the bound one (in grey paper with the title printed on it in green) and a limited edition of fifty copies in leather. Of these one has been printed for you with your name in it. But the printers printed this very special edition so badly that it cannot be used. It must be done over again. So then you will receive another "M. L.", and I will send you a bound one for the sake of completeness. . . .

Now tell me if you are content with everything. . . . Goodbye. . . .—RAINER MARIA.

47. *To Rudolf Kassner*

LAUTSCHIN
17 *August* 1910

MY DEAR KASSNER,—The "little Malte" has not answered, I know nothing of him; do not concern yourself with him overmuch, lest I grow jealous.

Everything has come different; I foresaw that it would be hard — it was harder. Since July I have been away from Paris, I had to yield this time, I couldn't bring myself to do anything. Never have I done myself so much violence.

I was in the neighbourhood of Bremen, it went badly with me. Only now are things beginning to get better; I have been in Lautschin since Saturday, with the Princess. Life is once more gathering into some sort of future. I am tending towards goodwill without too much exertion. Once more I can imagine what it is to be happy. My heart has bad patches but here it found resting-place at once.

Even if this wonderful change had not come, thanks to my new and happy surroundings (the Prince too is kindness itself to me, I enjoy the largeness and naturalness of this relationship, nothing could renovate me more deeply and more simply) — even, then, without this wonderful change I would reproach myself less than before, perhaps, on account of my obdurate heart.

If only the great and necessary things are done — that is what matters, not who does them. And you have worked for so many of us, for all those who, despite everything, however bad things may look with them, are pure in heart. I count myself among their throng, I do not deserve to be singled out, but even for me you have worked a little, dear Kassner. May God reward you.

The Princess has been reading your little book on 'Dilettantism' aloud to me, and yesterday and the day before I went on and on — past the cover, I had almost said! For it seizes hold of you, always you read it in some new, inward place. For us it is much indeed — just how much time will shew. For you I conceive it to have been something absolutely decisive: a great resolve, a new entrance into the kingdom you have made your own, a veritable earnest of all that you have before you. The presentiment of unending tasks.

It is wonderful; now you will be able to make order — already one feels how thorough you mean it to be. I am sure the world must have gathered itself together over your little book: were you to express it now, every word would be of the same density. Always you were entitled to authority; but now your certitude and experience combine to point into so mighty a direction that you need no longer worry about your right to it: it lies outstretching behind you, into infinity, and now, I would like to say, you are free and can go forwards in all directions from that source.

May new good come to you always.—Your RILKE.

48. *To the Princess Marie von Thurn und Taxis-Hohenlohe*

SCHLOSS JANOWITZ, BEZ. SELČAN
BOHEMIA, 30 *August* 1910

DEAR PRINCESS,—At this moment I am engaged in imagining how this letter will reach you in Duino, in your little realm, a world thickly populated with memories, with a window opening out into infinity; there is something final in this arrangement which draws the Near very near so that the distance shall be left alone with itself. Proximity then means a great deal, and the infinite grows singularly pure, free of meaning, an unadulterated depth, an inexhaustible store of intervening space that can be used for the soul.

But however well I can imagine all that, I still catch myself hoping with every post for a card from you, just to tell me that your trip has done you good and that you found the days to your liking. Is the Prince with you, and how is Prince Pasha? You must sometimes feel how I inwardly prolong that life at Lautschin. Prague interrupted me for a few days, I arrived here almost ill, but now everything is continuing again; yes, I can really say that things are going on somehow. Lautschin was a great watershed, and now my waters are flowing down differently, I know not where, I cannot see ahead; things have taken hold of me completely, so that suddenly all my springs are there, making use of the new gradient and flowing on. This is, however, by no means true of my work, which is lying fallow, but deep inside my life something is stirring, my soul is learning something, it is beginning some new elementary lessons, and the best thing of all is to see it so unpresumptuous. Perhaps I shall now learn to become a little human; hitherto my art has really only come into being at the price of my insisting always on *things*; this was self-willed of me and, I fear, arrogant — Heavens, how appallingly greedy I must have been! I am a little horrified when I think of all the violence I put forth in *Malte*, how in my consequent desperation I plunged clean through to the back of things, behind death itself, so to speak, so that nothing more was possible, not even dying. I do not think anybody has ever experienced more vividly to what an extent art goes against Nature; it is the most passionate inversion of the world, the return journey from infinity on which you encounter all the honest, earthly things; you now see them in their complete shape, their faces draw close to you, their movement acquires particularity: yes, but what is Man that he should do this, that he should travel in the opposite direction against them all; what is this timeless reversal with which he deceives them, causing them to think that he had already got somewhere, reached some end, and now had leisure to return? . . .

49. *To the Countess Lili Kanitz-Menar*

SCHLOSS JANOWITZ, SELČAN
BOHEMIA, 7 *September* 1910

DEAR FRIEND,—I ought not to keep you waiting too long; to the best of my ability I want at least to thank you for your kind and warm letter which only reached me three days ago. So our dear "Malte" pleased you and went to your heart — well, he could scarcely do less; it was the least he could do for you who have always believed in him and expected so much of him. As for me, I breathe a sigh of relief when I think that this book is there; indeed it had to be there, I was committed to it beyond all speaking, — choice I had none. But now I feel rather as Raskolnikov did after his deed, I haven't the least idea what is going to happen now, and I am a trifle appalled when I reflect that I have written this book; *with what strength*? I ask myself; *with what right*? I would almost like to ask. . . .

58. *To Lili Schalk*

PARIS, 77 RUE DE VARENNE
14 *May* 1911

. . . You write of *Malte Laurids Brigge*. This heavy, heavy book. Do you know that sometimes, as I approached the end, it all seemed to me such a hard and culminating labour that I fancied I was comprehending all my tasks in it and running them into myself, like someone who, in the thick of the fray, turns all the opposing spears against him from far and wide and renders them, in his own self, harmless for everybody else? Whenever I tried to look out beyond this work, I saw myself doing something quite different on the further side of it, no longer writing. All the same I have dawdled over my attempts to do something else, something I have not learnt, and thus I have reached a backwater where there is no current. Can you understand this? And tell me whether either of these alternatives is arrogant, and which: to give up work, step aside as though something had already been achieved, or, despite all drought in me, to persevere with it, because all that has been realised is scarcely even the beginning of that to which one deemed oneself boundlessly committed ? . . .

59. *To the Princess Marie von Thurn und Taxis-Hohenlohe*

PARIS, 77 RUE DE VARENNE
16 *May* 1911

. . . I take counsel with myself why I am still not working, it is high time, this long drought is gradually reducing my soul to starvation. How comes it ? It is as if I had completely lost the ability to bring about the conditions that might help me ; whenever I reach out for them I find new aggravations and excuses, the days pass, and who knows how much of life ? Ought one not to devise some grotesque figure solely to bring in this sentence : " He spent the last six or seven years doing up a button that always came undone again " ? . . .

PART TWO

1912-1921

65. *To Lou Andreas-Salomé*

SCHLOSS DUINO BEI NABRESINA
28 *December* 1911

DEAR LOU,—Let me pretend that you are on the point of expecting a letter from me — otherwise there will be no accounting for this huge sheet of paper, and I cannot really take a smaller one. There are prospects about this time of your being at home and having some peace, it was always like that between the two Christmases, — so let me launch out on a tale of some pages' length.

I heard of you through Gebsattel,[1] in the autumn, but as you can imagine he did not give me any complete pictures of you, he is like one of the mirrors doctors use for examinations ; so nothing entire could be learnt from him, but I understood nevertheless that you are well, and this agrees with all I know of you, news apart.

You can see that I am, as always, in a hurry to get to myself ; I always assume that this theme is of interest, — would you like to find your way in again ? Please, please do so, I will help you as best I can, maybe it will be badly, — yet a clue is there : *Malte Laurids Brigge.* I do not need answers to my books, you know that, — but now I need fervently to learn what impression this book has made on you. The good Ellen Key, of course, confused me with Malte and gave me up ; no one but you, dear Lou, can distinguish between them and shew whether and to what extent he looks like me. Whether he, who is in part compounded of my own dangers, perishes in order to keep *me*, as it were, from perishing ; or whether I have only now, with these notes, really got into the current that will sweep me away and dash me to pieces. Can you understand that this book has left me stranded like a survivor, my soul in a

[1] Viennese psychologist. See letters dated January 14 and 24, 1912.

maze, with no occupation, never to be occupied again? The nearer I approached the end the more strongly did I feel that it would mean an indescribable cleavage, a high watershed, as I always told myself; but now it is clear that all the water has flowed towards the old side and that I am going down into a parched land that grows no different. If this were all! But the other one, the one who perished, has somehow used me up, has defrayed the colossal expense of his ruination with the strength and the objects of my life, there is nothing that was not in his hands, in his heart, he appropriated everything with the fervency of his despair; hardly does a thing seem new to me when I discover the fault in it, the jagged edge where he broke off. Perhaps this book ought to have been written as one detonates a mine; perhaps I ought to have sprung away the moment it was ready. But probably I still cling too much to my possessions and cannot achieve that boundless poverty, although this appears to be the deciding task for me. I was ambitious enough to put my whole capital into a lost concern, yet on the other hand its value could only become apparent in the loss, and for that reason, I remember, the longest period of *Malte* did not strike me as a decline so much as a strange, darksome ascent into a remote and deserted part of heaven.

Nearly two years have gone by: dear Lou, only you can understand how wrongly and miserably I have spent them. When they began I thought I had a long, long patience, how often since then have I patched it up, what have I not unravelled and stuck on to it! I have gone through so much bewilderment, experiences like finding that Rodin, in his seventieth year, has simply gone to the bad, just as though all his unending work had never been; that some niggardly thing, some tenacious trifle such as he must have kicked from his path by the dozen in earlier days, not giving himself time to finish them off properly, — has lain in wait for him and wantonly overpowered him, and now makes his old age more grotesque and ridiculous every day — what am I to do with such experiences? A moment of fatigue, a few days of slackness, and Life rose up round him fully as unaccomplished as round the merest schoolboy and drove him, just as he was, into the next wretched mistake. What shall *I* say, with my little bit of work which I am always falling off from, when *he* was not saved? Is it not to be wondered at that life-size life treats me with utter contempt during these interludes? And what in all the world *is* this work, if you cannot learn and experience everything in it, if you can stand outside it and let yourself be pushed and pulled, seized hold of and dropped again, entangling yourself in happiness and falsehood and never understanding anything?

Dear Lou, things are going badly with me when I *expect* people, need people, look round for people: this only drives me still further into my misery and puts me in a false position; they will never know how little trouble I really take on their account and of what ruthlessness I am capable. So it is a bad sign that often since Malte I have hoped for somebody who would be there for me; why is it? I had an incessant longing to lodge my aloneness with some person, to place it in his protection: as you can imagine nothing came of it. With a sort of shame I think of my best time in Paris, that of the *Neue Gedichte*, when I expected nothing and nobody and the whole world streamed towards me only as an ever greater task which I answered clearly and surely with pure achievement. Who would have said then that so many relapses were ahead of me! I wake up each morning with a chill in the shoulder, just where the hand ought to seize and shake me. How is it possible that I now, ready and trained for expression, remain without a calling, superfluous? In the very years when Ilya von Murom[1] has sprung up I sit down and wait, and my heart knows no occupation.

What will you say, Lou, when you read this? Did you foresee it? I remember a passage in your last letter, which I haven't got with me: "you still go so far", you write. And if I don't, what must I do so as not to go bad in this stagnation? What to do?

I think less than I did formerly of a doctor. Psychoanalysis is too fundamental a help for me, it helps you once and for all, it clears you up, and to find myself finally cleared up one day might be even more hopeless than this chaos.

[1] Hero of the *Bylines*, Russian epic.

On the other hand I still occasionally think of pursuing something or other consistently at a small country university. — You smile, you well know how little I say is new, and the unfortunate thing is that certain of my plans and perhaps also my best and worst qualities have sense only in conjunction with a definite age and, failing that, are simply absurd. Already it is almost too late for a university, but you know what I mean ; the terrible thing about Art is that the further you progress in it the more it saddles you with the extreme, the all-but-impossible ; there supervenes psychologically what, in another sense, the woman in Baudelaire's poem alludes to, when she suddenly cries out in the great silence of the full-mooned night : *que c'est un dur métier que d'être belle femme.*

Here, Lou, is another of my confessions. Are the symptoms those of the long convalescence which is my life ? Are they the signs of a new illness ? I wish I could be together with you for a week sometime, listening and talking. It is such ages. I get around so much, isn't it possible for us to meet, just once ?

Do you know that last winter I was in Algiers, Tunis and Egypt ? Unfortunately there was so little in me that was fitted for it that I lost seat and hold and finally only tagged along like someone thrown by a bolting horse, bumping over the ground by one stirrup. That was not the proper way. Nevertheless a little of the East was instilled into me, on the Nile boat I even came to terms with Arabic, and the Museum in Cairo did perhaps, after all, make something of me, confused as I was when I entered.

This year I am a guest in this sturdy old castle (for the time quite alone), which holds you rather like a prisoner, it cannot do otherwise with its immense walls. And at least the *practical* disorder of my affairs will benefit by my being cooped up here for some months. Beyond that I know nothing and don't want to know.

Goodbye, dear Lou ; your heart, God knows, was in all truth the door through which I first came into the open ; now I always return from time to time and place myself against the very door-post on which we used to record my growth, long ago. Leave me this fond habit and love me.—RAINER.

One thing more: have you read Kassner's latest book on the *Elements of Human Greatness*? Some time ago I ordered a copy for you; can I send it?

67. *To Lou Andreas-Salomé*

Duino bei Nabresina
10 *January* 1912

Dear Lou,—The elder Prince Taxis has been here, it is only for a few days that I have been alone again, I am now thanking you at last for your good letter. I have, believe me, excogitated much for myself. I walked up and down in the garden with it as with something you want to learn by heart — what should I do without this voice: yours. I can't tell you how familiar and comforting it was, I am the only little ant that has lost its head, but you see the ant-hill and assure me that it is whole and that I shall find my way back again and make myself useful. And on top of all this came the surprise of your knowing this coast, so that your letter concerned not only me but my surroundings as well, it was directed towards everything and fitted everything. You are right, I have probably always been like this, but, you see, I exhaust myself in the process; just as someone walking on crutches always, at first, rubs his coat through under the arms, so my nature, worn on one side only, will one day, I fear, have holes in it while other places will be as new. During the last few years I have often felt that many artists have got themselves in hand by outwitting and exploiting their own known inadequacies much as they would have taken advantage of a weakness exhibited by somebody else. I stand too definitely on the side of my nature, I have never desired anything from it which it did not give forth greatly and happily from its very ownest impulses, almost as though I were not there. The most that any other technique leads to is facility in writing; I don't give a pin for that. The thing that oppresses me this time is perhaps not so much the length of the pause as a sort of dulling of the senses, an ageing almost, as though what is strongest in me had somehow received injury, were a little at fault, were *atmosphere*, — you understand, *air* instead of space. It may be that the continual inner distraughtness in which I live has bodily causes in part, is a thinness of the blood ;[1] whenever I become aware of it I reproach myself for having let it go so far. No matter what is ahead of me I still get up every day doubting whether I shall succeed in doing it, and this mistrust has increased mightily with the actual experience that weeks, nay, months may go by during which I only bring forth with the utmost exertions five lines of a completely insipid letter which, when at last they are there, leave an aftertaste of such incompetence behind them as a paralytic may feel, who can no more even give his hand.

Can I still go on, despite all ? If people happen to be there they offer me some consolation in that I can, more or less, be what they take me for, without first having to reckon with my real presence. How often does it come about that I step out of my room all of a chaos, and outside, received into somebody else's mind, I find bearings which are really his, and the next moment, to my astonishment, am uttering well-formed things, while a second ago everything in my whole consciousness was completely amorphous. To whom can I tell this, dear Lou ? I know, through you, that it is so, you see how little has changed, — and in this sense people will always be the wrong thing for me, something that galvanises my lifelessness without remedying it. Ah, my dear, I know so well that my earliest instincts are the decisive ones, I don't want to go against them, — but now I have been placed among men and have received real influences from them and worked my way in as though I were one of them. I am not speaking of the fact that, in one particular year when things simply could not go on, or rather, could not get started (for there was absolutely nothing there) — you came :[2] that can happen but once, just as there is only one birth, — but I have other, individual memories of people which I cling to ; if you speak of them they are quite unpretending as regards their content, and yet, can you believe it, in the long, complicated solitude, often pushed to extremes, in which *Malte Laurids*

[1] An astonishing premonition on Rilke's part ; he was to die fourteen years later of leucaemia.

[2] It was with Lou that Rilke went to Russia in 1898.

Brigge was written, I was absolutely certain that the strength with which I battled with him derived to a considerable degree from certain evenings in Capri when nothing occurred save that I sat together with two elderly ladies and a young girl and looked at their needlework and sometimes, at the end, received a peeled apple from one of them. There was not a trace of fate between us, it has not even been established how far precisely *these* people were necessary for that to arise which did arise ; name it has none, but I experienced from it something of the mystic nourishingness of the Last Supper ; while it was still there I knew that it was giving me strength, and later, in my arduous solitude, I recognised this strength among all the others ; it was strange, but it lasted the longest.

Dear Lou, when I wrote recently that I almost hoped for people, I meant that I have not felt *this* again since then and need it infinitely. Can't you conceive of there being someone who could give this, involuntarily, without intending it, and who could find pleasure in radiating his presence and expecting nothing ? Yet there are people who do that for the sick, when all their care leads at most back to health, — whereas here they would be starting, as it were, with the bloom of health and would reach God knows where. It was not in bad times like these that my need took shape ; during the stupendous concentration that carried the *Neue Gedichte* to their goal it received contour, and to a certain extent I wrote *Malte* to an end as though under the condition that this would be there. I'll prove it to you by something quite concrete. Just imagine me thinking, with this same sense of oppression, of trying a little furnished room in the rue Cassette again, or of returning to my own furniture which, in the last few years, has been completely metamorphosed into the scenery designed for the last act of *Malte*. Ridiculous as it is I struggle through these things of mine as though they were destinies, and that is why one day they get finished with, root and branch, and cannot be used again. Can you understand that I have some being in mind who would make the things I have driven to death ordinary and harmless once more ? Can this be ? You might think that the fable is coming true in me : I have sung instead of building, and now, when it grows cold, I remain without shelter. But no, look you, the thing I am thinking of could not have been *built* at all, it should be utterly miraculous, and I would have no right to count on it had not all the decisions in my life been as independent of my care and as impossible to plan and purpose. Perhaps someone who hears this will begin by asking what I, for my part, propose to contribute towards this relationship ? And here I must confess that I have really nothing to reply with, except perhaps my warmer and happier being, as possibly it manifested itself to those women in Capri. I believe it was in Naples once, standing before some antique tombstones, that it flashed through me that I should never touch people with more forceful gestures than is there represented.[1] And I really believe I am far enough advanced to express the whole surge of my heart without loss or disaster by laying my hand gently on a shoulder.[2] Would not this, Lou, be the only sort of progress which is thinkable within the framework of that " restraint " of which you remind me ?

It is half-past three, I have eaten hardly anything and have

[1] See conclusion of Second Elegy :

" Do you not marvelling gaze on the Attic tombstones,
seeing the caution, the care of the human gesture ?
Were not love and farewell so tenderly laid on the shoulders
as though different in substance from ours ? Think of the hands
how they rest without pressure, though power rears up in the torsos.
These Lords of the Heart, they knew that the heart has its boundaries,
that this is our human achievement, this mutual touching,
but more strongly the gods urge us on. . . ."

[2] *Collected Works*, vol. iii. p. 444 (*Letzte Gedichte und Fragmentarisches*) :

" Beside the sun-accustomed road, within
the hollow cloven tree-trunk which has long
become a trough renewing in itself
a water's surface — there I still my thirst.
I take into myself the origin
and laughter of the water through my wrists.
To drink would seem too much, too obvious ;
but with this quiet waiting-gesture comes
bright water flowing to my consciousness.

So I would still my spirit if you came,
only a light reposing of my hands
be it upon your young and rounded shoulder,
be it upon the swelling of your breasts."

spent nearly the whole day writing to you, and at the same time it is so difficult to make myself understandable that my head buzzes ; I barely move from the spot, I would like to start afresh and say everything all over again ; but what's the point ? I shall not convince you. You need only know what I mean by " people " : I do not want to give away my solitude ; it is only that, if it were a little less in mid-air, if it got into good hands, it would lose its morbid undertones entirely (which will have to happen sooner or later in any case), and I could achieve at least some kind of continuity in it, instead of being chivvied amid the din of shouting from pillar to post with it like a dog with a stolen bone.

Well, well, — once again your old mole has been burrowing and thrown heaps of dark earth across a perfectly good path. Forgive me. To you I speak my heart like the people in the Old Testament, a whole book of sayings : for what stands there in the burning bush of your life is the very thing that ought to have power over me.

Dear Lou, if all goes well I shall probably stay here till the spring, although neither the house nor the climate really agrees with me : this perpetual alternation between bora and sirocco is no good for nerves, and I exhaust myself by enduring first one and then the other. All the same, when I count up the individual advantages of this retreat a sizable total is reached, and I must deem myself lucky to have it at all. In my present state every place would have been a strain for me ; not everywhere, however, could I have plumbed the depths of my condition as I can here. It is only a pity that the scenery offers me practically nothing, even the sea leaves me indifferent, as though the stupid garrulousness of the Austrians took its uniform and monotonous character even from the landscape. It is scarcely to be expressed how much everything Austrian repels me. I long for Naples, or I would like to wander for hours in the snow through the woods and drink exquisite coffee with you afterwards. But one day that will really be. . . .

I am sending you Kassner's *Elements* with this letter. It will be very important for me to know what impression this little book makes on you. Kassner himself one cannot see

comes over the reader to collaborate and go forwards, it is a book that spawns notes in the margin ; I can imagine, side by side with the text, a man's whole evolution being deposited in addenda, exclamations of surprise or relief, and derivative ideas.

Ah, Princess, if only we can find time to read it quietly and deeply together we will grant ourselves long voyages of interpretation, — Heaven knows where we'll emerge.

A storm is blowing outside, and this sets me thinking of how lucky Nature is ; always she rinses and runs herself clean again. Enough, enough, — what a long letter : I hope it will hasten towards you.—Your RILKE.]

68. *To the Countess Manon zu Solms-Laubach*

SCHLOSS DUINO BEI NABRESINA
12 *January* 1912

. . . Artistic work has many dangers and in its individual phases often does not allow of any clear recognition whether one is making progress or being driven back by the pressure of the superhuman powers one has compounded with. Then it is a matter of waiting and persevering, and this has always been difficult for me because I have neglected everything outside my work, so that in the intervals I lack even the spot upon which a decision of this kind could be taken. Never have I looked more passionately than in the last year towards those who pursue some good, regular occupation which they can always do, which depends more on intellect, brain-power, understanding, skill — whatever it is — than on those mighty tensions of one's inner life over which one has no control. They are not exaltations, that much is certain, otherwise they could not induce such an indescribable reality in the spirit ; but they are so immeasurable in their impetuosity and recoil that one often thinks the heart could not bear such extremes on both sides. In *your* reality there are certainly no lesser powers, but they are differently disposed, fortunately ; I can scarcely conceive of a woman following art without doing hurt to her nature ; we are a fraction more remote, abstracted, apart. That's why we manage somehow. Only by means of some great aberration, probably, can art proceed from nature, — not without despair and, I would say, not without a Fall. . . .

69. *To Emil Freiherr von Gebsattel*

Schloss Duino bei Nabresina
14 *January* 1912

Dear Friend,—We haven't written to one another at all since Munich, I know you are not getting alarmed about it, but all the same I will now make use of this Sunday evening to ask you how you are and to tell you about myself.

How have things been since then ? I have many questions. If you replied by a similar question I would say that I have been here since the end of October but have only recently been alone, which was what was really intended. During this little new time I have not, of course, managed to do anything, yet, — there is little to say against the surroundings, at most that the climate, an incessant alternation between extremes of sirocco and bora, is not exactly typical of the inner stability I want. Therefore not entirely advantageous, — but on the other hand the advantages are so many that, if I set about it with some degree of sense, I could extract profit of a sort here. Mainly through my absolute solitude. The castle is an immense body without much soul ; obsessed with the idea of its solidity it holds you like a prisoner with its in-turned gravitational force ; it is a somewhat austere abode. On the steep cliffs an evergreen garden climbs up to it from the sea ; apart from that green things are scarce, we are in the Carso, and the hardened mountains have renounced the effeminacies of vegetation.

So much for the externals. As to the " internals " there is hardly more to say, — I long for work, sometimes I fancy for a moment that it longs for me — but we cannot come together. The fact that I have no plans is more pleasurable than disquieting. My furniture has now at last left the memorable, the long-lived-in, the strange house in the rue de Varenne and waits in a *garde-meubles* for my future . . . Marthe (of her I only hear indirectly from Frau W. who, it seems, has a more lively concern for her than ever), Marthe is learning to cook and has talent for it, in the evening she draws and for that, too, she has an eye that is scarcely credible ; now and then she visits the theatre with Frau W., all this, in her, becomes pure life, finds innumerable receptive places in her nature, — it will be a marvel. But I am almost too worried and concerned about myself, — it is evident that this place must lead to some kind of decision ; among the many things that pass through my head is naturally psychoanalysis also. Incidentally it occurs to me that we have never spoken of whether you thought it were actually applicable in my case ? I always have the idea that my work is really nothing but a self-treatment of this kind, how else could I (even at the age of ten or twelve) have got down to working at all ? My wife, from whom I receive only short and infrequent letters, thinks, if I do not err, that a sort of cowardice is frightening me away from psychoanalysis ; for, as she expresses it, it would be commensurate with the " trusting ", the " pious " side of my nature to take it upon myself, — but that is not right ; it is precisely my, if one may say so, piousness which holds me back from this intervention, from this great clearing-up which Life does *not* do, — from this correcting of all the pages Life has hitherto written, — pages which I picture to myself all scored over in red as in a school-book — a stupid conception and certainly an entirely false one, — but it has suddenly struck me.

In an earlier letter shortly after my departure from Munich my wife said so much that was right and positive concerning me that it moved me profoundly : true it is that many elements in me which were merely a bad habit, which I just cut through like so much bad air, do solidify, grow resistant and may the next moment turn into a wall shutting me in, — I know that things aren't going well with me, and you, dear friend, have noticed it too, — but, believe me, I am nevertheless moved by nothing so much as by the incomprehensible, the stupendous marvel of my own being which was so impossibly biased from the start and which yet travelled from salvation to salvation, as through ever harder stone, so that, whenever I think of not writing any more, this fact alone dismays me, the fact of not having recorded the absolutely miraculous line of this so strangely lived life. Ah, all round me I see unhappy destinies and hear of disasters and I have to wonder. Can you understand, my friend, that I am afraid of disturbing by any sort of arrangement and supervision, however palliative, a much higher order which I would be bound to justify by all that has happened, even if it condemns me to perdition ?

You know enough of my life to find examples of what I mean. You, better almost than any other, also know how I have been lying there for two years doing nothing except try to raise myself up, clutching now at this, now at that passer-by, and living from the time and ears of those whom I bring to a standstill before me. It is in the nature of this state that it should become completely abnormal if it lasts long, and I ask myself every day whether I am not under an obligation to end it one way or another at all costs. And yet, you see, it was never *I* who made the end, — the new beginning took it, just as it was, out of my hands.

My dear friend, with all this I must have made myself copiously present to you. Write me some time, tell me, and if you care to mention it, let me read how you regard this creature from the standpoint of analysis. Perhaps my going from here will be the next thing on the list ? I ask nothing. Ask yourself sometime. Let us be prepared, let what can come, come, and things may solve themselves.—With all my heart, Your RILKE.

70. *To Lou Andreas-Salomé*

SCHLOSS DUINO BEI NABRESINA
20 *January* 1912

Do not be alarmed, Lou, at my being here again so soon : it will only be a little visit, if it doesn't suit you put me aside until tomorrow, the day after — when you like.

Providence caused me to find your letter together with Gebsattel's, which I enclose, on my writing-table this morning. I beg you to read it ; here, very quickly, a few data which will make it comprehensible to you.

You know that the thought of undergoing a course of psychoanalysis comes up in me from time to time; and although what I know of Freud's writings is uncongenial to me and, in places, hair-raising, yet the essential thing that runs through all his work has its genuine and powerful side and I can well believe that Gebsattel makes use of it with care and influence. As for myself I have already told you that my feelings rather fear this clearing-up and that, my nature being what it is, I could hardly expect anything good to come of it. Something perilously akin to a disinfected soul is the result . . . and yet, dear Lou, as things are at present I hardly have the right to suspect any help that is there and holds itself in readiness — merely on account of my feelings. I knew more or less that Gebsattel would be prepared to carry out the entire exhumation on me, but I had never actually asked him whether, in so far as he knows me (and during a certain period in Paris we were very intimate at a time that was, for me, desolate and wearisome) the application of psychoanalysis would seem to him appropriate in my case. The letter I sent him on the 15th of this month contains this question and at the same time some of my misgivings. The enclosed is his reply. It seems to me that he is wrong in some things ; nevertheless it is now time, in view of his willingness, to give the course real consideration. The fact remains that I find myself thoroughly insupportable on purely physical grounds. . . . The hypersensitiveness of the muscles, for example, is so great that a little gymnastics or any strained posture (as in shaving) immediately results in swellings, painfulnesses, etc., symptoms to which in turn, as though they had only been waiting, fears, explanations, torments of all kinds subjoin themselves : I am ashamed to admit how, often for weeks on end, this vicious circle spins about me, each anguish aiding and abetting the other.

Perhaps you know, dear Lou, that Gebsattel has more or less been treating my wife since the spring, — with her it is different, her work has never sustained her, whereas mine was by way of being a self-treatment from the start ; anyhow to the same degree that it develops and grows independent it loses more and more of its therapeutic and tutelary qualities and makes demands ; any soul destined to seek harmony with the immense hyperboles of art ought to be permitted to count on a body which mimics nothing from it, which is precise and nowhere exaggerated. My physique runs the risk of becoming the travesty of my spirituality. Dear Lou, if it is not too much, give me a few words of advice. (Under certain conditions I would go to Munich, do one or two things at the University and at the same time try the psychoanalysis.) Your letter I will answer soon, thank you for it, you see how my mind goes up and down and to and fro : what's to be done ?—RAINER.

71. *To the Princess Marie von Thurn und Taxis-Hohenlohe*

DUINO, 21 *January* 1912

Now at last, dear Princess, always to remain at your side, the little green book comes back to you, obdurately inscribed with the first work[1] in Duino (and the first for ages !), for which precisely it was made.

Take it to you, be good to it as you were from the first moment, although then, strictly speaking, it only purported to be " The Foundations of General Religious Teaching " from the year 1801, which it contained. But we both saw that it had a higher, mysterious purpose. Is it now fulfilled ? You will decide.—Your DOTTOR SERAFICO.

72. *To Annette Kolb*

SCHLOSS DUINO BEI NABRESINA
23 *January* 1912

DEAR FRÄULEIN KOLB,—Rarely does such good luck befall me. Only in Paris, on the Quai, does it sometimes happen that, with an accuracy which no amount of purposiveness could compass, I stretch out my hand towards the very book I want — so, miraculously, has your essay arrived just at the right moment — I read it three times yesterday with ever-increasing agreement and now fling myself across this page to thank you.

How often have I been near to thinking precisely this, — as a subject it is so hugely present, it hangs in the air, it exudes from the pores of things : *mais moi, je ne pense guère au fond, j'avale mes pensées toutes entières sans en détailler le goût, je les ai dans mon sang avant d'en tirer le profit immédiat qui s'impose. . . .*

[1] The First Elegy in its first version.

And then : I have no " window on to people ", in the last analysis. People manifest themselves only in so far as they find words in me, and there, for the last few years, they have conversed with me almost entirely under the similitude of two figures, from whom I refer back to humanity in the mass. That which speaks to me of humanity, speaks immensely, with a calm authority that enlarges my hearing, is the phenomenon of " the youthful dead " and, more absolutely, more purely, more inexhaustibly — " the girl lover ". With these two figures humanity is mixed into my heart, whether I will or no. They rise up in me with the distinctness of the marionette (which is an " Outside " charged with verisimilitude), and at the same time they appear as exclusive types beyond which there is nothing more, so that a complete natural history of their souls could be written.

Let us take the lover, — here I mean not so much Saint Theresa and marvels of that sort, — she (the lover) reveals herself to my mind much more explicitly, more purely, in a manner less *adulterated* and, if I may say so, less *utilitarian*, in the persons of Gaspara Stampa,[1] Louize Labé of Lyons,[2] certain Venetian courtesans and, above all, the incomparable Marianna Alcoforado[3] in whose eight heavy letters the love of woman is

1 Of Padua (1523–1553). She wrote a number of sonnets to the Count Collaltino di Collalto. See also the First Elegy :

> ". . . Have you
> sufficiently pledged to remembrance Gaspara Stampa,
> so that some girl whom the loved one has left
> might feel from this lover's augmented example :
> Would that I grow as she ? . . ."

2 The 24 Sonnets of Louize Labé of Lyons (1555). Translated by R. M. R. 1918, now in *Collected Works*, vol. vi. pp. 187-210.

3 It must remain an incomprehensible mystery how anyone of Rilke's discernment could have been bamboozled by these famous *Portuguese Letters*. They are in remarkably bad taste. One can only conclude that Rilke managed to read something of his own magnanimity and idealism into them, for nowhere do they indicate that the wretched Marianna had the remotest conception of the love which Rilke never tired of attributing to her. Far from being " love " letters they might serve as an example of " hate " letters, and of how NOT to love ! Fuming away in her convent with rage and mortification, Marianna achieves nothing but arrant self-pity in these deplorable screeds, which even in Rilke's translation are only supportable by reason of their comical *naïveté* or a flash of desperate wit, pointed by the malice that is always the

laid bare feature by feature for the first time, without display, without exaggeration or relief, as if by the hand of a sybil. And here, great heavens, it becomes evident that as a result of the irresistible logic of the feminine heart this line, finished and perfected on earth, could be continued no further, could only be prolonged into infinity towards God. For now, with this utterly irrelevant Chamilly as an example (whose stupid vanity Nature employed in preserving the letters), in the sublime words of the Nun : " my love no longer depends on how you treat me " — the man, as Beloved, was finished and done with, *loved through*, if one may express it so ruthlessly, loved through as a glove is worn through. And it is miraculous that the man lasted out as long as he did, since all the time he only participated in this love with his thinnest places. What a doleful figure he cuts in the history of love : he has scarcely any strength but the noble birth which tradition ascribes to him, and even this he wears with a negligence that would be simply outrageous did not his absence of mind and heart often have weighty causes behind them which partly justify him. But no one will dissuade me from the conclusion to be drawn from this extreme lover and her ignominious partner : that this relationship clearly shews that whatever there is in love of achievement, of suffering, of consummation is on one side only, the side of the woman, as contrasted with the utter inadequacy of the man. She receives, to put it in a crudely obvious way, the diploma of love as it were, whilst he has in his pocket the elementary grammar of this discipline whereof a few wretched syllables have penetrated his mind, syllables from which he occasionally constructs sentences, beautiful and thrilling as the well-known sentences on the first page of primers for beginners. The case of the Portuguese nun is so wonderfully pure because she refrains from projecting the current of her feeling further and further into the Imaginary, but with infinite strength leads the genius of this feeling back into herself again : bearing *it*, nothing else. She grows old in the nunnery, very old, she

reverse side of such orgies of self-commiseration. We need, however, feel no qualms about Marianna's future ; it is certain that in a short while she succeeded in wholly eliminating the perfidious Count from her system and that she settled down to a series of more accommodating (and less sensitive ?) lovers.

does not turn saint, not even a good nun. It goes against her exquisite sense of tact to apply to God that which was not meant for him from the beginning, which the Count Chamilly was permitted to scorn. And yet it was all but impossible to check the heroic course of this love before its final leap and *not* become a saint with such a vibration in her innermost being. Had she, glorious beyond all measure, given way for an instant she would have plunged into God like a stone into the sea, and had it pleased God to do to her what he does to the angels continually — casting their radiance back into themselves again [1] — I am certain she would have become an angel on the spot, just as she stood there in this grievous convent, an angel deep inside her, in her deepest nature.

You call me back, but I have not strayed so very far from your essay. You will see at once that we are in the middle of it. Woman has something of her very own, something suffered, accomplished, carried to an end. Man, who always has the excuse of being busied with more important things and who (let us say it openly) is not adequately equipped for love, has not entered into love at all since classical times (saints excepted). The troubadours knew very well how small was the distance they could go, and Dante, in whom the need was really quite great, only skirted round love with the huge curve of his gigantically evasive poem. Everything else is, in this sense, derivative and second-rate. But you can understand, such being my persuasion, how very remarkable and thrilling the view from your window was to me. I take your word for what you see, and now that you have so brilliantly placed me in the run of things I know what I am really expecting. Look you, I am expecting the man, the man " with the new heart-beat ",

1 See Second Elegy :

" God's earliest triumphs, O you, Creation's spoiled children,
summits and peaks and morning-red ridges
of all things created, — pollen or blossoming godhead,
hinges of light, passages, stairways, thrones,
spaces of being, scutcheons of ecstasy, tumults
of stormy enchanted sensations and suddenly, singly,
mirror on mirror, which catches the torrent of beauty
that streams from each angel and pours it back into his countenance."

who for the time being is getting nowhere, to take upon himself after a few centuries of healthful rest an evolution towards " the lover ", a long, difficult and, for him, completely novel development. As for the woman, dear Fräulein Kolb, the excellent, the really unique position of your window allows one the assumption that she will probably, withdrawn into the beautiful contour which she has made for herself, find the composure to wait for this slow lover of hers without getting bored and without too much irony, and receive him.

Posting-time ! Greetings and thanks.—Yours, R. M. RILKE.

74. *To Emil Freiherr von Gebsattel*

SCHLOSS DUINO BEI NABRESINA
24 *January* 1912

DEAR GOOD FRIEND,—Do not take this as my very last word — it's not that I'm proposing to wriggle out of a decision again, I am only endeavouring to be quite precise with regard to your great, and for me very important, offer of help. — This is how things are : it is only since Epiphany that I have been entirely alone here. Now I feel that this not, as yet, very protracted solitude is doing all sorts of things to me, daily a little more. And I would only like to reserve for myself the possibility of confirming, after a few weeks, say at the beginning of March (if it lasts as long), what I am attempting to write to you today, — or of retracting it. And here let me say at once that the first has more prospects.

The fact is, after the most serious reflection I have come to the conclusion that I could not allow myself the loophole of psychoanalysis unless I were really determined to start a new (if possible, uncreative) life on the other side of it, a change such as I sometimes promised myself on the completion of *Malte Laurids Brigge* and often since then in tired moods, as a sort of reward for all I have gone through. Now, however, I must confess that these plans have really never been quite serious, that beneath such evasions I still feel bound with infinitely strong ties to what has been begun, to all the happiness and misery it entails, so that, strictly speaking, I can wish for no change, no intervention from outside, no relief save that which is inherent in endurance and in the ultimate triumph. Maybe certain of the misgivings I recently expressed are very exaggerated ; judging by my knowledge of myself it seems certain that if my devils were driven out my angels also would receive a slight, a very slight (shall we say) shock, and, you see, I cannot let it come to that pass at any price.

What I am going through is at bottom no worse than what I have successfully gone through many times before, and added to that my patience is now much maturer and more reliable than it was some years ago. The length of the pause might, if need be, find its explanation in the deep schism which came as a result of my gigantic culminating labours on *Malte*. Yet even if this were but a small part of the lull, might it not still be that there is only one thing right for my nature : to hold out ? I fancy that time and time again I shall be in the position of Sinbad the Sailor, who in the fateful days of extremity abjured all voyaging and then one morning always girded up his loins anew and set out, he knew not how. So it is with me, my dear friend. Your kind letter did much to bring me to this sort of clarity, which is not exactly radiant, one must admit : but one can read by it and write and persevere, and it would be inquisitive and arrogant to demand more all at once.

Enough, dear friend.

Please sense through all the limitations connected with paper and ink my good and living gratitude.—With many greetings, Your Rilke.

77. *To N. N.*

Schloss Duino bei Nabresina
8 *February* 1912

Now it is my turn to thank you, not for Pierrot, Heavens above, no ! it would be his ruin, Pierrot's ruin, and the saddest story in the world. How do you think I could prevail against his immense home-sickness ? ! Furthermore, apart from the torment of helplessly watching it, I should have the added torment, peculiarly painful to me where dogs are concerned, of not sacrificing myself to him : they touch me very closely, these beings who rely on us so utterly and in whom we have helped raise a soul for which there is no heaven. Although I have urgent need of my heart it would probably end, end tragically, by my breaking off little bits at the edge, then increasingly bigger bits towards the middle (as dog-biscuits) for the wailing Pierrot, who couldn't understand life without you; after a few hesitations I should give up my career and live wholly for his consolation; — such, you see, would be the consequence, a terrible and hopeless consequence indeed, for it would remain like that; existence, for him, would be at your side, nowhere else, — in a word, I lack the strength to paint the picture further.

So, not for Pierrot. But hear what I am thanking you for, and say yourself whether thanks can be spared: for the *Harzreise im Winter*; not the Brahms version (I know practically no music), but the Goethe poem which is sheer magnificence. Most erudite maiden, who increases daily in wisdom, what will you think of me when you learn that I did not know these great verses of truly *classic* proportions (for otherwise they would lose themselves for us in the Disproportionate) — till yesterday evening? In your letter I found the one very beautiful passage you quoted, that made me curious, — thus I came to it. Thank you.

I must tell you that it is only now, gradually and amid all manner of precautions, that I am coming to admire Goethe, indeed, when my admiration does appear, it is very great and quite unqualified. Till recently I knew very little of him, my need never turned towards him instinctively; as well as being more accessible, greatness has been more akin to me in other high places; — but this *Harzreise* ranks with the strongest and purest things I know, it is one of the most sterling of poems: what harm could any age do it? Of course you shouldn't open the commentary, where old Goethe returns the compliments of "Herr Dr. Kannegiesser, Principal of the Academy at Prenzlau", — this offends, it has nothing to do with the tranquil verses, just as the scrawling of visitors on the stones of Strassburg Minster has nothing to do with the superior being of the cathedral.

But now I will tell you quickly how I too had a meeting with Brahms years and years ago in Aussee. I was then just an ordinary young person, sixteen or seventeen perhaps, on a visit to a female cousin who was ill, in which connection it may be explained that we sat the entire time morosely in the garden, patching together our mutual boredom till it stretched round the whole day. However, as soon as they let me out of their sight, I withdrew from this pious occupation and thus, one afternoon, raced from the spot like a thing broken loose, out and away into the open, the big, the real, presumably without hat, or if a hat was there it certainly played no very important part. The road sloped uphill, full of stones, but I had started off with such impetus that I was as little conscious of this fact as of any other obstacle ; I charged forwards in such an elemental way that my activity ceased being anything personal ; to express it, you would have to say that "it ran", just as you say "it rains", "it thunders". And as a matter of fact both these things were now imminent. What convinced me of this in the most unexpected fashion was a sturdy old man who was corpulently coming down the slope and had obviously been computing for quite a while how our collision could be arranged most mildly, — to avert this altogether was, owing to the initial velocity with which I had discharged myself and the slow bulk of my opponent, physically impossible. Thus it came about that he suddenly fended me off with a grunt, he had ample cause to curse me, and when I, violently alarmed, looked up at him I had the impression that he was very angry. But after we had glared at one another for a while his indignation resolved itself into a gentle sort of growling, which finally changed into a warning about the darkly-gathering storm he indicated over his shoulder : and sure enough, clouds were already pushing ominously over the mountains.

Now it would be right and proper for me to have apologised and then thanked him sincerely for the great-hearted attention he had shewn me, despite everything, — but, alas, to be quite truthful, my memory hands me no such details. It is more likely that, babbling out something chaotic, I swerved to the right and careered on like one demented, for I now felt it was an immeasurable freedom and rather heroical to run straight into this impending storm, while the stones grew pale beside me. — This is my story. A few days later they pointed out the old gentleman in the town to me, on the promenade, and told me his name: Brahms. But I do not believe he saw me (fortunately).

Adieu, thanks and hearty greetings.—Your Rainer Maria Rilke.

78. *To Arthur Hospelt*

Schloss Duino bei Nabresina
11 *February* 1912

It is Sunday, who knows what tomorrow will bring, so it is best to take this moment in hand at once and thank you for your letter which came today. It was a pleasure to read of yourself and be told of your endeavours, also to recognise in your lines the good heart for which I was prepared by the few poems you have let me see. Over and above this you bestow on me a friendly confidence which I cannot but note with gratitude, though at the same time, since you make particular mention of *Malte Laurids Brigge*, I am almost inclined to direct you away from me towards some other books, I know not which; for the "Notes" are, in a certain sense, more seductive than beneficial. With the knowledge one gleans from them one might, under certain conditions, go on living and even go quite far, for it is a great, hopeful knowledge demanding active achievement and one arising in the teeth of insuperable obstacles; but one should never forget that, within this book, such knowledge has become the constituent of a moral decline, so much so that there will certainly be many who, because of its obliquity, will be blind to the high altitude of its individual points and will fling *Malte* aside as the despairing book of a defeatist. Naturally it is a question of taking it *en masse*, for the powers which come to light in it are not altogether destructive even if they sometimes lead to disintegration; this is the reverse side of every great power, what the Old Testament expresses when it says that it is not permissible to see an angel without dying of it. However, I am almost persuaded that you understand *Malte* in this ascending sense, which is its true and definitive one; all the same it is always possible that the book will shew its disastrous face to the reader in a careless moment, and I do not think it out of the question that it might then, in a certain measure, have an injurious or uselessly depressing effect. For some time I have realised that I must rigorously warn those people whose spiritual development is tender and questing, against finding analogies in the " Notes " for what they are suffering ; whoever gives way to temptation and goes parallel with this book must of necessity sink down ; in its essence it will be pleasurable only to those who undertake to read it *against the current*, as it were. Strictly speaking, however, I would not place it in anybody's hands, I would *let it be simply there*, seeing that it has the good conscience not to have fashioned itself irresponsibly. Certainly there is nothing to *learn* from it, as we ordinarily understand this word ; for that you must keep to the *Neue Gedichte*, where you can at least feel how every object may turn into work and, once resolutely and honestly mastered, reveal itself in absolute grandeur. — But finally, why all this ? Why cannot we, who are still living, lie fallow for a spell without being questioned, when there is so much lucidity in the older literature, which ought by rights to exert the temperate influence that lies hidden in its depths, rich and wonderful ? To a remark in a recent letter I am indebted for Goethe's *Harzreise im Winter* which I (barely experienced in Goethe) did not yet know : what a magnificent poem, in its freedom as well as its submission to that happy metre. I wish that such things may find their way into your hands and heart. And friendly greetings.—Yours, R. M. RILKE.

84. *To Lou Andreas-Salomé*

SCHLOSS DUINO BEI NABRESINA
1 *March* 1912

Ah, Lou, when I think that I am once again in the midst of life after all this, my heart plans so much ; it is dreadful to have been for the second time and for so long on the very spot that should have marked an end. And I am still not past it, I know ; but I cannot see the people working in the garden below without fancying that I am silently doing the same. Yet, in the last analysis, my soul *must* have got bigger, but why do I not live in it if there be room in the spirit, why do I hear every noise in my body and why am I confused and distracted by it and all tangled up in wretched trivialities as though I were living in the company of petty people who squabbled? This is so ignominious and pitiable; if ever for an instant there glides through my feelings a movement that wants to go infinitely far, my feelings do not go with it, they remain stuck in some unevenness of the body, grow stale and decay. Now, what with all my reading, I am like someone who smacks his lips with joy over his food; but every time, as more and more of the plate beneath becomes visible, he is horrified at his bad, damaged and battered crockery and falls to brooding. I used sometimes to be amazed at the way the saints insisted on imposing bodily afflictions on themselves; now I understand that this desire for pain, even to the tortures of martyrdom, was a precipitate and impatient craving no longer to be molested and disturbed even by the worst that can come from this side. There are days when I look at the whole of creation with the fear that some agony may break out in it and cause it to scream, so great is my terror of the abuse which the body, in so many things, wreaks on the soul, which has peace in the animals and safety only in the angels.

I am reading (and Goethe has it on his conscience that I have busied myself with them very violently of late) the *Annals of Italian History* which Muratori (not at all dry, but full of zest and good humour) compiled in the 18th century from numerous chronicles, many of which he had brought to light; I am deep in it, — but, Lou, I am seriously alarmed at my lack of memory, not only because I know next to nothing of the past, but also because from day to day it slips out of my head, despite all my exertions; in my way of receiving things there is something that consumes them without trace, I feel it not only from this book but from my own knowledge as well, everything passes into my blood, mixes itself there with God knows what and is in danger of getting lost. A plant would read like that, but a plant has its calm, pure sap and would drive it into blossom without trouble; but on the other hand nobody knows anything of his blood, I am everlastingly alone with mine, I lack the object to interpose between it and me. If only I could begin to make such an object for myself!

I marvel, marvel at this fourteenth century,[1] which was ever the most remarkable for me, so exactly the opposite of our own, where increasingly everything internal *remains* internal and is played out to the end there without any actual need, almost without prospect of finding external equivalents for its various states (hence the laboriousness and insincerity of present-day drama and the quandary it is in). The world is devouring itself; even for *their* part things are doing the same: transposing their life more and more into the vibrations of money and developing a sort of financial spirituality which is superseding their tangible realness. In the age with which I am dealing money was still gold, still metal, a beautiful thing, the handiest and most understandable of all. And a feeling set no store by behaving nicely in some "interior" and evolving within those bounds; scarcely was it there when it leapt into the next manifestation and filled the world, which was already full of the Visible, the world against which the great Death of 1384, intoxicated with so much vitality and no longer his own master, hurled himself at full tilt. I am engrossed in Venice, but the Venice of those times was so extensive that I travel around diligently, am now in Avignon, now in Naples, everywhere discovering little bits of myself, only in Constantinople do I have, unfortunately, to take things on trust. Adieu, dear Lou. (If only I could find one or two people from whom I could learn something more about it!) Formerly there were always such people, and Goethe was well provided. If it goes on like this I shall have to tackle Latin also; if only we had learnt betimes that the pudding grows cold if you have to make the spoon first, nay, if you have to learn how spoons are made! In such a situation am I. What to do?—RAINER.

88. *To Elsa Bruckmann*

SCHLOSS DUINO BEI NABRESINA
11 *April* 1912

VEREHRTE FREUNDIN,—Even if you mentioned it only in passing the most memorable thing about your letter before I re-read it was that you were plagued with headaches, — with

[1] As depicted by Froissart.

all my heart I hope they have diminished more and more with the new season, and that you hardly remember what this affliction was like. It is insufferable to be obstructed by one's body, I could never understand how people could pretend to make spiritual use of any sort of malaise ; whenever they befall me I feel them as the veriest outrages, and only in extreme cases can I conceive of a great application of such sufferings (having become immeasurable) in martyrdom, when there is hardly any alternative but to cast the whole mass of pain that can no longer be physically accommodated into the soul with all its urgency : for there pain, no matter where it comes from, instantly turns into pure power, just as in a work of art hardness and even ugliness, through the sheer *being* they then assume, reveal themselves as strength, determination and fullness of life. But to suffer bodily in little things, in patches, is senseless, something I fear as much as I fear being distracted. I am only writing this so that you may feel how much cause I have to wish you betterment and recovery, and I hope that in the meantime these have set in and struck root. . . .

At Easter I had a big letter from Ruth ; happiness radiated from every one of the large lines, chiefly because she is now really going to Munich with her Mother : she has been looking forward to it so long. I can see in advance with what trust and joy she will fling herself upon you ; may you, too, gradually be able to feel yourself her friend. The little girl does not have an easy time with her parents, I am amazed at the magnanimity and patience she displays towards us, but for the last few weeks I have been thinking almost exclusively of her immediate and prospective future : ten years one could let her grow like this, it is not a bad foundation, but the next ten years must be all the more ordered and considered ; after letting her experience a world that is simply *capacious*, they must give her a hundred introductions and openings into a more useful one. Will it succeed ? And how ? You can understand my not wishing to disturb too much the joy that both would have in a life together ; nevertheless I am keeping all sorts of other plans ready for Ruth, fearing that my wife may be undertaking too much in wanting to manage her own, so little assured life, and at the same time that of this dear child, which has still to be lived from the very beginning.

All the more reason for me to come to Munich again ! If only I could act in other directions too, and with reason ! But you would not believe how much it is characteristic of me to let my life be determined beyond all reason, and however much this pure calling has abandoned me during these last years I still cannot decide to hold any other flag before me than that one beneath which I have done my earliest, and indeed all, my feats of arms.—Your RILKE.

91. *To the Princess Marie von Thurn und Taxis-Hohenlohe*

VENICE, SAN VIO, PALAZZO VALMARANA
12 *July* 1912

To be precise, dear friend, I have not one single definite need beside the need to write to you, and to know what you think of my present mode of life ; but I cannot attempt to describe what an embargo is in the air and in the limbs on all forms of activity, it is a season fit for healthy infants : just as certain conjurers manage to pull never-ending ribbons out of their mouths, so from the cracks of my closed eyelids I pull yards of day-dreams ; scarcely has one dream come to an end when out lolls the grey or mauve tab of another, and so entangled am I in all these slow-forming ribbons of sleep that it is like living in a net that grows all the tighter with every effort I make to get free.

It's all very odd, one's conscience is not improved by it, and yet I don't want to slash through everything and burst out, rather keep on waiting, just let things happen to me, and what comes will take on the habits of a dream and have its dimensions.

Here on my table lies a little key (yes, it is really lying there) : it opens the huge, strange hall of the Casino dei Spiriti in the Fondamente nuove ; whenever I wish myself there I can go, — but what an expense, what an exaggeration to wish.

The Duse — even to wish myself with her, or her with me, even that is like a mirage in the bright, overexcited air — as you can imagine we were like two people coming into action in an old mystery play, spoke, as in the recitation of a legend, each one his gentle part. A meaning emanated from the whole and instantly passed out beyond us. We were like two bowls and together we made a fountain and only shewed each other how much continually escaped us. And yet we could scarcely avoid telling one another of the splendours of such fullness, and perhaps we both thought at the same moment of the pulsing, upright jet that rose above us and descended (ever afterwards) and filled us so full. — Coward that I am I hardly dared look at her ; it caused me a sort of pain to find her so stout and sturdy, her muscular body like a setting from which the stone has fallen. My fear of seeing some distortion, or simply something that is no longer there, is to blame for it that her mouth is practically the only thing I remember, this brooding mouth which looks as though nothing but an impassive fate, a fate not her own, could move it, just as for certain swords the hero must come, the demi-god who shall lift them. And the smile, of course, surely one of the most famous that have ever been smiled, a smile that needs no space, calls nothing back, covers nothing, transparent as a melody and yet so full of oncoming life that one is tempted to stand up when it makes its entry.

Hardly less moving than the event itself was the fact that this meeting, which for several years has been almost my greatest wish, came about suddenly without my agency. For some time past I have lost the accuracy required for wishing (wishing is like shooting at targets, but I stand under heavy fire over against an invisible enemy), — yet, as on more than one occasion in my life, involuntarily I took the fact of things gently coming true as a proof that I am on my way, despite all, — otherwise this region, so often visited on the map, could not have materialised.

My experience with Rodin has made me very apprehensive of all change, all diminution, all failure, — for once you have recognised these sorry fatalities they can only be endured so long as you are capable of *expressing* them with the same strength with which God allows them. A little while and I could work, perhaps ; but Heaven forbid that I should be required (at least right away) to look into anything more painful than was laid upon me in *Malte*. It would simply be a weeping and gnashing of teeth and not worth the trouble.

Yesterday I wrote straight down in my diary :

" *Ah, when we waited for help from people — angels rose soundlessly, crossed with one stride over the fallen heart.*"

Here Moissi entered suddenly, coming from the Duse, I knew she was expecting him yesterday ; he rushed, pushed, burst in, at first I thought it was his tempo, something he had in him, sui generis — but now, now I almost fear it is just the tempo of Reinhardtism : heavens, what an " actor " he has become, I soon spotted him at it with the Duse, we were standing at the window, she came past with her friend, Madame Poletti (who is writing the *Ariadne* for her), we went down to her into the gondola and glided slowly towards the Lido. Today, the Duse was splendid, deep in a sadness such as lofty cloud-pictures have, you brood over them wistfully, yet really there is nothing but an immense space, not serene, not desolate, — just great. Later we dropped Moissi, but we stayed together, I ate with them in the house on the Zattere, it was companionable, full of friendship, full of intimacy, and once more a pure significance came out of the simplest things and passed over into greatness. Now it is late, I am closing a letter which would otherwise have continued quite, quite differently, but it is more complete so, for today she and I have seen one another truly and without fear, graveness confronting graveness, and melancholy melancholy : it seems that we cannot harm one another. (And the world is so different from Moissi.)

This must be enough ; we sent a telegram to Placci, he ought to come tomorrow ; a thousand greetings to everybody, especially the Prince and you, honoured friend ; often I think of how much you are implicated in everything that befalls me, and here also, — how nothing would have happened without you.—Your D. S.

(All the rest next time.)

92. *To the Princess Marie von Thurn und Taxis-Hohenlohe*

VENICE, SAN VIO, PALAZZO VALMARANA
23 *July* 1912

Ah, dearest friend, how hard everything human hits me, what labour, what weariness wherever I enter : instead of helping me, making me a little new and harmless, it sets me to the galleys, I ply the oars, caulk the seams, scrub the decks, and (God forgive) have learnt nothing. I spend a good deal of time with my great neighbour, a place is laid for me every evening, I can always come, and it is obvious that I should come. She is marvellous, expressing the human things more mightily than any other ; she has no wish to make herself understandable, her gestures assume from the start that they are understood and proceed from there. We others gesticulate, say things by halves, regret it, take it back, try anew ; she speaks, shews and refuses to shew herself, and from the very outset it is one thing, a whole thing, final, in a higher order, as on the pediment of a temple. What splendour and what waste ! No poet in all the world, and she passes by. No one has ever had so great a need. Without scenery, without artifice, she magnifies our dailiness, our life in the raw ; small, fleeting, ephemeral events come into their own in her gestures, transcend themselves, — they would start at their own image could they see themselves in her, would halt, stand, no longer flow away. And she stays bearing, motionless, unrelieved, loaded down, — because there are never spectators enough to relieve her of the fullness of her entry ; every other moment she is like a ripe vine, — one would have to send away thousands of labourers again and again under the load of her grapes. . . .

94. *To the Princess Marie von Thurn und Taxis-Hohenlohe*

VENICE, SAN VIO, PALAZZO VALMARANA
3 *August* 1912

. . . I must tell you that recently I had a letter from an unknown young person in Saxony, who writes me a mass of details about my family, things I of course knew ; but (and this was what interested me) he also knows well the territory in which the one-time possessions of my ancestors are dispersed ;

this property extends far into the mining districts of Freiberg, and in actual fact Rilkes were among the first to exploit the lead-pits; their fortunes, which already in the 13th century were established in Carinthia on similar foundations, had their heyday in Saxony, in Meissen, in the March of Brandenburg, — but suffered radical injury in the Thirty Years' War and, eighty years later, collapsed completely: those were the days of the trek to Bohemia — into exile, into the unknown future. And now this strange young man subscribes himself Rülke and informs me, quite modestly, at the conclusion of his letter, that in his family the tradition has been handed down from mouth to mouth that at the downfall of the old house one Rilke, instead of migrating with the rest, descended into the mines as a simple miner and that their lineage runs from miner to miner from this original subterranean survivor. You will laugh, but I envy him this legend just as it stands, — was it not a truly magnificent solution to vanish darkly and a little defiantly into the earth, through whose veins the strength of the house had been drawn up all through the centuries, instead of taking the dreary road of emigration, with memories one may not think back on, degraded but not extinguished, a compromise, at bottom, in the worst taste? Here I sit and it strikes me that it is I who have need of being descended from that other dogged Rilke, who with one wrench dragged the sumptuous heart of his forebears under the earth, while it still glittered, — and look you, it remained there, it was preserved unexamined from father to son, only becoming a little drowsy on the surface with the pure rhythm of elemental work — and I, one and a half centuries later, augmented by so much darkness, could have brought this heart back to consciousness in me instead of finding it attenuated, suburbanised, with so many false fronts.[1]

[1] See Tenth Elegy:

"But far off in their home in the valley an Elegy-Elder
takes the youth under her wing when he plies her with questions.
We were a great family once, she murmurs, we Elegies.
Our fathers, they worked the great mines far away in the mountains.
Among men you may sometimes see fragments of polished
primordial sorrow, or haply the ashes of anger,
the petrified heart of a wrath-bearing ancient volcano.
Yea, it all came from us. Once we were rich."

I wrote to the young man (the name is quite possible, since the Rilkes wrote their names, latinised, Rüliko, Rülicke, Rülke) wishing him that the tradition may somehow recollect itself in him and that he may draw strength from it.

Before closing, I am reading your dear letter again (of the 27th and 28th), thank you, when it came it did me no end of good, — there was, fortunately, no more talk of the *Weisse Fürstin*, for me it is finished and done with, it would have been the sheerest anarchy to devise any kind of plans for it. The Duse — if it is not too late — can only portray something perfect, one or two great states of soul leading into one another purely. But where is this work, and what will keep her from ruining herself beforehand ? Now she wears herself out, treats her own body like a cheap lodging-house, having no other place to live. In September she wanted to come back here, but the house she had in mind has not been found, also half an hour is sufficient for her to wear a flat to shreds, even the ceiling can't be used any more. A distaste for living issues from her in certain moments which is so piercing that it shakes the teeth out of everything in her vicinity.

For Placci a thousand greetings ; he saw her again on that wonderful afternoon about which he will have told you. Ah, it all seems as though it were five hundred years ago when I think back (and I am no longer young). But enough, as many greetings as possible and to everyone. To you, kindest friend, daily thoughts.—Your D. S.

96. *To the Princess Marie von Thurn und Taxis-Hohenlohe*

TOLEDO,[1] *All Souls' Day*, 1912

Princess, for you the first word, let it be " Hope ", and if a wish may be uttered in the same breath : may no other thing discover itself to me for a long time, so that I can make my

[1] In September 1911 Rilke had written to the Princess Marie von Thurn und Taxis-Hohenlohe (Collected Letters No. 62, 1907–1914) :

". . . Princess, do you know, I have rather a longing to go to Toledo. Last night, suddenly, I fancied us doing it, I was half in a dream and let myself journey far in both realms. . . . All day long I had been thinking of the Grecos I saw in Munich, saw over and over again, experienced, lived through ;

home here innocently and without bounds.

Never shall I be able to say what this place is like, dear friend (that would be language such as the angels use among men), but the very fact that it *is*, that it exists, you must believe me blindly. It couldn't be described to anybody, it is utterly right, yes, in a flash I understood the legend that God, when he took the sun on the fourth day and placed it, set it exactly above Toledo: so sidereal is the situation of this prodigious city, so outward, so much in space — I have gone round everywhere, have impressed everything on myself as though I should have to know it tomorrow for always, the bridges, both the bridges, this river and, ravished beyond it, this open mass of landscape spread out before the eye like something that is still being created. And the joy of your first walks, this feeling of being taken and led with indescribable sureness, — imagine it, I took the street of Santo Tomé, then the street of the Angel (Calle del Angel), and it brought me face to face with the church of San Juan de los Reyes, on the walls of which the chains of liberated prisoners hang in rows and rest in peace on the cornices. P. had told me in Munich that he had once seen in Baedeker that there was such a church with chains, — without remembering having seen it himself. Now I find it first thing. And from then on nothing accidental, almost you have the desire to look round when making such discoveries in order to find out exactly who is watching, whom you are giving pleasure to, just as children look round when they are learning something.

I wrote you about them but probably did not get as far as telling you that this strange *Laocoön* was there.

"Imagine a capacious picture and in the foreground, on brown stony soil that has been swiftly and tragically darkened by clouds, Laocoön, enveloped by a serpent which he is struggling to hold off behind him; one of his sons felled; another standing to the left, cowering back and yet all rigid in the mighty arc of the second serpent which is already reaching up to his heart; two sons to the right barely comprehending as yet (so quickly has it all rushed down upon them and gained the upper hand), — and seen through this chaos of standing and falling and striving, through the dramatic lulls in the cataclysm — Toledo, as though cognisant of this agony, thrusting up on its uneasy hills, cadaverous with the glow of the heavens crashing behind it. An incomparable, unforgettable picture. It must be marvellous to see this city and the Greco together. But I rave, of course — such a thing would mean more than a round-about trip, God knows what it would mean. . . ."

It troubles me not to be able to strike the tone of the place; here for the first time I can imagine people going and tending the sick; how, advancing daily through the streets, they might turn off somewhere and busy themselves unobtrusively in some narrow den, — everything here stands at the uttermost limits, — one cannot get beyond it. But again, outside, scarce a hundred paces beyond this unsurpassable town, you can imagine yourself meeting a lion on one of the unhidden paths and binding him to your will by some involuntary trait in your bearing. Somewhere between these two gestures life here must lie.

My God, how many things have I loved because they tried to be like this, because a drop of this blood was in their heart, and now I am to have it all — can I bear it?

No more today, Princess, — I arrived at ten this morning; in Madrid (which displeased me almost as much as Trieste) just driving from one station to another; it is now about seven in the evening and the day in between was as long as a day out of Genesis. My hotel is called Hôtel de Castilla, is supposed to be the best here and seems habitable.

Many, many greetings to you and the Prince, where are you? How are things? This morning it was very, very cold, I was alarmed at having come so late in the year, but by day the sun fills out everything that can be shone on. Enough, a justifiable weariness is breaking over me and withdraws me from you. Adieu, adieu.—Your D. S.

98. *To N. N.*

TOLEDO, SPAIN, HÔTEL DE CASTILLA
17 *November* 1912

You see, it is not my fault if I am only now answering you, — or my fault only in so far as the porter in Venice did not have my address and your letter had thus to come by various stages. But it has survived the journey, I received it this morning, — and even if it had not come I would still have written to you one of these days so as to make it possible for your good news (which I felt must come soon) to reach me safely and directly.

What you call my "world", dear child, would not suffice

at present to nourish or keep anybody, indeed, you ought to weight the balance against it if you are to *be* wholly. It is possible that from such fragments as we gradually gather together before us, sometime, as we survey them, something like a world will be granted, — but this is still a good way off, I am now more than ever on one plane, the lament has prevailed many times over, but I know that we may only use the strings of lamentation so exhaustively if we are determined, later on, upon *them*, by their means, to play the whole paean of praise which swells up behind all heaviness, anguish and suffering, and without which the voices are not complete.

You will be astonished to find me here, an old wish has at last been fulfilled, and I saw at once, the very first day, that there are many things here which I have long needed. Only this for today, many wishes, many greetings and confidence in all things.—RILKE.

99. *To the Princess Marie von Thurn und Taxis-Hohenlohe*

RONDA, 17 *December* 1912

I long for a letter from you, dear Princess, God knows where it is wandering — and the last that I wrote you seems all wrong in my memory ; what was alive in it was nothing but a rehash of the one I wrote in Cordoba, in thought only ; for the rest, nothing has left any mark save my discontent with Seville, with myself, with myself and ten times with myself. Once more there has been a succession of oppressive days, bodily pains and my spirit so little disposed to endure them that, had I by chance had a home, I should undoubtedly have gone back to it, for any journey, particularly a journey through Spain, demands a certain balance, a knowledge that you can rely on yourself, — but for me the world collapses every other minute, in my blood ; and if then there is any strangeness outside it is a strangeness beyond all measure. I intend, Princess, to get to the bottom of this malaise and discover the source from which again and again sickness issues ; scarcely have I found a little boat anywhere when this gloominess rises up and overwhelms it and leaves me hopelessly stranded. And I know that a doctor could help me if only he were the right one, — not I, with me everything is too much of a piece, so that I cannot suffer in one spot and create in another, fundamentally I do not enjoy being miserable, my pain darkens the earth for me, — for this reason I have absolutely no qualifications for sainthood and have not the slightest prospect of ever substantiating so worthy a rumour (indeed you recognised this and said so, it was incontestably right).

Moreover you must know, Princess, that since I was in Cordoba I have become an almost rabid anti-Christian ; I am reading the Koran — in places it strikes a chord in me and I echo with all my powers, like wind in an organ. Here you are supposed to be in a Christian country, well, here too it has long been overpassed, — it was Christian so long as you had the courage to kill somebody a hundred paces outside the town, where the innumerable unassuming stone crosses flourish on which stands simply : Here died so-and-so — that was their version of Christianity. But now an immeasurable indifference reigns over all, empty churches, forgotten churches, chapels that starve ; really, they ought not to sit any longer at this denuded table and dole out the last remaining finger-bowls for food. The fruit is sucked dry, — all that is left for us is, speaking crudely, to spit out the rind. And yet Protestants and American Christians *will* go on making a brew of this weak tea that has been drawing for two thousand years — the next to come was in any case Mahomet ; like a river bursting through a mountain he bursts through to the one God, who can be gloriously apostrophised every morning without the aid of the telephone " Christ ", where all the time you bawl " Hello, who's there ? " — and no one answers.

Now just imagine, Princess, I am three hours away from Gibraltar, five, when the weather is good, from Tangiers, — in my present mood nothing tempts me so much as to go over to Morocco ; on the other hand I am afraid of a dazzling brightness superimposing itself like a whitewash on the dark-red clay of Spain. At the moment I am in Ronda (have been here a week), I sent P. a couple of postcards at once, it seemed highly likely that the unforgettable vision of this town, piled up on two steep rocky escarpments separated by a deep and narrow gorge, would conform to his dream-picture ; it defies description, the whole thing girded round by a spacious valley busied with its level fields, evergreen oaks and olive-trees, and over against it, soaring up in the distance, the pure mountains, tranquil, peak behind peak, making the most superb perspective. As for the town itself, in such surroundings it cannot be anything but individual, rising and falling, here and there opening so precipitously on to the abyss that no window dares look out ; little palaces behind yearly incrustations of white, each with a doorway set off in colour, and underneath the balcony a coat of arms with a somewhat dejected-looking crest but the shield distinct, detailed and full like a pomegranate.

This naturally would have been the place to live in true Spanish fashion, were it not for the time of year, were it not for my own weary reluctance to let myself in for any troubles other than the most necessary ones (inborn or assiduously cultivated) ; to make my cup quite full the devil has inspired the English with the idea of building a really excellent hotel here, in which of course I am now living, tame and expensive though it be and just what many people would wish, and yet I am shameless enough to give it out that I am travelling in Spain. . . .

Today, when I saw these mountains, these slopes outspread in purest air as though leading a choir in song, I had to tell myself of the raptures to which it would have moved me three years ago, how it would have utterly transformed me with joy, — but now it is as though my heart had gone on miles ahead of me, I see many things starting out and travelling in that direction, but I do not experience their arrival. Ah, I have still not got over expecting something new as a result of human intervention, and yet what's the good, since it is my lot to pass all humankind by, as it were, to reach some uttermost extreme, the very edge of the world ; for instance recently in Cordoba an ugly little bitch-dog in the last stages of pregnancy came up to me ; it was not a very deserving hound and was sure to be full of casual puppies over whom no great fuss would be made ; but seeing that we were quite alone she came across to me, despite the difficulties it caused her, and lifted up her eyes enlarged with worry and wombfulness and implored my looking, and in her own there was in very truth everything that probes beyond the solitary soul and goes God knows where, — into the future or into that which passeth understanding. In the end she received a lump of sugar from my coffee, but over and above that, unspeakably so, we read as it were the Mass together ; in itself the action was nothing but giving and receiving — yet the meaning and solemnity and our whole communion were boundless. This sort of thing can only happen on earth ; it is good in any case to have passed through life willingly, even if uncertainly, even if guiltily, even if not at all heroically, — at the last one will find oneself wonderfully prepared for the godly conditions.

How the littlest bird-voice hits and concerns me ! Would to God it were spring and I could cast myself with all my senses upon Nature, — I have discovered such a strange valley, a sort of hunting-park belonging to the Marquis de Salvatierra, hardly laid out at all, only rearranged so that the hares cannot quite find their way about in it, as though it were all in a dream or the *Elective Affinities* ; I go for long, long walks, — but mostly I come upon my good fortune only in the *first* excursions I make in any one place, — even in Seville where everything else went wrong I began, God knows why, with the Almshouse for the Aged ; it was morning, in the long cheerful rooms the old fellows sat round the braziers or simply stood about, ready, like playthings ; two of them were lying on a bed taking a rest from life, as though they had no need of the exertions of dying — but on each of the other beautifully-made beds, everywhere on the same patch of flowery coverlet lay two enormous pale loaves of white Spanish bread, peaceful in their self-evident profusion — sheer reward and no longer to be eaten in the sweat of the brow.

Here too was the Church of San Francisco, out in the southern suburbs, the first I discovered and about which I will tell you another day ; it is high time I closed and said Happy Christmas, my thoughts will go to you, — I have not seen the newspapers but hope that you have no more fears of war ; I see from the Prince's kind good letter, which arrived with the first post to catch me in Ronda, that he feels hopeful and that nobody really understands why a war would be a good thing.

Princess, your letter! It has come in the nick of time. I am writing straight off without reading or criticising the poems (I must first get the feel of the German text in my memory so as to compare them); but as I have spent six days dawdling about in Seville I want this to be with you by Christmas, whether it be festive or not. It is terrible how the war danger is still in the wind; politics in general only worry about speed and it is a wry joke when they go as slowly as the good God himself.

As for Seville, up to the very last there was no understanding between us, none at all, although the inhabitants take the Festival of the Virgin very personally and a whole series of ceremonies was impending, whose beginning I shared. But I found the cathedral thoroughly repulsive, indeed hostile, — it is never serious, there is something hazy and imponderable about this high-blown overweening dome, an *out-trumping* spirit that seeks to out-trump God himself and seize him as it were from above. And the infamous organ makes the interior so sweet with its treacly tone that the colossal pillars grow quite faint; it leaves you unmoved, this deliquescent architecture, a tour de force — it can go and do what it likes with itself.

Do you ever see any books, Princess? Sometimes in the evening (my eyes are so suffused with blood that I cannot read much) I dip into the German version of *Don Quixote* and find him rather childish; artistically speaking this book has no limits except perhaps those which a witty and inventive extravaganza may have in the world of reality — and these are wildly and frivolously overstepped. But Christmas: greetings to you, the Prince, the Mzellers with all my heart. Do you know that there is a full moon exactly on Christmas night? How that white world of yours will match her silver dress!—All love and thanks, Your D. S.

100. *To Lou Andreas-Salomé*

RONDA, SPAIN, HÔTEL REINA VICTORIA
19 *December* 1912

DEAR LOU,—Softly, without looking up, Christmas approaches, here also, — let me write to you. Once again I have myself on my heart, with all my weight and with the heaviness of I know not what things. . . . It stands to reason that I should look back a year to the time when I began writing to you again, and honestly it seems as if I had not budged since then, unless I have gone in a circle, — God knows. I can see a sort of tide-mark in a passage from the *Instructions* of the blessed Angela da Foligno ; I noted it down a year ago and when I chanced to open it again the day before yesterday, it applies to me just as much now, so that, by writing it out I bring the whole of my condition to light : "*Quand tous les sages du monde et tous les saints du paradis m'accableraient de leurs consolations et de leurs promesses, et Dieu lui-même de ses dons, s'il ne me changeait pas moi-même, s'il ne commençait au fond de moi une nouvelle opération, au lieu de me faire du bien, les sages, les saints et Dieu exaspéreraient au delà de toute expression mon désespoir, ma fureur, ma tristesse, ma douleur et mon aveuglement*".

The good, generous sanctuaries of which Duino was one and Venice immediately after, did not help me much ; also the singular conformations of these surroundings demand so much adaptation, they have their being in conditions that are too multifarious and strange, and if ever you do manage to belong to them it is only a make-believe belonging that is achieved. Till well into the autumn I was in Venice, held there by kind and friendly connections, but really staying from day to day, from week to week because I did not know where to go ; at last from despair, from instinct, from impulses I had dragged about with me for years, the decision formed itself in me to make this journey through Spain, actually only a stay in Toledo ; and arriving there, breathlessly exposed to this infinitely longed-for town which yet infinitely surpasses all longing, — I believed myself jerked out of my dejection and already on the road to participating once more in the ultimate realities. There are no words to tell you how superlatively this town stood before me in all its untamed scenery,. absolutely immediate, something that could not have been endured a moment before, chastising and comforting at once, like Moses when he came down from the mountains with the Tables, — and yet gradually reminding me of all that was necessary, strong, pure and dependable in my life.

But from the fact that I did not stay (I was there for four weeks), that the cold, my old pains, the rush of blood to forehead and eyes, that one discomfort after another cropped up alongside so mighty and for me so eloquent a Present, absorbing my attention and distracting me, — from all this you can see that I could not endure what was destined perhaps to bring about "*la nouvelle opération*" — I journeyed south, I stood marvelling in Cordoba, I had time to realise that Sevilla meant nothing to me, something drew me to Ronda, — and here I now am and await in these no less stupendous surroundings first of all a better distribution of my troublesome blood under the influence of the high pure air, which sweeps across from the open circle of mountains everywhere into this steeply perched town.

When I wake up in the morning, before my open window, reposing in the pure spaces, lie the mountains : how comes it that this does not stir me inside — even four, five years ago a sunset on the crossing from Capri to Naples could transfigure me with joy from head to toe, joy that was quite new, that had never been there before, leaping out of me and running towards everything like a new-found spring ; and now I sit there and look and look till my eyes ache, and point it out to myself and say it over and over again as though I had to learn it by heart, and yet have not done so and am clearly a person in whom such things do not thrive.

Dear Lou, tell me why it is that I spoil everything, — sometimes it seems to me that I apply too much force to my impressions (which, in fact, is what I do do on so many occasions), I stay too long in front of them, I press them into my face, and yet they are after all impressions of Nature, are they not ; but even if you let them lie for a while quite quietly, — *au lieu de me pénétrer, les impressions me percent.*

I go for long, long walks in the open, sometimes for an hour or so the sun is such that you can rest under an evergreen oak, then a little bird-voice sings for me, or the rushing from the deep ravine makes everything that was and everything that will be, superfluous. But as I walk I brood on so much, — from January 1st a studio in Paris belongs to me ; I foresaw that, however this trip might turn out, the most important thing for me would be to go to some independent place of my own immediately after, and I was certainly right. And whether Paris, which has gnawed at me so much, will be needed any longer or is advantageous in any way — time will have to shew. I realise that you mustn't leave a plaster on all your life because it has once done you good, also if possible I do not want to go back to Paris until the worst of the winter is over.

I must tell you, Lou, I have a feeling that what would help me would be an environment similar to the one I had with you in Schmargendorf, long walks in the woods, going barefoot and letting my beard grow day and night, having a lamp in the evenings, a warm room, and the moon when it suits her, and the stars when they are there, and, for the rest, just sitting and listening to the rain or the storm as though it were God himself. On your travels, dear Lou, bear this in mind and let me know if you see a place where it could be done. Sometimes I think of the Black Forest, the Triberg district, Rippoldsau, then again I think of Sweden, what it would be like for example with Ellen Key (but I would rather not be " with " anybody) — or near her by a lake in the woods or near a small university town in Germany ; then of course it would be fine to have books, preferably some person also with whom one could learn something. Do you know whether it is true that the books of Moses are completely different in the original text from the content of the Greek and Latin translations ? I've been reading some remarkable volumes by this extraordinary Fabre d'Olivet (beginning of the nineteenth century) ; this discovery caused him to reconstruct a whole new Hebrew grammar (just as all his life was spent in the preparations for some gigantic master-work which he never began —) ; here I dip into the Koran and marvel, marvel, — and want to tackle Arabic again. If I could do that with your husband, Göttingen for instance might be considered — but I rave, you see, and there's no end to it.

Where are you, dear Lou ? In Vienna ? Do you see Kassner ? Where will you spend Christmas ? There is a full moon exactly on Christmas night, think of me among your good thoughts.—RAINER.

102. *To Lou Andreas-Salomé*

RONDA, *Epiphany*, 1913

" Actually he had long been free, and if anything prevented him from dying it was perhaps only the fact that he had somehow overlooked Death, so that he did not, like other people, have to go on towards it, but back. His existence was already outside him, was in the confident things children play with, and perished in them. Or it was rescued in the glance of an unknown woman who passed by, at least it left her at its own risk. But the dogs, too, ran past with it, uneasy and looking round to see whether he would not take it away again. When, however, he stepped up to the blossoming almond-tree he was terrified at finding his life so completely at a remove from him, passed over, self-absorbed, gone from him ; and he himself not sufficiently face to face with it and too dull even to reflect this part of his being. Had he become a saint he would have drawn a serene freedom from this condition, the imperishable joy of poverty : for it was thus perhaps that Saint Francis lay there, consumed, having been enjoyed, and the whole world had the pleasant taste of his being. But he had not peeled himself properly, had torn himself out of himself and given away bits of skin, and had often (like children with dolls) held himself up to an imaginary mouth and smacked his lips, and the morsel had fallen to the ground. So now he looked like refuse and was in the way — however much sweetness had grown in him."

I wrote this early this morning in my pocket-book, you will see whom it is about. Your good letter came yesterday. Yes, two Elegies are there, — but only by word of mouth could I tell you what a small and bitterly truncated fragment they form of what was once given into my power. With conditions and powers like those when the *Stundenbuch* was begun — what could I not have achieved ! *If only we could see one another, dear Lou*, that is my great hope now. Often I tell myself that it is only through you that I am linked with mankind, in *you* they are turned towards me, know of me, breathe at me ; everywhere else I emerge behind their backs and can never make myself known.

Greet the Beer-Hofmanns from me (and Kassner) and comfort me in your heart — you.—Your RAINER.

105. *To Karl von der Heydt*

Paris, 15 *March* 1913

My dear Friend,—It would not accord with the passionateness of the angels to be spectators, they excel us in action to exactly the same degree that God is more active above them; I regard them as the aggressors par excellence, — and here you must give way to me, I have paid the price: for when I, coming deep down from things and beasts, longed to be instructed in mankind, behold, the next stage, the Angelic was infused into me, and that is why I have overleapt people and now look back at them with compassion. . . .

106. *To the Princess Marie von Thurn und Taxis-Hohenlohe*

Paris, *Good Friday*, 21 *March* 1913

Your letter was an elixir, your beautiful letter (and thank you for all its news), but everything works slowly on me now, I shall often re-read it; at present I go about, *à quelques exceptions près*, thoroughly depressed, somehow amazed that the new beginning, new as it is, fits on to the old end so exactly; one and a half years of absence have deposited themselves on it only like the thinnest glaze.

What, what must be done to me if I am to feel it? Duino, Venice, Toledo which snatched at my heart-strings so violently, all have gone, like an interruption, like an hour of deep sleep in the open. God knows — it may be the force with which Paris has again received me, taken possession of me, sucked me into the centre of her being; although sad, although confused, although utterly unenviable I sometimes feel as I walk a smile on my face, a reflection of this large open air, — bright, bright I am, no different from the house that shimmers at the end of the street, while the saddest things may be happening in it unobserved. What reality is in this city, ever and again I gape at it, pain is there, misery, horror, each like a bush, and blossoms. And every stone in the pavement is more familiar than a pillow elsewhere, is stone through and through, hard to the touch, yet as if stemmed from that stone which Jacob laid under his head. *La mort du pauvre qui expire, la tête sur une de ces pierres, est peut-être douce quand-même.*

You ask about Marthe : I have seen her twice already, as a matter of fact, the first time all night. It was mi-carême, two days after my arrival I drove out to Sceaux, Frau W. had gone away so I went into the park and knocked at the studio of the Russian. He appeared at the door himself, a little, fair, Christlike peasant, surrounded by the vague, huge proportions of his darkening studio ; we did not know each other, I told him my name, a clear smile fought its way through his face, he called my name breathlessly into the air as a bird calls its being, a tall curtain on the right was seized from behind and impetuously flung aside, Marthe rushed out, leaning forward like a deer, a gold ribbon round her temples, in a strange tanagra-like robe, — but absolutely swallowed up in the enormousness of her eyes. It appeared that she wanted to go to Paris and dance ; the whole day she had done nothing but wash, comb and dress herself, and all the time, she said, having a premonition that it was not for the ball only, for much more. The night was sad, I took her to Bullier's, we missed the last train to Sceaux, my flat was not yet in order, so we drifted round the streets till morning and in inhospitable cabarets, in a ghastly neighbourhood (my clumsiness in not knowing anything better !). She had insisted on going barefoot in her sandals, so as to be truly Greek : this gave her a touching, improbable look (rather like that of a beggar in heaven) ; at Bullier's and in the street where she trotted with odd little steps on the coloured snow of whirling confetti, wrapped and draped in her tunic, people stared at her puzzled and embarrassed, je dirais même avec une espèce de respect timide. Tellement elle était autre que tout ce monde à l'amusement entêté et facile. Parmi toutes ces filles plus ou moin scabreuses elle avait l'air d'une petite mourante qui sera une Sainte quelques années après sa mort. On la prenait comme une petite femme, à peine osait-on l'engager, elle était comme tombée d'un nid très haut et qu'elle ne retrouvera jamais. Elle ne s'inquiétait pas beaucoup de danser si peu, elle n'avait que le besoin de parler et celui de manger infiniment. Elle avait faim, elle mangeait avec peine et effort, avec désespoir, comme un revenant qui se matérialise. Et en même temps elle voulait quitter ce monde pour entrer complètement dans mes yeux et dans mes oreilles ; elle se penchait sur moi comme une petite fille sur un lac, désireuse d'y trouver son image même au risque de s'y noyer. Elle parlait beaucoup de sa vie, de sa vie tellement provisoire, tellement incompréhensible et qu'aucun événement ne vient avancer. Elle vit auprès de ce Russe comme une sœur, dit-elle, soulagée immensément de ne pas l'aimer, car " la femme qui l'aimerait il la traînerait par les cheveux ". C'est un sauvage, un Mordvin[e], un Sibérien, bon et terrible, et qui rend définitivement malheureuses les personnes qu'il aime. La langue mordvine, sa langue à lui, ne possède que quelques mots pour les objets les plus élémentaires, parlant quelque peu le russe, il s'est créé depuis qu'il a dû quitter son pays pour des raisons politiques, un mélange de son idiome et de l'italien (ayant vécu quelques années à Milan), langue de fantaisie, dont Marthe semble très au courant. Son atelier vaste, dont une partie sert de dortoir, est d'un désordre tel que, sans doute, on l'appellerait un paysage si par hasard cela se trouvait en plein-air. On dort sur des grabats parmi un tas de choses éparpillées là et oubliées. — Marthe, toute fière, m'a montré des bulbes d'hyacinthe qui ont commencé de pousser parmi les couvertures à la chaleur innocente de ses pauvre pieds. Pour le moment, le Russe a quelques amateurs qui s'intéressent à ses travaux (je me souviens d'avoir vu un Christ à la Croix, gigantesque, exprimant avec ce trouble musical que les Slaves introduisent dans la sculpture, l'agonie finale), — il a quelque argent, mais sa bonté et sa négligence font disparaître les deniers avec une rapidité d'eau qui coule, — les jours et les nuits, on les emploie sans organisation aucune, on dort de temps en temps, on mange rarement, seulement lui fume toujours, depuis qu'il vit a l'étranger en exil, — par nostalgie. Marthe tout en profitant de cette irrégularité qui doit lui sembler presque idéale, s'aperçoit tout de même qu'il est difficile de marcher dans la vase de la liberté. Je crois qu'elle souffre beaucoup, qu'elle se consume, aussi m'a-t-elle dit qu'elle ne voudrait plus accompagner le Russe, s'il va maintenant en Italie comme il se le propose. Elle ne voit aucune existence pour soi-même, pour le moment elle se promène sur le dos des vaches. Ayant travaillé depuis sa quatrième année, faisant toutes les petites besognes qui tombent entre les fentes des métiers, elle ne se voit plus de travail à entamer et tous les chemins lui semblent fermés par l'ombre épaisse du " patron " qu'il faut traverser les yeux fermés si on veut arriver à des emplois profitants et durables.

And I, you understand, Princess, I don't know what to advise, can only let things take their course and go there from time to time; I am neither the wise counsellor who can help with his resource, nor the lover gripped by the inspiration of his heart. I am no lover at all, it touches me only from the outside, perhaps because no one has ever really shaken me to the depths, perhaps because I do not love my Mother. Poor as poor I stand before this rich little creature in whom a person with a nature less cautious and imperilled than mine has been of recent years could have blossomed forth and found boundless delight. All love is an effort for me, an outlay, *surmenage*, only for God have I any facility, for to love God means to enter, to walk, to stand, to rest and everywhere be in the love of God. . . .

113. *To Gertrud Ouckama Knoop*

HOTEL MARIENBAD, MUNICH
7 September 1913

LIEBE GNÄDIGE FRAU,—Last night I was on my way to Munich, and my thought was always this: will my friend Knoop be there? And now that I have arrived, with a certain uneasy haste quite foreign to me I open the paper and read with my first glance the grave, the immeasurably negative answer to the question that has been engaging me during the night. And read it time and again and have difficulty in understanding and can hardly write to you with any ordered words. So he is not here, the good, true friend, scrupulous in his love, in his feeling, in his wishes, is no longer with you and the children, has been taken away from all his likings, taken away from his work.

And yet even now, even in this first overwhelming sense of anguish, I feel, how shall I say it, that his seclusion has only been augmented a little, that the change which withdraws him from us was carefully provided for in that quiet, smooth-running spirit of his: us it drives back, but him it will have received gently, full of friendship for the heart that had read so deep, that in his last years had powerfully, fearlessly and with the modest pride peculiar to him, pored over Life and Death equally. He probed into the one as into the other, his experiences turned nowhere back, did not grow afraid, listened at no doors, everywhere went forward gentle and erect like ministering sisters accustomed to action where others only complain. When I saw him a year ago, so rich, so simple, as ready for joy as for the most painful knowledge, he gave me the impression of a hero, a hero such as men can be today, absorbed in the most steadfast action, serene, accomplishing his triumphs in the deepest and most hidden part of him, — and for a whole multitudinous year it attended me helpfully: to have seen him so. That he was good to me and took a clear-sighted interest in my work I count among the few successes I would like to have had.

To you and the children I would not venture at this moment to write a word of comfort, — I myself have the comfort of feeling how in us, in his work and life, he has raised himself to true permanence, to the most incontestable Being.—Ever, Your Rilke.

115. *To Lou Andreas-Salomé*

Paris, 17 rue Campagne-Première
21 *October* 1913

Dear Lou,—I cannot be entirely unhappy with all the bonds of sympathy which, you have made me feel, reach so far above us and so deeply below us, — and in my heart of hearts I am as happy as I can be. You have shewn me that somehow I am still the same, the same in a more strengthened way, that none of my old advantages has actually been laid waste or lost, perhaps they are really all there only I don't know how to use them at present.

This time Paris was just as I had expected: difficult. And I myself appear like a photographic plate that has been exposed too long, for I still remain "exposed" to this violent influence. My room was full of the past June, threatening, waiting for me to live to the end all the things I had begun in it. Last Sunday in terror I went straight to Rouen. It takes a whole cathedral to drown my misery. The French provinces always have a soothing effect on me; there are so many old houses in which, as I pass, I play at being at home in thought, and if I look, most of them in actual fact are to be let.

Would you believe that the glance of a woman passing in a quiet street in Rouen moved me so much that I could see practically nothing afterwards, had no mind for anything? Then gradually the marvellous cathedral was there, the legends of its crowded windows where earthly happening grows translucent and you can see the blood of its colours.

I think I can only stay in Paris if I pretend I am entirely without responsibilities, have come for a few days just to take events as they befall. . . . If only I can succeed in keeping hid as much as possible, so that I can get accustomed to myself again in the good old sense: contented. Doing a little reading, resting, looking out of the window, I would be content with everything if only it were wholly mine, without overflowing into longing. I am terrified when I think how I have lived beyond myself, as though ever standing at a telescope, ascribing to every passing woman a serenity that could never be found with any of them: *my* serenity, the serenity, long ago, of my loneliest hours. I have to think so much of the poem from the *Neue Gedichte* which, I believe, is called *Der Fremde* — how well I knew the essence of the matter:

> To leave all this behind without desire . . .

I, who do nothing else but desire. — Start afresh. Of course, even in the school-books it helped to turn to a new page; this page, Paris, is full of the most humiliating mistakes, scored over and over with red, and what with all my chopping and changing the finally corrected answer now stands on a spot that is nearly rubbed through, on the merest skin of a hole.

Dear Lou, somehow you have helped me infinitely, the rest is now for me and the angel, if only we cling together, he and I, and you from afar. . . .—RAINER.

120. *To the Princess Marie von Thurn und Taxis-Hohenlohe*

PARIS, *December* 27, 1913

It will sound odd, but all the same I cry: do not come, Princess, do not come, and it is not the jealousy of the Giocondo lady that makes me cry like this (I don't want to see her at all); but I have taken an oath to see no one, not to open my mouth except inwardly; if you came I should either have to observe this condition I have imposed, which would be absurd — or if I abandon it I am afraid, Princess, that I would immediately start travelling again or would speak to other people once I allowed myself a single nice exception. I am in the chrysalis stage, dear friend, threads of gossamer blow about in my room what with all the stuff I spin out of myself day and night, entangling me so that I am no longer recognisable. Please, please wait for the coming butterfly — you saw in the autumn, in Berlin, how bilious and frightful the caterpillar was, an abomination. If no butterfly comes in the end — well and good, I shall stay put in this squalor and dream quietly to myself of the sumptuous robe of grief I once had the prospect of becoming. If I do not fly out somebody else will, God only wishes that flying should be done; as to who does it he has only a passing interest.

Laugh at me, Princess, or scold me. Do both, I am an outrageous bird, there I sit on my pole, moulting and shabby, the feathers fly into my own beak, and this brazen beak shrieks at you: don't come, don't come! — for a New Year's greeting. Of course a little vanity is also playing its part, vanity at being seen like this by you. . . .

Dear Princess, I have here a newspaper page with a repulsive illustration, it is the only thing I have seen of Schrenck-Notzing's[1] and, in very truth, it is disgusting enough. I have not had his book sent me, my dealer told me about it as soon as it appeared, I considered it, but this is not the right sort of thing for me. (You can imagine what *is* right.) I am willing to give ear to any spirit if it has to expand and needs to break into my life, for then it will have something sensible to say of which neither of us need be ashamed; but to scatter this ghost-bait about so

[1] A spiritist. Cf. letter to Nora Purtscher-Wydenbruck, August 11, 1924.

that a rabble of God knows what outcast and excommunicated spirits may creep up and, like the wild men dragged over from Africa, make an exhibition of their customs and mysteries which belong to no conceivable world — that is tasteless and sullies both This Side and That Side with its sediment. . . . No, despite all the protestations of the clairvoyante, I do not like this business and shall take care not to lead my little waters into those dubious canals where they would stagnate into a swamp and where bubbles and will-o'-the-wisps play in the foul air.

But you, Princess, are immune, for you *know* something of these things, are not dependent on your feelings and would not let yourself be duped by any spirit, because you know the spirits from the inside and can judge just how much more helpless and limited a spirit must be that tries to approach us from without. I can well imagine how remarkable it was for you when you went to see Prince Schrenck ; formerly at least he must have been a not insignificant figure. Though the least experience of one's own, if one *must* experiment, would be infinitely more helpful, I should think, than this frenetic hodge-podge of sensations.

Is Kassner with you now ? Give him all my fondest greetings.

I see nobody, it has been freezing, there was ice, it rains, it pours — such is the winter here, always three days of each. I am sick to death of Paris, it is a place of damnation, I have always known it, but formerly the pains of the damned were explained to me by an angel ; now that I have to explain them myself I find no commendable interpretation and am in danger of making my once great conception mean and petty. If God has any understanding he will let me find a couple of rooms in the country soon where I can rage on my own and where the Elegies can howl at the moon from all sides, to their heart's content. Added to this, the possibility of my going long solitary walks, not to speak of the person who, sister-like ! ! ! (oh, oh) will keep house and have no love at all or so much that she demands nothing except to be there, active and sheltering, on the borders of the Invisible. Herewith the quintessence of my wishes for 1914, 15, 16, 17, and so on.

But for you, dear Princess, and for the Prince I have a special corner ready in my heart, — may Heaven dispose of whatever wishes are there.—Absolutely, Your D. S.

131. *To Lou Andreas-Salomé*

PARIS, 17 RUE CAMPAGNE-PREMIÈRE
20 February 1914

DEAR LOU,—I have just read your three *Letters*[1] with great avidity, I had no idea one could say *so* much, and yet it is only the first tiny beginnings of real utterance. Many things pass through the soul as one reads — could I have understood it, as you now present it to Reinhold, had I been his age ? Does he only understand it because he grew up in these days and not then, — above all, you yourself would not have been able to say it then either : thus we are just as we are, and our own childhood seems more puzzling to us for having been surpassed. . . .

In place of anything coherent I shall only write down one or two notes just as they came to me during my reading, all pointing beyond the edge of the *Letters* at us, at me.

I understood, more beautifully than had ever been shewn to me before, how the evolving creature is translated out of the world further and further into the inner world. Hence the delightful position of the bird on this inward journey : her nest is practically an external womb granted to her by Nature, a womb which she only furnishes and covers up instead of containing entire in herself. Thus she is the one creature to have a very special feeling of trust in the external world, as though she knew herself to be in harmony with its most intimate secrets. That is why she sings in it as if singing in her own inwardness, that is why we receive a bird-note so easily into our depths, we seem to be transposing it without residue into our feelings, for a moment it turns our whole world into an interior landscape, because we feel the bird does not distinguish between her heart and the world's. — On the one hand animals and humans gain greatly by the relegation of the maturing being into a womb :

[1] *Three Letters to a Boy* (1918).

for the womb becomes more world the more the world outside forfeits its share in the process (just as the world, being deprived of this share, has become more insecure), — on the other hand (you will remember the question in my diary, written last year in Spain) : " *Whence comes the passionate inwardness*[1] *of the rest of Creation ?* " From the fact of *not* having matured in the body, which means that the non-viviparous creatures never really leave the protecting body at all. (Enjoy lifelong environment of womb.[2])

[1] *Innigkeit.*

[2] This conception should be of interest to the psychoanalytically-minded, who will doubtless be able to find references for it in the works of Freud. The sudden break of the young mammalian creature from the parent body, the forlorn sense of responsibility that ensues, and the consequent desire to return even in adult life to the womb, or at least to create in the external world a set of circumstances comparable to the womblike shelter and security — all these ideas are elaborated in the Eighth Elegy, which is dedicated to Kassner. Contrasted with this desperate and nostalgic clinging of the human animal, either in mind or in actual fact, to the " Mother " in the widest sense, *i.e.* the " Mater ", the materia or material, is the enviable state of the bird which, having been born already in the little external world of the egg and merely hatched out into the bigger external world, has never really left the mater-materia-matrix at all, or only far back in its evolutionary history, as a germ-cell.

Among the many speculations that crowd into the mind perhaps the most significant in this connection is the fancy that the whole endeavour of man, even in quite normal man, is to get back to these womb conditions. Some sort of mater(ia) he must and will have : many find it mainly in the live warmth of marriage, in which state responsibility is at least shared by the partner, — others in work. Rilke certainly regarded his work as an all-environing, all-nourishing circumstance ; he was as dependent upon it for his physical and psychological well-being as a child upon its mother. Hence, in all probability, his constant terror of his work being invaded and disrupted by the outer world, and the spiritual disasters that overtook him whenever (as during the war) no work was vouchsafed him.

See also the Eighth Elegy :

" Yet deep within the warm and watchful beast
is weight and care of some great melancholy.
For to the beast as well is wont to cling
what often overwhelms us — Memory :
as though that goal to which we strive was once
nearer and truer and in tenderest
communion with our blood. Here all is distance,
there it was breath. For after that first home
the second seems a hybrid thing and windy.
O rapture of the *little* creature, which
stays ever in the womb that brought it forth ;

Very beautiful is the passage about the " two secrets " : the secret for the sake of what is within and the secret that excludes what is without.

What the plant-world demonstrates so beautifully — that it makes no secret of its secrets as though knowing they would always be safeguarded — is exactly what I felt when standing before the sculptures in Egypt, and what I have always felt since then with all things Egyptian : this laying bare of the secret that is a secret through and through, on every spot, so that there is no need to hide it. And perhaps everything phallic (as I intuited in the temple of Karnak, I could not *think* it even now) is only an exposure of the human " private-secret " in the sense of the " open-secret " of Nature. I cannot bring to mind the smile of the Egyptian gods without the word " pollen " occurring to me. . . .

135. *To Lou Andreas-Salomé*

PARIS, 17 RUE CAMPAGNE-PREMIÈRE
8 *June* 1914

DEAR LOU,—Here I am again after a long, broad and heavy time, a time that has lapsed past me like a sort of future, not lived strongly and reverently but tormented to the very end until it perished (a feat no one will succeed in imitating very easily). If ever I could plead during these last years that certain attempts to obtain a human and natural foothold in life were dashed because the people concerned did not understand me, because they heaped violence, injustice and injury upon me, one after another, and made me so discomfited — now, after these months

---

bliss of the gnat which still, even in marriage,
interiorly leaps : for womb is all.
And see the half-assurance of the bird
which almost, by its ancestry, knows both ;
as though it were some old Etruscan soul
fleeing the space in which is housed the dead,
his resting figure wrought into a lid.
And how dismayed is that which has to fly
whose origin is womb ! As though its own
self were aghast it flashes through the air
as when a crack goes through a cup. So rips
the bat-trace through the porcelain of evening."

of suffering, I stand condemned in an altogether different sense : being forced to see this time that no one can help me, no one ; and if any came with the justest, the most forthright heart and proved his worth to the very stars and sustained me even where I made myself never so heavy and stiff, and if he bore himself purely and unswervingly towards me even where I shattered his ray of love ten times over with the murk and opacity of my underwater world — I would still (I know this now) find a way to strip him of the abundance of his ever-renewed, ever-resurging help, to shut him up in a region of suffocating lovelessness so that his support, unavailing, would grow overripe on his own self and wither and hideously mortify.

Dear Lou, for a month I have been alone and this is my first attempt to regain consciousness — you see what a plight I am in. In the end something will have been learnt, — at present of course I realise only this : that once more I was not proportioned to a task that was pure and joyous, a task in which Life again stepped up to me, guilelessly, forgivingly, as though it had not had any ill experience of me at all. Now it is clear that this time too I have muffed my exam and that I make no progress and must still sit for another year in the same agonising class and day after day, right from the beginning, be given those same words on the blackboard whose accents I thought I had learnt from the very bottom of my heart.

What eventually befell so completely to my misfortune began with many, many letters, light, beautiful letters which ran trippingly off my heart ; I can hardly remember ever having written such letters before. In these (as I understood more and more) a spontaneous vivacity welled up as though I had struck a new, brimming ebullience in my own being which now, unloosed in an inexhaustible spate of communication, poured itself forth over this happy gradient whilst I, writing day and night, felt its joyful streaming and at the same time the mysterious repose which seemed naturally prepared for it in the recipient. To keep this communication pure and limpid and to feel or think nothing that could be excluded by it : this suddenly, without my knowing how, became the law and measure of my doing, — and if ever a spiritually turbid person can become pure again, I was that person in those letters. The daily round and my relation to it became, in some indescribable manner, sacred and responsible, — and from then on a powerful confidence seized hold of me, as though an alternative to my sluggish drifting had at last been found in some fate-like permanence. How much, from that date, I was involved in changes I could also note from the fact that even the Past, whenever I spoke of it, surprised me by the way it rose up ; if, for instance, it was a question of times I had often talked of earlier, the emphasis fell on otherwise unnoticed or barely known places, — and each assumed a pure visibility innocent as a landscape, was there, enriched me, belonged to me, — so that I seemed for the first time to be the owner of my life, not through the appropriating, exploiting and understanding of the Past by analysis, but just because of that new truthfulness which flooded through my memories.

9 June 1914

I am sending you these pages I wrote yesterday : you will understand that what I there describe is now long overpassed and gone from me ; three months of (undone) reality have laid something akin to a stout plate of cold glass on top of it, beneath which everything is as unpossessible as in a museum show-case. The glass reflects, and I see nothing in it but my face, the old, aforetime face which you know so well.

And now ? — After a fruitless attempt to live in Italy I have turned back here (a fortnight ago today) with the wish to plunge head-first into some kind of work ; but I am still so dull and numb that I can do little more than sleep. If I had a friend I would beseech him to work a few hours with me every day, no matter what it was. And when, in between, I think with heavy heart of the future, I like best to imagine some work that is disciplined from the outside and is removed as far as possible from productivity. For I no longer doubt that I am ill, and my illness has infected everything about me and now lurks in what I used to call my work, so that for the present there is no refuge in it. . . .

137. *To Lou Andreas-Salomé*

PARIS, 20 *June* 1914

Lou, dear, here is a strange poem written this morning, I am sending it at once because I involuntarily called it *Wendung* [*Turning*], and because it represents the turning that *must* come if I am to live, and you will understand how it is meant. . . .

TURNING

" The road from passion to greatness lies through sacrifice."—KASSNER.

For long he triumphed through looking.
Stars fell to their knees
under his wrestling gaze,

or he gazed kneeling,
and the scent of his instancy
made weary a thing divine,
that it smiled at him, sleeping.

So gazed he at towers that they
were afraid :
building them up again, suddenly, all in a flash !
Yet how often the landscape,
day-burdened,
sank down to rest in his tranquil perceiving, at evening.

Beasts stepped with assurance
into his open vision and grazed there,
and the imprisoned lions
stared in as though into incomprehensible freedom ;
birds flew straight through him,
the ensouled. Flowers
looked back at him greatly,
as though into children.

And the rumour that a Seer was there
touched the less
fallibly visible beings,
touched the women.

Gazing how long ?
How long already fervently fasting,
imploring deep down in the gaze ?
When he, the expectant, sat amid strangeness,

the inn's ungathered, averted room
sullen about him, and in the shunned mirror
again the room,
and later, from the agony-bed,
again :
then in the air,
impalpably in the air
was discussion
concerning his palpable heart,
concerning his still, through the painfully smothered body,
yet palpable heart,
discussion and judgement :
that love was not in him.
(And refused him further ordainment.)

For behold, to gazing there is a bourn,
and the more gazed-upon world
fain would flourish in love.
Work of the vision is done,
do now heart-work
at those images in you,
the imprisoned. For you vanquished them,
but now you know of them not.
Behold, inner man, your inner maiden,
this maiden attained
from a thousand natures, this
till now but attained, never
yet beloved creature.

142. *To Clara Rilke*

MUNICH, HOTEL MARIENBAD
21 *August* 1914

. . . Frau Stieve told me of your good, kind proposal that I should live in your flat : I would have accepted it gratefully had I been staying in Munich ; but before long I am going to the country (Irschenhausen, Post Ebenhausen, Pension Landhaus Schönblick, Isartalbahn). — Stauffenberg, with whom I am undergoing elaborate physical (*not* psychoanalytical) treatment, absolutely commands this, and so I shall try to gather a little strength before it is my turn to apply it to the heavy, the stupendous common task. During the first days I sent you a telegram from here but received reply by telegraph that you had gone away. So I did not write, also any voice for writing is quite crushed under these conditions ; may you both, you and Ruth, find a calm inner patience and confidence ; for the present I am endeavouring to work until it becomes clear where one is more needed and what demands the indecipherable future will make.—Your R. M.

COLLECTED LETTERS : 1914–1921

1. *To Thankmar Freiherr von Münchhausen*

Feast of the Assumption, 1914 [15 *August*]

MY DEAR THANKMAR,—Your Mother could have done me nothing more agreeable than send me this envelope in which I am now enclosing a hurried word of greeting, together with a few lines of poetry [1] from the first days of this tremendous August.

Through Hellingrath (who joins up tomorrow as a volunteer) I had already heard of the splendid chance you have of taking part in the action of this momentous year as a standard-bearer ; for no one is it more difficult than for him who stays behind inactive : will he ever understand the new time that is coming, that will be so different ?

Now your indecisions have been taken away from you by a decisive and universal fate — I can imagine that this must be an unforgettable joy, suddenly to be under *one* dominion and *one* feeling, especially after the time of many wills that has confused and wearied us so long.

In spirit and heart I am faithfully at your side, dear Thankmar.—Your RILKE.

4. *To Anna Freifrau von Münchhausen*

LANDHAUS SCHÖNBLICK, IRSCHENHAUSEN
29 *August* 1914

DEAR GOOD BARONESS,—Yesterday I had my first card from Thankmar, dated August 20 : it came via the Insel Verlag, consequently it took somewhat longer than usual. I saw from it that my letter from Munich had not yet reached him. Could I but send him something soon from a more uplifted heart, — he rides out so bold and gloriously young, it is indeed wonderful that this knightly fate should come unawares over a young man today.

[1] " *Fünf Gesänge, August 1914* ", *Collected Works*, vol. iii, pp. 389-97.

Gradually I am beginning to feel dismayed and resentful at having remained behind after so many departures : the first days swept my spirit along in the great universal current, — in its way it could play its part ; then my thoughts turned to myself, unutterably alone, to my old, unchanging heart (which I cannot give up), and now I find it very difficult, alone as I am, to attain the true and, somehow, if it be possible, the fruitful attitude towards our tremendous common fate. Happy are those who are in the thick of it, whom it sweeps away, whom it overwhelms.

Till now, despite the circumstances I have lived according to my plans : was in Munich undergoing medical treatment and consultation, came out here on Monday on the doctor's advice ; but this is now the most insufferable thing of all, to align yourself with your unconscious nature and thus get exemption. Even as I try it impatience and discontent grow in my breast and I shall not be able to endure it long. Probably I shall go back to Munich again, and after a while to friends in Bohemia : could I not make myself useful from there and leave " recovering " and " getting strong " till later, till we (when ?) are over the terrible mountains and are in the inscrutable future, which no one can imagine. . . .

9. *To Helene von Nostitz*

MUNICH, PENSION PFANNER, FINKENSTRASSE 2
21 *October* 1914

LIEBE GNÄDIGSTE FRAU,—When was it (I often ask myself) that I got Johannes Kalckreuth to point out your house — I can still see the quiet street it is in and the simple face it shewed from the garden, — when was it ? A few days afterwards fate broke loose from a darkened world—this universal din which has drowned our memories overnight and beyond which we may not yet think. Not even now, when so much dreadful execution and progress have been done on all sides. Who can tell what is really happening to us now and what sort of human beings the survivors of this year will prove to be ? To me it is an unutterable torment and for weeks I have understood and envied those who died earlier, so that they did not have to experience it from here; for somewhere in space there must be places from which this enormity appears only as Nature, as one of the rhythmic convulsions of a universe which is sure of its existence even when we perish. And of course we perish into it, into purest existence — this is why we have to contemplate the fullness of perishing and suddenly know about death, — perhaps this is what is meant by this terrible war, perhaps it is an experiment going on before some unguessed spectator, if it be conceivable that there are unerring eyes, the gazing, fathoming eyes of a discoverer who examines it like the hardest rock, and establishes the next degree of life's hardness underneath this seething Death.

Only now do I begin to ask with a certain longing about my friends: where are you, where is Herr von Nostitz, where is your Mother? Is there any prospect of receiving a little news from you? In truth I long greatly for some. . . . Your RILKE.

11. *To Karl and Elisabeth von der Heydt*

MUNICH, PENSION PFANNER, FINKENSTRASSE 2
6 November 1914

DEAR FRIENDS,—My Mother was on a visit here, — hence I could not thank you at once for your card à deux, which shewed me how actively and readily you are doing the hard and mighty will of the times, each one according to his powers.

You ask after me with touching concern. I will only tell you hurriedly that I left Paris on the 20th July, anticipating nothing; leaving behind me all my goods in the usual way, as I thought, for two months. These I have long since surrendered and abandoned to fate, for it is a fundamental trait of mine not to take possessions too literally. Of course two or three things, the daguerreotype of my father, an old ikon that had stood before me since childhood, certain letters and some few of my several hundred books that are irreplaceable, all these follow me in the distance and wave farewell, and I wave back to them. . . . But it will pass; individuals, as one may learn, are obviously not the point, though at the same time I see no sign of the fellowship that *ought* to be the point, probably there is no point at all, but fate is right, and behind fate the everlasting stars. All visible things have once more been cast into the seething abyss to be melted down. The Past is left behind, the Future trembles, the Present is without foundation, but the hearts, should not *they* possess the power to soar and hover among the great clouds? In the first days of August I was smitten by the phenomenon of War, of the War-God (in the Insel war-almanac you will find a couple of poems sprung from this experience), now the war has long grown invisible to me, a spectre of visitation, no more a god but a god's unchaining over the peoples. The only thing we can work for now is the survival of the soul; distress and disaster are perhaps no more prevalent than before, only more tangible, more active, more visible. For the misery in which mankind has lived daily since the beginning of time cannot really be increased by any contingency. But there may still be an increase in our understanding of the unspeakable misery of being human and perhaps all this is leading us towards it; so much calamity — as though new dawns were seeking distance and space for their unfolding.

. . . Give your wife my fondest messages, good friend, and greetings to all your house; I hope we shall see each other when the days pause for breath: perhaps we are all learners, and if we come through there will be heart-holidays as never before.—Your old friend, RILKE.

24. *To Thankmar Freiherr von Münchhausen*

For the time being (extremely provisional) WIDENMAYERSTRASSE 32/iii
28 *June* 1915

GOOD FRIEND,—It was wonderful to reach out for the card on which, at long last, I recognised your writing again! Thank God you are comparatively well, and that the not too insistent incursions of fate have brought you some rest and weeks together with your Mother, — they will have been good and productive for both of you in these times which, one thinks, exaggerate the good as well as the bad.

For anything as good as seeing people again must have a sweetness one never thought of ascribing to it before; this monstrous catastrophe creates a new range of feeling ; since it goes down so deep it mounts up higher, but is what one feels really *more* ? Or does one simply read life in terms of Fahrenheit instead of the usual Réaumur ?

People like us, dear friend, who have stayed non-combatants, have much time for doubting : probably always, we say, all suffering and all misery have been there to the utmost. Always the whole of misery has been in use among men, as much as there is, a constant, just as there is a constant of happiness ; only the distribution alters. Anyone who did not know that there is so much misery is liable to be shattered now. But who, if he were truly alive, did not know ? Wonderful, of course, is the evidence of such vast misery suffered, accepted and achieved on all sides, by everybody. Greatness comes to light, steadfastness, strength, a facing of life *quand-même*, — but how much in such conduct is stubbornness, desperation and (already !) habit ? And the fact that so much greatness is displayed and maintained can hardly lessen the pain of knowing that this chaos, this ineffectual blundering, the whole dreary human muddle of the trumped-up doom that has befallen us, in a word, this unmitigated catastrophe was actually *necessary* to extort proofs of courageousness, devotion and grandeur. Whereas *we*, the arts, the theatre, aroused nothing in these selfsame people, brought nothing to the top, could change nobody. What other avocation have we than the laying down of causes for change, true and broad and free ? Have we done this so badly, so half-heartedly, so unconvinced and so unconvincing ? For nearly a year this has been our question, our torment, — and our task : to do it more mightily, more inexorably. How ? !

Dear Thankmar, that's how it is with me, inside. Outwardly I am making ready to go to the country so soon as a little country-house can be found such as I seek (for myself alone) ; for the time being I sit in the flat of some acquaintances (who have gone to the country) with the loveliest of all Picassos (the *Saltimbanques*) in which there is so much of Paris that I sometimes forget.

Write to me again and give your good Mother all my devotion.—Your RILKE.

26. *To the Princess Marie von Thurn und Taxis-Hohenlohe*

MUNICH, WIDENMAYERSTRASSE 32/iii
9 July 1915

MY DEAR PRINCESS,—Nearly a month since your last letter! Thank God, I said, thought, felt at the news of Duino and still did not dare to say Thank God out loud, for so long as there is destruction in the world who may breathe, who may hold anything safe, spared, saved? In personal matters as in universal it is a surrender, a sacrifice of all possessions, but to what end? If only there *were* an end, if only this question did not arise, who would not cast himself away and all that he had, did he but understand, did he but guess that some pure essence of survival needed this foothold in order to mount up the higher? —We, some of us, have long felt continuities which have nothing in common with the wasting of history; even beyond this disaster the Past and the Future will still communicate, but we, hemmed in between yesterday and tomorrow, shall we ever again be caught up innocently, quietly, serenely, in the swing of the great affinities? Or shall we remain below affrighted, with the brand-mark of an age upon our shoulders, knowers of unforgettable details, guilty alike of the great and the merely terrible, consumed by this suffering and achievement and endurance: shall we not later also, and for always, as now we are learning to do, postpone all knowledge, deem humanity's plight inextricable, history a primordial forest whose bottom we never reach because it stands finally, layer upon layer, on piles of wreckage, a mirage on the back of ruination? . . .

28. *To Elsa Bruckmann*

WIDENMAYERSTRASSE 32/iii
13 *July* 1915

VEREHRTE FREUNDIN,—After a few days of quietness a curious impulse has suddenly come to me: to give a public reading from the *Stundenbuch*. When I read it to myself it sustained and exalted me in such a remarkable way that I thought, if only I could express it movingly and convincingly, it would surely have a similar effect on others.

You once proposed a reading of the *Cornet*, perhaps you will think over the matter of the *Stundenbuch* and tell me whether an evening like this — soon — (the sooner, the better) could be arranged under the auspices of the "War Aid Society" (and to its benefit, of course). In Ludwigstrasse or at Steinicke's? It would suit me best to find myself facing not merely a knowledgeable and aesthetically minded *group*, but ordinary human beings, hence a cheap admission fee and a discreet, but none the less informative advertising of the project would be desirable. The audience, however, not above 200 if possible.

Are you in the country? In town? I suppose now one thing, now another; if you are here we could talk it over, but it must be soon, for I may be going away before long into the country or further off.—With a hand-kiss for the good Princess and greetings to Herr Bruckmann, Always yours sincerely, RILKE.

29. *To Elsa Bruckmann*

WIDENMAYERSTRASSE 32/iii
19 *July* 1915

LIEBE, VEREHRTE FREUNDIN,—Since our conversation by telephone I have realised more and more completely that I have roused your good enthusiasm with the most irresponsible haste: we must give up the reading we planned or at least postpone it until after the summer; as yet I am not capable of it. I told you how the impulse arose, in an hour when I found myself reading the *Stundenbuch*, but this impulse, as immediate as it was unforeseen, cannot be transplanted or gathered together for a definite evening, at least not as I see things at present. What I had invoked with this reading was the crowd *in myself*, and it is before this crowd and no other that I shall have to act and take my stand for a long time to come. I only became aware of this gradually during the last few days, when I realised that I could scarcely read even the third part of the *Stundenbuch* before a public gathering without letting myself in for a number of prefatory explanations concerning the inner reasons for this lecture. Cogitating just *how* this foreword would have to be framed, I set in motion such a mass of untouched and hitherto unexamined ideas and feelings that I saw at once that the planning of these words would necessitate a terrific rearrangement and re-clearing of ground in myself, a process so arduous and multiform that I could only venture to undertake it independently of all aims and objectives. Assuming, however, that it could be done, all in the space of this week, and that I could cast some part of the results into this address, this in turn would grow into something quite other than an apologia for the *Stundenbuch*, and although it would not have the presumption to attack the present state of things it would nevertheless give rise to such unqualified disagreements, one after another, that it would have little prospect of not offending the censor ; and to say anything that was toned down to suit the censor would be painful to me, just as it would, on the other hand, hardly be in keeping with my nature to pander to any spirit of reaction. For when I proceed from my innermost and most central convictions I see myself in no way called upon to express motives of this kind unless they be an integral part of my hardest production, where, if God wills it, they are removed from all the censors in the world and are of so mysterious an influence that no hand can restrain their working. Till then and to that extent I am (as is once more clear to me) committed to that positive silence which for many months has been my own, and my most personal, affair. It was more than a caprice that caused me to disquieten you, it was a strong wish to have a share, momentarily at least, in other people and their lot ; but on closer inspection I must hold wishes of this kind to be not genuinely mine. Forgive me if I do not come tomorrow to the War Aid, you want to leave town and I should only detain you pointlessly and furthermore I myself am going to the country (if the weather's good). I should prefer to come and see you in Starnberg one day soon.—Best wishes to you and yours, Your RILKE.

31. *To the Princess Marie von Thurn und Taxis-Hohenlohe*

MUNICH, WIDENMAYERSTRASSE 32/iii
2 *August* 1915

DEAR PRINCESS,—How should I not always be at your side with all my heart, when it is so natural to me to share your sufferings and your hopes? I do not understand this present hell, but I do understand how you bear it and struggle through with it, — there are few constants in human life, how many people have become different, incomprehensible — have taken on the colour of an age which itself could not say whether it had a colour or not, I believe it is being played out in a hitherto undiscovered part of the spectrum, in an ultra-red that goes clean beyond our senses.

I was just thinking of Count Wallis when your letter arrived; he must be one of the people who have surrendered nothing, whose good sense, however individual, this madness, general as it is, seems unable to confound. I should like to have a talk with him. — Ah, and sit with you, Princess; if I did not have an indefinable fear of crossing "frontiers" I should probably have emerged in the Victorgasse by now.

Munich is getting empty, I suppose it has almost its usual summer appearance; outwardly I enjoy the most regular days imaginable, but inwardly there is an abyss, one lives on the edge of it, and down below there lie, smashed perhaps, who knows? — the things of one's former life. Was it this, I ask myself a hundred times, was it this that lay on top of us all these years like an immense weight, this frightful future which now constitutes our hideous present? I have to think how one day I said to Marthe: "*Marthe, il n'y aura devant moi que des désastres, des terreurs, des angoisses indicibles: c'est avec vous que finissent les bontés de ma vie*" — this burst forth as though a gale had wrenched it out of me in the middle of a lull, I listened as I heard myself saying it, I was only thinking of my own crumbling fortune and did not guess that the whole world would bring forth ruin. And Marthe made an unforgettable gesture of taking me into protection. Only now do I see that this was precisely how the few mighty old men went about, Tolstoi and Cézanne, emitting warnings and threats, like the prophets of an ancient order that would soon be broken, — and they did not wish to experience the break. Whatever comes, the worst is that a certain innocence of life in which we grew up will never again be there for any of us. The years ahead, however many they are, what else will they be but a descent with trembling knees from this mountain of pain, up which we are being dragged further and further. . . .

32. *To the Princess Marie von Thurn und Taxis-Hohenlohe*

MUNICH, WIDENMAYERSTRASSE 32/iii, [1915]

DEAR, GOOD PRINCESS,—The last two batches of news (letter and card) are still unacknowledged, and yet each time I snatch everything that comes from you with the greatest need. Your letters belong to the very few things that mean a continuity of past and future, I stretch myself across them, as it were, — if only I knew to what end ! The fact that I have not written lies with the blankness and listlessness of my nature from which I can wrest nothing unless it be worry or complaints, and how should I come to you with those ! Neither is there any sense in coming to you with joy over the safety of Duino so far, for . . . There will only be sense in our joy and hope and suffering when we have to do with more understandable, more human things again. Ah, Princess, a few years earlier and I might perhaps have called up in my heart — it was not so decayed then — elements which might have endured even such a time as this, a *Stundenbuch* attitude which might have had the power to equate the utterly incomprehensible with what, in its essence, transcends all understanding ; for what more do I seek than that one point in which, as in the Old Testament, the terrible merges with the greatest, — and to declare it now : it would have been like the lifting up of a monstrance over all those who have fallen and risen again and yet again. For although no one likes to admit it out loud, consolations are needed, the great inexhaustible consolations whose possibility I have often felt in the depths of my heart, almost startled at holding them, the boundless, in so restricted a vessel. Certain it is that the divinest comfort is lodged in humanity itself, for we could do but little with a God's comforting; but our eyes would have to be a shade more seeing, our ears more receptive, our tongues savour more completely the taste of a fruit, we would need to have a more vigorous sense of smell and to be more present in spirit when we touch and are touched and less forgetful, if we were to extract from our most immediate experiences those consolations which are more compelling, more overmastering, and more true than all the suffering that can ever shake us. . . . We live amid the most tremendous currents, often I have to turn round, asking myself what powers are even now passing behind us towards their work, each one to its work, and the path of so many of them leads straight through the centre of the heart (*qui n'est pas une auberge, mais un fameux carrefour quand-même*). Dear Princess, what abuses have I wreaked on this heart of mine that it does not now bear witness to our powers of comforting! For years past I have spoken accusingly of this heart to you, reviling it, degrading it to the least among us, — but still too kindly, still too hopefully. Could I say of it that it overflows with bitterness, that it is stiff with pain, but no, it is as though its contents had simply been battered into a formless mass, and thus I carry it about with me. The alternative is to call it sick, and some days I am really nothing but that, sick, a little thing enough, and I imagine that the good Stauffenberg could have changed it; for that was why I came here. A year ago, — *this* year ago! You can see, dear Princess, I am unbearable today, I wish we were sitting in your boudoir in Duino or hiding in the chapel where I once read to you from my pocket-book, for to bewail by mouth is always more considerate, but to bewail on paper is cowardly, I know — and yet . . .

Princess, like everybody else I have been puzzling my head on the quiet about our common future, the future of all of us, wondering whether I am dependent on fewer premises than the man in the street, for history is dark to me, also I suspect that it is not history that can be known and from which we can draw deductions, but an odd assortment of accidents and laws in which we recognise ourselves, because the continual interplay of both is the most familiar feeling we have. But now it is suddenly, breathlessly autumn, at least here ; from unfamiliar windows I see the tree-dotted banks of the Isar turning yellow, and beneath the cold rain the yellows deepen, not in turn but all together ; suddenly the penultimate tones are there, then comes the shedding of leaves. With rainy nights and winter outside the door, — with these the world-wide misery grows into something of my very own, into bewilderment about my tomorrow and the day after, — whither, whither ? A year in Munich has gone, I have not made much of it. On the contrary, I seem to have retrogressed in every respect, how shall I do better now ? My heart is so inhospitable that I cannot undertake to lead you around in it, indeed it is probably blocked and inaccessible, — *restons dehors*. My entire knowledge is confined to the extremely negative realisation that I ought not remain in Munich any longer, the people here make too many demands, you must be " finished " or pretend to be, — *et moi, si j'ai encore quelque avenir, ce sera en recommençant humblement que j'y parviendrai*, for anything in my books that might (to a certain extent) be regarded as finished is also finished and done with for me ; I stand there like a beginner, like one, naturally, who doesn't begin. Well then, begin, — but how ? !

My position has, so to speak, been clarified by my learning yesterday that all my property in Paris, that is, roughly everything I possessed, has really been lost : the entire contents of my flat were auctioned in April ! You know that I do not take this hard, I have long been disposed to regard all the things that have congregated round me for the last twelve years in Paris, as the effects of the late Malte Laurids Brigge, and it may be that with these things that knew of him, and the books and the few heirlooms, my obsession with this figure has been taken away from me, though I was absolutely determined, in the end, to avert my eyes from him. And yet, dear friend, to you I may confess it, ever since this news from Paris I have been wandering about with a queer feeling, rather like someone who has had a fall, has got up painlessly and who cannot somehow rid himself of the suspicion that an after-pain will suddenly break out in his bowels and cause him to scream. In a general way I had long given up everything and schooled myself to test out my renunciation on the few objects that I valued most, — it worked ; but now I see they were nevertheless always there ; now that I know everything has gone a strange fear stirs in me, that it might be possible suddenly to be seized by the memory of a lost object that is absolutely indispensable, a little sheet of paper perhaps, a picture, a letter in one of the hundred bundles of letters, how do I know what, — that some little thing you loved might be missed, something that was bound to the core of your being by a light, fine thread, now broken. . . . Ah, Princess, how strange, how unforeseeable is the pattern of experience, I am only writing this down because it surprises me and makes me feel something I could never have invented or ascribed to anybody. I am detached enough now to suppose that this curious sensation will quickly be overcome, in reality it has been overcome already since I am giving an account of it here. Probably it would not have appeared at all had my belongings been actually annihilated, for with annihilation we have the profoundest and most absolute affinities, but there is something particularly rueful about losing one's possessions, no matter how peculiar they are, to other people, to strangers. I am quite unable to imagine what happens in such a case to a box full of letters and papers ?

Dear Princess, once again my heart has tumbled out, *voyez quels débris*, — perhaps I shall go to a small university, perhaps to Berlin, perhaps to Janovič and Sidie Nadherny ; it is so difficult to decide because it is, I know, a question of winning an *inner* resting-place ; only, an impressionable person like me takes it for granted that the right conditions outside will help the inner ones. *Je suis un enfant qui ne voudrait autour que des enfances toujours plus adultes.*—A thousand greetings to your family, Always, Your D. S.

33. *To Fräulein A. Baumgarten*

MUNICH, WIDENMAYERSTRASSE 32/iii
22 *August* 1915

LIEBES GNÄDIGES FRÄULEIN,—As large time-gaps are customary between us it will not surprise you if I answer your letter of the

26th April so late. My lateness is not to be construed in the sense of my feeling this token of your continuing sympathy any the less — on the contrary. A real good was thereby vouchsafed me, and we do not have to give each other any special assurances at this juncture of how high the value of the good now stands.

You can, if you remember the young person whom you once met, easily imagine that the homeless and in a sense ageing soul he has become cannot find his way in this forsworn, crumbling and self-lacerating world! The state of mind he would have to regain is so deep, so fundamental; he would have to get back to himself again through all the length and breadth of his childhood; everything he ever was would have to be there in him; in some unparalleled sense he would have to take possession of his entire heart, — if he were not to notice the losses, if he were to have that place in himself which is also a world-place and not a spot hedged round by a hundred limitations. Certain prisoners known to history managed, in times of complete and utter privation, to win their own souls in the depths of their being, and inexhaustible freedom, — could one but succeed in that now! But to win a consciousness so great our present isolation is not prison enough; even for one who has no part in it, it is too immediately fateful, too uncertain and chaotic, shot through with too much pain and hope, too full of forebodings, too agitated and too unhappy. And although you admit all this, almost you want to complain that it is not enough so. What a conspiracy of silence there is in the cities, how much of the worst sort of distraction, what hypocrisy in our ordinary everyday living, abetted by a money-grubbing literature and an execrable theatre and fawned on by a loathsome press, which certainly is much to blame for this war and still more to blame for the trickery and lies and treachery that turn this monstrous event into a sickness, whereas it might have been a pure frenzy. But premature, false, malicious and completely irresponsible reports and vile propaganda have so often in this last year been the undoubted cause of actual happenings, lies by the hundred have bred facts by the thousand, and now all the splendour, the sacrifice, the determination that ceaselessly unfold have been sucked into the welter of misery and deception, swallowed up in the " task " of this war, which is supposed to bring profit — glory ? Oh no, all such notions have become meaningless under the abuse of the papers, — the world has fallen into the hands of men.

What am I thinking of, writing to you like this, perhaps bursting in upon quiet summer days ! Probably what I once told you in the mailcoach was just as inconsiderate, only then I had the excuse of extreme youth, whereas now this outburst depends solely on the indulgence which you may perhaps concede to one who is more lonely than ever before. Indeed I hope so. And thank you as—Your ever devoted R. M. RILKE.

34. *To Ellen Delp*

MUNICH, 22 *August* 1915

. . . What excellent words you have found for the fate of the lighthouse birds — final ones. This is how it should be seen, in the sense of life ; and yet I, I who have so often penetrated into the *reverse* side of this sense, the side turned away from life, cannot get over the fact that an error in perception can bring about such rapture and such ruin merely because of the existence of something that belongs to the human world, that would not exist at all in the world of these birds, ought not to exist — for to their senses it is an exaggeration, a sort of music ; actually it destroys them because it does not exist for them (rather as a ghost would destroy *us*). And then, what is life doing when a misapprehension has the power to call forth Reality from rapture, ecstasy and death, — is life making a mistake ? And further, the most terrible thought for me : all the dramas that are enacted before our eyes may produce, in the invisible realms between man and man, in their hearts, in their spirits, in those soaring domains that make up the essence of our experience, even *there* they may continually produce, out of the subtlest misunderstandings, the most profound destruction and reeling ecstasies ; for we also, in our innermost immanent hearts, may not become aware of the truth at all, but only of that which does not belong to us, of that which *ought not* to be there, of those lighthouses that send out signs beyond us, do not mean us, do not know us, are nothing but the incomprehensible overflows of some power contained in us like a question-mark, which consumes us by the force of its crushing answer. But of course I know that if one thinks far enough, the Divine itself is only thinkable outside our boundaries, as just such a lighthouse in a space that is more than ours ; so that it may only be a matter of waiting for the greatest, the most transcendent of all possible misunderstandings in order to perish, jubilantly, in that flame which is the most inconceivable and the deadliest of all, and in no less. Is this life ?—Your grateful and devoted RAINER.

35. *To Ellen Delp*

WIDENMAYERSTRASSE 32/iii
10 *October* 1915

DEAR ELLEN,—I have a period of not very fruitful planning behind me which I pursued with a remarkable lack of faith ; this has now become understandable since I have heard that a further section of my class has been called up. In consequence I shall, for the time, be spared all arbitrary intentions, for as I am now in the lists it is best for me to wait here and submit to the next disagreeable decision. But in this way time again becomes explicitly a time of waiting ; nothing is more agonising to me.

I must leave these rooms tomorrow as the owner is coming back from the country, and with them the marvellous big Picasso with which I have now lived for nearly four months. Four months — what times have passed and what with them ? For me, they pass with increasingly melancholy insight into the universal distress and dementia in which everything drives relentlessly forward, human strength and human life (whose purpose cannot be put into words), being squandered on blatant and distorted slogans. What chaos there will be afterwards, when all our credulously accepted ideas are cast down from the pedestals upon which we displayed them, and the bewildered survivors want to link up again with the abandoned laws of their inner being. Can no one prevent it and stop it ? Why are there not two, three, five, ten people who would stand together and cry out in the market-places: Enough! and be shot down and at least have given their lives for it to be enough, whereas those out at the front only perish so that the horror shall go on and on and there be no end to the perishing. Why is there not one person who *will* bear it no longer, who refuses to bear it, — if he cried for but a single night in the midst of the false beflagged city, cried and would not let himself be silenced, who would dare call him a liar? How many of us hold this cry back with an effort, or don't they? If I am wrong and there are not many who would cry so, then I do not understand human beings and am not one myself and have nothing in common with them.

Forgive me, Ellen, but I have been feeling like this for nearly a year, I let fly at you like this because you are a girl and in harmony with the great things and because your heart is full of balance after your rides through the golden translucence of autumn and far into its new distances . . . so you can bear it if one's bitterest heart overflows.

I have lost not only Paris, I have lost all my things there, all my possessions which were for the greater part inner ones, — at the instance of the proprietor they auctioned them all in April, not out of malice, he merely wanted to collect his rent, for no one could assure him that I still existed and would pay. I do not complain, for who may complain now, when losses are the least of our ills, over a loss of property, — but it cannot be denied me to remark with pain, even from this incident, the worthlessness into which the present time has plunged our closest realities.—May you keep well, even now, in this inhospitable autumn! Affectionately, RAINER.

36. *To Ellen Delp*

MUNICH, KEFERSTRASSE 11
27 October 1915

Had you not, Ellen, happy Ellen, made your way so surely and triumphantly through the almost impassable present, I would have reproached myself for having brought this boundless catastrophe so powerfully and insistently before you in my last letter. But I feel it has not harmed you, since you have come out again on innocent ground " through the thick of it " (as you say), into deep and eternal Nature, in which your being has its harmony.

Would this way have been possible for me too ? I push on, but I still hold back too much, the Nature that lies ahead does not lure me enough, — " Season, Tree and Beast ", these no longer have that immediate magic over me which once, like a pure call to happiness, had dominion over my heart however beset it was. " Work in accordance with Nature " has made all existence into a *task* for me, to such an extent that it is only very seldom, as if inadvertently, that a thing addresses me fruitfully and yieldingly without there being evoked an equivalent and powerful demand in myself. The Spanish landscape (the last that I was to experience absolutely), Toledo, carried this attitude of mine to its extreme limits : for there the outward things themselves — tower, mountain, bridge — instantly possessed the unparalleled, unsurpassable intensity of the inner equivalents through which one would have wished to portray them. Appearance and vision everywhere merged in the object, in each a whole interior world was revealed, as though an angel who encompassed all space were blind and gazing into himself. This, a world no longer seen from the standpoint of people, but *in* the angel, is perhaps my real task, at least all my previous endeavours would be united in it : but in order to start this task, Ellen, how sheltered and resolute one would have to be !—RAINER.

38. *To L. H.*

MUNICH, KEFERSTRASSE 11
8 *November* 1915

Your letter gives openings in so many directions, almost every sentence provokes ten letters in return — not because one would have to set answers against all the questions it asks (and what in it is not question ?) — rather because they are all questions which have always been countered with more questions or have, at best, grown more transparent under the influence of others which shed their own illumination about them ; they constitute a great dynasty of questions — and who has ever answered them? What is expressed, what is suffered in *Malte Laurids Brigge* (forgive me if I mention this book again, as that is what has started us off) is ultimately nothing but this question asked right from the beginning and with all the means available and in the light of all the evidence: how is it possible to live when the fundamentals of this our life are so completely incomprehensible? When we are always inadequate in love, wavering in our determination and impotent in the face of death, how is it possible to exist? In this book, written under the profoundest inner compulsion, I have not managed to conquer my amazement over the fact that for thousands of years humanity has been concerning itself with life and death (not to speak of God) and yet, even today (and for how much longer?) stands in front of these primary, these immediate tasks (strictly speaking the *only* ones we have — for what else have we to do?) so helplessly, so pitiably, caught between terror and evasion like the veriest beginners. Is it not incredible? My amazement over this fact whenever I give way to it drives me into the greatest confusion and then into a sort of horror; but behind the horror there is something else, something so immediate and yet transcending all immediacy, something so intense that I cannot decide with my feelings whether it be like fire or ice.

Once, years ago, I tried to tell someone whom this book had frightened how I myself sometimes regarded it as a negative, as an empty form, the hollows and depressions of which were all pain, despair and saddest insight but whose cast, were it possible to produce one (like the positive figure obtained with bronzes) might perhaps be happiness, the most definite and certain serenity. Who knows, I ask myself, whether we do not always emerge as it were at the back of the gods, separated from the sublime radiance of their faces by nothing save their own selves, quite close to the expression for which we yearn but standing exactly behind it? Yet what else does this mean except that our face and the face of the gods look out in the same direction and are at one; how then should we approach the gods from the front?

Does it confuse you that I say God and the gods and juggle with these propositions (just as one does with ghosts) for the sake of comprehensiveness, thinking that some image must form in your mind too? But take anything supernatural. Let us agree that since the dawn of time man has fashioned gods in whom only the deadly, the threatening, the annihilating and the terrible elements of life were contained, its power, its fury, its daemonic possessiveness, — all amassed in one dense, malevolent concentration — something alien to us, if you will, yet at the same time permitting us to recognise it, to suffer it, even to acknowledge it for the sake of a certain mysterious kinship and involvement with it: this also was part of us, only we did not know how to cope with this side of our experience; it was too massive, too dangerous, too multitudinous, it piled up over our heads into a superabundance of meaning; it was impossible, what with the many demands of a life contrived for use and action, always to take account of these unwieldy and imponderable factors, and so mankind agreed to extrude them. But since these factors were an overflow, were Power, were indeed *too* powerful, the violent, inconceivable, tremendous life-forces — how could they fail, concentrated in one spot, to exert an influence and have ascendancy over us? And, what is more, from without. Could not the history of God be treated as a completely unexplored tract of the human soul, one that has always been stored and saved up, only to be neglected in the end, one for which time, will and address had been there but which, relegated to an external plane, gradually charged itself with such a tension that the impulse of the individual heart, continually dissipated by petty usage, was absolutely powerless against it?

And so, you see, the same thing happened with Death. Experienced and yet not to be apprehended by us in his reality, always overshadowing yet never quite acknowledged by us, violating and surpassing the meaning of life from the very beginning, he too was banished and excommunicated so that he should not continually interrupt us in our search for this meaning. He, who is probably so close to us that the distance between him and the inner centre of our hearts cannot be registered, he was made into something external, something to be held daily at a greater distance, something that lurks in the outer voids ready to pounce this man or the next with his baneful choice. More and more the suspicion grew up against him that he was the antithesis, the opponent, the invisible opposite in the air; the end of all our joys, the perilous glass of our happiness from which we may be spilled at any moment. . . . Nature, however, knew nothing of this banishment which we have somehow managed to accomplish — when a tree blossoms, death blooms in it as well as life; every field is full of Death, who reaps a rich harvest of expression from its prone countenance, and the animals pass patiently from one to the other; all round us Death is at home, he peers out at us from the cracks of things, and the rusty nail that sticks up out of a plank does nothing but rejoice over him day and night.

And love too, which bedevils our arithmetic so as to introduce a game of Near and Far, — in which we always shew ourselves so far, indeed, from one another that it seems as if the universe were crowded and ourselves alone full of space — love too has no regard for our divisions but sweeps us, trembling as we are, into an infinite consciousness of the whole. Lovers do not live from any sundering of the Actual; as though a partition had never taken place they break into the boundless capital of their hearts; of them one can say that God is nourishing to them and that death does not harm them: *for they are full of death because they are full of life.*

But this is not the place to speak of our experiences; they are secret, not a secret that locks itself up, not one that demands to be kept hidden, it is a secret that is sure of itself, that stands open like a temple whose portals exult in being portals and whose towering pillars sing that they are the gateway.

All the same (and it is here that I come back to your letter at last) what are we to do to prepare ourselves properly for the experiences which affect us in our human relationships, in our work, in our sufferings and for which we dare not be imprecise, because they are so precise that in them we meet ourselves in antithesis, never anything fortuitous. You have discovered several paths of learning for yourself and one can feel that you have pursued them attentively and thoughtfully. Thus the shocks of which you write have shaken you more closely together and not overwhelmed you — and I would like, so far as I can, to strengthen your absorption in death from the biological side (by drawing your attention to Wilhelm Fliess[1] and his very remarkable researches : I am sending you a little book by him in the next few days) as well as by directing you to one or two significant human personalities who have meditated very purely, quietly and augustly on the phenomenon of death. Tolstoi, first of all.

There is a story by him called *The Death of Ivan Ilych* ; the evening your letter came I felt a very powerful desire to read those extraordinary pages again. This I did ; and because I was thinking of you I almost read them out loud to you . . . Can you get hold of the book ? I could wish that much of Tolstoi were accessible to you — the two volumes containing *The Cossacks*, *Polikuschka*, *Three Deaths*. His enormous experience of Nature (I know of hardly anyone who was initiated so passionately into Nature) put him wonderfully in a position to think and write from a total standpoint, from a life-sense through which death was so finely diffused that it seemed to be contained everywhere for him, like some rare and characteristic seasoning to the pungent savour of life. But it was precisely because of this that he knew such a profound and helpless fear when he realised that somewhere death in the pure state existed, — as it were a flask full of death, or this hateful cup with the broken handle and the insensate legend " Faith, Hope and Charity ",[2] from which we are compelled to drink of the bitterness of undiluted death. This man had observed in himself and others many forms of the death-fear, for his natural self-possession enabled him to be the observer of his own terrors, and his relationship to death was such that his fear must have been marvellously permeated in the end, a regular fugue of fear, a gigantic building, a tower of fear with corridors and stairways and landings without banisters and vertiginous drops on either

[1] *Vom Leben und vom Tode* ; biological disquisitions.

[2] See *Der Tod*, Coll. Works, vol. iii. p. 413. The reference in both cases is to a vision which Rilke had about this time in the Englischer Garten in Munich. This death-cup, he said, suddenly appeared to him standing on the back of his hand.

hand — yet the intensity with which he still felt and admitted this prodigal fear of his may in the last moment — who knows ? — have turned into some unapproachable reality, may suddenly have become the solid ground beneath this tower, the landscape and the sky overhead and the wind and the birds wheeling round it. . . .

40. *To Anna Freifrau von Münchhausen*

MUNICH, KEFERSTRASSE 11
15 *February* 1916

MEINE GUTE GNÄDIGSTE BARONIN,—Since December in Vienna, since the beginning of January when I joined up, I have been and am reft away from everything mine, smothered under the landslide of the universal cataclysm.

I have now succeeded in getting sent here " officially " for four days, in the uniform of a militiaman, which I now am. All my mail has been reposing on my writing-desk for two months, great piles of it : your letter underneath (whose enclosure I am now returning), two letters from Thankmar, one of the 17th December, one of the 7th January ; but even if they had reached me I could not have spoken.

I have done three weeks of barrack and field training ; now I sit, idly for the moment, in the War Department and, I fear, am not finding it any easier, spiritually, to do what is expected of me there than I did, physically, before. But it must be done with patience, forgetting as much as possible all that one is. When will one be oneself again ? And finally, who ?

I am going back to Vienna today and shall write to Thankmar from there ; here also several people who think fondly of him wanted to write to him again.

When the spring comes, when other and succeeding times come, surely they must bring some future at last into our unending and incomprehensible present.—Kissing your hand, dear Baroness, I remain in devoted friendship, Your RILKE.

42. *To Hugo von Hofmannsthal*

VIENNA 13, HIETZING, HOPFNERS PARK-HOTEL
28 *March* 1916

MY DEAR HOFMANNSTHAL,—You cannot know (or do you feel it ?) how much, even that same afternoon, I reproached myself for having expatiated to you on Saturday about my affairs, mostly about antiquated ones which ought to be completely forgotten, — this self-abandon really demands a special apology. But so often during the past months I have wished and imagined a talk with you, feeling that nobody could understand my position more rightly than yourself, — with the result that my mouth overflowed unrestrainedly at long last.

Not to continue this outpouring, on the contrary, to take away the last afterthought of it, I shall now tell you what happened yesterday. As I see it the most important thing is that Lt.-Col. V. sent for me, asked about my affairs and finally instructed me to send the decree issued by the Munich General Command — which arrived late — to the War Department Archives. It would have been called in already had they only known where to ask for it. Once the document was there he could then see what could be done with it, and he hopes to get me quite free by its means. So from this side it is certain that everything possible will be done. This solicitude of my superiors is extraordinary, and obviously I can no longer complain about remaining inactive here, since it is only an express part of the general move to get me eliminated from the whole apparatus to the point of complete extrusion.

So I would beg you, dear Hofmannsthal, not to alarm yourself about me and to say nothing to anybody of my complaints, for what with these extremely well-meaning efforts I must admit that my position is endurable, no worse than any other time of waiting. Naturally I still do not give myself any too absolute assurances, — who knows how far the powers of the Munich dispensation extend ? — but if the directorate of the War Department does not succeed in its purpose, one can rest assured that nobody could have succeeded in doing anything.

However burdensome I may have made myself the other day for *me* the hours with you were extraordinarily pleasant, forming a happy link with those first distant hours of long ago. Everything went wonderfully well and I think of your Picasso with admiration.

Nothing from Kassner yet? To your wife and to you, dear Hofmannsthal, the very heartiest greetings and thanks (in haste at my work-table).—Your RILKE.

46. *To the Countess Aline Dietrichstein*

MUNICH, KEFERSTRASSE 11
12 *September* 1916

. . . Today I am sending you the little edition of Jacobsen's *Six Tales*, because the hurrying autumn may perhaps bring an evening when this echoing prose has just the right voice; the edition, outwardly bad, deserves indulgence in so far as the translation given in it, the oldest, by the deceased Maria von Borch, has not been rivalled by any later one. You will soon see that the parable you are already familiar with can be read more rapturously here; but now let the first thing I recommend to you be *Frau Fönss*, for me it is the most haunting tale of this inexhaustible book.

You surprise me when you say that you have already begun the *Intérieurs* of Maria Grubbe. One should know Danish to feel the sheer force of the language: Jacobsen, by imitating the style of the 17th century, not only recreated the spirit of the times, he also evolved an individual medium for portraying life altogether more forcibly and sensuously. But is not the most marvellous thing about him perhaps this: that the more he advances in clarity, colour, and density the more he gains in gentleness and tenderness too? The figure of Maria Grubbe will naturally have remained strange to you: your own direction and aspiration have too much of an *upward* tendency for you to accompany a life with such a contrary movement. Here a descending, yes, a falling fate is depicted, the fall of a woman's heart, abandoning itself simply to its own weight, — only after all these years do I understand with what purity this plunging curve is drawn against the dense and massy arabesques of history.

Ah, dear Countess, this profound innocence of the human heart which enables it even in its irresistible downfall, even on the road to perdition, to describe a pure line : — for me this will be the one quality I shall steadfastly keep before me when the time for "making good" has at last come. For in this redemption the most active among us will be those who possess this inexhaustible innocency (women, girls . . .), and we others only in so far as we are capable of implicitly believing them. . . .

52. *To Imma Freiin von Ehrenfels*

MUNICH, KEFERSTRASSE 11, VILLA ALBERTI
20 *February* 1917

DEAR BARONESS IMMA,—Ever since it was there, that devastating certainty, I have had a daily impulse to write to you, and every day I have failed ; for how ill-proportioned every ministering word must seem to you. Today I have at last wrung a few lines to Frau von Hellingrath out of my stony inner silence, and now I will at least come to you with the assurance that I am thinking of you and that this profound shock has brought me as near to you as you may deem possible for a person whom you have not often seen.

I knew Norbert so well and had such an affection and regard for him that I can feel something of your condition by reason of my own. Your lot is at once harder and more creative than that of mother or sister. These may find rest from the burden of grief in long memories of what has been and deeds done ; but of you, who seem robbed of all promise and of all future, it is demanded that you should hold yourself in perpetual sublimation ; yet by those very means you become capable of turning your grief — how inadequate is the name ! — into a pure experience of the spirit, and thus you may enter into that vanished future as though into a great and immeasurable legacy.

It is in the nature of all ultimate love sooner or later to reach the beloved only in the infinite. May your deep spiritual communion with Norbert, and your youth, help you to see in your fate not a denial of the past but always only this extreme, this greatest, this inexhaustible task.

The only thing for which I have words is to beg you, Baroness Imma, in hallowed remembrance to let the bond continue between us in the years to come.—Your devoted R. M. R.

58. *To the Countess Aline Dietrichstein*

CHIEMSEE, HERRENINSEL
26 June 1917

MY DEAR COUNTESS ALINE,—It's just like it was in Munich — there are always too many acquaintances who draw me into conversation ; now, with my inner tension so diminished, there is hardly enough for writing — to the same degree that I have to be communicative in personal intercourse my writing capacity decreases : this only by way of explanation why I have not written you more promptly. I have thought of you a great deal, of this I may assure you, and have seen several delightful things as it were on your behalf, such as yesterday a squirrel which ran straight towards me down the garden path in the big castle terrace, right up to my feet, — there only did suspicion and bewilderment outweigh his curiosity and venturesomeness, he scuttled off across the lawn and made a wide circuit, and an extreme one at that, — not over level ground, but translating his fugitive arc high into the branches and leaping from tree to tree into the denser brushwood. Herewith I have mentioned the lovely terrace which is disposed in a gentle curve, like a veritable hanging garden, in front of the so-called " old castle ", formerly St. Augustine's Abbey ; three paths run parallel with its façade, raised up a little, and in between, lawns and bright-standing plane-trees ; the whole thing facing a square of limes — now a restaurant garden shut in by a thick curtain of beeches, so that you step through it as into a light hall under the plane-trees, there being no colour except vivid green and the grey and yellow spotted trunks of the planes, only along the edge of the castle a strip of begonias before a row of taller fuchsias : so here you have the terrace, and, from its outermost path, across the meadows lying beneath it, you look out over the lake, and in the lake are the two islands for which I found the right simile at the end of my last letter : oval-shaped they lie there, self-enclosed and wistful as medallions. You must picture the Fraueninsel much smaller than this one here with its regally tended woods ; and of the Herreninsel one would have to say that its tall trees have grown so huge from pride, perhaps not without defiance ; the sheltered life of the monks found its vindication in these beeches and ashes and pines and exalted itself vaingloriously and thrust up towards heaven, while the famous lime-trees (they are now in blossom) which stand over there on the convent meadow, they grew so great from centuries of tranquillity and devotion. The Herreninsel is a single wooded park, now entirely open to the public ; the Fraueninsel, still conventual today, even now holds a world of privacy within its many walls and inaccessible places, into whose pure, sunny ordering a trellis-gate sometimes hesitantly vouchsafes you the privileged peep. What, apart from this, makes up the outdoor population of the island, is small guilds of artisans, fishermen, carpenters, locksmiths and gardeners who have always been associated with the nunnery ; these, with their flower-thronged little gardens and inquisitively windowed houses, form a candid worldliness which, through the medium of Nature herself, passes over imperceptibly into the discreet and mysterious domain of the nuns. The transition is formed by the flowery churchyard, laid out to the right and left of the path ; behind the hedge there is a gently sloping field once, but no longer, used for graves, on the highest point of which the age-old clock-tower has remained, standing alone — between it and the church an ancient elder-tree pours over in flower. With this tower, as soon as you see it, you know that the little island together with all the fervour of its heart is bound to the past ; the tower marks the dates and again effaces them, because ever since it has been standing it has chimed out Time and Fate over the lake, as though comprehending in itself the visible portions of all the lives that have here been surrendered, and evermore discharging their transitoriness into space, invisibly, in the sonorous mutations of sound. The quintessence of innumerable lives has vanished in this ringing and crumbles away inside the church in the drifting voices of ever other women who, from the choir of nuns, lift up their chant towards the altars and pillars and apses. Sometimes you think, sitting alone in the church at evening, when the twilight, raying in through the two rustic lattice-windows of the hindmost chapel, lingers there as though in a drawing-room, you think that from so many perished voices some visible thing must once again beat down ; but if you then pass along the side aisle and enter the adjacent chapels, it is just light enough for you to discern here and there the figure of an abbess in the inscribed frame of some commemorative tablet, ever and anon a single austere woman who bears witness in her figure and in her robes to the fact that she has succeeded in becoming the silent, sovereign representative of all those given over to her charge. Somewhere on the Tyrolese estates of the convent the red marble was quarried from which these tablets are fashioned, generally depicting the Abbess herself, surmounted by the luxuriant spirals of her tall sceptre, clad in her sealed, seignorial vestments which point down in parallel folds to where, at her feet, her illustrious coat of arms appears, carved by the side of the ancient cloistral shield — two crossed water-lily leaves in varied field. But even of the lady-regents of Frauenwörth, how little has their death allowed to survive in this form. Only a few of the more important stones, or those spared by accident, have been preserved, whereas tradition, harking back to the Carolingian Kings' daughters, numbers fifty-two abbesses. After a temporary eclipse of the convent in 1803 the renewed line continues, and just think, this delightfully secluded community of nuns has now (since 1913) been administered by a Freiin von Eichendorff, the Abbess Maria Placida, granddaughter of the poet.

Have I somehow managed to fill in the oval I shewed you, Countess Aline ? I doubt whether these individually observed details have managed to struggle through my lines into a real picture ; it is as though these anarchic times prevented me from effecting the proper synthesis in myself, — I note that even in my conversation and my thoughts I always get stuck in particularities. So be indulgent towards my not very able pen if these pages only help you to shorten an afternoon and to call up images and memories, and above all the promise of future travels and impressions. Yes, but now I ought not to leave you in a haze about the second medallion, the other island which I can see from my window and from the plane-tree terrace : this is the Island of Plants, since olden times a garden dependency of Fraueninsel, on which the monastery and the other inhabitants have continued to retain their old rights to garden and vegetable land. You can row over from here by boat in twenty minutes, but it is nicer to look across, specially in the evening, or when a storm wraps the two islands in darker contours.

I have now been here for a fortnight and must be back in Munich before the 1st, when the disbanding of my flat will make my days restless. There it will also be decided what sort of complexion my summer will have, whether I shall spend it in Munich, in temporary lodgings, or whether I can travel. As for your summer, the plans are sure to be firmly established ; whatever they are you will doubtless feel and experience the season profoundly, with the right of a convalescent.—Always with many wishes for your good, Your sincere and devoted RILKE.

69. *To Clara Rilke*

HOTEL ESPLANADE, BELLEVUESTRASSE
BERLIN W., 19 *November* 1917

MY DEAR CLARA,—Yesterday I wanted to write to you a little birthday letter when the news of Rodin's death reached me ; as you can imagine everything was subordinated to that. Now my greetings stand in front of this background which is, however, common to both of us, infinitely so, — like me, you will be in remembrance and mourning, and will have to bear this all too final bereavement along with Paris and all that has been lost. I do not know what Rodin's death would have meant to me in normal circumstances, — perhaps something reconcilable after all, — but now confusion prevails in me all the more because such an intimate affair as this has to run its course, immitigable and limitless, against the chaos of the times, and behind the unnatural and terrible ramparts of the war these familiar known figures sink away from us, who can tell where ? — Verhaeren, Rodin, — the great wise friends, their death becomes blurred and unrecognisable. . . . I feel only this : they will no longer be there when the dreadful fumes draw off, and will be powerless to succour those who have to rebuild the world and tend it again. Yesterday and today I received a couple of good warm-hearted letters about Rodin, — if only I could genuinely believe in the strength of human feeling amid this prevailing inhumanity. . . .

76. *To Bernhard v. d. Marwitz*

MUNICH, HOTEL CONTINENTAL
9 *March* 1918

MY DEAR HERR VON DER MARWITZ,—How many times in my life could I have responded fruitfully to a token of your affection ! But to let you have even the smallest share in my life now would mean casting you into a poverty so great that my faculties are quite unable to describe it. In the mighty and tremendous conditions of your present life the only thing that could make letters desirable is the certainty issuing from them that we at home have not forsworn our spiritual continuity. And it is precisely this for which I am unable to give the least proof. On the contrary, as for myself, circumstances in general and extreme personal difficulties have conspired to interrupt any sort of current in me and have separated me from the nourishment that, even in my most evil days, once used to rise up to me from unperturbed roots. The closer the calamity came the more I began to cast round for bearings in these disastrous times, but this very search made me more wretched than ever. For where can we find landmarks in this distracted world ? Loaded down as we are with the year-long consciousness of all the catastrophes that are being enacted in it, you would think that in the end we would be bound to reach a spot where people fell on their knees and shrieked, — this I could understand, I too would throw myself down and have my cry under the protection of theirs. What " doing your bit " in this visitation actually means, for us at home, is reading the newspapers, — letting yourself be stuffed full of the fictitious, bogus events that are amassed daily, so that in the end you can only conceive of pain and anxiety in the version which the papers impose upon everything. Frightful as the war itself is it seems still more terrible that its pressure has nowhere contrived to make man more recognisably human, to urge him towards God, either the individual or the mass, which was the genius of the great misfortunes of olden days. On the plane that has arisen meanwhile, the plane on which the papers present an unscrupulous cross-section of all these happenings (a hodge-podge of exaggerations and conjectures rubbing shoulders with actualities, commercial news with the most imponderable factors) — on this plane all tensions are perpetually levelled down and humanity is all the while being dragooned into accepting a world of news instead of realities, which nobody has time or leisure to leave alone to grow great and heavy in their season.

I have never been and cannot now be a newspaper reader. Today I enquired of a friend whether he could furnish me with a quiet room in the country where I need see no one and speak with no one, — conditions which have often proved favourable for my spirit and my work. I am afraid of becoming ill in the absence of such a change for solitude and in the absence of a union with nature and the seasons. There may come a time when Friedersdorf or a forester's cottage in the neighbourhood might offer me a refuge of this kind ; I shall always need such a shelter now. But first I want to have been there with you.

You see, your letter has made itself felt in my heart ; may mine not wholly fail to do the same.—Your R. M. RILKE.

80. *To Joachim von Winterfeldt-Menkin*

MUNICH, AINMILLERSTRASSE 34/IV
16 *September* 1918

Again and again, my dear Herr von Winterfeldt, since the arrival of your letter, I have taken up my pen and tried and am not master of the words which the moment demands. What are they ? Have we not long ago expended those which used to meet the various dictates of mourning ? If we were to say anything more now we would have to break off a portion of our hearts, — it lies on the further side of exaggeration, beyond the utmost that was ever possible in words, and the superabundance of lamentation that would then burst forth presupposes in us, if it were to be proportionate, a spirit infinitely enlarged, such as cannot be developed in so turbulent and trammelled an age.

What am I to say: I know, I feel, you have lost a young friend, and all the incomparable treasures that are implicit in those two words. Among the thousands of young people who have offered up their lives in the heavy destiny of the war, Bernhard von Marwitz will remain, to those who have known him, one of the most unforgettable. The monument you raise to him in your heart is more than personally true: for the "youth" and "friendship" of this noble-minded and great-spirited young man had a more than personal meaning, they were in a sense the measure of that German Youth which, had it not been for the outbreak of these dread disturbances, would have founded our future in the large world of the spirit. The continuing evil of the war has called forth more and more rebellious voices, young people who think they can build the world more purely on a negation of the past. In Marwitz, on the contrary, tradition was operative and at the same time a complete readiness for responsible freedom: if any future is to be born of our German Youth it must rest on an ideal very closely akin to his own, which would characterise it. Thus the thought of his survival is, it seems to me, bound up with our deepest hopes of regeneration.

How much I regard myself as having suffered an indescribable loss you may discern from the fact that one of von Marwitz's magnificent letters (written on the 9th of August) has not only absorbed me continually for weeks, but bespeaks a human affection such as has not fallen to me from any other association. Ever since this letter came (which I, tired and inhibited as I was, put off answering until a more capable hour), I have felt the certainty of possessing in young Bernhard von der Marwitz a friend, an intimate friend, and I regarded this friendship as an untouched legacy whose future riches seemed all the more precious because men have so seldom essayed an intimate attachment with me. So the hopes that have been left unfulfilled on my hands are at least as numerous as your own broken and orphaned memories

— may this keep a lasting bond between us, my dear Herr von Winterfeldt. . . .

Had you not expressed the wish to grant me an advisory glance through your friend's posthumous writings, I would have made just this request : feeling that this mutual and almost unpractised friendship would entitle me to make amends, with gentle after-love, for any intimacy I had missed.

Now I am going to ask a real favour. If there is anyone in his immediate family (I fancy he spoke to me with particular attention of a sister) who stood close to him in genuine understanding, it would satisfy a deep longing in me to direct a few words of sympathy and sorrow to this person, and assure him of my devotion, understandable enough in one who has been left behind with his affection wholly unexpended. If you know of such a person and advise me to write, please tell me the name and address.

If we meet again, and I now desire it all the more ardently, I shall not be able to keep back a number of questions concerning his last days, just as I shall always be thankful for everything you may do to bind me to his memory, which I hold in honour and love.—I give you both my hands and am with all my heart, Your sincere R. M. Rilke.

82. *To Marie von Bunsen*

Munich, Ainmillerstrasse 34/iv
22 September 1918

Ah, in conversation I can still manage sometimes (though only, I fear, with the strength of my former self !) to be sociable and alive — but everything to do with writing is beyond me, — only thus could it have come about that I put off replying to your kind letter of the spring until now, the summer ; but the summer passed, it passed me completely, neither did it bring me the good hours in which I had hoped to write to you more fruitfully and, if possible, more joyfully. For plaintive and miserable words wrung from an arid soul are so manifestly the wrong ones with which to approach you, who have the secret of keeping a clear vision and finding a savour in life no matter how distorted and despoiled the world may be ; you who can understand history in that noble traditional sense in which even the present, be it never so irresponsible and impenetrable, will one day have to reveal itself in its true proportions.

Your last letter again gives proof of your clear-sightedness : still you hold the works of man dear, still you can trace in him some proven and indestructible order, still feel the brooding presence of castles and see in the simplest peasant house an achievement, a solution, a satisfying harmony from which a spirit of fellowship, from which *consolation* proceeds ! How lovelessly, lovelessly by contrast did I journey a few days ago through Ansbach. I looked, I remembered, I tried to marvel : but with all this evil confusion how sinister everything has become for me right back into my past ! Scarcely can I stand before old and beautiful things without being appalled by their forsaken look, by the abandon into which they have fallen, woefully persisting among these wide-eyed, gaping people who have placed beside some lovely, noble and prodigal thing not even a thing of use, no, a blatant emblem of their ill-usage and desecration, of their nonentity, their nothingness ! One thinks, does one not, I asked myself, that one is living in a world whose most precious heritages have for centuries passed through greedy fingers : for what gives every heritage its significance is something almost imperceptible ; it is like a zero mark, but when this vanishes off the scale the entire system loses its spiritual value, its diversity, its direction and tension and polarity. Isn't that so ? Surely something must have vanished, fallen away from the proportions of a door or window, from the sequence of a staircase, from the bend of a lattice, before such an unholy age as ours could have become possible ? . . .

I long for people through whom the Past with all its great lines remains wedded and related to us : for how very much at this juncture does the future, the more boldly and adventurously you think of it, once more depend on whether it falls in the direction of our deepest traditions and moves and radiates out from them (and not from negation). Two cherished young friends were snatched from me in August and September by the war, friends whom I lament infinitely in the interests of the hoped-for future, — young Keyserlingk and that rare and excellent young Marwitz of Friedersdorf, whom perhaps you also knew. I was on the point of gaining his love. . . . Losses, losses . . . if only every one of them were an inexorable pledge enjoining upon us a more serious, a more responsible life, more in touch with the mysteries !

Committing myself as always to your goodness of heart, your RILKE.

84. *To Clara Rilke*

MUNICH, AINMILLERSTRASSE 34/IV
7 November 1918

DEAR CLARA,—The great free breath of your letter (of 28th October) blew on ahead of events ; we in the city have now to put up with all these alarms and excursions and the many newspapers, the hundred and one loathsome rumours, — and at each pause in the march of what has at last come, one's heart stands still, as if the future, still struggling on foot through the tumult, might fall or turn back once more.

I was so taken up with looking and listening, nay, above all with *hoping*, that I failed to notice how long it must be since I wrote to you. Now, faced with your telegram, I reproach myself for having alarmed you by my silence : there was no reason for it.

Meanwhile I have had the picture-book of Old Munich sent to Ruth (it will probably have arrived by now), and I imagine you both looking through it on the family table by the evening lamp ; it is quite entertaining to envisage to oneself how countrified and Bavarian the city looked even eighty years ago, when it ended everywhere at its gates.

In the last few days Munich has given up something of its emptiness and quiet, the tensions of the moment make themselves felt even here, though they do not comport themselves in an exactly edifying manner among these " *boarisch* " temperaments. Everywhere huge gatherings in the beer-halls nearly every evening, speakers all over the place, among whom Professor Jaffé is obviously first-rate, and where the halls are not adequate, gatherings under the open sky in thousands. I also was one of the thousands on Monday evening in the rooms of the Hotel Wagner. Professor Max Weber of Heidelberg was speaking, a political economist considered to be one of the best heads, and a good orator, and after him, discussing the anarchy and the wearing strain, more students, fellows who had been four years at the front, — all of them so simple and frank and " of the people ". And although you sat round the beer-tables and between the tables in such a way that the waitresses could only eat through the dense human structure like weevils, — it was not in the least oppressive, not even for the breath ; the fog of beer and smoke and people did not strike you as uncomfortable, you barely noticed it, so important was it and so clear above everything else that things could be said whose turn had at last come, and that the simplest and truest of these things, in so far as they were presented more or less intelligibly, were seized upon by the immense crowd with heavy and massive applause. Suddenly a pale young worker rose up, spoke quite simply : " Have you or you or you, have any of you ", he said, " made the offer of an armistice ? And yet *we* are the people who ought to have done it, not these gentlemen at the top ; if we could get hold of a radio station and speak as common people to the common people over there, Peace would come at once." I cannot say it half as well as he did, but suddenly, when he had said this, a difficulty struck him, and with a touching gesture towards Weber, Quidde and the other professors standing on the stage beside him, he continued : " Here, these professor chaps, they can speak French, they'll help us to say it properly, as we mean it. . . ." Such moments are wonderful, there have been all too few of them here in Germany, where only intransigeance found words, or submission which in its way is only a participation in violence by the oppressed.

I have just seen Ramberg.[1] Just think, I may be able to go to Switzerland after all. I have announced in Zürich that I want to give a lecture on the 25th November, but have reserved the final decision. Now Ramberg tells me he can give me permission without further formalities. And I am thinking it over. Sidie

[1] Austro-Hungarian Consul.

has given me much encouragement and has invited me for as long as I want. I almost think I shall do it. Enclosed is a not too unpleasing letter from Grandmama Phia, — it says much for the Czechoslovaks that she feels herself more or less incorporated and secure in the new state.

Are you still in Fischerhude ? Ruth too ? Are the schools still closed ?—All the best, and love, RAINER-MARIA.

(Postscript, 7.11.18)

We have a remarkable night behind us. Here also a council of soldiers, peasants and workers has been set up with Kurt Eisner as the first President. The whole front page of the *Münchner Neueste* is given over to a decree issued by him, according to which the Bavarian Republic declares that Peace and Security are promised to the populace. A gathering on the Theresienwiese preceded the night's business, attended by 120,000 people. It only remains to be hoped that this extraordinary upheaval will give rise to reflection in people's heads and not a fatal intoxication once it is over. Up to now all seems quiet and you cannot do otherwise than admit that the times are right in trying to take big steps. . . .

87. *To the Headquarters of the North-eastern Provincial Government, Vienna*

MUNICH, 17 *Dec.* 1918

The undersigned begs to make known the following deposition : When in May of this year he learned through the papers that he had been awarded the Order of Merit it was his immediate resolve to decline it ; for it has always been his intention to refuse any decoration that might be offered him. At the time informed friends drew his attention to the fact that, as he still stood under the jurisdiction of the Army, he had no right to exercise such a refusal.

The official notification of the award of that distinction and the Order itself have only now reached the undersigned, at a time when he is free to act according to his convictions : may it be permitted to him therefore to return the Order together with all enclosures to the place of issue.

The undersigned would suffer from a sense of injustice were his action in this matter attributed to a lack of respect; his refusal rests solely on his desire to maintain that personal humility to which he is absolutely committed by his work as an artist.—R. M. Rilke.

94. (*Poem enclosed in a letter to Frau L. Tronier-Funder*, 1919)

O hard is the descent to God. But spend
not all your care upon your empty bowl:
if suddenly you play the woman's rôle
it brings contentment to him without end.

He is the water: fashion to the brim
the vessel purely from two outstretched hands
and kneel you down: then God, o'erflowing, stands
beyond your most embracing thought of him.

95. *To the Countess Stauffenberg*

Munich, Ainmillerstrasse 34/iv
23 *January* 1919

Verehrte gnädige Gräfin,—Ever since the last days of the year that has gone the *Insel Almanac* has been meant for you, now it is so late that it can no longer plead the New Year as an excuse for its arrival! I would scarcely have ventured to remind you of my existence in this impromptu fashion had not the choice of my contributions to the Almanac been determined by that hard event of long ago which I regard as having bound me to you.

The lovely poem by the Countess de Noailles, my own two little efforts, but particularly the page from a diary published under the title *Erlebnis* [*Experience*] [1] —each of these pieces embodies

[1] *Collected Works*, vol. iv. pp. 280–84. The prose passage given below was written later as a tailpiece and sent to Lou Andreas-Salomé (November 1925 ?).

in its own way an approach to the sense-frontiers of life, and they all strive towards that final equilibrium which we can only guess at and which I once found in its most perfect form in a fragment of ancient music. Romain Rolland, who played it to me, discovered it in a Gregorian Mass. As I heard and harkened to it again and again, I had the impression of two scales which, softly swinging, came to rest against one another. I described my feeling to Rolland and only then did he confess to me that it was an ancient epitaph in musical notation : the most startling corroboration of this being the fact that it could be apprehended and understood under so strange a simile.

What I call the *Erlebnis* befell me in exactly the same way, in the now ruined and blasted garden of Duino (near Trieste) ; a year after this remarkable occurrence, in Spain, I tried to make a record of the facts with the greatest possible acuity and precision, but in so doing the domain of words did not seem to be really sufficient. I know that I got stuck in my inadequacies — I even failed in the last analysis to make myself intelligible. Experiments of so extreme a nature may nevertheless have some claims to indulgence.

If in the general darkness and incertitude that have descended upon all things human and upon public life in particular I can still see one paramount task before me, independent of all else, it is this : to use the deepest joys and splendours of life to strengthen our trust in Death, and again to make him, who was never a stranger, more known and felt as the silent sharer in all life's processes.

Forgive this elaborate commentary and permit me, dear Countess, to commend myself to your goodwill and remembrance.—Your ever sincere R. M. R.

Extract from a Diary

"Later he thought he could remember certain moments in which the strength of *this* moment was infolded as in the seed. He brought to mind the hour in that other southern garden (Capri), when the call of a bird was simultaneously outside him and in the depth of his being, for, not breaking off, as it were, at his body's bounds, he was able to comprise both in a continuous space in which, mysteriously sheltered, there dwelt only a single area of the purest, profoundest consciousness. Then he closed his eyes lest he be beguiled in so lofty an experience by the contour of his body, and the Infinite passed into him from all sides so trustingly that he fancied he could feel the stars which had come out meanwhile, gently reposing in his breast.

It also recurred to him how much he had valued, leaning in like attitude against a fence, his awareness of the starry sky seen through the mild branches of an olive-tree ; how the universe confronted him like a face in this mask, or how, if he but suffered it long enough, everything dissolved so perfectly in the clear solvent of his heart that the savour of creation was in his being. He thought it possible that such ecstasies might be discerned far back into his heavy childhood : he need only be reminded of the passion that always seized him when he had to bare himself to the storm, when, striding across the great plains with heart exhilarated, he broke through the wall of wind that he everlastingly renewed, or when, standing at the prow of a ship, he let himself be borne blindly through the solid distances which closed up more firmly behind him. But if even then the elemental rush of air, the pure and multitudinous behaviour of water and the heroic procession of the clouds had moved him beyond all measure, or had actually (since he could never grasp them in human terms) borne down upon his soul like fate, — it could not now escape him that with his recent experiences he was finally delivered up to such kinships. Something gently separative maintained between him and people a pure, almost luminous interspace, and though single details might reach across, it nevertheless engulfed every relationship and, saturated with it, hid the figures from one another like a driving mist. He still did not know how far the others had any notion of his seclusion. As for himself, it lent him a certain unwonted freedom in his attitude towards people ; the first beginnings of poverty made him lighter and, among all these innumerably hoping and worrying creatures who were bound to one another in life and death, gave him a mobility of his own. He was still tempted to hold out his lightness to their loadedness, although he realised how much he would be deceiving them, since they could not know that he (unlike the hero) had attained to his kind of triumph not in the midst of their encumbrances, not in the heavy air of their hearts but outside, in a spaciousness so little adapted to humanity that they would not call it anything but the " void ". All he could turn to them with was, perhaps, his simplicity ; it was left him to speak to them of Joy when he found them too much ensnared in the counterparts of happiness, and also to disclose to them some aspects of his communion with Nature, things they had missed or had only noticed on the side."

101. *To Elisabeth von der Heydt*

MUNICH, AINMILLERSTRASSE 34/IV
March 20, 1919

. . . You won't have time to read letters. Just this quickly about Ruth. For two months she has been, so to speak, a peasant lass ; that was *her* conception of the revolution ; she longed to work, and only the most concrete thing would satisfy her. She started on the 15th January in the very coldest days, moved into a little maid's room up north, without a stove, begins her daily housework at six o'clock in all seriousness, and sinks into her crude, square peasant bed at half-past eight, dead tired. Dead tired and bursting with happiness. Never have I received more joyful letters from her. When after a few weeks I made another suggestion, she considered and then turned it down : for, she wrote, her pleasure lay in not doing school things any longer, but something quite real and full-size ; it was sheer bliss for her, she said, to be *needed* in that little place of hers, — and since there was not exactly a superfluity of happy people just now, she would insist all the more on having her own way. Could anything be better ? . . .—Your RILKE.

104. *To the Countess Aline Dietrichstein*

SOGLIO, SWITZERLAND
9 *August* 1919

MY DEAR COUNTESS ALINE,—You wrote to me on the 14th June, — three days previously I had gone to Switzerland — a long hoped-for and, when I had almost ceased to think of it, at long last completed project, in the midst of which I now stand. You can imagine how necessary it was for me to get away from Munich : in reality and in point of fact we did not have to suffer too badly, the newspapers exaggerated many things like all their kind, — but one's senses were aware of an indescribable and, worse still, ultimately futile tension on all hands. For behind so much upheaval, bombination and malicious muddle there was in the end absolutely no will for real change and regeneration, in which one would have been only too ready to cooperate and take one's part. From the outset the Man of the Spirit must needs be the opponent and controverter of all revolutions, it is precisely he who knows how slowly all changes of lasting significance reach maturity, how unprepossessing and how, just because of their slowness, well-nigh invisible they are, and how Nature, in her constructive activities, hardly anywhere brooks a spiritual violence. And yet on the other hand it is this same spiritual man who, by virtue of his insight, grows impatient when he sees the muddles and bungles which human affairs acquiesce in and lend themselves to : indeed we all experience continually how this and that, how practically everything could be altered from the very roots ; how Life, so rich, so gracious, and cruel only because it is inexhaustible, is in many cases quite incapable of asserting its true values nowadays, crushed as it is beneath a mass of irrelevant and antiquated superstructures : who then would not yearn for a great storm to tear down everything obstructive and decadent so as to make room again for the creative, infinitely youthful, infinitely benevolent powers ? There is no doubt that many such pure and vigorous impulses worked together at the dawn of the revolution, for it would have been the one conceivable counterbalance to that terrible war if a new and transvaluing sentiment had appeared in mankind, and prevailed here and there, at isolated points, in the shaken and bewildered world. For a moment one hoped. But the predominance of material ambitions and evil and vindictive secondary motives played havoc, even in the earliest hours, with this originally joyful, then desperate and at last completely senseless urge, which has now sucked many innocent people into its maw and practically *all* those who thought they were anticipating a noble though premature vision of humanity. Strictly speaking, anyone of clear spirit in this wild confusion, which was only darkened and deepened as the poisons of the war seeped back into the land, could be on *nobody's* side, neither with the unthinking insurrectionaries, nor with those who countered the often criminal outbreaks of madness with antiquated and no less unjust and inhuman measures. The future lay neither with the one nor with the other, and the spiritual man is now bound and sworn to it not in the sense of the revolutionary, who would presume to establish from one day to the next a liberated (what is Liberty ?) and happy (what is Happiness ?) humanity, but in that other patient sense in which he prepares those soft, mysterious, quivering transformations in people's hearts, changes from which alone can proceed the harmonies and unities of a clearer horizon. If you now, my dear Countess, measure by these thoughts the dismal and daily more hopeless events that have been brewing since November, and furthermore take into account with what lack of foresight and reflection, how *soullessly* they have been opposed, — you will understand how I have suffered. Not so much from privation and uncertainty as from disillusion and worry, which stretch far beyond one's own life and its realisations. But in the end I had to think of my own life again and of the tasks that are laid on it, although it has been staring at them for five years, frustrated and paralysed, without plucking up courage for its innermost achievement. And so there grew with every day the wish for a radical outward change of the kind that has always been of the most telling influence for me, — the wish for a journey to a foreign land not stricken directly by the war, to its countryside, towns, rivers, bridges and forests : for the loss I have most suffered under in these last agonising years was precisely this former intimate connection with Nature. The men of this war and the contemporaries of these men, myself included, seemed so far removed from the world of Nature, — to draw close to a tree, a field, the grace of evening, appeared selfish and truthless to me, for what did the tree, the field, the evening-scape know of these hapless, devastating and slaughtering men ? It is true that these things have really no part in us even when our minds are at peace, building and blest, — nevertheless there exists an inexpressible bond between the quietly creating spirit and the holy, deep self-absorption of Nature.

. . . Here then (to my mind) a yawning gulf had become visible, which was the more sensible to me since that silent unison, that attunement with natural things somehow belongs, as I realise more and more, to the first conditions of my productivity, indeed to my daily life itself. If Man only ceased invoking the cruelty of Nature to excuse his own ! He forgets how innocently even the most terrible things happen in Nature, she does not treat them as a spectacle, does not hold aloof from them ; in the Terrible she is entire, also her fruitfulness is in it, her magnanimity; it is, if one may say so, nothing but the expression of her plenitude. Her consciousness consists in her totality, — because she contains *everything*, she contains horror also, — but Man, who will never be capable of comprehending everything, is never certain when he chooses the Terrible — murder, shall we say — of containing the opposite of this abyss, and so in the same instant his choice condemns him (since it makes of him an exception) to be an isolated, one-sided being who is no longer subjoined to the Whole. The good, steadfast, adequate person would not, of course, be able to exclude evil, fate, suffering, disaster and death from these polarities, but where one of them struck him or he became a cause of them, he would only stand there like one afflicted in the midst of Nature, or working affliction against his will, — he would be like the ravaging stream fed by plunging head-waters, whose confluence into himself he cannot close up. . . .

But you ask me about Switzerland. No, it is not at all easy to travel after five years of immobility ! At first it seemed as if I no longer could. Where did your letter reach me ? — in Geneva, if I am not mistaken. I came straight from Nyon, where I was granted my first days in Switzerland under the kind hospitality of Countess Mary Dobrzensky (née Wenckheim), and to that little villa by the lake which the Countess has been living in for the last eighteen months or so, I hope one day to return. First, however, I had the desire to make use of my freedom and see the country, which it is true I have always in other years regarded only as a country of passage, being somewhat mistrustful of its too famous, too obvious and too pretentious "beauties". Mountains, to begin with, are not very easy for me to grasp, — I managed to see the Pyrenees, the Atlas mountains in North Africa belong to my sublimest memories, and when I read of the Caucasus in Tolstoi I felt the indescribable fever of their grandeur. But these Swiss mountains? They still seem to me something of an "obstacle"; there are so terribly many of them. Their shapes rise up conflictingly; I can make out with some satisfaction that somewhere a contour runs pure against the sky, — but, how shall I put it? — I lack the simile, the inwardly perceptible parallel to them which alone turns an impression into an experience. First I approached, tentatively, the towns: Geneva (which is but a motor-drive's distance from Nyon) — then Berne, and that was very, very lovely. An old, settled, in some places quite unspoiled town with all the marks of a sturdy and active citizenry, even to the high self-assurance that shews out of the unanimous-looking houses, preening themselves above their porches with an aloof air where they face the street, but towards the river Aar, with a more communicative and open mien where the lovely gardens lie outspread. By good fortune I had friends who were native to the place, with such beautiful, old-inherited houses, and this at one stroke delivered me from the hotel atmosphere and has helped me to experience things from the heart of the country, even here, where I, situated as I am among strangers, have to find my way about from their bearings. About Zürich, this politically cheerless town, there is hardly anything to say, — it roused in me the desire to get away from the cities, in my mind's eye floated a countryside with if possible southern skies above it, — and now this has been fulfilled for me here, for a while. A map of Switzerland will easily shew you the situation of Bergel, and the haste this valley has to debouch into Italy; above the valley, half-way up the mountain, lies this little snuggery embedded in slabs of gneiss, a church (unfortunately Protestant and also empty) on the slopes, very narrow streets; I live in the middle of it, in the old family house of the Salis', even the furniture is there, and out of sheer abundance the palazzo has a French garden-terrace with old stone balustrades, traditionally clipped box with a riot of summer flowers in between. Another time, however, I must tell you of the chestnut woods which dip down the slopes towards Italy in marvellous beauty.

But now I have only room enough to commit to this letter the heartiest greetings for you, dear Countess Aline, and your husband, to whom it is also directed, — and the assurance of ever the same attachment, — Your RILKE.

106. *To the Countess M.*

SOGLIO, BERGELL, GRAUBÜNDEN
13 *August* 1919

. . . My letter of the 4th August will have described to you where I am living, — and now of course there is more prospect of this summer bringing me to you. But even here the summer will have been much, much too short! This is partly the fault of my slowness, which cannot be exaggerated. Everywhere I have to begin a new life and must surrender to the fancy that, provided the places I find are in any way supportable or sympathetic, endless Pasts have been enacted upon them which want to thrust at least one of their branches towards me and into me, as though they were my own or those of my family. It was like this, even before the war, in Spain; so insidious was the effect that I went away after six months only with the greatest effort of will, — and so it is again in this singular mountain-eyrie which I think I mentioned to you not long ago. Old houses, old things exercise the most compelling power over me, the smell of old wardrobes and old chests of drawers has such a *familial* atmosphere about it, I told you of all the stuff that's collected here, — I described the woodwork, knick-knacks, my four-poster bed, did I not? and the old garden within whose border of trimmed box hedges the wild flower-summer teems and throbs — but I had not then met the crowning seduction of all; just think what was now revealed — an old library, otherwise inaccessible to the guests, the ancient Salis library preserved intact! An old-fashioned room, quiet, facing the garden (which now glimmers green and murmurous in through the little opened windows); over the fireplace the gigantic scutcheon of the Salis willow,[1] in front of it an antique spinet;

[1] The following, *Die Weide von Salenegg*, is conjectured by J. R. von Salis (see Appendix I) to be Rilke's last poem:

Heraldic willow planted long ago,
you put your question to the future's sun:
the living and the dead both seemed to know
that here the growth they hoped for was begun.

It grew and flourished. And the powerful earth
confirmed the tree's heredity and breed;
for always when another spring had birth
the heavens blessed the urgent, waking seed.

Is not a symbol or a faith expressed
here in the tree's all-overcoming might
and in the stem's endurance manifest?
Where there endures a loved thing in our sight

we too endure with it: thus grew the tree.
Out of the bole's firm building, year by year,
ever it flung its green felicity
into the glad, accordant atmosphere.

But growth means growing old. And in the end
the aged tree-form gave itself away,
and you with heavy heart might apprehend
the quiet, self-stilling process of decay.

Soon in the rugged bark there came a cleft
and through the fissure in the shrunken skin
you saw the empty, of all life bereft
and sap-abandoned darkness deep within.

Ever more gaping stood the hollow, through
the wind and tempest of the winter's stress,
until into this sombre cavern drew
a ruin that was strange and shelterless.

Yet through the artery of one last root
hanging forgotten in that hollow cell,
the joyous festival of flower and fruit
seemed granted for a little longer spell.

Nobody tended to this fragile arm,
it slipped unnoticed past the gardener's ca
dwelling beside the constant threat of harm
a miracle's sweet song we cannot share.

It triumphed. For a living vigour stirs
in anything that piteously decays:
mysteriously the voices of the years
rose up within and filled this throat with praise.

Out of its sap the new stem slowly came, —
and now the rotted trunkage only stands

in the middle of the room a solid square table of the 17th century with an almighty sofa opposite, Louis Quatorze style, with all the old embroidered upholstery ; near one of the three windows a genuine iron chest (with the enormous, multifariously bearded key lying on it) — and what besides ? books, books, books. Rows and rows and cupboards full of them. Books of the 17th century, many volumes bound in hog-skin and little books of the 16th century (among them some of Aldus and Elzevir) ; memoirs of the 18th in delightful leather bindings, the whole of Linné and of course lots of Swiss stuff, also the poets : Albrecht von Haller, whom I peruse by day — just look at this stanza from a poem entitled *Morning Thoughts* in which God is apostrophised : " *Dem Fisch, der Ströme bläst und mit dem Schwanze stürmet,/hast du die Adern ausgehöhlt ;/Du hast den Elephant aus Erden aufgetürmet,/und seinen Knochenberg beseelt*" *! ! !*) — and Salis-Seewis (in the 1800 edition), — where else could one read him ! I save him for the evening hours, whenever the more wistful minutes come. Then I read him, the forgotten one, out loud in this library, and it touches me to see how he finds his voice there, not exactly a great voice but nevertheless singing in the loveliest, purest lines, dolorous and nightingale-like as befits that age and the garden which outlives him, which is more enduring than the poet who was moved by the Eternal long, long ago. Now you will understand, dearest Countess, how beguiled I am. What can I do against this room in which every day brings a new discovery, — and then the garden calls me and I think of the chestnut-woods : there is no escape and no end to it. But you will understand. How lovely these moments are with this Venusberg encompassing me, where Venus is a rose run wild and the books glitter like tantalizing gems in the dark mines, all this has me spellbound, I don't want to make any plans, don't want to think of the

---

there like a shield, as round a struggling flame
one holds the curving hollow of one's hands.

ENVOI

May now the willow weave its robe of flesh
in every generation, every sun :
here with the tree the meaning springs afresh,
and here the many mysteries bloom as one.

winter at all, for I can imagine neither abode nor manner of living. Of Munich I have no thought, — but where ? Where ? —With greetings of warmest friendship, Your RILKE.

108. *To Anni Mewes*

SOGLIO (BERGELL, GRAUBÜNDEN), SWITZERLAND
12 September 1919

MY DEAR ANNI MEWES,—Your carefully and beautifully sealed little parcel had difficulties in reaching me : on its arrival in Munich it had to begin its real travels, long and protracted, but they did it no harm, and this very morning it brought me the keenest joy : how glad I am to feel you near me with your kind and affectionate thoughts, and with how many fond and good things would I like to answer you !

The Vogeler pamphlet you sent me was, it appears, already known to me in another, evidently earlier, version ; at that time it was not entitled *The Silver Horse*, but called itself *Love's Expressionism* — both being about equally incomprehensible. The underlying motive I understand well enough, who does not feel it, who does not desire the world's making good and becoming different, the immediate and universal resolve towards " mankindliness " ? But no such resolve has yet been made, neither in Russia nor elsewhere, and it cannot be made because there is no God behind it to drive it forwards. Arming itself under the cloak of this new brotherhood is still the same old war, the same destructive element, still prowling about and far from pacified ! This frenzy, now grown completely demented, lets fly some slogan like " brotherhood " and contradicts it in the same instant — for it is nothing but the reverberations of the war, the after-storm of the war-years when the avenging furies run amok and overreach themselves, all the while believing that they are harnessed to some greater purpose — as though a train flying off the rails were a picture of freedom. Vogeler is anything but consistent, he is easy to pick holes in and I am sure the immediate conditions round him pick holes in him every day. But I, who have been permitted to be his friend for so many years, am still touched by this outburst of his quiet and genuinely shy nature: what upheavals, what havocs, what earthquakes must have taken place in this man, caught in his web of delicate day-dreams, for him to cry out from his very bowels like this and see himself compelled to act? Again and again this sentence grips me: "A state of affairs such as man has never known is in the process of evolving — Peace". In this statement there is all the fervour of the early Vogeler, augmented by something infinite: by a real tribulation, a having been in hell and, afterwards, Hope, — the emotional experience from which these words proceed is immensely real, as though they were uttered by one rising from the dead, who can no longer be led astray although he comes from the grave and mounts reeling into chaos. None of these voices help. The expressionist, this explosive spirit pouring its boiling lava over all things and insisting that the arbitrary form into which the crusts harden is the new, the future, the veritable outline of being, — is a desperate soul, and the honest ones among them we must leave alone to rave. It is possible that these startling and obtrusive manifestations (which are only wholly repulsive when used commercially) are turning our eyes away from the tender growth of what, by and by, will really become the Future. It is so easy to understand why men have grown impatient, — and yet, what is more needed now than patience? — wounds take time and do not heal by having flags stuck in them. The world must arrive at a more stable consciousness by some other road, and maybe the first thing through which it will come to itself again will be something quite unpretentious, something certainly that cannot be expressed! It seems to me that the *littlest* reconstruction, what each one does in his own place, the carpenter who simply uses his plane again, the smith who hammers again, the merchant who reckons and deliberates again — these are the progressives, these are the pure revolutionaries the longer, the more quietly and actively and work-lovingly they ply their trades, each at his last.

But, dear Anni Mewes, of yourself you write next to nothing, and now only this little fragment of the page is left to tell you of myself; or have I nothing to tell? Not much more than the fact my address has already betrayed to you and of which you know more or less everything, if it has caused you an involuntary smile of pleasure. It was three months yesterday since I left Munich behind me, and I confess I prefer to think forwards into the unknown rather than back *there*, even if this is, in a certain sense, ungrateful. . . .—Dear Anni Mewes, sincerely and devotedly, Your RILKE.

109. *To Gertrud Ouckama Knoop*

SOGLIO (BERGELL, GRAUBÜNDEN), SWITZERLAND
Sept. 12, 1919

MEINE SEHR LIEBE GNÄDIGSTE FRAU,—The impulse to send you a few words from abroad has been with me from the first. I am only ashamed at succumbing to it so late. Yesterday it was three months since I crossed the frontier, three months, a whole summer lies between then and now — how and where has it passed for you, Lilinka and Vera? I hope you were not all the time in Munich, — but I don't know quite where I would wish you to have been. My memory has only a small sickle-moon for Munich; it shines into other pasts much more brightly; this last one I have left behind me so misspent that I can only hastily avert my eyes from it. Towards what? That is the imponderable question.

Can you imagine, being abroad was something of a strain at first? You no longer knew how to set about it; you (or was it only I?) spent half the day reading the names Houbigant, Roger & Gallet and Pinaud over the drug-stores; yes, for a moment *this* was freedom, — who would have thought it possible? The confectioners did not impress me half so much, so far I have bought no chocolate, but the soaps did for me, I was entirely defenceless against the hygienic shop-window displays in Zürich's Bahnhofstrasse. By these devious routes, however ridiculous they were, I gradually got to the other things; to the French book shops and art salons, to the bustle of streets and business, and with some effort, even to Nature. It's a pity that she only seems to reveal herself to me in Switzerland in exaggerations; how pompous these lakes and mountains are, there is always too much of them, they have been weaned from the simplicities. The admiration of our grandparents and great-grandparents seems to have worked on these regions — they journeyed down here from their own countries where there was " nothing ", so to speak, and here there was " everything " in luxury editions. Heavens alive ! A sort of parlour-Nature, all ups and downs, full of prodigies, duplicates, underlined objects. A mountain ? behold, dozens of them on either hand, one behind the other ; a lake ? but of course, and a very refined lake too, best quality, with reflections in the purest water, a whole picture-gallery of reflections and the Almighty explaining them one by one like a curator, if, that is to say, he is not at the moment doing his film-director stunt and training the search-lights of the blood-red evening on to the mountains, where the snow clings day after day far into the summer so that we shall have all the " Beauties " en masse. For the winter naturally has special beauties of its own, and this is the final triumph — not to be deprived of those while you feel yourself safe and snug amid the central-heated delights of their opposite. I can't help it, the easiest way for me to approach this penny-plain-tuppence-coloured version of Nature is with irony, and I remember the good old days when, passing through Switzerland, I drew the curtains of my compartment, whereupon the rest of the travellers greedily devoured my share of the view in the corridors, — I am sure there was nothing left over.

Now you will say : why has this person grown so ungrateful all round, wantonly so ? He is ungrateful about Munich which, despite everything, was a not unfriendly refuge in those insurmountable times, and now he is ungrateful about his new and enviable freedom, which he scorns instead of using modestly for his convalescence. No, things aren't as bad with me as all that : I even believe that I am beginning to understand Switzerland in its peculiar pertinacity and inherent unity. This I owe to Berne, where the most hospitable weeks were afforded me, and in Berne too you can feel these landscapes with their piled-up barriers and obstacles with a remarkable clarity and translucency. Berne's history is full of Nature's strength, and the people, when they collect in groups, have something of the consistency and hardness of the mountains about them, and their sturdy wills have always, at every crisis, been like an extension of the indomitable force with which the wild mountain streams plunge down into the valley. And this skilled and proven strength has led to a shapely self-assurance in the cities : Berne stands there all of a piece, every house above its cross-hatched arcade, drawing even the traffic into its protection, so that only the market-places remain outside and the wonderfully representative fountains, which are so typical that even the water serves a civic purpose ! You can easily account for the Swiss man as part of this civicness : you then understand his outline and composition ; in essence these seem to be actually moulded out of the average mass and cut out of the whole — so that in each person the People is present (a thing one misses so much with us, where we are continually dealing with bits and pieces or with complete anomalies, regarding individuals as exceptions). Strange, though, that psychoanalysis should have grown here (at least in Zürich) to the most impressive proportions : nearly all these clean and angular young persons are being psychoanalysed. And now puzzle this out for yourself : a completely sterilised Swiss whose every cranny has been swept and garnished — what sort of inner life can he have with his soul all disinfected and glaringly lit up like an operating theatre ! . . .

I have been here six weeks, if I am ever to get back my senses — how slowly ! — some sort of home and season must be given me for a long, long time ahead. And in conclusion I ask : Munich ? What are the prospects ? What will the winter be like ? (It will be my winter too, I fear.) — Affectionate greetings to Vera and Lilinka, and with hearty wishes, Your R.

116. *To Leopold von Schlözer*

Locarno (Tessin), Pension Villa Muralto
21 *January* 1920

My dear Herr von Schlözer,—Fancy your remembering me, and on Christmas evening ! Your letter took some time to reach me, it came yesterday evening and suddenly it was lying on my table : that — the resumption of contacts on all sides (Switzerland has granted me many of them, also some remarkable links with my life in Capri and Rome) — is the only sign so far of the healing I need so much. As for me, I have no choice but to impress myself long and passionately upon the violent and fearful breaks of the year 1914 until the skin grows over again ; it was then that I began (back in 1912) my great, perhaps my greatest and most decisive works ; the sheltered spot where I started them the war has transformed into a heap of ruins above the graves of countless soldiers : the old castle of Duino (near Trieste) where it was granted me to do such glorious days and nights of work. All that has gone, and Paris too, which is so indispensable to me — and yet I don't want to, *can't* give it up, anything, any of it ; there is not a single point in the last five years that I can cling on to, not one, the abyss is so steep that I cannot strike root at the edge, neither is there air or nature or heaven above me, nothing but the smoke of doom. . . . Practically all through the war years, *par hasard plutôt*, I was waiting in Munich, always thinking it must come to an end, understanding nothing, nothing, nothing ! *Not understanding* : that, indeed, was my sole occupation, and I can assure you that it was not easy ! For me an open world was the only possible one, I knew no other : for this I had Russia to thank, — it made me what I am, from there my inner life proceeded, the home of my instinct, all my deepest origins are *there* ! How I thank Paris, and shall never cease to thank her. And the other countries ! I cannot retract anything, not for a single moment, cannot reject or hate or suspect anything anywhere. The abnormality of the general situation has dictated an attitude that brooks no exceptions : no one people can be charged with a lack of standards, for this very lack of standards has its cause in the bewildered lostness of all. Who helps ? Everywhere there are only the profiteers of misery, nowhere a helper, nowhere a leader, nowhere a great thinker. There may have been such epochs in the past, full of corruption and decay, but were they so without form, so without a coordinating centre that set up its own tension's — but now tensions and counter-tensions are produced without that centre which alone could make them into a constellation, an order, an order *of decay* at least. My part in all this is only suffering. Suffering shared, suffering anticipated and suffering remembered. Soon I shan't be able to suffer any more. Please do not believe what Pater says about the " bestiality " of the French in the Rhineland, — we must stop vilifying people, — it's only the general chaos that throws up licence and rebellion now here, now there, — nobody's fault. *C'est le monde qui est malade, et le reste c'est de la souffrance.* Since June I have been in Switzerland, here, there and everywhere, without abode. I want to spend two more winter months on Swiss soil, then go back, — but where ? Although I have never made use of my nationality I now feel the homelessness of the Austrian. I have done no work. My heart has stopped like a clock, somewhere the pendulum struck against the hand of misery and stood still. Very many greetings to your wife (in 1917 I saw her brother, Baron v. d. Ropp, in a club in Berlin and I asked about you then). May things go as well with you as possible.—Sincerely, as of old, Your RILKE.

120. *To the Countess M.*

PALAZZO VALMARANA A SAN VIO
VENICE, 25 *June* 1920

This morning, my dear Countess, your letter from Basle reached me, — but before you do anything else look *where* ! In Venice, and not only in Venice but in the old and unchanged mezzanino of the Palazzo Valmarana which has been kept safe and sound for the Princess Marie Taxis, so that for the first time since the war she was able to spend a few weeks here in the summer. It was to see her that I came down on June 11th, the Prince was also there and another visitor ; the Princess could not put me up, but immediately after her departure early this week I moved into the beautiful rooms which, for me, are filled with so many moving and exquisite fragments of the past. The charm of these Venetian mezzanines : nowhere else can low rooms be so big, so spacious, so harmonious in their proportions (for all space, in the world as in the self, is a question of proportion) — as though they had imposed the limitations of lowness on themselves out of sheer bravado. And the Princess, who from her childhood has remained a part of Venice, has furnished this *pied-à-terre* with especial care and feeling. I myself had contributed a few trifles in 1913 when I made a long sojourn here, — a couple of glasses, a set of little Italian books of the 18th century in uniform bindings, even the escritoire at which I am now writing to you : it was like a dream to touch these forgotten things again, I noticed at first how great my inner renunciation had in fact been, I had to take back a relinquishing gesture in myself to countermand it, so as truly to become aware of them. Strange, all is as it was, and as I sit here I could easily attune myself to the surroundings, the noises and the very atmosphere of the year 1914 — even the Countess Valmarana upstairs (who without a thought at once received me into the stream of her old friendship) whenever she thinks of the last time I stayed in the mezzanino involuntarily speaks of "*l'année passée*". . . . But if I hoped to find everything unaltered I must confess that this wish has been granted with the exactitude with which the fairies are wont to beguile us mortals when they grant more than enters into mortal calculation. In the fairy tales the wish is always something hasty and incautious — so was mine : for I did not intend that I also should feel so absolutely unchanged as regards everything about me. My life was stopped and turned off at the main by the war and it must have undergone a sort of hardening (I wished it so, for it was my only means of surviving the monstrous distortion that everywhere prevailed !), but now, seven years later, it is hard indeed to be more aged and more worn-out than ever, and with no evidence of those successive inner changes which ultimately are the very essence of living. Perhaps I am mistaken about the degree of my unchangedness, — and have somehow grown different after all, that remains to be seen ; since I've been here I have lived on the edge of recovery, things are being forced into the present, but still under the guise of a cousinship — all too close ! — with the Past. Nevertheless I am glad of this escape from Switzerland, which I can still only regard as a waiting-room with a couple of Swiss views hung up on the walls. . . .

Monday, 26 June 1920

This letter has been left, dear Countess, on purpose, for I wanted to write a bit more ; but for the last three days we have been supplied with such sweltering heat that I shan't get very far; I see that I feel the resulting enervation more than I did some years ago; a bathe on the Lido would be the remedy but the *vaporetti* have been on strike for a week, one would be thankful for their absence were it not that gondolas have become unobtainable. Most Venetian families, my house-mates the Valmaranas included, have given up theirs, and so all travelling, except for what can be done immediately inside the Calli, has become extraordinarily difficult. I would have liked to make a trip to the garden of old Mrs. Eaden on the Giudecca — the last to survive of the once charming Giudecca Gardens; tall trees standing by ones at the edge, but inside, a garden made up of vineyards, little stone-bordered pools, lawns, pomegranates with blossoms all aflame, and in the flickering shadow-play of the vines, enormous mallows; hedges and an old wall with weatherbeaten stone figures in niches ring round this garden of contentment, while beyond it a plain strip of lawn runs to meet the lagoon — and as you step out of one of the little gates you feel at first that it is singularly empty and austere, belonging to the sea rather than the garden, and leaving room for the wide savannahs of ocean which heave in an infinite agitation of renewal beyond the plain brick balustrade. I have always admired the great tact of the 18th century which decreed that the bright profusion of the garden should not be carried forward to the edge of the sea water; nothing is more affecting than this strip of world between, whose purpose is seemingly to wean you away from the pluralities of the garden and prepare you for the simplicities of the eternal. How Eleanore Duse, who has always loved this garden, would have come into her own had she stepped out of the garden's masking and obliterating fullness into myriadfold freedom — in that utter isolation, alone upon a length of meadowland, forsaken — what a figure she would have been! At certain seasons of the year this ribband of seabord, pathless and turfy and quite silent underfoot, is like a Shore of Farewells, — never have I known the feeling of farewell undergoing such a sea-change, such a spatial transformation; now, under the gathering rays of summer, a sense of easement also reigns there — the lagoon dazzles you and involuntarily you turn back to the garden and dwell in the consciousness of its undisturbed joy. The lovely old trees in the background shape themselves aloft against the pellucid sky, and over them, in pale shades of rose and grey, the walls and domes of the Redentore! I know, dear Countess, that this is not a description — no more than a face, a view, a feeling can the Giardino Eaden be described, only experienced, — indeed in the end this is true of Venice as a whole, there is nothing you can take up with vessels or hands, only as though with mirrors — it is all beyond your grasp and you are merely made the confidant of its evanescence. All day long you brim over with pictures, but you would be hard put to it to point to any one of them — Venice is an act of faith; when I first saw it in 1897 I was the guest of an American. It's different now, and so that a little reality should enter into this insubstantial world I was bitten by a particularly virulent flea and am now more or less localised round the itch! . . .

121. *To the Princess Marie von Thurn und Taxis-Hohenlohe*

SCHÖNENBERG BEI PRATTELN, BASEL-LAND
23 *July* 1920

. . . Dostoievski's biography was awaiting me here, written by his daughter and translated into German from the French manuscript. I am having the book sent to you tomorrow, Kassner too (in case he does not know it, though the woman who did the translation lives in Munich) will find it most interesting. Especially the short introduction; here Madame Dostoievskaya, continuing the Slavophile associations of her father, gives the most marvellous and visionary interpretation of the present state of things in Russia: the Russian moujik, she says, who is the enduring and constructive element of Russia, is already at work creating vast and profound relationships with the East, and Bolshevism is only being used as a "scarecrow" to hold off the Westerner and his destructive and interfering dogmatism. Even if it doesn't look like that today I am certain that Ljubov Dostoievski is only seeing prematurely, through the eyes of her father, things which must come sooner or later, and then the whole world will have to stand and pause. Of all future movements, however, this will be the most magnificent and the most just. . . .

127. *To the Countess M.*

HÔTEL FOYOT, RUE DE TOURNON
PARIS, 27 *October* 1920

You won't be able to gasp enough, I think, my dear Countess, when you see this address! You have always credited me with being able to take the most far-reaching steps, but look, just look! What can I say, everything is good, completely and absolutely good; for the first time since those terrible years I am feeling the continuity of my life, which I was on the point of renouncing: for even Switzerland only perpetuated (more mildly, more pleasantly, more hiddenly, if you wish) the breaks, but here, here — *la même plénitude de vie, la même intensité, la même justesse dans le mal*: apart from the political muddle and pother, everything has remained great, everything strives, surges, glows, shimmers — October days — you know them.

I fit on to all the breaks, and now I no longer feel them. If I could stay here I would have my life back again tomorrow, all its dangers, all its raptures: my whole life — *ma vie, depuis toujours mienne* — But the exchange prohibits this: it will only be four, five days, — but even so it is right, I love it: now I *know* again, my mind has thrown off its fetters, I have ceased being rooted to one spot, I circle once more in my consciousness. *One* hour here, the first, would have been enough. And yet I have had hundreds, days, nights, — and each step was an arrival. . . .

129. *To Hans Reinhart*

SCHLOSS BERG AM IRCHEL, KANTON ZÜRICH
19 *November* 1920

MY DEAR HERR HANS REINHART,—The fact that I often wanted to write to you can only offer the smallest excuse; the bad thing is that I have not done so!

But if *you* complain that various business affairs prevented you from getting down to your work, how much worse it was for me: all work apart, my circumstances were such that I had to leave practically all my correspondence in arrears, the good as well as the tedious ; this always takes its revenge one day, for arrears use up the strength that ought to belong to the present. But now I hope to get straighter. The good fortune on which I was counting when I entered Switzerland, although there was no sign of it then, has now come almost unexpectedly; I was able to withdraw into the most gracious hospitality you can imagine ; the little Schloss Berg, thanks to the kindness and understanding of its owner, is now to be at my disposal for the winter, and that perfect and undisturbed seclusion may perhaps be granted which alone can help me towards the inner recovery that became more and more urgently necessary with the years of hideous interruption. And, so that nothing should be lacking for my return into the spirit — that quietest and austerest of dwellings — Fate, even before I entered my retreat, made possible something else, equally unexpected : a journey to Paris, the result being that I can now exercise a whole consciousness over my life again. The journey was a risk ; for the visit might well have given rise to a sense of loss, a separation, an aversion, but the most happy opposite was the result, everything blossomed again from the first moment under the influence of impressions which, I can assure you from personal experience, have forfeited nothing of their richness and force. It may be that a person who had renewed contact with this city through business or social channels would have noted some alteration ; I am in the fortunate position of appealing to *things* always ; these and the air that danced and sparkled across from them had the same undiminished power over me which, for almost twenty years, has been the most formative and propitious for my work, so that once again I have hopes of attaining with perseverance and concentration a continuity without too great a loss.

You know that saying : "*Cella continuata dulcescit*" : in my mind's eye I see it over my two doors and shall not move anywhere recklessly. But you, dear Herr Reinhart, should not fail — if your health allows of it — to attend Pitoeff's production of your play : his work is so strong, so integrated, so enjoyable because it is wholly constructive, evoking and setting free in you the equivalents of pure creation. I shall always remember that evening in Geneva with Mlle Blumer, when Pitoeff shewed us how he thought of casting the parts in Chavanne's play (since produced), the *Bourg St. Maurice*. He had spent the whole afternoon over it, and now every movement, bend, turn and modulation of those puppet-like characters had grown to such a perfect pitch of expression in him that he was able to embody each separate figure, instantly and wittily, in himself, at the same time continually projecting into the room, with a fixed, trenchant look, the large auditorium he had inside him. His power of transference was so irresistible, the cut of his gestures so clear that I asked myself whether the actual production, in which he would have to leave so much to instruments less ebullient and enthusiastic than himself, could ever be as thrilling as this incomparable hour : also, one must bear in mind that this vision, so subtly communicated, lay on the imaginary plane of the joy he himself felt while he was giving us that inspired presentation. What stage could possibly be, the whole time, as true and as full of imagination as the creative joy of his heart, which continually threw out space, framework and background and varied them as the tension and situation demanded ? And perhaps this remains the most wonderful thing of all, — that side by side with this joy, wedded as it were to his acting, an overflow of absolutely childlike bliss shone in his face — as though he could still find time to be the richest and most gift-laden spectator of all these inventions. Yes, he sat there in front of himself in the front stalls, enchanted, breathing himself in again, he was the whole show — I had to think : this is how the world plays and never runs down.

You can see that I have a very great admiration for this extraordinary man, and it is a calamity for him to be hemmed round with restrictions which make it impossible for him to realise, through his fellow-artists, all that he forms and transforms in his own heart. For that he would have to be in the position once enjoyed by Stanislavski, independent of material worries and limitations — and I am positive that in three years his theatre would become the theatre of Europe. What productions he would give us ! — while as things are he is in the invidious position of having to fill the box-office with pieces he doesn't really believe in, which will only obscure his ideas and diminish his priceless talents. Nowhere is complaisance more dangerous than in the theatre : for here, where the spectator participates more directly than in the other arts, the tyranny of the public is also more palpable and more disastrous ; finally, by ignoring them or applauding them the playgoer " makes " the plays that please him. One has only to think of any other art in such dependence to understand how outrageous and disreputable this state of affairs is — and fundamentally it has long been general on all our public stages ! . . .

130. *To R. S.*

(who sent MS. with particular reference to his loss of sight)

Schloss Berg am Irchel, Kanton Zürich
Switzerland, 22 *November* 1920

Your letter of October 16th had to go a long way round to reach me, so my lateness is not quite so great as may seem.

As for my answer, it must direct itself more to your letter than to the works you enclose. My conscience will not permit me to pass " judgement " since I know how much I lack the shifting scale necessary to assess the worth of artistic endeavours; I am bound to the manifestations of art by nothing save my sense of wonder ; all my life I have been the pupil and acknowledger of the Great, so that I cannot now find it in me to give counsel to those who have not, perhaps, worked their way fully into their tasks. To them I wish that they may keep joyfully to the road of long learning until that deep, hidden self-awareness comes, assuring them (without their having to seek confirmation of others) of that pure necessity, by which I mean a sense of inevitability and finality in their work. To keep our inward conscience clear and to know whether we can take responsibility for our creative experiences just as they stand in all their truthfulness and absoluteness : that is the basis of every work of art, and art such as this could be produced even if we cut away all ground from beneath our feet, provided that we kept our inspiration continually at concert pitch.

The great and ultimate sorrow that has befallen you is a special inducement to those winged promptings which alight wherever we have suffered a loss greater than any conceivable possession. You cannot do other than set this perfect sorrow which, as you note, attracts to itself the Invisible and the Spiritual, — in the very centre of your reordered consciousness ; it will rightly remain the unchanging measure of all the voyages and dimensions of your soul. But once this adjustment has been made it must be your steadfast practice to endure this central sorrow more and more namelessly, so that it could no longer be seen from your work as an artist *what* infinite restriction it was that underlay the perfect balance you had conjured yourself to attain. Art can only proceed from an anonymous centre. But for your life also (whatever it is destined to bring forth) this act seems to me decisive : it alone would make the core of your renunciation. By bearing your sorrow as a nameless and finally unnameable thing you would grant it freedom to be not sorrow merely but — Fate, even (for we cannot see its end) Fortune. Such indivisible destinies have a Deity of their own and are thereby forever set apart from those manifold, complex misfortunes whose privations are not profound enough and not massive enough to serve as a mould for so mightily proportioned a figure.—R. M. R.

131. *To the Countess M.*

SCHLOSS BERG AM IRCHEL, KANTON ZÜRICH
25 *November* 1920

. . . Schloss Berg am Irchel. . . . How has it come about ? It has come about by a miracle, — there is no other explanation. How can I hasten enough to tell you all the incomprehensible things that have happened to me ? Just think, the good fortune that allowed me to go to Paris has had, so to speak, a second act in which the little, old, out-of-the-way Schloss Berg was offered to me (to me, all by myself !) as a winter residence the very moment I returned ! You can just make it out on the enclosed map : a bluff old house of hewn stone dating back in its final form to the 17th century, with a toothed gable when seen in side view, — in front, a rather neglected park where avenues of tall, lopped beeches flank the unbordered " *pièce d'eau* ", in whose centre there stands, like a dancing tree (*un arbre de luxe*), day and night the slender figure of a fountain. (And with its ever modulating changes of key this is indeed the measure of all the sounds here, seldom does anything reach beyond its plashing.) If you look, in a contrary direction to that shewn on the map, out of one of the windows (mine are on the ground floor) into the garden, you see it, beyond a receding avenue of old chestnuts, passing over without a break into the landscape, into meadows which slope up gently to the foot of the Irchel, a cosily wooded hill that rounds the picture off without perceptibly limiting it. — My rooms are beautiful, large, full of old, delightful things, — great tiled stoves and a fireplace take care of the heating — and, whenever there is sun it shines in radiantly through all my windows. A quiet and understanding housekeeper looks after me just as I want, and does not seem to mind my being so silent and sealed (for I have to remain like this in order to get down to work !). — I am telling you a fairy story, am I not ? Yes, and what have you to say about my being the centre of this fairy story, all unawares ? Am I really happy ? No, my heart thumps with apprehension : shall I be able to wrest from these extremely favourable and congenial circumstances the work which they should permit me to do and which I (after all the distractions and disturbances of the last few years) await urgently and inexorably of myself ? Now there is no excuse ! Shall I be able ? Shall I be strong, pure, fruitful, fecund ? My meeting with Paris — which was so healing — puts me under an obligation, and now this obligation looms up all round me, clear and categorical, — if I fail this time, in Schloss Berg — I am past help. A stranger coming in — his first word would be : What a lot of work could be done here ! — Shall I be able ? My fear (my cowardice, if you care to call it that) is as great as my joy, — but this joy is truly immense. . . .

No — I was not long in Paris, six days. It was so perfect that time didn't matter. Even in the first hour there descended on my heart, on my spirit, on all the passionate memories of what I had won and struggled for in that city, such a wonderful and positive benediction that I could have left after that hour had run its course, without sensible privation. I have long accustomed myself to accepting the things life gives me according to their intensity without, as far as is humanly possible, worrying about their permanence, — it is the best and wisest way of enduing them with every quality — even that of permanence. But if you begin with this demand you spoil and falsify all experience, indeed, you inhibit its inmost fruitfulness and genius. Things that lie beyond our prayers can only come to us as gifts, — so I thought now ; often in life it is but a question of the longest patience ! . . .

134. *To General-Major v. Sedlakowitz*

(one-time instructor to the Military School at St. Pölten)

SCHLOSS BERG AM IRCHEL, KANTON ZÜRICH
9 December 1920

VERY MUCH TO BE ESTEEMED HERR GENERAL-MAJOR,—Your two letters were forwarded to me by the Insel Verlag as soon as I, after many months of travel, could be reached at a more stable address.

Had I followed the reaction which your distant memory aroused I would have thanked you at once, — and you also, as your second letter shews, were somewhat nonplussed not to find my answer forthcoming.

Meanwhile the emotion which made up my inner agitation was of so complicated a nature that I had to let some weeks of dawning understanding pass if my thanks were not to be more superficial and, in a certain sense, more embarrassed, than they already are, — and this would have in no way satisfied your sincere approach to me.

Any voice (it is the first of the kind ever to attempt to find me !) that harks back to those remotest of years, could not fail to strike me as being — forgive my directness — unworthy of belief. I do not think I could have lived my life (or those fragments which I may call by that name) — had I not, year after year, disowned and thrust out all memory of the five years of my military training ; yes, what have I not done to thrust them out ! There were times when the least influence of that rejected Past would have shattered the new, fruitful and individual consciousness for which I strove, — and whenever such an influence rose up in me I had to pass over it as over something that belongs to an alien and utterly unrecognisable form of existence. — But later also, when I found myself more surrounded and sheltered by things increasingly my own, that long and mighty visitation of my childhood, out of all proportion to my years, seemed even then incomprehensible to me, — and I could as little understand its impenetrable darkness as I could the miracle which finally, perhaps at the last moment, delivered me from that pit of undeserved misery.

If you, Herr General, find my bitterness exaggerated — without which I cannot even today record the facts of my early youth, — I would beg you to remember for a brief moment that, on leaving the Military High School, it was as an exhausted, physically and spiritually violated, backward, seventeen-year-old youth that I faced the gigantic tasks of my life, cheated of the most innocent portion of my strength and at the same time of that irretrievable foundation which would have laid firm and healthy footholds for the ascent I now had to begin, weakened and maimed, upon the steepest walls of my future.

You hear me saying all this and you will finally ask how I could possibly make up for the enormous loss of time and flow into those channels towards which my original impulses, weary as I was, nevertheless drove me. Probably it was this question that has caused you so long to doubt my identity with " that pupil, René Rilke ". I myself have no idea how anyone like him could make good, were it not that life is made to surprise us (when it does not wholly appal us !). Of course I looked round in those years of consternation for help ; much as I remained apart — for my contemporaries were all in normal and incomparably easier circumstances and association with them could not be considered — I still drew comparisons and realised ever afresh what utterly different channels I might have expected for my talents. That did not help me. But even today I can recall how I clenched my teeth and found a sort of help in the fact that those foul and fearful years of my childhood had been so completely horrific, without the least mitigation.

Do not, esteemed Herr General, think me unjust : I have an idea that I have sketched it with a certain moderation and I have no greater wish than that I should one day be able to see the brighter spots in the illimitable sufferings of those years, some friendly happening that came by pure chance, because things couldn't get any worse. For the struggles of Nature work far into the Unnatural and an attempt to achieve balance may sometimes take place even there. But how slight it was, measured by the daily despair of a ten-, twelve-, fourteen-year-old boy.

Hence in the last moments of my youth it helped me to sum up those events of long ago as one unbroken and atrocious purgatory from which I was cast out as from a destructive and turbulent sea, which cares not whether it leaves a live man or a dead on its ravaged shores.

When, in more meditative years (how late I came into the realm of books, reading them calmly and receptively instead of making up for lost time !) I first got hold of Dostoievski's *House of the Dead*, I would seem to have been initiated into all the terrors and despairs of prison from my tenth year ! — Please discount this statement of all pathos. It seeks to express nothing other than the simple recognition of an inner state, whose outward causes — that I admit at once — were of course entirely different from the surroundings of Siberian convicts. Yet when he endured the absolutely unendurable Dostoievski was a young, but mature, man ; for the soul of a child, if it used the measure of its hopelessly deserted heart, the prison walls of St. Pölten might take on roughly similar dimensions.

That is twenty years ago ; then I stayed for some time in Russia. An understanding which had only been fostered in the most general terms by a reading of Dostoievski's works became incontestably clear to me in that country which was my spiritual home ; it can be formulated only with difficulty. Something like this, perhaps : the Russian has shewn me in so and so many instances how even an enslavement and a visitation that continually overwhelm all powers of resistance need not necessarily bring about a degeneration of the soul. There exists, at least in the soul of the Slav, a degree of submission which deserves the epithet perfect because even under the most massive and annihilating pressures it creates for the soul a secret arena, a fourth dimension in which, however grievous conditions become, a new, endless and genuinely independent freedom can now begin.

Was it presumptuous of me to imagine that I had accomplished a similar absolute surrender, instinctively, in my earliest years, when a solid mass of misery was trundled over the tenderest shoots of my being? I had, it seems to me, some right (on a different scale, of course) to such an assumption, since I cannot point to any *other* means by which I could have survived that monstrous, over-life-size injustice.

So you see, Herr General, that I long ago undertook to come to terms with my earlier fate. Since this fate did not destroy me it must, at one time or another, have been added as a weight to the scales of my life, — and the counterweights, which were destined to tip the balance, could only come from that purest achievement on which I found myself determined after my sojourn in Russia.

Hence if I did not completely thrust out the prehistoric days of the Military School, I could only admit them in vague and general terms, somewhere far behind me. My powers, otherwise engaged with a view to the future, would never have sufficed to examine, or even form a picture of, the details. So if you refer me, as you do in your letter, to a particular memory it seems so bizarre that I am quite at a loss to describe it.

The irony you entertained for my literary work will certainly have been very just and disciplinary, — even the fragment of the letter written in 1892(!) shows how right one would have been to lop off, ruthlessly and severely, the ragged and frilly edges of my style!

The fact that you have preserved that letter among your papers and were even able to find it again fills me, my worthy teacher, with a strange emotion, which I can conceal all the less since, in all these crude explanations, I have nowhere thanked you for your last sympathetic enquiry. I do so now, believe me, without the least reservation.

Must I, in conclusion, reproach myself for having set all this down in such elaborate perspective and, moreover, so vehemently? Could I have taken your letter's link with me in a more "inoffensive" way?—No; I think I had only one choice: either to hold my peace or to involve you very thoroughly in that commotion which the only voice ever to reach me from over there could not fail to evoke.

If, Herr General-Major, you can take this unusual answer in that just and indulgent sense, you also will feel that it cannot end otherwise than with the expression of sincere wishes for your good health. How should I not see a peculiar favour in the very fact that your memory should ever allow me to utter such a wish!—Very sincerely yours, R. M. RILKE.

144. *To the Countess M.*

SCHLOSS BERG AM IRCHEL, KANTON ZÜRICH
10 *March* 1921

. . . Ultimately, each of us experiences only *one* conflict in life which constantly reappears under a different guise,—mine is to reconcile life with work, in the purest sense; and where it is a question of the infinitely incommensurable work of the artist, the two directions stand opposed. Many people have helped themselves by taking life easily, by snatching what they needed from it *apart from* the conflict, or by turning life's values into an intoxication whose wretched enthusiasms they hurriedly flung into art; others have no alternative but to withdraw from life—asceticism—and *this* way is of course much cleaner and truer than that rapacious cheating of life for the sake of art. But for me even asceticism cannot be considered. Since in the last analysis my productivity proceeds from the plainest adoration of life, from the daily, inexhaustible wonder of it (how could I have been productive otherwise?)—I would see it as a lie to reject any one of the currents that flow towards me; in the end every such failure must express itself in your art—however much art may gain potentially from it—as a certain hardness, and there take its revenge: for who can be open and affirmative on such sensitive ground if he has a mistrustful, restrictive and anxious attitude towards life ! So one learns, oh how slowly, that life travels over endless starting-points — to what end, finally, can one apply one's little abilities ?

Rodin often brooded on this in his old age. Sometimes, at five in the morning, I found him standing in the garden, lost in contemplation of the slopes of Sèvres and St. Cloud which slowly rose out of the wonderful autumn mists of the Seine, as though they were coming into the world faultlessly fashioned, — there he stood, the old one, and pondered : " What end can I serve when I gaze in wonder at the richness of it all, this morning . . .? " A year later, and he did not understand even this, simply *could* not understand it, had long been unable to, for an influence, a fatality far inferior to him had wrapped him round and swallowed him up in darkness and confusion from which no ray of splendour shone !

Dear Countess, I only wanted to give reasons for my silence, — where have I got to ? . . .—Thanking you always with all my heart for your friendship, I am, dear Countess, Your RILKE.

145. *To the Countess Maria Victoria Attems*

SCHLOSS BERG AM IRCHEL, KANTON ZURICH
12 *March* 1921

VEREHRTE GRÄFIN,—Your letter, which has just reached me, I am all the more eager to answer since I remember that once, some time ago, a note in your handwriting was forwarded to me in — if I am not mistaken — Paris. I must ask your indulgence if it remained unanswered ; but immediately afterwards the letter got in among books and papers when I was packing — and these were not accessible later — so, as I had not noted your address I could no longer get in touch with you.

Faced with the friendly interest which is apparent from your few lines I find it rather difficult to admit to the attitude of mind, or prejudice, which I nevertheless must confess if I am to be sincere about your enquiry.

I do not know *which* of my works you refer to through the medium of your art, — but fundamentally it holds good for all of them that I have, alas, a deep-seated aversion to any accompaniment of my productions either in music or design. For I am concerned to fill out with my activities the *whole* of the artistic field which presents itself to my subject. I would not have it that in that territory (assuming that the representation in the very highest sense succeeds) there should still be room for another art, itself interpreting and amplifying. Illustrations are particularly fatal for me because they impose certain despotic limitations on the free play of the reader's imagination : but in his appreciation of a true work of art (to the lesser, or merely entertaining, categories the pictorial element may be conceded) it seems to me an essential part of its effect that the reader should preserve his individual freedom entire. Hence I cannot conceive of the various arts as being separate *enough*, and this point of view, which I admit at once is exaggerated, may perhaps have its most cogent cause in the fact that I myself, having a marked leaning towards pictorial expression, had to decide in my youth which art I would follow in order to avoid dispersion, — with the result that this decision was made with a certain passionate exclusiveness. At any rate it is my experience that every artist must, for the sake of intensity, while he is actually working, regard his means of expression as the only possible ones, otherwise he might easily arrive at the supposition that there were portions of world which were altogether inexpressible through his mediumship, and thus fall at last into the anomalous interspace between the individual arts, which is yawning enough in all conscience and which only the dynamic tension of the supreme masters of the Renaissance really knew how to bridge. *We* are confronted with the task of determining, fairly and squarely, each one his own unique means of expression, and this form, conditioned by one faculty only, is weakened and imperilled by any succour derived from the other arts.

Whatever conclusions you draw from this explanation, dear Countess, may they not be unfriendly ones ! Please be gracious enough to forgive along with the disclosure of this letter its haste also : my house is so secluded that the postal facilities are extraordinarily limited, the next post will not leave Berg before Monday noon, so I want to get this ready for today's collection : there are only ten minutes left !

It would indeed ease my mind to know that I have somehow made myself understood and not lost your good graces ; is it too great an immodesty to ask you to confirm that for me, sometime, with a favouring word ?—Yours very sincerely, RAINER MARIA RILKE.

PART THREE

LETTERS FROM MUZOT

1. *To the Princess Marie von Thurn und Taxis-Hohenlohe*

Hôtel Château Bellevue, Sierre (Valais)
25 *July* 1921

July runs to an end, and I am not with you. Do not get a room ready for me yet, but do not on the other hand pass the death-sentence on my coming : in August, perhaps.

During these last few weeks I have often been on the point of announcing my arrival, and a strange current came into my sluggishly flowing feelings whenever I thought of doing so ; what, however, keeps me on the other side is this wonderful Valais : I was imprudent enough to come down here to Sierre and Sion ; I've told you what a singular magic these places exerted on me when I first saw them a year ago at the time of the grape-gathering. The fact that Spain and Provence are so strangely blended in the landscape affected me deeply even then : for both those countries appealed to me in the last years before the war more powerfully and more decisively than anything else ; and now to find their voices united in a wide-spreading Alpine valley in Switzerland ! And this echo, this family likeness is not imaginary. Only the other day I read in a treatise on the plant-world of Valais that certain flowers appear here which are otherwise only to be found in Provence and Spain ; it is the same with the butterflies : thus does the spirit of a great river (and for me the Rhône has always been one of the most marvellous) carry gifts and affinities through country after country. The valley is so broad here and so magnificently filled with little eminences within the frame of the great bordering mountains, that it affords the eye a continual play of most bewitching modulations, like a game of chess with hills. As though hills were still being shifted about and grouped — so creative is the rhythm of what you see, an arrangement new and startling with every change of standpoint, — and the old houses and castles move all the more pleasingly in this optic game since most of them have the slope of a vineyard, the woods, the glades or the grey rocks for a background, blent into it like the pictures on a tapestry ; for a sky that is absolutely indescribable (almost rainless) has its share high up in these perspectives and animates them with so ethereal a radiance that the remarkable correlation of object to object, just as in Spain, seems to shadow forth at certain hours the tension we think we can perceive between the stars in a constellation.

But now for the particulars of my enchainment here : when, some three weeks ago, I left Etoy (with my visitor), the prospect of a little house in these parts (we didn't want to stay long in the hotel) was held out to us, which proved useless at the first glance ; we looked at one house after another in the neighbourhood, time passed, — until suddenly an object of the greatest temptation discovered itself. This old manor, a tower whose walls date back to the 13th century and whose timbers and in part also the furnishings (chests, tables, chairs) derive from the 17th, was to be sold or let. At a very cheap price, but still far exceeding the possibilities I could realise in Swiss francs. Well, last week one of my friends who had long known this so-called Château de Muzot (pronounced " Muzotte ") — one of the Reinharts of Winterthur, — rented the house so as to place it at my disposal ! And now I am moving out there tomorrow and shall make an attempt to live in these stony and castellated surroundings, which press on you like a suit of armour ! I simply had to do this, hadn't I, the way things have turned out. The presence of my lady friend makes it possible to run a small household until some serviceable soul can be found, — if all goes well I could then take up my abode in Muzot with a housekeeper for a while. It lies some twenty minutes above Sierre, set pretty steeply in a less arid, but happy countryside gushing with many springs, — with views of the valley, of the mountain slopes and far into the most marvellous depths of sky. A little rustic church, situated above it to the left among the vines (not present in the postcard), also belongs. The postcard does Muzot injustice, the growing trees in the garden have got much taller meantime, also you cannot see the magnificent old poplar which must be imagined a few paces further on, above the right-hand edge of the picture, and which characterises the look of the castle wherever you see it from. I myself say " castle ", for this is the perfect prototype of the sort of mediaeval manor that still lingers on everywhere hereabouts ; these " castles " only consist of such a single solid house-structure which comprises everything. The entrance is from the back, where you see the sloping roof jutting out : this floor (the one with the long, built-on balcony) comprises the dining-room, a little boudoir and guest-room, also the kitchen (in a modern annexe) ; the former kitchen was buried underground, a single gigantic room (now abandoned and used for storing garden-tools, etc.). On the next floor I have ensconced myself. My little bedroom is there, lighted through the windows on the right, but it sends out a little balcony on the other side, straight into the tree. The double window beside it with the adjoining window in the sunny west-front round the corner belong to my study, which we more or less finished furnishing yesterday with the conveniences at hand : it has all kinds of promises and attractions for me with its old chests, its oak-table of 1600 and the old dark rafters, in which the date MDCXVII is engraved ; when I say " attractions " I am not being quite accurate : for actually the whole of Muzot, while it somehow holds me, nevertheless drives a sort of worry and oppression into my heart ; as far as possible I have made myself familiar with its oldest history ; the de Blonays are supposed to have built it ; in the 15th century it was in the possession of de la Tour-Chastillon ; at the beginning of the 16th, a year before the battle of Marignan, the marriage of Isabelle de Chevron with Jean de Montheys was celebrated here (we still know all the guests for these three days of festivity and their various goings-on). Jean de Montheys fell at Marignan and was brought back to the young widow in Muzot. Thereupon two suitors immediately burst afire for her and in their ardour came into such violent opposition that they ran one another through in a duel. The hapless Isabelle, who seemed to bear the loss of her spouse with dignity, could not get over the demise of her two swains between whom she had not yet chosen ; she lost her reason and only left Muzot by night, deceiving the vigilance of her old nurse Ursule ; almost every night you might see her, "*très légèrement habillée*", wandering towards Miège to the grave of her two combustible wooers, and the saying goes that finally, one winter's night, she was found in the churchyard at Miège dead and stiff. — So somehow we shall have to resign ourselves to the ghosts of Isabelle and of Jean de Montheys returning like pendulums from Marignan, and not be surprised at anything. The Château de Muzot since we cleared it up has gained everywhere in brightness and snugness. As in all these mediaeval houses the rooms have something honest and peasant-like about them, rough and ready, with no reservations. . . . However, — and lest I forget, besides my bedroom on the upper floor there is the so-called old "chapel" facing the back, a small whitewashed room accessible from the hall through a strikingly low doorway which is still quite gothic and mediaeval, and in the wall above it, done in powerfully raised relief, not a Cross, but — a huge swastika! So here you see me, Princess, beguiled by Muzot from the start: I must try it. If only you could see it! When you approach it from the valley, each time it stands there like an enchantment high up above the rose-pergolas — already withering — of its little garden, set deep in the hues of the ancient hewn stone which has grey and violet tints in it, but which has baked and browned itself golden in the sun, again like certain walls in Andalusia.

And now, please greet everybody very much, — the Prince, Pascha and particularly Kassner; as I said I am still not abandoning all hope of coming to you. My chief worry is to find, this winter, i.e. autumn as well, a sort of Berg Irchel for quiet seclusion and work. Now it will be shewn whether Muzot has the character to become and remain so for a while. The winter is supposed to be mild and favourable here, and apart from that Muzot has one of those marvellous country tiled stoves made of the grained, grey *pierre olaire*. If Switzerland could once again offer me a congenial winter refuge, so that I didn't have to seek it abroad, I would probably not travel further afield, for time will be short and I want to enter upon my autumn hermitage as soon as I can so that it may lead slowly over into a long winter. . . .

I must end, dear Princess. How long does Kassner think of

staying? The thought of finding him still with you would naturally do much to decide my future, should I start travelling again. Etoy was lovely and friendly to the last.—In thought ever with you, Your DOTTOR SERAFICO.

2. *To a Young Girl* [1]

. . . You must know that I am not one of those who neglect the body so as to make of it an offering to the soul, for my soul would have no wish to be served in such a manner. All the soaring of my spirit begins in the blood, for which reason I let a pure and simple mode of living, free of narcotics and stimulants, go on ahead of my work like an introductory prelude; in this way I am not deceived of that true spiritual joy which is to be found in a happy and radiant communion with the whole of Nature.

. . . A little while, and it may be that my mind will no longer grasp the conditions out of which those chants arose, the Duinese Elegies begun so long ago. If one day you get to know some of these works, you will understand me better; it is so difficult to express oneself.

When I look into my conscience I see only one law, inexorably commanding: to enclose myself in myself and to complete at a stroke the task that was ordained from the centre of my heart. I obey. — For you know that in coming here I wanted only that, and I have no earthly right to change the direction of my will before I have done my act of sacrifice and obedience.

Now I have almost finished the preliminaries, that is, I have remedied the incredible arrears of my correspondence. Think of it, I've written — I counted them this morning — 115 letters, and not one had less than four pages, and many comprised eight, or even twelve, in close writing. (Naturally I do not count what has gone to you. That is not writing, it is breathing with the pen.) Masses of letters! There are so many people who expect I don't really know what from me: help, advice, from *me*, who find myself so helpless in face of life's imperious urgencies. And

1 From *La nouvelle Revue française*, Année 14, Nr. 161, Ier février 1927. German text by Kilian Kerst.

although I know that they are deceived, go astray, I still feel — and I don't think it is vanity — tempted to give them something of my experience, some fruits of my long solitudes. Young women as well as young girls are terribly deserted even in the heart of their families. Young married women appalled at what happened to them. And then all these young working people, mostly revolutionaries, who come out of the state prisons without any bearings, flee into literature and write rabid, malicious poems. What am I to say to them ? How raise up their despairing hearts, how form their formless wills which have been temporarily falsified by the rush of events and which they now carry about with them like some strange force whose use they barely know.

Malte's experiences oblige me now and then to answer the writings of unknown persons. *He* would have done it, if ever a voice had reached him. . . .

At any rate it is he who compels me to continue this sacrifice, challenges me to love all the things I would shape, with all the capacities of my love. This is the mighty strength whose exercise he left behind for me. Imagine a Malte who had a beloved or even a friend in that Paris he found so terrible. Could he then have entered so deeply into the confidence of things ? For these things (as he often told me in our few intimate conversations) whose essential being it is your wish to recreate, ask you first of all : " Are you free ? Are you ready to devote your whole love to me ? To bed with me as St. Julian the Hospitable bedded with the leper, in that uttermost embrace which can never be consummated in the common fleetings of mortal charity, but which has Love, the whole of Love, all the love that exists on earth, for its impulse ? " And when such a thing (so Malte told me) sees you occupied, even with a sliver of interest, it shuts up in your face. Perhaps it will grant you a word of precept, make you a small, distantly friendly sign, but it refuses to yield up its heart, to come to you with its patience and starry constancy which make it kin to the constellations of heaven.

If a thing is to speak to you, you must for a certain time regard it as the only thing that exists, the unique phenomenon that your diligent and exclusive love has placed at the centre of the universe, something the angels serve that [every ?] day on that matchless spot. What you are now reading, my dear, is a chapter from the lessons I received from Malte, my only friend during so many years of suffering and temptation, and I see that you say absolutely the same thing when you speak of your drawings and paintings, which only seem valuable to you by reason of the enamoured compulsion with which *brush or pencil carry out the embrace, tenderly taking possession.* Do not alarm yourself over the word " fate " which I used in my last letter. I call Fate all external events (illness, for example, included) which unavoidably and by their very nature interrupt and annihilate the direction and discipline of the spirit. Cézanne doubtless understood it when he removed himself for the last thirty years of his life from everything that might, as he expressed it, " hook on " ; when he, who was so faithful and devoted to tradition, refused to go to the burial of his mother lest he lose a day of work. This pierced me like an arrow when I heard it, but like a flaming arrow which, though it seared my heart, left it in a blaze of vision. There are few artists in our day who understand this stiff-neckedness, this violent obstinacy. But I believe that without him we would have remained on the outskirts of art, and though these may be rich enough to afford us some pleasant discoveries we stop there at our peril, like a player at the green table who, while he may occasionally succeed in making a coup, is still given over to Chance, which is nothing but the docile and sedulous ape of Law.

Often I have had to take away Malte's diary from young people, forbidding them to read it. For this book, which appears to reach the conclusion that life is impossible, must be read against the current, so to speak. If it contains bitter reproaches they are by no means levelled at life. On the contrary, they are the declaration that because of our lack of strength, because of our spiritual dispersion and hereditary faults we forfeit nearly all those countless riches of earth which were intended for us.

Try, my dearest, to run through the overfulness of these pages in this spirit. It will not spare you tears, but will help to give all your tears a clearer, as it were more transparent, significance.

3. *To J. H.*

(a working man who submitted some poetry)

Dear Herr H.,—The " T—— Magazine " you sent me came as a surprise : my thanks today arrive late ; I am even later in returning your manuscript, which I was at a loss to recommend anywhere. Luckily I find an edition of your collected works announced by the publishers at the end of this same magazine, so that a reference to another firm would in any case have been superfluous.

To speak quite candidly, I would have found it difficult to recommend your poems, — they move in the speech of a time that is yours perhaps, but whose conditions I can only view from outside, and with no lasting attachment. People like us will not easily be dissuaded from thinking that the boiling flood of productions which now swamps us flows not out of fullness but out of disaster and disorder, having burst the banks of what has been not so much a *limitation* for us, as a *standard.* I don't want to add anything more to your distress and confusion at a time when the immediate circumstances of existence are hard and refractory : — but, in the end, as much must be said as you yourself have involuntarily demanded. I do not know what trade you have learnt, — but as a worker the experience of a certain proficiency must nevertheless dwell in you, and the joy of making a thing well cannot have remained entirely strange. If you look out for a moment from this good, reliable ground towards the lurchings of your literary achievements, it will not escape you how great a part *accident* plays with you there and how little you have schooled yourself to use the pen for what it is above all else : an honest, accurately controlled and responsible tool.

You will surely not find it unfriendly of me to answer the sincerity of the attention you paid me in a similar manner, — that is, with sincerity. For the rest, I have the best and most earnest wishes for you ; one may always hope that when times are absolutely hopeless and unendurable the turn for the better lies just round the corner. May your heart find not only the endurance to await the good, but also the resource to draw it towards you.—R. M. R.

9. *To Gertrud Ouckama Knoop*

CHÂTEAU DE MUZOT SUR SIERRE, VALAIS
26 November 1921

VEREHRTE FREUNDIN,—How touched I was by your warm-hearted voice, and how gladly I recognised its quiet and dependable accents !

At first I found it rather tiresome to see my place of residence betrayed by that widely circulating notice of Ruth's engagement, just at a time when I needed seclusion more than ever. But it has turned out well after all. Firstly because it is a good thing to be assured of faithful relationships on one's entry into a period of retirement, but particularly in regard to Ruth. Even her oldest friends who knew her only as a little girl and later hardly more — even they can now form a time-picture of her, something comparatively precise and distinct, — and for her also, who grew up along the straight line of her heart, something we had long foreseen has come true. Thus all who know and knew her must agree that her present decision is right and reassuring — you yourself do, I see — and as for me (little as I know of the details and, from this distance, *can* know) I have a well-wishing and sometimes happy confidence in her choice and in all that may come of it. Clara will have told you that Ruth is marrying into the Westhoff family of her grandmother, who grew up on the neighbouring estate of Liebau and left it in her day with many tears. I think Ruth will become a squire's wife, and this steady and active life would suit her inclinations and capabilities very well (it is possibly the one which I, without really expressing it, have always wished for her).

If I should stay in Muzot for the coming summer, I am thinking of inviting Ruth over for a few weeks in the spring, which starts very early here : in the glorious surroundings of this great landscape and in quiet daily association with me, I fancy her girlhood might run fruitfully to its end.

Till then my solitude, so I hope at least, will continue uninterrupted, I see nothing I need so much, — for I am far from having bridged over the deep gaps left by those fateful years, — although much has been done and more help is all the time being vouchsafed me than I — to judge by results — can account for. (Ah, dear friend, the masses of help I have used in my life ! Is such extravagance allowed ?)

Munich — when you tell me I am " still avoiding " it, I see quite clearly that I don't really want ever to go back there, — proved to be of no avail. Often during the last two and a half years when I was just over the border, people looked everywhere in Bavaria, in Württemberg, even in Carinthia for a country place for me, but with little prospect of finding the congenial, the exact spot, — and so it was an incredible relief when the miracle of Swiss hospitality, to which I cling blindly, opened up a new chapter — perhaps its strangest one.

For the Valais (why is it not included when one counts Earth's loveliest places ?) is an incomparable country : at first I did not understand the truth of this because I *compared* it — with the most significant things in my memory, with Spain, with Provence (with which it is indeed, via the Rhône, related by blood), but only since I admired it for its own sake has it revealed itself in all its grandeur and at the same time, as I gradually came to see, its sweet gracefulness and its strong, passionate tradition. You remember the evenings when one sat as a child over the bound magazines in which tales of travel were told, not very well, perhaps, but accompanied by alluring pictures into which one put the whole meaning of what one would later experience, together with an almost wistful impatience at being separated from it by so many years of growing up. Yes, and perhaps there was an added fervour in this devoted contemplation, the inexpressible fear of dying before all these things could be felt and fulfilled : well, these very panoramas and everything you put into them, these scenes of sunny afternoons and winter evenings, — they are being fulfilled here, imagine it ! Here are the bridges, the gates, the lovely, graceful and thrilling pathways winding round the hills like silken ribbons, with the rustic railings to the left and right which the draughtsman did in such intriguing perspective and which, like the fountains, have remained unforgettable. The hills have castles on them and even the towns, seen from a certain distance, gather together into something proud and stately : not a romantic fancy but an undreamable reality.

Shrines, crucifixes at every cross-road, uplands ribbed with vineyards and in late season all curly with their foliage, fruit-trees, each with its tender shade and (oh, so rightly !) single fully-grown poplars dotted about, exclamation-marks of space crying "Here !" — and no figure, no peasant-woman (dressed, of course, in country costume) who does not give the place its character, its accent and metre ; no cart, no mule, no cat even whose presence does not make everything larger, opener, airier ; and this airiness looping thing to thing, this nowhere-empty world, and the carillon — how you fancy you can hear it chiming in your imagination, dropping its benediction berry by berry in the ear and again reminding you of the grapes ! Goethe journeyed through the Valais, and I imagine there must be pages of his, carefully sensitive sketches in which he puts his unique stamp on the overpowering presence of details, one leading to the other, all interlinking and swinging away into the distance.

It is possible that my Muzot may appear in one of those pages, not as a subject by itself but as a phase that dips and drops into dimness, as a gradation of the background, which is so beautiful, so gentle, so aerial, quite without density, well-nigh weightless, although a mountain !

So much for the Valais. But a desire to tell you why Munich would be less profitable has been present all the time. For had there been but a single person with me, and that a very discreet person who kept to himself, I could not have shewn you all this as I have. I would shew it to him and translate it for him, this near and intimate person, — and a little would be left over to be shaped and passed on, but not much. This (call it weakness if you will) makes all places more and more impossible where people might become so dear to me that I would overflow too joyfully and too copiously on their account. The rivalry between environment and work was made pitilessly manifest during the war years, — formerly my home had been Paris where I saw some eight persons in all those years (and they more giving than receiving) — such was the natural isolation (and what a provision it was !) of my inner domain. But now things are such that I must keep a strict hold on my expenditure, for life passes and the idea comes that the years of which the war and its aftermath cheated me *might* have been, to judge by my age and position, the most responsible ones for my work. But they stand empty ! Oh, empty : are overflowing with terror and grief. Actually I do not see things in the light of this worry, time and age have become less and less essential for me. Heavens ! when I think of it, how my life floods over the edges of childhood, — and can I assert that my youth was ever at an end ? And what of life and death ? How open are the roads that lead us from the one to the other, how close we are to knowing it, how nearly expressible is that word in which life and death rush together in an (as yet nameless) unity. So this does not trouble me, neither (if only one keeps the grace of giving) the way things are given, whether to my closest friends who take it at my side, or in my own work : the difference will not be so very great in the end. Nevertheless communion with my own work is somehow older in me, unspeakable memories gather round it from my whole nature, — it insists on its own rights, and ultimately I have no choice but to concede them. In the meantime may the " work " really come, or at least the inner state of mind that corresponds to it in intensity and purity — both are equally valuable — and then the solitude in my old tower would not have been altogether wanting. For much as the artist in us is concerned with *work*, the realisation of it, its existence and duration quite apart from ourselves — we shall only be wholly in the right when we understand that even this most urgent realisation of a higher reality appears, from some last and extreme vantage-point, only as a means to win something once more invisible, something entirely inward and unspectacular, — a saner state in the midst of our being. (How deeply may such cogitations have moved Gerhart Ouckama Knoop at certain times.)

Another page, the fourth ! Is it too much that I let myself go, spend a whole evening writing to you ? But how else am I to make amends for the fact that years have slipped by without my having sat with you at the high table in that chair which, despite my too infrequent use of it, I may still call mine : for how willingly and solicitously it has received me each time. Anyhow when, seeking *points d'appui*, I cast my mind back to

Munich, it is not my various flats that I remember (which, if it does not sound ungrateful, were really only sham-flats), but some such chairs, the above-mentioned before all. If it had been granted me to occupy it today I would have talked to you roughly like this, — then, perhaps, we would have got on to Regina's[1] book (where she has accomplished something extraordinary, indeed perfect, in the *Tale of the Old Inn Sign*)[2] — to books exclusively, and by now you would have made many remarks and suggestions, — and right at the end, in the hall (as generally happened) I would have thought of Paul Valéry, a most significant person whom you ought not to miss. Maybe you have already come across the name ; it is only since this spring that I have known its contents, but since then it has ranked among the first and greatest, — the very great. Here is a man, belonging to the Mallarmé circle and, it must be said, of his school, who came early to the fore with some remarkable observations loosely grouped round the figure of Leonardo, and single poems, — he was not unnoticed at the time — but who then, declining all work for two decades or more, studied mathematics and only appeared again before the public about 1919. Completed. A poet who seems to have acquired from those studies new measures and exactitudes so as to give incontestable expression to the majesty of his feelings and experiences. Perhaps I can send you a fragment of the dialogue *Eupalinos ou l'Architecte*, which is printed in one of the more recent numbers of the *Nouvelle Revue Française*. There is nothing of these last few years, so far as I can see, that I would like *more* to know was in your hands. . . .

How very much, as always when I talked with you, Vera is present, not only *facing* the words as she was once, but *in* and *behind* them. The time will come, won't it, when you will tell me of her, quietly ; the last and extreme question of hers about my coming has earned me the right, small though it is, to take part to the very end — and make up for what I have missed.

And here is a request I have long been weighing, but in which I am now fully emboldened : with the passing of years some sort of tenure will once more grow up round me, it has

[1] Regina Ullmann. [2] *Erzählung von dem alten Wirtshausschild.*

already begun, and a roof will one day be fixed over me again, so that no harm need ever befall it : put aside (so that I can receive it with my own hands) some little thing that was dear to Vera, if possible something that she often had with her. — Thank you.

And now, for the time, goodbye.—Very cordially, Your devoted RILKE.

11. *To Xaver von Moos*

CHÂTEAU DE MUZOT SUR SIERRE, VALAIS
12 *December* 1921

MY DEAR HERR VON MOOS,—Your letter, which could have been got at so easily, reached me only after a long and roundabout journey, — and although I am not to blame for its lateness I would nevertheless feel open to blame if I tried to postpone any further its acknowledgement and answer.

I would like to speak first of your poems : let me say at once that these brought me surprise and joy. There is no sufficient reason to give special prominence to any one of the four you have let me read, somehow they balance one another out, they are all good, precise and pure in their technique, no cheating. If I may keep the text that lies here before me I will take it up again from time to time ; but I am already quite sure that the beautiful first impression will hold good. Believe me, it is not often that I see myself justified in approving such work sent in by a younger man : all the more delightful is the exception that for once permits this. All the more " enchanting ", Verhaeren would have written ! For he was enchanted whenever he found a success ; no one who has experienced his rapture will forget it ; when the spirit and power of a young artist burst upon him and convinced him he would exult over every line that stood there pure and four-square, and then his acclamation was unqualified, unshakable, he shewed it with all the strength of his body, with all his consciousness, with his whole being. Judge from this just *what* his confidence, what his encouragement could do ! I had the good fortune, during the years of our acquaintance, to receive both in the highest degree ; although my language was a closed book to him and he could never really know any of my works, he *believed* in my achievement and gave me the whole support of his mighty nature. And I do not know whether this was not the most precious thing of all, that, without having tangible proof of what remained inexpressible between us, he credited my work with being true, with being necessary, and treated me accordingly from the very first moment. — To this friend I owe much strengthening of purpose, and it bore fruit in me all the more since I came to experience masculine friendship only comparatively late in life. For this reason his and Rodin's were infinitely affecting, and I myself could in no way overlook what the waters of these two influences have wrought in me.

My admiration for Verhaeren was considerably older than our acquaintance, — his earlier books, specially the *Villes tentaculaires*, had engrossed me continually during the first years of my (almost twelve-year) stay in Paris. The first of his books, which he came to place in my hands himself, was the volume called *Multiple Splendeur*, and I was ready to receive it with a full heart. From then on we saw one another often and yet (measured by the cruelty of his loss) not nearly often enough. He lived outside Paris in St. Cloud, but only a few winter months each year : sometimes, when his walks into the city had landed him in my neighbourhood, he dropped in unexpectedly (each time was the right time for me !) — and the wonderful movement of his heart came at me like a storm. Sometimes, following a sudden impulse, I (whose life in Paris was always of the loneliest) drove out and pulled the old-fashioned bell-rope at the door of his restricted but friendly flat. And what a guest you were as soon as you stepped across his threshold ; what traditions of Welcome were awakened in you : so large, so open, so perfect was his reception that you became a great guest, the guest from afar, the guest incarnate, the guest of all guests—if only to balance his huge hospitality.

Enough.

Since you have sunk yourself deep and lovingly in the works of Verhaeren, you will not be a stranger to the book in which his industrious German translator, Stefan Zweig, has tried to recollect the figure of the poet and his own close association with him. At the moment, unfortunately, I cannot obtain this publication, — but perhaps M. de Poncheville's little book is not yet known to you, so I am enclosing it now (requesting you to give it back in due course). The chaos of the war inevitably intrudes into this last, and when it was written the Terrible had already occurred : Verhaeren lived no more.

Of the poem I read you two years ago in Lucerne I am enclosing three copies ; it is not irrelevant to take into account the note which indicates that the volume called *Les Flammes Hautes*, although it appeared only in 1917, was finished in the summer of '14, before the war.

It would give me pleasure if these pages should help to render the theme of your lecture, and above all the figure of that great poet whom we both admire, closer to you and more worthy of your love. And let me read your work again.—Your sympathetic and devoted RAINER MARIA RILKE.

14. *To Ilse Blumenthal-Weiss*

CHÂTEAU DE MUZOT SUR SIERRE
28 December 1921

Towards Christmas, so I had planned, a small token of my remembrance was to be with you, for your letter of that Sunday in November still lay there unacknowledged ! But I had such enormous arrears of correspondence to put to rights that my pen could not make its way towards you in time. And just as I was about to put it to paper and wish you at least a " happy New Year ", behold, your parcel surprises, overjoys me. You had intended it for the fourth, which I am not celebrating in any way — it would take up too much time ; but now your present (with more right than my birthday can lay claim to) comes in the midst of Christmas, which we can never quite outgrow and which still (even if we allow it no festivities) fills us with a certain traditional expectation.—Warmest thanks for it and for your nice accompanying letter.

You certainly overestimate, in the matter of my books, their power and effect on you ; no book, and no encouragement either, can work anything decisive unless he whom it concerns is prepared by wholly unforeseen factors for a deeper reception and acceptance : unless the hour of communion with it has *never-theless* come. Then, any old thing is enough to push that hour into the centre of consciousness : sometimes a book or an object of art, sometimes the glance of a child, the voice of man or bird, yes, in some cases the sound of the wind, a creak in the floor, — or, sitting by the fireplace (as I have done now and then in my life) gazing into the changing shapes of the flames. All this and many more trivial things, seemingly fortuitous, may cause and lend strength to such a finding and refinding of oneself as you are now solemnising, — the poets, ah ! from time to time even they may be among these good causes. . . . Not from modesty, by no means, but because his extraordinarily impressive work has remained so significant for me all these years and has so often led to comprehensions in my own heart, I would opine that JACOBSEN is much, much more deserving of your wonderful experiences and your development than I. Give *him* the honour, and then, if truly you want to, to me, but as to one who is nameless among a hundred innominate powers.

Faith ! There is no such thing, I had almost said. There is only — Love. This forcing of the heart to regard this and that as true, which is ordinarily called Faith, has no sense. First you must find God somewhere, experience him as infinitely, prodigi-ously, stupendously present, — then whether it be fear, or astonishment, or breathlessness, whether it be, in the end, Love with which you comprehend him, it hardly matters at all, — but faith, this compulsion towards God, there is no place for it once you have begun your discovery of God, a discovery in which there is no more stopping, no matter on what place you have begun. — And you, as a Jewess, with so much immediate knowledge of God, with such ancient Fear of God in your blood, ought not to have to worry about " faith " at all. But simply *feel*, in your presence, His : and wherever He, Jehovah, wanted to be *feared* — that was only because in many cases there was no other means for mutual closeness between Man and God, *except* fear. And fear of God is only, as it were, the *rind* of a state whose interior does NOT taste of fear, but which can ripen into the most unspeakable and ineffable sweetness for him who loses himself in it.—Do not forget that you have one of the mightiest gods in the universe in your ancestry, one to whom we cannot just convert ourselves as we can to that god of the Christians — one to whom we *belong* because of the People, because from everlasting they have been moulded and fashioned in the fathers by Him, so that every Jew is ingrained in Him (and in him whom none dares name) : un-uprootably implanted in Him with the very roots of his tongue !

I have an indescribable trust in those peoples who have come up against God NOT through faith, but who experienced God through their own nationhood, in their own tribal sources. Like the Jews, the Arabs, and to a certain extent the Orthodox Russians — and then, in a different way, the peoples of the East and of ancient Mexico. For them God is Origin and hence also Future. For the others he is a derivative, something they struggle away from or struggle towards as though he were a stranger or had become estranged, — and so they are in perpetual need of the Mediator, the link, someone who translates their blood, the idiom of their blood, into the language of Godhead. The achievement of *these* peoples is then naturally faith ; they have to conquer themselves and school themselves to *deem* true that which *is* Truth for those sourced in God, and that's why their religions slip so easily into ethics, — whereas a God experienced from the fountain-head does not sunder Good and Evil and discriminate between them out of regard for human beings, but he does so *for his own self*, passionately concerned only that men should be close to him, cling to him and belong to him, and about nothing else ! Religion is something infinitely simple, simple-souled. It is not knowledge, not the content of feeling (for every kind of content is admitted at the outset when a man enters into collusion with life), it is not duty and not renunciation, it is not a limitation : but, within the perfect amplitudes of the universe it is — a direction of the heart. Just as a man can go and wander off to the left or right, and bang himself and fall and get up again, and do wrong here and suffer wrong there, and here be maltreated and there harbour evil in himself and maltreat and misunderstand : so all this passes over into the great religions and preserves and enriches in them the God that is their centre. And Man, who lives at the outermost periphery of such a circle, *belongs* to this mighty centre, even though he has only once, perhaps at dying, turned his face towards it. When the Arab turns at certain hours towards the East and casts himself down, that *is* religion. It is hardly "faith". It has no opposite. It is a natural animation within a being through whom the Wind of God blows three times a day, as a consequence of which we are at least — supple.

I think you must sense and begin to feel what I mean, — may it somehow make its way into the quiet and open state of mind which you call your "convalescence" and work there to your assurance and joy.—Your RAINER MARIA RILKE.

When are you going to write me again ?

[The following letter, the notorious "Worker Letter" about which there is considerable controversy, may best be inserted here, both for chronological reasons and because in many respects it is cognate with the foregoing. The reader who would jump to conclusions, however, is reminded that it cannot be held to represent Rilke's views on Christianity in any definitive form, since Rilke himself made no use of it either as letter or essay, and it was published only after his death.]

IF I HAD BEEN A YOUNG WORKER, I WOULD HAVE WRITTEN YOU SOMEWHAT AS FOLLOWS :

Last Thursday, at a meeting, they read out some of your poems, and I keep on thinking, Herr V., I have no other counsel but to write down for you what is occupying my thoughts, as well as I possibly can.

The day after the recitation I found myself by chance in a Christian meeting, and perhaps just that has been, so to speak, the spark of combustion generating the motion that propels me towards you with all my powers. It is a tremendous exertion to begin anything. I cannot *begin*. I simply leap clean over what ought to be beginning. Nothing is so strong as silence. Were each of us not born into the midst of speech, it would never have broken.

Herr V., I will not speak of the evening on which we received your poetry. I will speak of the other one. I am driven to say : *Who*, yes, — just now I cannot express it otherwise — WHO is this Christ who insinuates himself into everything ? Who has known nothing of us, nothing of our work, nothing of our affliction, nothing of our joy such as we, today, accomplish, endure, and summon up in ourselves, and who despite all this, it seems, always demands to be the *first* in our lives. Or do we only put that in his mouth ? What does he want of us ? He wants to help us, we're told. Yes, but he places himself with singular helplessness in our presence. His circumstances were so completely different. Or is it really not a matter of circumstances at all, — if he were to come in to me, here in my room, or there at the factory : would everything immediately be different and good ? Would my heart open out in me and as it were proceed on to another plane and always towards him ? My feelings tell me that he *cannot* come. That there would be no sense in it. Our world is not only externally another one, — it has no entrance for him. He would not shine through a ready-made suit of clothes, it isn't true, he would not shine through. It is no accident that he went about in a robe without seam, and I believe that the core of light in him that made him shine so strongly, day and night, has long been dissolved and differently distributed. Yet this, I think, if he were so great, would be the very least we could demand of him : that he should somehow have been consumed and left nothing behind, yea, nothing, — not a trace.

I cannot imagine that the Cross should *remain*, which was never more than a Crossroads. Certainly it should not have been stamped on us everywhere like a brandmark. It should be extinguished in his own self. For it isn't like that — he wanted merely to create the higher tree on which we could ripen better. He, on the cross, is this new tree in God, and we should be warm joyous fruits high up in its top.

We should not always speak of the Heretofore, it is rather the Hereafter that ought to have begun. This tree, it seems to me, should have become such a unity with us, or we with it, *on* it, that we should not have to be everlastingly concerning ourselves with it, but simply and quietly with God, into whom the more purely to uphold us was always the tree's intention.

When I say God, it is a great, never truly learnt conviction in me. The whole of creation, I feel, says this word without thinking, if often out of profound meditation. If this Christ has helped us to utter it with clearer voice, more fully, more authentically, all the better, — but for Heaven's sake leave him finally out of the game. Do not always drive us towards a relapse into the toil and distress which it cost him, so you say, to " redeem " us. Let us, at last, take possession of this redemption. — Otherwise the Old Testament would be more to the point, which is full of index-fingers levelled at God wherever you open it, and there, if any of us become heavy and fall, it is right into the middle of God. Once, too, I tried to read the Koran, I did not get very far, but I understood enough to know that here again is such a mighty index-finger, and God stands at the end of its direction, caught in his eternal ascent and in an East that shall have no end. Christ wanted the same, surely. To point. But men here have been like dogs who do not understand any index-fingers, and think they ought to snap at the hand. Instead of going onwards from the Crossroads where the signpost was raised high into the night of sacrifice, instead of going onwards from this Crossroads Christianity has encamped there and declared that it was there living in Christ, although there was no room in him, not even for his Mother, and not for Mary Magdalene, as is always so with every Signaller, who is but a gesture and no lodging-place. And for this reason they do not dwell in Christ, these obstinate ones of the heart, who reinstate him again and again and live from the setting-up of crooked or completely overturned crosses. They have this multitude on their conscience, this assemblage on the surfeited spot, theirs is the blame that the journey does not continue in the direction of the Cross's arms. They have made a trade out of Christianity, a bourgeois profession, *sur place*, a pool that is alternately let out and filled up again. Everything that they themselves do in accordance with their own irrepressible natures (in so far as they are still living) stands in contradiction to this extraordinary position of theirs, and so they sully their own waters and must always renew them afresh. They are so eager to make bad and worthless the Actual, which ought really to have our desire and our confidence, — and thus they deliver the Earth more and more over to those who are ready to extract at least a temporary, quickly profitable advantage from it, deficient and suspect as it is and not fit for anything else. This increasing exploitation of life, is it not the result of a devaluation of the Actual continued throughout the centuries ? What insanity to side-track us towards a Beyond, when we are here surrounded by tasks and expectations and futures ! What treachery to purloin the images of actual delight so as to sell them behind our backs to Heaven ! O it is high time the impoverished earth collected all those loans we have raised on its splendour, in order to furnish something " beyond the future " with them. Does Death really grow any more transparent because of these fountains of light we have slipped behind him ? And is not everything that has been taken away from here, since a void cannot maintain itself, replaced by a deception, — is that why the cities are so full of ugly artificial light and noise, because we have handed the true radiance of the song over to another, later enterable, Jerusalem ? Christ may have been right in speaking bad of the Earthly in an age strewn with dilapidated and ungarlanded gods, although (I cannot think otherwise) it amounts to an affront to God NOT to see in what has here been granted and conceded us — if only we use it properly — a thing to delight us to the very limits of our senses ! The right use, that's the thing ! To take the Actual truly in our hands, cherishingly, lovingly, wonderingly, as ours, ephemeral, unique : that is, to put it crudely, at once the great directions-for-the-use-of-God, and this it was that Saint Francis of Assisi believed he was declaring in his Song to the Sun, which, as he lay dying, was more glorious to him than the Cross, which only stood there to *point into* the sun. But what we call Church had in the meantime swollen to such a babel of voices that the song of the dying man, everywhere outsounded, was only caught by a few simple monks and infinitely affirmed by the landscape of his own gracious valley. How often may not such attempts have been made to effect a reconciliation between the negation of Christianity and the obvious friendliness and gaiety of the earth ! But apart from this, even inside the Church, yea, in its very crown the Actual enforced its abundance and its inborn prodigality. Why does one not praise the Church for being sturdy enough not to collapse under the live weight of certain popes, whose thrones were loaded with bastard children, courtesans and murdered men ? Was there not more Christianity in these popes than in the crusty old curators of the gospels, — something vital, irresistible, protean ? Naturally we do not know what will become of the great teachings, we must only let them stream on and leave them alone and not be frightened if they suddenly plunge forward into the cloven nature of existence and roll under the earth in unrecognisable courses.

I once worked a few months in Marseilles. It was a very special time for me, and I owe it a great deal. Chance brought me together with a young painter, who remained my friend till his death. He suffered from lung trouble and at that time had just returned from Tunis. We were much together, and as the conclusion of my work there coincided with his return to Paris, we were able to arrange a few days' halt in Avignon. They have remained unforgettable. Partly because of the town itself, its buildings and its environs, but also because during those days my friend held an undisturbed and somehow intensified communion with me over many things, particularly his inner life, speaking with that eloquence which, it seems, is peculiar to such invalids at certain moments. All that he said possessed a strange soothsaying force ; through everything that raced along in almost breathless discourses you could see, as it were, the bottom, the stones on the bottom. . . . I mean, more than something merely ours, Nature herself, the most ancient and enduring part of her which, despite all, we touch at so many points and on which we are probably dependent in our most driven moments, since its gradient determines our own proclivities. A love-affair, unexpected and happy, came too ; his heart was held unwontedly high for days on end, and the darting beams of his life swung over on the other side to unusual heights. To apprehend an extraordinary town and a more than pleasing landscape with somebody who finds himself in this mood, is a rare privilege ; and thus, when I think back, those tender and at the same time passionate spring days appear to me also the only holidays I have known in my life. The time was ridiculously short, for anyone else it would have sufficed for but few impressions, — but for me, who am not accustomed to spend free days, it seemed ample. Yes, it almost feels wrong to call " time " what was rather a new state of freeness, tangible truly as *space*, an encompassment by the open, no evanescence. If one can so express it, I recovered childhood and a little of my former youthfulness, the which to accomplish in myself there had never been any time ; I looked, I learnt, I understood, — and from these days too, dates the experience that to say " God " was so easy, so genuine, so — as my friend might have said — so problemlessly simple. How should the house which the popes had raised up for themselves NOT appear mighty to me ? I had the impression that it could not contain any interior at all, but must be piled up out of solid blocks, as though the intention of the excommunicated had been to heap the papacy with all its super-weight into the scales of history. And in very truth this churchly palace towers up over the antique torso of a statue of Hercules immured in the rocky crypts. " Has it not ", said Pierre, " sprung up tremendously as from this seed ? " It would be far more comprehensible to me to regard *this* as Christianity in one of its phases than to discern its strength and its flavour in that ever-weakening infusion of tisane which is said to be prepared from its first and tenderest leaves.

Are not also the cathedrals the body of that spirit which they want to persuade us is the true Christianity ? I could believe that beneath some of them there rests the shattered statue of a Greek goddess ; so much blossoming, so much vitality has shot up in them, even if, as though in a terror arising contemporaneously with them, they struggled away from that hidden body into the heavens, which the music of their great bells was intended to keep perpetually open. — Since my return from Avignon I have gone much into churches, in the evenings and on Sundays, first alone . . . later . . .

I have a lover, almost a child still, who is employed as an outworker, so that when there is little doing she often gets into a bad way. She is clever, she could easily find employment in a factory, but she is afraid of the boss. Her conception of freedom is boundless. It will not surprise you to learn that she feels God, too, as a sort of boss, an " Arch-boss ", she once told me laughingly, but with such fear in her eyes. It took her a long time to decide to go with me one evening to St. Eustache, where I liked to enter because of the music during the May ceremonies. Once we went off to Maux together and looked at the tombstones in the church there. Gradually she noticed that God leaves you in peace in the churches, that he demands nothing ; you might think he wasn't there at all, — yet the very instant you want to say that kind of thing, said Marthe, that he is not in the church, — something holds you back. Maybe it is only what people themselves have brought into this lofty, curiously fortified air through so many centuries. Maybe it is only that the vibration of the sweet, mighty music can never quite get out, it must long have penetrated into the stones, and they must be extraordinarily animated, these stones, these pillars and arches ; and even if a stone is hard and difficult to find access to, ultimately it is shaken, again and again, by the chanting and the onslaughts of the organ, by the cannonades, the tempests of song every Sunday, the hurricanes of the great festival days. A lull in the storm, that's what reigns in the old churches. I said so to Marthe. A lull. . . . We listened, she understood at once, she has a wonderfully listening nature. Since then we have gone in here and there occasionally whenever we heard singing, and stood close together. It was nicest when there was a window before us, one of those old windows with pictures, with many segments, each one packed with figures, big people and little towers and all sorts of happenings. Nothing was too strange for them ; here you see citadels and battles and a hunt, and the lovely white stag appears again and again in the hot red and the burning blue. Once I was given a very old wine to drink. It is like that for the eyes, these windows, save that the wine was only dark-red in the mouth, but this is the same in blue and violet and green. There is *everything* in the old churches, and fear of nothing as there is in the new ones where, so to speak, only the good examples are represented. Here is also the bad and the wicked and the terrible, the crippled, that which is in distress, that which is hideous — and the unjust, and one would like to say that it is loved somehow for God's sake. Here is the angel, which is not, and the devil, which is not ; and man, which is, is between them, and, I cannot help it, their unreality makes him all the more real to me. What I feel when somebody says " Man " I can apprehend better in there than on the street among people, who have nothing recognisable about them. But this is difficult to express. And what I want to say now is even more difficult. As far as the

" Boss ", or Might, is concerned (all this, too, slowly became clear to me in there, when we stood wholly in the music), there is only one remedy against it : to go farther than it goes. I mean it thus : we should make an effort to see in every sort of Might that claims a right over us, *all* might, the whole of might, might itself, the Might of God. We should say to ourselves that there is only ONE might, and understand the lesser, false, defective kind as though it were something seizing us rightfully. Would it not become harmless in this way ? If in every might, even in one that is evil and maleficent, we saw always Might Itself, I mean that which in the end insists on its mightiness, would we not triumph, unhurt, so to speak, over unauthorized and irresponsible might as well ? Do we not take up our position with regard to all the great unknown forces exactly like this ? We experience none of them in their purity. For a beginning we accept each of them with its faults, which are perhaps proportioned to our own. — But with all scholars, explorers and inventors, has not the assumption that they were dealing with great powers suddenly led to the greatest of them all ? I am young, and there is much rebellion in me ; I cannot be certain of acting in accordance with my understanding in every case where impatience and aversion carry me away, — but in my innermost heart I know that submission leads farther than resistance ; it puts tyranny to shame, and contributes indescribably to the glorification of true mightiness. The being that resists struggles out of the attraction of one centre of might, and he may perhaps succeed in leaving the field of conflict ; but out beyond, he stands in a void and must look round for another gravitation to draw him in. And this is generally even less legitimate than the first one. Why not, therefore, in every might in which we find ourselves, instantly perceive the greatest of all mights, unconfused by its weaknesses and vicissitudes ? Somewhere or other irresponsibility will strike its own law, and we save energy if we allow it to convert itself of its own accord. This, of course, belongs to the slow and lengthy processes which stand so completely in contradiction to the extraordinary precipitancies of our time. But beside the swiftest movements there will always be slow ones, of such extreme slowness, indeed, that we are quite unable to experience their passing. But it is just for this, isn't it, that mankind is there, to wait for what transcends single individuals. From humanity's point of view the slowest is often the quickest, that is, it proves that we only termed it slow because it was something immeasurable.

Now there is, it seems to me, something utterly immeasurable, for the sake of which men will never tire of muddling themselves with measures, standards, and regulations. And here in that love which, with an insufferable mixture of contempt, lasciviousness and curiosity they call " sensual ", here are to be sought probably the worst effects of that degradation Christianity thought fit to wreak on the Earthly. Here everything is distortion and derangement, although we proceed from this deepest of occurrences and ourselves possess in it the centre of all our transports. It becomes more and more incomprehensible to me, if I may say so, how a doctrine that puts us in the wrong just *there*, where the whole of creation enjoys its most blessed right, is permitted, if nowhere to prove itself true, at least to declare itself with such persistency.

Here again I think of the animated talks I had with my dead friend in the fields of the Isle of Barthelasse in the spring, and later. Yes, in the night preceding his death (he died the following morning shortly after five o'clock) he opened out to me such pure vistas into a realm of the blindest suffering that my life seemed to begin anew in a thousand places and my voice, when I wished to reply, was not at my disposal. I did not know that there were tears of joy. I wept my first, novice-like, into the hands of this man who was to die on the morrow and I felt how the torrent of life surged up once more in Pierre and overflowed when these hot drops were added to it. Am I extravagant ? True, but I am speaking of an *excess*.

Why, I ask you, Herr V., if people want to help us, us who are often so helpless, why do they leave us in the lurch at the roots of all experience ? Anyone who assisted us *there* could be confident we would demand nothing further of him. For the assistance he would infuse into us would grow of itself with our life and would become greater and stronger simultaneously with it. And would never go out. Why do they not set us into our deepest mystery ? How we have to sneak round it, and finally get in like burglars and thieves into this fair sex of ours, in which we go astray and knock ourselves and stumble, in order, in the end, to rush out again, as though caught red-handed, into the twilight of Christianity. Why, if guilt or sin *had* to be invented because of this inner tension of the soul, why didn't they attach it to some other part of our bodies, why did they let it fall just there and wait till it dissolved in our pure fountain, to poison and sully it ? Why did they make our sex homeless for us, instead of transferring thither the whole festival of our birthright ?

Good, I will admit that it ought not to belong to us, who are unable to accept responsibility for such inexhaustible bliss and control it. But why then do we not belong to God from that very spot ?

An ecclesiastic would refer me to the fact of marriage, although it would not be unknown to him how things are with this institution. Neither is it any use slipping the will to propagation into the light of heavenly grace, — my sex is not turned to posterity only, it is the secret of my own life ; and only because, apparently, it is not allowed to take up a central position have people pushed it out on to their edge and lost their balance over it. What's the good ! The terrible truthlessness and uncertainty of our times have their cause in the unacknowledged ecstasy of sex, in this strange, warped vilification of it which always increases and separates us from the rest of nature, even from the child ; — although, as I learnt in that unforgettable night, its, the child's, innocence does not lie in its having as it were NO sex, — but, so Pierre said almost expressionlessly, that inconceivable rapture which wakens for us on *one* spot in the midmost fruit-flesh of the sealed embrace, is unspeakably dispersed everywhere over the whole of its body. In order to designate the proper position of our sensuality one would have to say : once we were child *all over*, now we are child only on one spot. But if there were only one among us who was aware of this, and who possessed the ability to shew proofs for it, why do we suffer one generation after another to come to consciousness under the wreckage of Christian prejudice and stir like the cataleptic in the darkness, in the narrowest of spaces between sheer abnegation ? !

Herr V., I write and write. Almost an entire night has passed over it. I must pull myself together. — Have I said that I am employed in a factory ? I work in the writing-room, sometimes I have to handle a machine. Formerly I was able to study for a while. Now, I will only say how I feel. I want, look you, to be applicable to God, just as I am ; what I do here — work — I want to go on doing in his direction without getting my rays broken, if I may express it so, not even in Christ, who was once the water for many. The machine, for example, I cannot explain that to him, he cannot grasp it. I know you will not laugh when I say this so naïvely, it is better that way. God, on the other hand, I have this feeling, I can bring it to him, my machine and its firstling or else my whole work, it goes into him without hindrance. Just as once upon a time it was easy for the shepherds to bring a lamb to the gods of their lives, or the fruit of the field or the fairest grapes.

You see, Herr V., I can write this long letter without once having need of the word " faith ". For it seems to me an elaborate and strenuous concern and none of mine. I do not want to have myself made bad for Christ's sake, but be good for God's. I do not want to be addressed straightway as a sinner, perhaps I am not. I have such pure mornings ! I could speak with God, I need no one to help me compose letters to him.

Your poems I know only from that recital the other evening, I possess but few books, and they deal mostly with my profession. One or two, naturally, about Art and history which I was able to procure for myself. — But the poems, with this you must let yourselr agree, they have evoked this movement in me. My friend said once: " Give us teachers who will praise the Here and Now for us." You *are* such a poet.

16. *To Frau Amann-Volkart*

CHÂTEAU DE MUZOT SUR SIERRE, VALAIS
[Undated]

MEINE VEREHRTE GNÄDIGSTE FRAU,—What a nice thought of yours it was to give me such a comprehensive and optically evident picture of the elements of " catkin-science " in the book you sent me and the explanatory letter ; after this I have no need of further or more precise information : I am convinced ! So there are, then, no *hanging* willow-catkins (remarkably enough), and even if there were any rare tropical exception it would be of no use to me. The poetic passage [1] I wanted to control for objective correctness, stands or falls by the reader's perceiving and seizing, with his *first* feeling, the *falling* quality of the catkins, otherwise the image employed there has no point. Hence the absolutely *typical* appearance of the inflorescence must be called up, — and it became clear to me at once, looking at the very instructive illustrations of your little book, that the bush which, years ago, gave me the impression which I have now woven into my work, must have been a hazel ; its branches are densest *before* the leaves come out, and are furnished with long, perpendicularly hanging *lamb's-tails*. So I know what I ought to have known, and am substituting " hazel " for " willow " in the text. . . .

[1] The difficulty need not arise in English, since " catkin " is the popularly generic term for the inflorescence of both the willow and the hazel. More strictly speaking, of course, the catkin refers to the willow only (" pussy-willow "), while the absolutely correct name for the inflorescence of the hazel is " lamb's-tail ". The letter is of interest because it shews that Rilke, contrary to the general belief and also to his own repeated statements that the later Elegies were all " of one birth ", was quietly working away at the final Elegy some time before the " tornado " broke loose.

17. *To Lou Andreas-Salomé*

Château de Muzot sur Sierre, Valais
29 December 1921

. . . More than ever I feel companionship as the rival of my work, which is probably the case with everyone whose purpose grows more and more single and who in his giving, be it inwards or outwards, accordingly gives forth the same, unchanging thing. A few days ago a dog was offered me; you can imagine what a temptation it was, particularly as the lonely position of the house makes the presence of a watch-dog almost advisable. But I felt at once that even this would result in too much relationship if I had dealings with such a house-companion; anything alive, that makes demands, arouses in me an infinite capacity to give it its dues, from the consequences of which I have to beat a painful retreat when I see how completely they use me up. . . .

18. *To Xaver von Moos*

Château de Muzot sur Sierre, Valais
30 December 1921

Dear Herr von Moos,—What with very urgent business it is only today that I can thank you for the kind words with which you acknowledged my letter.

No, I am not in the least disappointed that you write poetry "extremely seldom" and that you do not give way to hopes of achieving anything complete and final in this field. On the contrary, I am glad to see this restraint in you at a time when nearly all the boundaries of art have been torn down and overrun by those who want to make everything common. Embarking on another distinct and specific profession (which one do you wish to join ?) will not prevent you (in whom the medium of creative language is ready-formed) from doing something responsible and necessary when the hour has come. I would like to stress that my confidence in you is, in this sense, extraordinarily sure. Also you have examples enough, if needed, to shew that no harm is done if you fulfil the highest and most splendid function of the spirit in some side-function: think of Mallarmé,

— or, and this lies much closer to you, your great Spitteler, whose most enduring poetry came, if I am not mistaken, at a time when he was still far from devoting the whole of his strength to this mighty service. And Paul Valéry, who was absolutely silent for twenty years, even studying mathematics, I believe, alongside his career as an official — does he not, perhaps, owe the composure and finality of his words to this long-suffering abstention?

When, in his time, my father expected me to pursue the art to which I thought myself destined, as a hobby (side by side with the career of officer or lawyer), it is true that I burst into the most violent and persistent refusal: but that was entirely the fault of our position in Austria and the narrower milieu in which I grew up; a milieu, moreover which was still so close to the sophistications of the '80's that it would have been utterly unthinkable to have accomplished anything real or resolute in art with one's strength divided; indeed, in order to begin at all, I had to detach myself altogether from the conditions of my home and country, counting myself among those who, only later, in the lands of their choice, might test the power and fertility of their blood. Since then so much has changed. A great deal of pioneer work has been done, art is set free, air and space were (at least before the War) there for any who inwardly needed them. . . . And just as I myself have regretted, often and often, *not* having some daily profession which, independent of the streamings of grace, is always, every day, purely feasible, — so I would advise every young person to penetrate at least some distance into this kind of task before he identifies his existence wholly with the inexorable demands of Art.

I send you the heartiest greetings and wish you a year of good progress and fulfilment,—Your R. M. Rilke.

20. *To Gertrud Ouckama Knoop*

[Undated]

Verehrte Freundin,—What am I to say? — As little as you were able, after writing down those notes,[1] to add a few words for me at the side, so little can I now speak with you while I am

[1] On the progress of Vera's illness.

still the reader of those pages, bent over them, always, despite all my uplooking. I had no idea of all this, from the beginning of the illness I knew hardly any of the details, — and now, at one stroke, I am initiated into this heart-rending, shattering, overwhelming experience. If one read of this and it concerned *any* young girl one had not known, it would still be moving enough. And now it is about Vera, whose dark, strange, fiery loveliness is so terribly haunting and so prodigiously easy to evoke that at this very moment of writing I am afraid to close my eyes, lest I should suddenly, here and now, be utterly overcome by it.

How completely she experienced, with all her being, those things to which these memorials of her agony bear such deep and irrevocable witness, — and how marvellous, how unique, how incomparable a human being is ! For, when everything in her should have been consumed, suddenly there rose up enough for a whole life : a great flood of light in her heart, and in it appeared, shining, the two extremes of her understanding : that pain is a mistake, a blind misapprehension of the body, driving its wedge, its stony wedge, between earth and heaven, which are one ; and, on the other hand, the oneness of her wide-open heart with the living and everlasting world, this harmony with life, this joyous, throbbing communion to her very last breath with the delights of earth — ah, only with the earth ? Nay (and this she could not know in the first anguish of division and farewell) — with the Whole, with much more than the Earth. Oh how she loved it, how she reached out with the antennae of her heart far beyond anything that can be seized in an earthly embrace, — in those sweet, soaring lulls of suffering which, mingled with dreams of recovery, were still granted to her. . . .

It seems, dear friend, that Fate has deemed it necessary to lead you, each time on some overhanging crag of life, past the customary bourne of things to the Valley of Death, and always with heart more bared. Now you live and see and feel from infinite experience.

But for me it has come as an immense obligation to my innermost and gravest self and (even if I only attain it from far off) to my serenity, that I am allowed, on the first evening of a New Year, to take into my possession *these* pages.—Your RILKE.

26. *To Gertrud Ouckama Knoop*

Château de Muzot sur Sierre, Valais
7 February 1922

Verehrte, liebe Freundin,—In a couple of thrillingly impassioned days, when I was really thinking of settling down to something else, these Sonnets were given me.

You will understand at first glance why you must be the first to possess them. For, tenuous though the relationship be (only one sonnet, the penultimate XXIVth,[1] summons Vera's own figure into the rhapsody which is dedicated to her), it nevertheless governs and animates the march of the whole sequence and — even if so secretly that I only became aware of it bit by bit — inspired with its presence this irresistible and convulsive birth.

Receive them kindly in hallowed remembrance of her.

Should the *Sonnets to Orpheus* be published, some two or three which, as I now see, probably only served to conduct the current (the XXIst, for instance) and remained empty after its passing, would have to be replaced by others. Then there would also be the question of what form you wish the dedication to take (in the sub-title). In the first copy I made there stands, pending closer agreement with you, only: V. O. K.—Your Rilke.

[1] Now Sonnet XXV, Part I :

Once again I will summon you back to me, O you anonymous,
fairest among the lost flowers that in memory lie,
and now to the world I will shew you, you who are gone from us,
playmate sublime of the last ineluctable cry.

Dancer you were who, with limbs full of lingering, halted
— as though of a sudden her youth had been poured into bronze —
grieving and listening. Then from the powers exalted
music fell into her heart, like a singing of swans . . .

Sickness was near. Seized already by shadows and night
her blood surged more darkly, yet as though unaware of its plight
it blossomed forth into its natural springtime once more.

Again and again, in a downpour of darkness and sobbing
it gleamed as of earth. Until after its terrible throbbing
it stepped through the comfortless open door.

27. *To Gertrud Ouckama Knoop*

CHÂTEAU DE MUZOT SUR SIERRE, VALAIS
9 February 1922

Here, following immediately on my letter of the 7th, comes an addendum, for, dear friend, it causes me such great uneasiness to think of that XXIst poem, the " empty " one in which the " transmissions " occur (" *O das Neue, Freunde, ist nicht dies . . .*"), so please paste it over at once with this " Child's Spring Song " [1] written today ; it enriches the symphony and, as a pendant, is not a bad match for " The White Horse Offering ".

This little song, as it came to me this morning on waking, complete down to the eighth line, and the rest immediately after, — seems like an interpretation of a " Mass ", a real mass joyfully accompanied by hanging garlands of sound : some convent children sang it, I do not know to what text, but in this sort of dance tempo, in the little convent church at Ronda (in South Spain), sang it, I believe, to the tambourine and triangle ! — It fits, does it not, into the sequence of *Sonnets to Orpheus* as, if you like, the lightest spring note among them ? (I think so.)

(Does the paper match more or less ? I hope it is the same.)

Only this — and only because that twenty-first sonnet was a blot on my conscience.—Affectionately your RILKE.

1 Springtime is come again, brimming with flowers.
The earth is a child that is lesson-wise.
She can say many poems. . . . And the tedious hours
are fully redeemed in the joy of the prize.

Strict was her teacher. The snowy hue
in the beard of the old man pleased us well.
What is the meaning of green or of blue ?
She can tell if we ask her, O how she can tell !

Earth, happy earth, on your holiday play
awhile with the children. We'll chase you along,
merry earth. The merriest wins the day.

What the teacher taught her, those many things,
and all that is written in roots and in long
difficult stems : she sings them, she sings !

28. *To the Princess Marie von Thurn und Taxis-Hohenlohe*

CHÂTEAU DE MUZOT SUR SIERRE, VALAIS
February 11 (*evening*), 1922

At last,

Princess,

at last, the blessed, how blessed day, when I can announce to you the completion — as far as I can see — of

The Elegies :

Ten !

From the last one, the great one (with the opening begun long ago in Duino : " O that I may at the end of my terrible vision/ sing a great song of exultance to angels accordant . . ."), from this last Elegy which, even then, was meant to be the last, — from this — my hand is still trembling ! Now, on Saturday, the eleventh, at six o'clock in the evening, it is finished !

All in a few days, it was an unspeakable storm, a tornado of the spirit (as in Duino), the very fibres and tissues cracked in me — there was never a thought of eating, God knows what nourished me.

But now it is done. Done.

Amen.

So here is the triumph I was holding out for, through everything. Through everything. This was what I wanted. Just this and nothing more.

One I have dedicated to Kassner. The whole thing is yours, Princess, how should it not be ! It'll be called :

" The Duino Elegies."

In the book (for I cannot give you what has belonged to you from the beginning) there will be no dedication, only :

" The property of Marie . . ."

And now, thank you for your letter and all its news ; I was longing for it.

Of myself, only this for today . . . it is, at last, " something ! "

Goodbye, dear Princess.—Your D. S.

A kind letter from the Princess Oettingen has just come.

Recommend me, please, to her good graces. I'll write soon.—All the best to the Prince, Kassner, etc.

P.S. Please, dear Princess, do not think it merely a subterfuge on the part of my laziness when I tell you why I am not sending you a written copy of the Elegies now : I am jealous of your reading them. I feel that *I* ought to be the first to read them to you. When ? Soon, I hope.—D. S.

29. *To Lou Andreas-Salomé*

CHÂTEAU DE MUZOT SUR SIERRE, VALAIS
February 11 (*evening*)

LOU, DEAR LOU, look :

At this moment, Saturday the 11th of February, at six, I lay my pen aside behind the last completed Elegy, the tenth. Behind the one (even *then* it was destined to be the last) whose opening was written in Duino : "*Dass ich dereinst am Ausgang der grimmigen Einsicht/Jubel und Ruhm aufsinge zustimmenden Engeln* . . ." What there was of it I had already read to you, but now only the first twelve lines have remained, all the rest is new and : yes, very, very, very wonderful ! — Think of it ! This is what I have been struggling for. Through everything. Miracle. Grace. — All in a few days. It was a hurricane, just as in Duino : all that was fibre in me, tissue, scaffolding, cracked and bent. There was no thought of eating.

And just imagine, there's *something else*, in another, earlier connection (the *Sonnets to Orpheus* — twenty-five sonnets written suddenly, in the mutterings that heralded the storm, as a memorial to Vera Ouckama Knoop), I wrote, I *created* the horse,[1]

[1] But to you, O Master, what gift can I bring,
who have taught all creatures the ear ?
A memory of Russia, a day in the spring,
and a horse, as the evening drew near. . . .

He came from the village, the stallion all white,
and hobbled he was at the hock ;
came to frisk by himself in the meadows that night
and his mane stood out in a shock

and beat on his neck as he galloped and pranced,

you remember, the prancing happy white horse with the stake at his hock, that galloped towards us one evening in a meadow by the Volga :

HOW,

oh, how I made him, an " Ex-voto ", for Orpheus ! — What is time ? When is Now ? He leapt across the many years, with his load of happiness, right into my wide-open feelings.

So they came, one after another.

Now I *know* myself again. It was like a laceration of my heart that the Elegies — *were* — not there.

They are. They are !

I have gone out and stroked my little Muzot for having guarded all this for me and at last granted it to me, stroked it like a great shaggy beast.

That's why I didn't answer your letter, because, all these weeks, without knowing why, I have been holding my peace for *this*, wrapping myself more and more closely round my heart. And now, only this for today, dear Lou. You shall see directly. And your husband too. And Баьа — and the whole house, even to the good old sandals ! — Your old Rainer.

P.S. Dear Lou, the pages I wrote, breathlessly, yesterday night, these two, could not go off by registered post this morning, Sunday, — so I have turned the time to account by writing out for you *three* of the finished Elegies (the sixth, eighth, and tenth). The other three I'll write by and by, and will send them soon. I like to feel that you have them. And apart from that it eases my mind to think of them existing somewhere outside, kept safe in a fair copy.

But now I must take the air for a moment, while the Sunday sun is still in it.

Прощай

---

dragging the troublesome hobble along !
O how the fountains of horse-blood danced !

He snuffed the wide winds, and loud was his song !
Your cycle of sagas, O master mine,
is closed in his image :
my gift at your shrine.

30. *To Lou Andreas-Salomé*

CHÂTEAU DE MUZOT SUR SIERRE, VALAIS
20 *February* 1922

Thank God you are there, dear, dear Lou, to bring it home to my very soul !—As I read your good, so understanding letter it overpowered me anew, this assurance from all sides that my work is at last there, shaped long, long ago, from everlasting !

I had planned to write out the other three Elegies for you today, as it is Sunday again ! But now, just think, in a radiant after-storm, another Elegy has been added, the *Saltimbanques.* It puts the most wonderful finishing touch to the others, only now does the circle of Elegies seem really rounded off. It is not joined on as the Eleventh, but inserted (as the Fifth) before the " Hero Elegy ". The fragment that has stood there hitherto did not seem, owing to its different structure, entitled to that place, although it was beautiful as a poem. This is going to replace it (and how !), and the supplanted poem will come under the section *Fragmentarisches* which, as the second part of the " Book of Elegies ", will contain everything contemporaneous with them but which time wrecked as it were before birth or so amputated in form that the broken edges shew. — Thus I even have the *Saltimbanques* who affected me so when I was first in Paris and have lain on me like a task ever since.

But not content with that, hardly was this Elegy on paper when the *Sonnets to Orpheus* went on further ; today I am arranging this new group (as Part 2) — and have written out one or two of the nicest for you — to keep ! All of them from these last few days and still quite warm. Only our Russian Horse (how he greets you, Lou !) is from the earlier first part, from the beginning of this month.

And herewith finish, for today. I must catch up with my letters ; several have accumulated for answering.

I know very well that there may be a " reaction " — after being thrown like this I may fall down somewhere ; but actually I am falling into the approaching spring, and since I have had patience long enough to get so far, how should I not manage a little further side-patience for the days that are not so good ;

and finally, my gratitude (of which I have never had so much) ought to outweigh all their aggravations and confusions !

Thank you for writing to me at once, despite all your work ! —Your old RAINER.

The 5th, 7th, 9th Elegies — soon !

35. *To Gertrud Ouckama Knoop*

CHÂTEAU DE MUZOT SUR SIERRE, VALAIS
18 *March* 1922

VEREHRTE, LIEBE FREUNDIN,—In view of the sad and wearisome distractions which, when you wrote me last (on the 20th February) were keeping you busy in Weimar, I deliberately held back all further news, — but I could not fail to do violence to myself by this abstention. For I would have liked firstly to thank you at once for your kind and warm-hearted acceptance of the *Sonnets to Orpheus*, and secondly to confess that the number of these poems has been doubled in the meantime ! As soon as my somewhat exhausted pen can muster strength enough for the copying, this new Second Part of the *Sonnets to Orpheus* will be placed in a booklet for you (matching the earlier one as far as possible). Today I am sending you only *one* sonnet[1], because it is the closest to *me* of the whole series and the most important one in it.

[1] Hurry ahead of farewell like a thing that's behind you,
speeding away like a winter about to depart.
For among winters one infinite winter will find you,
when you awake, with an all-overwintering heart.

Be ever dead in Eurydice, — rise up more singingly,
rise and regain that pure kinship to which you belong.
Here, in the realm of the vanishing, sing out more ringingly ;
be like a glass that shatters itself in its song.

Be — and yet know what you were before your creation,
sensing the infinite source of your spirit's pulsation
so that it may be perfected as never before.

To the depleted alike to the dumbly encumbered
store-rooms of Nature, the sum that is nameless, unnumbered
— add yourself to them exultant and reckon no more.

In addition I would only ask you to *replace* the VIIth (of which only the first stanza has remained, — the first version always pained me with its pathos and has since been deleted) by the enclosed variant.[1] The third sonnet which I am enclosing I have — for the time being at least — inserted as the XXIIIrd [2]. so that Part 1 of the *Sonnets* now comprises *twenty-six* poems (Part 2 contains twenty-nine !)

Only this for now, with sincerest greetings,—Your RILKE.

1 Praise is the thing ! Like one destined for singing
he broke like a bell from the tongueless ores.
O transient press of his heart, from whose wringing
the wine of mankind inexhaustibly pours.

His voice shall not flag in the dust nor decline
once the godly example possesses his mouth.
All becomes vineyard, all becomes vine
ripened and full in his sensuous south.

Not by sepulchres hoary with princes' mould
shall his song of exultance be gainsaid ;
nor by shadows that fall from the gods of old.

For he like a heavenly messenger stays
and holds far into the doors of the dead
vessels heaped high with the full fruits of praise.

2 Not till our flight shall uprise
guilelessly into the pure
pellucid quiet of the skies ;
no longer so sovereign and sure,

no longer flaunting its lines
as the tool whose prowess is proved,
swooping in slender designs,
playing the winds' beloved ;

not till its vainglory fails
and over the growing machine
at last a pure Whither prevails

will the airman, upborne by his gains,
hold in himself the serene
distance his flying attains.

36. *To E. de W.*

CHÂTEAU DE MUZOT SUR SIERRE, VALAIS
20 *March* 1922

LIEBE UND GESCHÄTZTE FREUNDIN,—Your letter, with its wealth of news, brought me the keenest joy even with the first lines ; yet I had feared that the long pause which I was obliged to let grow and grow all through the winter might have swallowed up your voice. This — and I thank *you* personally every bit as much as I attribute it to the nature of our relationship — was not the case : it was natural for us to take this pause as part of the rhythm of our friendship, which has been defined and regulated rather than interrupted by it. Your reaction is the guarantee of the constancy and certainty of our ties. Allow me to surrender myself with joy to this feeling.

Of course you, because of your experiences in your own work, must have come to terms with that state which follows the end of some long-continuing artistic tension — at first it seems an empty freedom ; it does not surprise me that you have got to know it so well. It is a dangerous state (one of the most dangerous for the creative worker), he becomes light the moment his wings are tired ; too light. It is the upswing of the spirit towards some kind of surface. In earlier years I found this sort of thing unspeakably confusing, for the *holiday* side of this unburdening is only one of its aspects ; it's no sooner there than it changes into a feeling that you have grown superfluous. To guard against these lurchings in too light a boat, I used to do everything possible to keep some reliable ballast always within reach, ready for such moments of disengagement, — but whether it was that my strength was not great enough to be divided in this way, or whether I had advanced, too late and in the teeth of too many difficulties in childhood and youth, towards my natural pursuits, or whether the age at which I took them up demanded of me a singleness and concentration on *one thing* alone : I still did not succeed, despite my beginning a number of studies, in really developing for myself a permanent counterbalance. Later I consoled myself with the thought, *tant bien que mal*, that my art — in any case a task too long for even the longest life — would suffer under a division of this kind, and Rodin's immense exhortation to work came just at the right time, enabling me to implant, in my innermost centre, *the will to wholeness and singleness*, and to obey its dictates to the end. But I did not have the, in this sense, so helpful *métier* that Rodin had, nothing that could have given me, with its continual presence, the support of the daily, tangible and reliable things of the visible world, — also I lacked the vitality of the great master which had gradually made it possible for him to meet his inspiration with so many ceaseless plans for work that it could not fail to enter into *one* of them, almost without any pause arising. This '*accord*', induced consciously and not without cunning, made the mighty artist so sure of his inspiration that he was able to deny its influence forthwith, its very existence even : for the vibrations of it, always accessible to him, were no longer distinct from his own powers, he reigned over them as over himself ; only in the last years of his life, when the lassitude of old age, at last descending, caused Rodin to become careless and inwardly wasteful and covetous, did this fact take its revenge just as every harnessing of the Too-Great, the Transcendent, the Divine, must one day take its revenge : then he created with the *technique* of inspiration, but without it, indeed, contrary to it . . . The imperilment of the artist is immense, and his peril grows round him like the multiple of his greatness.

However that may be, dear friend, I am not alarmed when you say of your art — which I value very highly — that for a long time you have been growing estranged from these strivings of your nature because of studies that can in no way be combined with them. Even if I do not understand what path you think of unlocking for yourself with a Doctorate of Law, this complete contrast between your two activities seems to me right ; for the more different one's intellectual, conscious and purposive world is in its essence and practice, the more readily does it protect the world of inspiration and the things that rise up incalculably, conjured out of the depths. (Where, on the other hand, two such activities, an artistic one and another one, are more or less contiguous, — say journalism and literature, and so many other examples — then the most fateful influences appear which obscure and corrupt the finer medium.) — Anyway, if I were young now, I would definitely look round for some daily, very heterogeneous sort of occupation and try to establish myself on some concrete territory in accordance with my strength. Perhaps one serves art today better and more wisely if one makes it the silent, secret avocation of certain days or years (which does not mean doing it on the side like a dilettante ; after all, to give a very lofty example, Mallarmé was an English teacher all his life . . .), but the " profession " itself is hag-ridden with intruders, with people who don't belong and who exploit this bastardised trade, and a regeneration, a re-orientation (in the absence of which a spectacular exposure of this kind would rapidly become ridiculous) can only come about through those silent *individuals* who do *not* count themselves among the crowd and who accept none of the usages which the literary fanciers have put into circulation. Whether such individuals are private persons or whether they hide modestly behind some skilled craft, they will play their part in remedying a situation that has long been impossible, all the more since their literary *silence* will look highly significant beside their deepest eloquence. For example, it will not remain a mere velleity for the poet to whom, of all the Frenchmen of my generation, belongs my greatest and most marvelling admiration — Paul Valéry — that, between his earliest publications and those magnificent poems and writings which have made him pre-eminent since 1919, he had the strength to interpose a silence of nearly twenty-five years. He was, if I am not mistaken, busied with mathematics, and was so much and so purely at home in this domain that he was able to perceive and proclaim Einstein's significance *before* the other French savants.

What I, at the time of *Malte Laurids Brigge*, thought I could discern in respect of the theatre, that all the offshoots and suckers would have to be cut away for many a year if it were to grow with its deepest roots into something greater and more necessary — that is now my opinion and warning as regards *all* the arts : they have run to seed, and it is not the encouraging, the tending gardener who is required but the chastising gardener, with shears and spade.

Enough — but so as to give you some little advance sign of the results of the winter, I am enclosing a sonnet (one dear to me), not from the corpus of the main work (the *Duino Elegies*, but from the so-called *Sonnets to Orpheus* : a little cycle of poems written as a memorial for a young girl.

With attentive ear, dear friend,—Your RILKE.

37. *To Rudolf Bodländer*

CHÂTEAU DE MUZOT SUR SIERRE, VALAIS
23 *March* 1922

How much, my young friend, I would have liked to give a *good* answer to your recent pages, — but words are difficult here. On the whole, I think I can see that you have the right attitude when you try to accept and endure this struggle as something intimately your own, intent on discovering what the physical and spiritual conditions are that renew the conflict and in which of their conjunctions it appears. Certainly this is the most responsible attitude, only you must definitely discount the irrelevant emphasis that would see it as an ignominious and vicious struggle. Good friend, this is important : fight without guiltiness. Nowadays nobody in our western civilisation can ever " get done " with it (as the expression goes) — for everybody this strange urge will become the cause of some conflict-group or other, — least of all has the superior town-dweller " got over it " who admits of so many dubious ways of escape, compared with which your own profound and tranquil perplexity must seem completely innocent. — In any case, do not forget that here we are wholly on *innocent* ground. — The terrible thing is that we possess no religion within which these experiences, literal and concrete as they are (yet at the same time so unspeakable and intangible), could be lifted up to a god, into the protection of some phallic Divinity, the *forerunner*, perhaps, of a whole galaxy of gods who may yet dawn upon mankind again after being absent so long. What is to succour us when the religious helps fail, when they hush up these experiences instead of transfiguring them, deprive us of them instead of implanting them in us more gloriously than we ever dared to imagine. Here we have been unutterably forsaken and betrayed : hence our tragedy. As the fire died out of the religions and more and more incrustations were laid down on the surface, they perished into moralities and drove this phenomenon, the very centre of their being and ours, out upon the chill soil of ethics and thus, necessarily, into the periphery. Gradually people will come to realise that *here*, and not in social and economic conditions, lies the great calamity of our time, — in this thrusting of the act of love into the periphery ; the clear-seeing individual now uses up all his strength in pushing it back again at least into his *own* centre (if it stood at the world's centre it would at once send the blood of the gods pulsing through the whole earth !). — The man who lives blindly, on the other hand, somehow rejoices in the " pleasure " that can be obtained at the periphery and (clear-sighted against his will) avenges himself for its worthlessness by seeking and at the same time reviling this pleasure. — Renunciation in superficial things is not progress, and it is useless to exert the " will " to that end (moreover the will is too young and too new a power, judged by the primordial right of instinct). Renunciation or fulfilment in love, both are wonderful and unequalled, but only when the whole love-experience with all its multiform yet equivalent raptures (which succeed one another so closely that, *precisely at that point*, it is no longer possible to distinguish soul from body) can take up a central position : there (in the ecstasy of united lovers or saints of *all* times and *all* religions) renunciation and fulfilment are identical. Where the Infinite (be it minus or plus) enters in its entirety the human sign drops away from before us, and, as after a journey completed, what remains is arrival, sheer Being ! — This, very roughly, dear friend, is what can be read (at a cursory glance) from our greatest, most passionate secret, when we ask. — I think it must, if you read it accurately, place your conflict on a new and unravaged plane. (And if, sometime, you should come to love somebody, read this letter together, unless you know it well enough by then to find its contents anew in yourself !) . . .

38. *To Ilse Blumenthal-Weiss*

CHÂTEAU DE MUZOT SUR SIERRE
25 *April* 1922

. . . As regards Beer-Hofmann's *Schlaflied für Miriam*, now that you mention it this poem does call up special memories in me ; I have known it more or less since its inception. At that time (about 1902) it was the *only* poem Beer-Hofmann had ever written ; — later, out of the wonderful rarity and fastidiousness of his work another, second poem was added, equally full, — I could not say whether the number of these exquisite things has increased in the meantime. If I admired the *Schlaflied* exceedingly on my first acquaintance with it (when it appeared in all its splendour in the pages of the one-time *Pan*), I was able (for I knew it by heart) to win unqualified admirers for it in later years also. When I lived six months in Sweden it even went to the length of people from other estates sending a carriage round for us, just as one fetches the doctor, solely in order that I should recite the verses to strangers who had heard of the extraordinary beauty of this poem : a summons to which I acceded each time with emotion and all the joy of my own admiration !

Here perhaps I may go on to another theme that was touched upon in your letter before last : the destiny of the Jews. Beer-Hofmann, unlike so many Jewish people who seem to display only the faults and anfractuosities of this hard fate, was always an example of its grandeur and dignity, of which nothing essential need be forfeited even in a long and grievous exile. — You know from one of my earlier letters (the one about " faith ") how much the Jew — besides the Arab and the Orthodox Russian, to go no further East — seems to me favoured by the inborn unity of his nationhood and religion, which time and again has secured him an obvious advantage. The fact that he had the ground cut from under his feet and had to maintain himself on a strip of borrowed earth has its good and bad points ; apart from a few great exceptions he was bound to abuse his advantages in order to overcome opposition and homelessness, — in most cases he was unfair to himself and others. With a cunning to which self-preservation schooled him he made of his non-attachment not a misfortune but a superiority, and wherever he misemploys this dearly earned superiority in a petty, greedy or hostile way, where he unwittingly *avenges himself* he becomes a pest, an interloper, a disintegrator. But where the same process, the same triumph over fate is accomplished in somebody with a *great* will, then out of the same inexorable conditions is born that nobleness of which Spinoza is a famous example. — The mobility and nomadism of man's inner centre, its independence (but at the same time its rootlessness, unless the mind be rooted in God) — this *spiritual vagrancy* came into the world through the fortunes of the Jews : a tremendous danger as well as tremendous freedom. And according as you stress the one side or the other of this Jewish dilemma you will either fear it or praise it ; in which respect it remains true that its consequences are ultimately necessary to all of us and are not to be thought or wished away. Perhaps this ferment, when it has worked long enough, will have to be drawn back again and collected in a vessel of its very own. The zionist consciousness that springs from purely Jewish impulses may be the beginning of the segregation I have tentatively proposed. This re-acquisition of the old ancestral soil, this new birthright would have to be conceived and interpreted literally as well as symbolically. If we, as is probable, have only known the Jewish race in its distortions, in its bewilderment, in its wayward and at times perverse obstinacy, and if we can deduce a measure of its strength from its endurance, we are alarmed at first when we realise the strength which it could not fail to exhibit once it were settled, secured, satisfied ! — The growth of these people so fruitful even in their *eradication* would then lead to an irresistible fruitfulness in God, — the continuation of that history of passionate and massy harvests for which the Old Testament, wherever we open it, gives us the occasion, the climate.

Enough. I send you, dear lady, my ever devoted and thankful greetings. Your letters bring me continual joy.

What now remains for all of us to wish is that the long-delayed spring may at last declare itself and more or less catch up with the date. For the winter was long enough.—Your R. M. Rilke.

39. *To Clara Rilke*

MUZOT SUR SIERRE, VALAIS
12 *May* 1922

MY DEAR CLARA,—Hearty thanks for your hurried lines of the 9th May, they came yesterday ; yes, you can imagine how much I am with and near you all in spirit, and how much the ringing of bells is in my ears. How could it be otherwise at this moment of crisis and decision. And my being with you will increase daily till the 18th.[1] — I am glad Bredenau [2] is becoming so beautiful ; it will still be festive when the festival is over, and the warmth of the celebrations of the 17th and 18th will make the little house all mellow !

I am enclosing two letters, for Ruth and Carl, which you can give to our children on the 17th or 18th, just as you feel. This was not the time to write *much*, — Ruth will have to create the consciousness and certainty of my participation more out of herself than out of any outward signs, and Carl must take it from her that I am sharing the solemn crisis with all my heart.

You yourself, dear Clara, know it deeply, — and I do not have to take pains to convince you. In a word : I am sincerely and fervently with you !

As for my own personal wedding present, I would like to decide about it when I visit the young couple in Alt-Jocketa and my own eyes shew me what is most gladly desired. I don't want to act into the unknown, vaguely.

It is altogether wonderful for me that the year 1922, memorable because of Ruth's wedding and the turning-point of her life, should also remain signalised and distinguished for all time by the completion of my great work — the *Elegies*.

Besides that the purchase of Muzot by that very friend from Winterthur, who has hitherto only *rented* the little castle, is being deliberated ; it is possible that he will come to a decision by the same date. This also holds a certain joyous significance for me. Werner Reinhart will not be able to live in Muzot himself for some time, — and so I, in common with other friends of his,

[1] Day of Ruth Rilke's marriage to Carl Sieber.
[2] Clara's house in Fischerhude.

will always retain the privilege of withdrawing from time to time into these old walls, which have granted me such fruitful shelter. . . .—With fondest thoughts of you. . . . Your Rainer Maria.

45. *To E. M.*

Château de Muzot sur Sierre, Valais
13 *September* 1922

The look of your writing alone, my good and dear friend, even before I had read it, made me fear that some heavy lot had befallen you, — and now it proves to be the heaviness that comes from joy : yet how can such heaviness come from such joy ? For you still remember how this joy loosened your spirit, set you free and gave you wings. For how long ? And why no longer ?

There are two ways of reading your letter : yesterday my conjecture was that you, perhaps both of you, had exposed one another too long to the strongest rays of your feelings, so long that the very rays that had brought forth growth and sweetness became excessive and began to destroy : for which you were now involuntarily taking your revenge.

Today I see it differently : perhaps because of this experience in which you are still standing and struggling you feel compelled to regard yourself as a person who, in his rôle of lover (once the wooing is over) seems condemned by his inner distresses to make use of the technique and instruments of hatred, quite unwittingly, as subserving a deeper and more enigmatic pleasure. . . . Of course you may find this discovery infinitely painful and confusing, — but you must not be appalled : it only means doing battle with the unsolved problems and mistakes of your inmost nature, — and who knows how far you might not be armed for this very conflict by those flights and triumphs of the spirit which unlocked the affection of her who surrendered to you ? If now you take fright when you feel yourself growing fierce and terrible towards the creature you once gained, and to her torment, — try, as against this, to understand that the acquisition and possession of a person for your own use and (often pernicious) pleasure — simply does not exist, that it may not and cannot be, — and you will see a distance, a reverence reviving within you which will cause you to measure your emotions afresh, with those measures which were yours during courtship. It often happens that a happiness such as you, loved and loving, experienced, not only liberates new powers in a young man but also lays bare altogether different, deeper layers of his nature from which the most mysterious discoveries leap out overpoweringly: but our conflicts have always been a part of our riches, and when we are terrified of their violence we are only terrified of the unsuspected possibilities and tensions of our own strength; and chaos, if we can but win a little detachment from it, instantly evokes in us the foreknowledge of new orders and, in so far as our courage can have any share in such prefigurements, the curiosity and desire to accomplish that still inscrutable future order!

I have written the word "detachment": if there is any sort of counsel I might find myself able to offer you, it is the surmise that you should now endeavour to seek *this* — detachment: both from your present perplexity and from those recent states, those enlargements of the spirit which, though you enjoyed them when they occurred, you have not yet taken essentially into your possession. A short separation, a parting for a few weeks, a re-beginning of yourselves and a new binding together of your overfull and loosened natures would hold out the most prospect of your retrieving what seems to be destroying itself. Whether my first interpretation of your letter is right, or whether I am closer now to the reality of the suffering which you endure and inflict, — or whether something quite different could be understood from your few lines: this advice could not, in any case, be wrong. Nothing fixes people so much in error as the daily repetition of that error, — and how many people who are bound to one another by a fate which is, in the last resort, paralysed, could have assured themselves by means of short, pure separations of that rhythm which would have sent the mysterious animation of their hearts pulsing inexhaustibly, from change to change, through their inner world.

This is all, the little I can do by way of repaying your trust in me. May you soon feel more assured.—R. M. R.

47. *To Ilse Jahr*

CHÂTEAU DE MUZOT SUR SIERRE, VALAIS
2 December 1922

YOU DEAR CREATURE,—It was a little miracle that your letter eventually reached me ; for more than twenty years I have not lived at the place you sent it to. But how glad I was of its pure voice ! How could the voice be too small for me when every creak in the floor goes to my heart ? Indeed you sense this : my world begins with *things*, — and thus even the least person in it is frighteningly large, almost an exaggeration. Nor are you so " little " either, you, with your girl's tenderness. You must know that I never read what " they " write about my work in the papers or magazines, or even in the books smacking of " Science " ; I pay no attention to them and so every real human voice finds the most bountiful space in my heart. But already I am directing you further afield, beyond me, to the figure whom I build more truly and more lastingly, outside. Cling to *it* if it appears great and significant to you. Who knows what I am ? I change and change. But that figure is the limit of my changing, its purest border : if it radiates love into your heart, well and good : let us both believe in it.—RAINER MARIA RILKE.

50. *To Prince Hohenlohe*

CHÂTEAU DE MUZOT SUR SIERRE, VALAIS
23 December 1922

. . . Proust, — you mention Proust : I am extremely glad that you have found relish and interest in his work. By an accident which I will tell you about one day, I was one of the first (in 1913 !) to read *Du côté de chez Swann*, hence one of the first to admire Marcel Proust, which was the natural and immediate reaction. On the occasion of his death André Gide reminded me recently that I had my place among the earliest admirers of this great writer, — and so you can imagine how breathlessly I travelled from volume to volume and how shocked I was by the death of this momentous personage. It cannot be estimated yet what these books have opened out for us and for the future, they are loaded with a wealth of discovery, and the strangest thing about them is the application, so quiet in its own way and so matter-of-fact, of the most daring and often unheard-of technique. Those lines linking event to event — any other writer could only have used them at his peril, as lifelines, — but with Proust they take on at the same time the beauty of ornamentation, and even as design they retain their validity and permanence. Launching out with bold, intuitive strokes into the most astonishing associations he seems only to be tracing the veins actually present in a piece of polished marble, and here again you are amazed by the perfect tact of his analysis, which pitches on no particular thing, playfully releases the very thing it seemed to cling to and still, with almost unsurpassable precision, everywhere admits and makes allowances for the ultimate mysteries. — In his wretched cork-lined chamber which he only left occasionally at night, this strange soothsayer must have seen life pass unceasingly before him, wide-open like a gigantic hand whose lines he understood so thoroughly in all essentials that they could not bring him any more surprises, — only unending tasks every day ! — How one must love work when one has got that far ! . . .

52. *To Lou Andreas-Salomé*

CHÂTEAU DE MUZOT SUR SIERRE, VALAIS
13 *January* 1923

MY DEAR LOU,—Today must be the Russian New Year ! But often of late, on the morning of the western New Year and also between it and Christmas, I have been with you in thought : I still thought, if I put off writing a little longer, that I could enclose the *Elegies* and *Sonnets* in my next letter ; I miscalculated badly : on the last day of the year there appeared, instead of the first copies of the *Elegies*, yet another set of proofs, still rather faulty, which took me just up to the threshold of the New Year. In the last echoes of midnight and in the pristine silence of 1923 I was in the middle of correcting and reading the fifth Elegy ! I am glad it began like that (if one may speak of time-divisions at all). And you ? I am often *very worried*, dear Lou, about you, all of you, when I hear of and picture to myself the increasing absurdity of things in Germany, with life and the cost of living practically impossible. It seems — and this was my impression in 1919 — that the right, the unique moment when everything might have led up to a general agreement, has been neglected on all sides; now the gap gets wider and wider, the sum-total of mistakes can no longer even be read, it has so many figures; bewilderment, despair, humbug and the typically modern desire to take advantage of catastrophe at all costs, even of this: such are the treacherous powers that bowl the world along. . . .

But maybe neither the world nor anything else can make headway in politics; hardly do you penetrate, no matter at what point, one layer below the surface when everything looks different, and you fancy that some mysterious process of growth, some incorruptible will, is only using these confusions to hide under and keep its curiosity, which is otherwise engaged, safe and whole. (In France especially, among people who don't dabble in politics, the deep workers — what a scene of change, renewal, stocktaking; a new orientation of the spirit suddenly, willy-nilly, grown thoughtful again. . . . I don't know whether you have been following Proust, his influence is colossal, — and not only is *his* influence at work but what *it* has brought about is simultaneously working in other and younger men. . . .) Here I am fortunate enough to be able to follow all this without much difficulty; I've been translating Paul Valéry and I felt my technique was so suited to his great poems that I have never translated with such certainty and insight before, despite the formidable difficulties. . . . And Valéry, although absolutely cut off from all things German by not knowing the language, wrote me when he was travelling through Switzerland in the autumn for his lectures: "*Vous étiez l'un des objets principaux de mon voyage*". How fate-like and irresistible all real relationships are! And yet, alas, I could not see him for the most fatuous of reasons: the impossibility of getting Austrian or German money sent out makes me more and more of a prisoner within the old walls of my Muzot, in them I have everything for the time being but each step outside, even to Lausanne, becomes increasingly difficult! But how should I not take this drawback comparatively lightly, when I think of the trials that would beset me and hem me about in a less remote and sheltered spot. You should not put too high a value on freedom of movement just now; it would only land you in disaster. In the summer I had all sorts of plans; but so many warnings immediately rose up at the edge of the least realisation of them that, on the contrary, I did everything to stay put in Muzot. Were the world less out-of-joint there would be some sense in making a change at this significant close of the chapter, and it might have good results. But it is best to hang on to proven data and be faithful and grateful to them. My health in particular is going through strange convulsions: every excitement, even that of work (which often does not let me eat *in peace* for weeks at a stretch) attacks more and more that centre in the pit of the stomach, the sympathetic centre, "the sun-web"; here I undergo a sort of interior cancellation and am having some weird experiences, what with the rivalries and agreements between the two centres, the cerebral one and the tummy one which is, presumably, *our* centre, after all — for the visible and invisible alike!

Meanwhile, I am not bothering too much about this queasiness of the central organs; at most applying my energies to "switching off" for meal-times the intensive vibrations that come from spirit or heart, just as I generally do for sleep. This great god, Sleep; I sacrifice to him quite regardless of time — what does he care about time! — ten hours, eleven, even twelve, if he will accept them in his sublime, mild and silent way! But unfortunately I seldom manage to get to bed early now; the evenings are my reading time. The presence of tempting books and the stillness of the old house — intense to the point of improbability — generally keep me awake until past midnight. Then the little private attentions of a mouse in the many undiscovered interstices of the thick walls do much to deepen the mystery which nourishes the immense landscape of night, eternally without care.

I have become curiously dulled — and to my amazement was so even in the summer — as regards this landscape whose marvels I have felt so deeply, yet I have to hold them before my eyes with an effort, deliberately, if I am still to partake of them. Does the flattening of our senses really go *so* far under the constant pressure of environment ? How manifoldly, then, may not habit put us in the wrong as regards people and things : is one to find comfort in the thought that the curve of enchantment runs on in oneself ; but how pursue it there, where it must inevitably get broken on the denseness of the medium and become unrecognisable, only leaving a mark where other curves, with origins similarly lost, cross it in the strange whirl of intersections ?

Dear, dear Lou — will word come from you soon ? Have you been abroad, and where ? — How were you able to keep alive in this surfeit of ills ? And of Russia, have you news now and then ? — Soon, please, write me, no year begins properly until I have heard you say a few words, in the new space.

Ruth, it seems, has been living in perfect and complete happiness since her marriage ; all her capacities for gladness and joy can now be applied and unfolded. And as they are living on that old farm on the estate of their " in-laws " they are not quite so dependent on the clamouring needs of these evil times as they would inevitably have been in any city !

Прощбй, dear Lou ! Many greetings to all your house.— Your old RAINER.

59. *To Ilse Jahr*

CHÂTEAU DE MUZOT SUR SIERRE, VALAIS
22 February 1923

. . . I must tell you that nothing was lost on me, although I kept silence : all the winter I have been a bad letter-writer despite my great solitude and my long evenings. This is because my pen (it is, alas, the same pen that has to do work and go the friendly pilgrimages of correspondence) wore itself out last winter with infinite tasks and now, this year, only has strength enough for the translations I have undertaken and for the most necessary writing which, with my correspondence enormously swollen, is still considerable.

But I am sure you will understand, you dear creature, when I ask you to keep your communion with me (whether you only feel it or, now and again, write it out) independent of my visible response ; as things are you cannot help but feel my response and replies, even if I am silent at first, even for a long time.

It may be also that you do not turn so much to him who *I am* — perhaps you address and rejoice with him who I *was* twenty years ago, when I wrote those books that have grown so close to you and become yours, so that you flowed through them towards the *man*, the brother in the human sense. . . . (This contact with the *human* neighbourhood I only experienced very late in life, and without those periods in my youth which I spent in Russia I should probably never have come to feel it as purely and perfectly as we must, in the end, feel it, if we are ever to be ushered into the whole glory of life without false gaps.) I began with *things*, which had been the veritable familiars of my lonely childhood, and it was indeed something that I was able, without outside help, to get as far as animals. . . . But then Russia opened out for me and gave me the brotherliness and darkness of God, in whom alone there is fellowship. That was how I named him then, the God who had dawned upon me, and I lived long in the antechamber of his name, on my knees. . . . Now you would hardly ever hear me name him, there is an indescribable discretion between us, and where closeness and penetration once were, new distances stretch out as in the atom which the new science also conceives as a universe in little. The Tangible slips away, changes ; instead of possession one learns the relativity of things, and there arises a namelessness that must begin again with God if it is to become perfect and without deceit. Sensuous experience retires behind an infinite longing for the perceptible world ; God, now become unutterable, is stripped of all attributes, and these fall back into creation, into love and death . . . perhaps this is what was accomplished over and over again in the *Stundenbuch*, this ascent of God from the breathing heart, covering the whole heavens and descending as rain. But any open avowal of this would be too much. Less and less can the Christian experience be considered ; the primordial Godhead outweighs it infinitely. The notion of being sinful and then needing redemption as a pre-condition of God is more and more repugnant to a heart that has understood the earth. It is not sinfulness and error in things earthly but, on the contrary, the pure nature of the earth that will lead to the most essential consciousness ; sin is certainly the most wonderful round-about way to God, — but why should those go a-travelling who have never left him ? The strong, inward, vibrating bridge of the Mediator has meaning only when the abyss between God and ourselves is admitted, — but even this abyss is full of the darkness of God, and if ever anyone feels it, let him go down into it and howl there (this is more necessary than crossing over it). Only for him to whom even the abyss was a dwelling-place will the paradise we have sent on ahead of us be retrieved, and everything deeply and passionately *here*, which the Church has pirated and pawned to a Beyond, come back once more ; then all angels will decide to sing the praises of the earth.

You are too young, dear child, to understand now, straight away, what I mean ; but look, one thing is more important to me than anything else : to be precise. I did not want your dear heart to seek me where I no longer am ; for this reason you should not lose track of me, on the contrary your interest even in my past ideas can only come to clearness when you know into what spirit they have unfolded. — The mysteries are greater than you now can guess, but you already know much of them since you could write that everything was beautiful on your " beloved God's earth ", but " differently " beautiful. Seize firm hold of this and do not let yourself be frightened or led astray.—And now, farewell for this time. RAINER MARIA.

64. *To Clara Rilke*

CHÂTEAU DE MUZOT SUR SIERRE, VALAIS
23 *April* 1923

. . . The spring. The Valais is not a country where it can breathe its true breath, find its proper depths ; for this a certain leisureliness is required. The March sun, already too violent, drags all the vegetation out of the hard grey earth as though with cork-screws. And then the climate has a terrible taboo about rain ; it is rain-shy to a degree I would never have thought possible ; every means by which rain can be frustrated and dispelled is justified, — in the summer this is pleasant enough in so far as you avoid getting wet, — but *now*, when the sky yearns to rain silently and fruitfully and write those long letters to the earth, you are driven almost to despair by the daily wrath of the gales which hurl the good clouds with indescribable virtuosity over the mountains. Often it frays your nerves and, still more, the poor flowers in the garden ; senselessly whipped and chastised, they lose their heads. . . .

69. *To Clara Rilke*

CHÂTEAU DE MUZOT SUR SIERRE, VALAIS
17 *November* 1923

MY DEAR CLARA,—Your news filled out my anticipations with such excellent details that I regarded them as having been exactly foreshadowed in my instinct! Those nights of expectation, — as though the star you saw from your bed above the forest trees were the same star that once glided through the empty vines, Ruth's birth star, now inherited by little Christine ! [1] The fact that Ruth was courageous and truly blessed and able at once to take her new happiness in her arms, fits in so absolutely with her sure and earthy nature, and it could hardly have been otherwise since the right help was on the spot. And of that, thanks to your and Carl's prudence, there was no lack. But it was she, I fancy, who involuntarily heightened the situation, making everything solemn. The scene was like a " Birth of Mary " : the many diligently active people in the very bright room, and then you seem to be looking behind it into the bigger room with the festal board, where they all get strong again and recover and congratulate one another.

It must have filled you with great excitement to have been busied in this intimate and fervent way : may you now celebrate your own birthday in equally good heart and feel how my wishes are there to speed and strengthen it for you. I imagine you will stay in Alt-Jocketa for the 21st, although (great-great)-Grandmama Phia writes me that you will have to return to Bredenau soon. (As for her, is it not an unutterable blessing that she has found this sheltered and congenial spot in Franzensbad ? ! We

[1] Christine Sieber, born November 2, 1923.

must do everything to keep her there, where she has food and shelter, and shield her from Prague ; you yourself will have seen from her letters how beneficial the change is.)

Please give me, before you leave the children, more news about how Ruth and little Christine are faring. It is splendid that she can feed her herself ; but will the fourteen-year-old maid be enough to look after the cooking and everything in the next few weeks and keep order, when Ruth certainly ought not to take too much on herself ? Could not some outside help be arranged, which would let her spend these weeks as quietly and contemplatively as possible ? That Carl has already harnessed himself so powerfully to his work again is, I hope, not bad for his health ; is he all right now ? Does he sleep naturally ? — Please tell me all this before you go. I will write to Ruth soon, when Muzot has entered upon its silent winter mood once more, with long undisturbed afternoons and evenings. Now everything is still rather in the transition stage ; arranging my huge apple-harvest and other domestic affairs distract me and demand attention. . . .—So all love, and with a fond embrace, dear Clara, for your birthday, RAINER MARIA.

76. *To Gertrud Ouckama Knoop*

CHÂTEAU DE MUZOT SUR SIERRE, VALAIS
13 *February* 1924

LIEBE UND WERTE FREUNDIN,—I thank you with all my heart that you did not wait until after Easter to give me the news which I have now received with attention and real need ; my silence, also, had continued far too long, — but even if the exchange creates no diversions here (at most when you are faced with the dire necessity of converting a flood of Czech or Austrian kronen, or even marks ! into the " frankish mould "), there were still other obstacles, calamitous and quite unaccustomed ones for me — far-reaching physical disturbances which I had always managed to get over by myself, became so acute after the summer that I had twice to visit nursing-homes (and shortly before Christmas again) ; I find this hanky-panky with doctors terribly confusing, not unlike suddenly having to commune with my soul through the devious agency of a priest : for my association with my body has, for twenty-five years, been so straightforward and of so strict an understanding that I feel this medical interpreter sticking like a wedge into our joint agreement. On the other hand it would be a new and painful thing for me were I obliged, with unwanted spiritual pride, to set myself above a failing body. I have never developed any counterbalances here ; on the contrary, I was convinced that all the elements of my nature worked together towards a pure harmony with creation issuing at the apex, springing forth from this abundance of common (physical and spiritual) gladness. My body, initiated into everything, has always had the power of attorney ; like its other responsible partners it could sign for the whole firm. A collapse of this business arrangement would be a disaster ; for however many great, indeed mighty examples were given me to the contrary, shewing the infinite consequences that have ensued from the conquest of the body, the ignoring of it, yes, even the exploitation of its infirmities, — this would still not be *my* way of attaining the same things, and I do not know what the solution is that I must work at in the situation I am now in. Well, perhaps it will not last long, and, if I am pressed hard enough, I may continue in my old attitude with some result !

You write nothing of grandmotherhood necessarily diminishing those faculties one credits oneself with, — so I too will regard *mon art d'être grandpère* (since the 2nd. of November last) simply as profit. Lilinka, to whom I send my wishes as well as to you, dear friend, has, it appears, thought a son the right thing, whereas Ruth, so far, has stuck to her own sex ; at any rate this little Christine does not seem to lag behind any boy in strength and lust for life. May everything, there and here, continue to thrive happily, without our grandchildren growing big too soon : for their own sakes they need to leave Time time to get better.

Russia : this : " лик богородицы "[1] — there also I hope that those who watch over its evolution will not retire too soon but be careful, very careful of it, wrap it round secretly and hide it until its splendour is ripe and the time ready to pass away !

[1] " Face of the Mother of the Gods."

I do not doubt for a moment that the seeds sown during the war will lead to new beginnings, but one trembles for them lest they shew themselves too soon and fall into the hands of the exploiters. First the days of the profiteers must have passed away.

I wish I could be with you for tea, one Sunday, in my usual deep chair, and tell you of all the wonderful things that come from France ; I am surrounded by them here. All that I can scrimp together I turn to the purchase of the books that are now being written ; for many of them are of such a kind that you ought not only to read them but open them again and again. *There* the frontiers have really fallen ; self-aware in a new and vital way, the French spirit is no longer afraid to assimilate foreign and distant things : suddenly — unheard-of occurrence ! — Italian, Spanish, Russian and Scandinavian, not to speak of English and even German art is being acknowledged and signally appreciated ; and the influences which, before the war, they thought they could do without (or would have misunderstood, spiritually marooned as they were), — these influences already appear, fully developed, in the work of the younger generation, the generation for whom the War was like some heroic puberty. There would be no point in my citing names at you : but there are a dozen or more books which clothe one's dreams with reality and thus (one may think) prepare from far off, perhaps from very, very far off, the corresponding *external* events as well . . . My confidence in this direction is great. . . .

78. *To Witold von Hulewicz*

(Dedication in a copy of the *Duino Elegies*)

Happy are they who know that behind
  all languages the Unspeakable stands ;
and know that some greatness from yonder will find
  rest in our full and contented hands —

dependent no more on these bridges we raise
  and build with the stuff of this various scene ;
so that from every enchantment we gaze
  into a kingdom broad and serene.

MUZOT, *February* 1924

TO THE FAITHFUL AND DILIGENT MEDIATOR
WITOLD HULEWICZ (OLWID)
IN GRATITUDE

RAINER MARIA RILKE

80. *To Alfred Schaer*

CHÂTEAU DE MUZOT SUR SIERRE, VALAIS
26 February 1924

DEAR DR. SCHAER,—A longish absence from Muzot, caused by my being unwell, has put me so far behindhand with my work and correspondence that I must reproach myself for my sorry negligence, towards you also ; your attentive letter bears the date of the 3rd of February !

If the kindness of your enquiry could not fail to put me under an obligation, my tardiness is all the more reprehensible because your letter contains two questions which merited a prompter reply.

To answer the first query is short and simple : since the two volumes of the *Neue Gedichte* (First and Second Parts) no publication of verse of any kind has come from my pen, except for the two new volumes which you know and name.

As for the second enquiry, however, you yourself know how difficult and lengthy a reply to the theme it broaches would be ; and I must confess at once that I do not really feel up to it. In my *earliest* days, twenty-five, thirty years ago, there might well have been a question of " influences " which could be adduced simply and specifically. The name of Jacobsen alone marks a clearly defined epoch of my life : he was really the " reigning sovereign " of my heavenly-earthly years. And when I think of Bang (the *Grey House* and the *White House*), a star of the first magnitude must be recorded, a star by whose light and position I found my way for quite a while in the darkness of my youth (which was differently dark and differently twilit from the youths of today). Liliencron's name was very wonderful for me in those years, Dehmel's hard and significant : Hofmannsthal proved that it was still possible to have the most absolute poet for a contemporary, — and in Stefan George's adamantine figure you glimpsed those rediscovered laws which none may now escape if he is concerned with the word as magic. Into this living fabric of experience came the Russians, Turgeniev at their head, and then the man who, by his personality as well as by the quiet competence even of his first works, had directed me to these masters : Jacob Wassermann. To know the *Michael Kramer* of Gerhart Hauptmann, with whom I also had personal connections, was my pride in those years. With my first journey to Russia (1899) and with the learning of the Russian language, through which I rapidly and almost without further hindrance came to know the magic of Pushkin and Lermontov, Nekrassov and Fet, and the influence of so many others . . . with all these crucial forces to assimilate the situation then changed so fundamentally that a tracking down of influences seems absurd and impossible : they are countless ! What has not worked in me ! Some because of their perfection, others because you immediately realised that they could be done better or differently. This, because you recognised it as belonging to you and having authority ; that, because it rose up like an enemy, unseizable, almost unendurable. And Life ! The actuality of life, suddenly and inexhaustibly revealed, which in Russia opened out before me like a picture-book, although later, after my removal to Paris in 1902, I felt myself really being drawn into it, everywhere partaking of it, sharing its dangers, sharing its gifts ! And Art . . . the arts ! That I was Rodin's secretary is no more than an obstinate legend, originating from the fact that I once, in passing, for five months (!) helped him with his correspondence. . . . But much more have I been his *pupil*, and for much longer : for at the bottom of all arts lies the same challenge which I have never accepted as openly as I did in my talks with that potent Master who, even in green old age, was full of living experience ; in my own profession I possessed a very great and glorious friend, Emile Verhaeren the poet, so human in all his hard splendour, — and, ever since 1906, my strongest model has been the work of a painter — Paul Cézanne, whose footsteps I followed after the death of the Master.

But often I ask myself whether things that in themselves are without emphasis have not exerted the realest influence on my development and productivity: the acquaintance of a dog; the hours I passed in Rome watching a rope-maker reiterating one of the oldest gestures in the world in his craft, as did the potter in a little village by the Nile;[1] to stand beside his wheel was inexpressibly and in a most mysterious sense fruitful for me. Or wandering through the Baux country with a shepherd, or hearing in Toledo, with a few Spanish friends and their women companions, an ancient novena sung in a poverty-stricken little parish church, a chant which once in the 17th century, when the handing-down of this custom was surpressed, was sung in the same church by angels. . . . Or being so familiar with the elusive phantasm of Venice that strangers in the labyrinthine windings of the Calli had only to ask me if they wanted to reach their destination, wherever it was . . . all this was "influence", was it not? — and perhaps the greatest of all has yet to be named: that I could be *alone* in so many cities, lands and climes, undisturbed, exposed to the new and unfamiliar with all the multiplicity, all the listening and obedience of my nature, wanting to belong and yet again compelled to lift myself away. . . .

No, books can have no very decisive bearing on the simple fulfilments that life realises in us, not when we are older anyway; so much of what they deposit in us like a weight may be counterbalanced by a meeting with a woman, by a shifting of the seasons, by the merest change in the air's pressure . . . by the knowledge, for instance, that to such-and-such a kind of morning, all unexpectedly "another" afternoon belongs, — or by anything else of the sort that is continually falling to our lot.

The question of "influences" is of course a possible and

[1] See Ninth Elegy:

"Praise for the angel the world, not the world beyond utterance,
him you cannot impress with your glorious feelings;
for in the universe where he more feelingly feels
are you but a novice; shew him, therefore,
a thing that is simple, that, fashioned through all generations,
lives as a heritage under the hand and the eye.
Tell him of things. He will stand there more marvelling, even as you
stood by the ropier in Rome or the potter who toiled by the Nile."

permissible one, and there may be cases where the answer would elicit the most surprising revelations ; but whatever the answer is it must instantly be referred back to the life from which it springs and be resolved in it anew. In accordance with this feeling I have tried, so as to give you an answer of sorts, to concoct some kind of " solution ". May it, dear Doctor, not appear too dilute in your test-tube and may it shew one or two properties which will reward the research and vigilance you wish to expend on it.—With sincerest regards, RAINER MARIA RILKE.

87. *To Lou Andreas-Salome*

CHÂTEAU DE MUZOT SUR SIERRE, VALAIS
22 *April* 1924

MY DEAR, DEAR LOU,—I can't tell you what a grand and marvellous Easter you brought me with your letter, which promised to be the more certain and full the longer it held back! Now it has come during this Easter Festival and was so mellow with good news and affection, more so than anything that has befallen me for a long time. Only when I tell you the story of the (third) winter I have passed in Muzot will you see how wonderful it is that you can report *just this* of your patients : I read it again and again and draw an indescribable comfort from it. That I needed this strengthening will be enough to shew you that my winter has not been a good one, indeed, almost hard. What you foresaw after the tremendous exertions of the first winter in Muzot, the recoil, has set in, and for a time it was so violent and bewildering that, shortly after Christmas, I left Muzot and went into the Val-Mont Nursing Home (above Montreux), incapable (for the first time in many years) of looking after myself. Those were peculiar weeks. Physically, the duodenum was the place attacked, but from there everything was thrown into disorder. I was three weeks in Val-Mont. Unluckily on the last day but one, just before my departure, the attentive and well-meaning doctor discovered on top of all this a goitre on the left side of my throat, and though he assured me that it was ten years old and had been neutralised, once discovered it worked on my consciousness all the more since the uprush of air from the duodenum itself gave rise to difficulties in swallowing and breathing which now, with this superadded cause, became still more noticeable and alarming. But this is a ' tale of woe ' which I will sketch in for you better another time, dear Lou ; at present the house is full of guests and in the next few days a succession of visitors will be coming (a really not unwelcome change after the loneliness of the long winter) . . . But I have not recanted, either, what I wrote you two years ago : that after so magnificent a triumph I would gladly bear anything that might be laid upon me by way of reaction. I am holding out. And have not been wholly inactive : a complete volume of French poems (an extraordinary experience : sometimes I took up the same theme in French and German, and it then, to my surprise, developed differently in both languages : which does much to belie the naturalness of translating) has unaccountably come into being, with much else besides, and my reading was lively all through the winter and most fruitful in its results. My old tower is so situated that French books in particular can reach me : one's astonishment over what is being produced there knows no end. First and foremost, Proust — he will certainly be a marvel for you as well. You know that I translated Paul Valéry the winter before last : this year he was one of my first visitors in Muzot, a fortnight ago on Easter Sunday !

Ever since your letter, Lou, do you know what I've been thinking ? That one day *you* will be here with me, this year ! Why shouldn't it be possible ? (except at the hottest season when it would do you no good and I shall probably go away). You know that I have a guest-room, a dear little attic, with very tiny windows it is true. Let us keep it in mind should the occasion offer — yes ?

I may soon have to exchange this singular and exposed solitude for that of Paris, which is differently grained and nurtured ; it may be that things here are beginning to be not so necessary as they were and to make themselves, like the climate, oppressive. The Valais sun only works on the wine, that is its *métier* : everything else, plants and people, it forces too much and bears down on them with all its incubative weight, which is perfectly adjusted to a wine-growing country. And so, by and by, a passing change at least will be needed.

Since November 2nd. I have had a grandchild, a fine and vigorous little Christinchen. Ruth asked me particularly to tell you. Of her, only good tidings ; and of Clara, everything good and wonderful, with lovely lightenings and lightings of the spirit !

And the good, steady news of you both, of 'Loufried',—how it moved me ! You mean so much to me, you dear thing, dear things ! Tell your husband how glad I am that he is rooted so quietly and firmly in the Unchanging, and greet him from my heart. . . .

Enough : I want to know much, much about you, your work, experiences, impressions, ideas, — there's nothing for it, you must come. Think what days we would have !

I must go to Sierre to await my guests, who have jaunted off to see Sion and return from there at six.—Your old Rainer.

91. *To Nora Purtscher-Wydenbruck*

Château de Muzot sur Sierre
11 *August* 1924

My dear Friend,—Your letter of June would have given me the strongest incentive to write to you at once, — if I nevertheless failed to do so, it lay with a caprice of my nature in having holidays, letter-holidays in particular ; I was really tired after a — for my health — not very good winter (which, strictly speaking, has not been followed by any improvement), so I gave way, — but now that I am at home (albeit for a short while) I am setting out before all else, leaving mountains of letters lying to the right and left of me, to thank and answer you.

Your letter found me in Ragaz, and, just think, it arrived in time for me to shew it to your aunt, the Princess Marie ! I had gone to this ancient spa for the express purpose of meeting her (and also the Prince again), since it appeared that the Princess would have to undergo treatment there instead of prolonging her Swiss trip to see me in Valais, as she has always done of late. The Princess charged me with so many cordial greetings for you that I am ashamed to carry out an order, which would assuredly have brought you much pleasure, with such signal tardiness.

If the whole of your letter, my dear Countess, was an object of interest to the Princess, her special attention was reserved for those remarkable passages in which you allude to your experiences in mediumistic writing. You may remember that whenever there was a reliable medium at the Taxis', serious and often continuous séances were held, — and in Ragaz we were engaged in reading through the more recent results of the sittings, parts of which were still unknown to me, so that what you had to tell me found itself in an atmosphere which allowed your words to work in all the fullness of their conjecture and sincerity.

The Princess asks me to tell you to go quietly and carefully ahead ; it may be that those communicating powers are ultimately willing to allow a record to be kept of their manifestations (in regard to which it is certainly important NOT to enter into any relations with Metaphysical Societies !), provided that one considers it one's duty to treat these manifestations in confidence and not use them in any way unpleasing to them. It is therefore of the greatest value to be able to read those communications through again, the meaning and validity of which often appear only after a time. As far as I myself am concerned, my own impressions in this mysterious territory derive, with few exceptions, from the experiments conducted at the Taxis' meetings, which I frequently attended until ten years ago as a spectator. Later on it was never possible for me to get in touch with a reliable medium, otherwise I would certainly have been eager to increase, on suitable occasions, the very remarkable experiences which have fallen to my lot. From this you can see well enough the nature of my attitude. I am convinced that these phenomena, if we accept them without seeking refuge there, and if we remain willing to incorporate them in the totality of our being — which, indeed, is full of no less miraculous secrets in all its workings — I am, I say, convinced that these phenomena do not testify to a false curiosity on our part but actually concern us to an indescribable degree, and, were we to exclude them, would always be capable of making themselves felt at one point or another. Why should they not, like everything else unknown or absolutely unknowable, be an object of our endeavour, our wonder, our awe and veneration?

For a while I was inclined, as you yourself seem to be now, to take the existence of "external" influences for granted in these experiments; I no longer do so to the same degree. However extensive the external world may be, with all its sidereal distances it hardly bears comparison with the dimensions, the *depth-dimensions*, of our inner being, which has no need even of the vastnesses of the universe to be itself all but illimitable. When, therefore, the dead or the unborn need a resting-place, what refuge could be more agreeable or more appropriate to them than this imaginary space? It seems to me more and more as though our ordinary consciousness dwelt on the summit of a pyramid, whose base broadens out in us and beneath us so much that the more deeply we see ourselves able to penetrate into it the more boundlessly do we seem implicated in those factors of our earthly, and in the widest sense, *worldly* being which are independent of space and time. Since my earliest youth I have entertained the idea (and have also, when I was adequate to it, lived accordingly), that if a cross-section were made lower down through this pyramid of consciousness, Being, in its simplest form, would become "eventual" in us, the inviolable presence and simultaneity of all that we, on the upper "normal" apex of consciousness, are only permitted to experience as flux. It once became a necessity for me in *Malte* to allude to a figure[1] who was capable of conceiving things past and to come as actual to the *n*th degree, and I am convinced that this conception corresponds to a *real* state of things, even though it be repudiated by all the conventions of our ordinary life.

Those séances, therefore, with all their disturbing and misleading secondary phenomena, with their fatal blunders, imperfections and (there can be no doubt of this) their countless misunderstandings, are on the road to such an intelligence, and could not, since this intelligence was already bodingly prefigured in me, have passed me by unnoticed. They have not changed my world-picture in any way, seeing that I was always disposed to concede a multiplicity of shapes to the Possible: it is simply

[1] Count Brahe. See *Collected Works*, vol. v. p. 40 *et seq.*

that I must have failed to observe manifestations of this kind. But just because this stupendous world was natural to me, being already an integral part of my inmost consent and compliance, I declined to have *more* concern with these revelations than with any other mysteries of our being : for me they are one mystery among countless other mysteries, which all have more part in us than we in them. Anyone who, within the framework of poetry, is initiated into the unheard-of marvels of his own depths, or is in any way used by them as a pure and unconscious tool, must eventually see in his wonder the development of one of the most essential capacities of the spirit. And here I must confess that my greatest, my most passionate wonderment lies with my own achievement in this respect and with certain movements in Nature rather than with any mediumistic occurrences, however much they have stirred me on occasion. But as regards these, whilst I accept them obediently, reverently, sincerely, I always feel impelled, as if by some extraordinary instinct, to call up counterbalances to them in my consciousness as soon as they pass over and into me : to my mind nothing would be more alien than a world in which these powers and intrusive elements had the upper hand. And the strange thing is : the more I act in this way (after each nocturnal séance trying, for instance, to see that the spectacle of the starry silent night is equally marvellous and true), the more I believe myself in harmony with the essence of those occurrences. They want, it seems to me, rather to be suffered than acknowledged ; rather not repudiated than invoked ; rather consented to and loved than questioned and made use of. I am, fortunately, completely unserviceable as a medium, but I do not doubt for one moment that, in my own way, I keep myself open to the influence of those often homeless powers, and that I never cease to enjoy or sustain their companionship. How many words, how many decisions or hesitations may not be ascribed to their working ! For the rest, it belongs to the original tendencies of my nature to accept the Mysterious *as such*, not as something to be exposed, but as the Mystery that is mysterious to its very depths and is so everywhere, just as a lump of sugar is sugar in every part. Possibly, conceived like this, it will under certain conditions dissolve in our being or in our love, whereas otherwise we only bring about a mechanical reduction of the Mysterious without it actually passing over into us. I am (and this might in the end be the only place in me from which a slow wisdom could sprout) completely without curiosity concerning life, my own future, and the gods. . . . What do we know of the seasons of eternity and whether it be harvest-time yet ! How many fruits which were intended for us or whose very weight would have caused them to drop into our hands, — how many such fruits have inquisitive spirits interrupted in their ripening, bearing away a precipitate and premature knowledge, often a misunderstanding, at the cost of crippled growth and nourishment later on !

But now I must make an end, my dear and valued friend, after having attempted to describe such a broad circle. Take out something for yourself and, if circumstances permit, keep me informed of the particular movements and impacts which are transmitted to you from the unknown. You also will not manage without calling up counterbalances, which happily you do not lack, since artistic work, house, family, nature and, last but not least, the *animals* urgently engage your heart and sympathies. Of course these, these companions in our knowledge of the Whole, the animals, who in a deeper layer of consciousness have intelligence of themselves, most easily lead us across again and are close to the mediumistic state.—Always in sincerest friendship to you both, Your RILKE.

103. *To Paule Levy*

CHÂTEAU DE MUZOT SUR SIERRE, VALAIS
4 November 1925

DEAR FRÄULEIN PAULE LEVY,—I stand before you as a complete ingrate — if only because of my long procrastination (excused by a hundred and one things). This might be made good in the end, for in its concluding sentences your letter gives me to suppose that I may find indulgence with you. But . . .

But, my case grows all the more complicated in that, answering you at last, I must shew myself still more ungrateful, wretchedly ungrateful !

Your French version of my '*Cornet*', adapted together with M. Derche, is the fifth or sixth translation which has been put before me in the course of the last few years ; unfortunately I have not been able to compare the earlier texts, which I have filed away somewhere, with yours, but I remember that I have always been inclined to refer back to the first of these translations should the (albeit not very desirable) occasion for a new impression arise. For not only does that oldest translation still seem to me the best and liveliest, but also it came from a friend's hand, a friend's feelings, — and for that reason continued to hold my preference. At present, having returned home after long months of absence, swamped with arrears and work of all kinds and ill to boot, — I have not yet succeeded in hunting up that old text from among my papers so as to compare it with the results of your labours ; but I hazard that I would have a predilection for it all the same : for, to be quite candid, your version seems to me to require many improvements and alterations ; in its present state it pleases me neither in wording nor in rhythm. It is true that I have some difficulty in recognising and detecting this : you must consider how far removed one feels from a precipitate work of one's youth, separated from it by thirty years, a whole life, — and its structure is so foreign to me today that I could not even say whether such a jumble, such a medley of prose and poetic false-starts is permissible at all ! I have tried to accompany the individual pages of your translation with suggestions, — but here I myself am uncertain ; were I sitting beside you and if we could come to some agreement about the various readings it would probably be only the work of an hour or so. But to go through your pages like this, pen in hand, a stranger to my own text, withdrawn from it for Heaven knows how long, — this seems to me a tedious and, in the end, not even a very reliable undertaking. What to do ?

I recall that M. Gaston Gallimard kindly told me of his interest in this old work, and I fancy I can deduce from your letter that the translation is intended for the *Nouvelle Revue Française.* Once more : what to do ? Is your and M. Derche's application to have been in vain ? I am on the fourth page of my letter, and, frankly, this *Weise von Liebe und Tod* does not seem worth so much expense : all your work, your letter, my letter. . . . From a single instant of robust youthfulness (the *Cornet* came to me in one autumn night) a movement of sorts may have flowed into those lines, a little something of ungiven and ungiveable happiness, a store that can still communicate with us even today : otherwise it is not to be understood how this very inadequate performance could have multiplied into so many hundreds of thousands of copies.

Meanwhile, I ask myself, does not this magic cling wholly to the German original ? In actual fact none of the translations into other languages (in so far as concerns those in which I can follow my wording) has really been able to convince me.

Thus I close, for this time, with nothing but question-marks. The content of this " poem " is so meagre, its language so undeveloped, that the only thing that could excuse its continued existence is just that glamour, that swing, that breathless voyaging for which clouds scurrying across the moon that night were more the model than anything I knew, and could know, by legend, of that forefather of mine. . . . And to render this anew in another language is difficult, if not impossible. It would be good to agree about one thing before all else : about the necessity of this extremely irrelevant book existing in French ?

Let me close for now — however late ! The words with which your letter ends, about the autumn flowers proffered me from the " great bouquet ", put upon me the full burden of my ingratitude. I can hardly venture to set the word " thanks ", which I have not ceased to contradict all through these hurried pages, — here in conclusion.—Relieve me of my humiliating position and believe, despite all, in the sincere regard of your RAINER MARIA RILKE.

105. *To Witold von Hulewicz*

MUZOT SUR SIERRE, VALAIS
10 *November* 1925

DEAR FRIEND,—I do not like doing anything " hurriedly " whatever it is, but this time I *rushed* through your question paper, urged on by my shocking dilatoriness and all the other, equally shocking, arrears by which I have been beleaguered since my return. . . . In *Malte* there can be no question of defining and substantiating the numerous allusions in it. The reader must communicate not with their historical or imaginary reality but, through them, with Malte's own experience : and even *he* was concerned with them only to the extent that a person may let a neighbour affect him, or a passer-by in the street. The connection lies in the fact that the people evoked exhibit the same " frequency " of vital intensity as vibrates in Malte's being ; just as Ibsen (we'll say Ibsen, for who knows whether he really felt this way ?), just as any bygone dramatist seeks visible testimony for an event that has become invisible in us, so the young Malte Laurids Brigge needed to keep a grip on life — which was everlastingly slipping back into the Invisible — by means of phantoms and images ; he finds these now in memories of his own childhood, now in his Parisian setting, now in reminiscences of his readings. And everything, no matter where experienced, has the same valuableness for him, the same duration and actuality. Not for nothing is Malte the grandchild of old Count Brahe who regards everything, past and future, as quite simply " present ", and in the same way Malte regards as present these reservoirs of his feeling which are fed by the above three channels of perception. His own days of affliction and the great days of affliction at the time of the Avignon Pontificate, when all the things that now strike *inwards* so grievously were projected *outwards* — are now put on an equal footing : it is of no consequence for us to know more of the figures conjured up than the searchlight of Malte's heart reveals. They are not historical figures or shapes of his own past, but *the vowels of his affliction* : hence one must bear with an occasional name which is not enunciated any further, as though it were but a bird-note in this country where the inner lulls are more perilous than the storms.

For this reason it would only be confusing to define more specifically the figures that are merely hinted at ; each must verify them in his own way, and whoever cannot verify them will still learn enough from the suspense of their anonymity.[1] . . .

[1] Here follows a lengthy question-sheet given over to the elucidation of certain passages in *Malte Laurids Brigge*.

Enough, my dear Herr von Hulewicz. . . .

The book is to be accepted whole, not taken up in single details. Only so does everything attain its proper accent and perspective. I wish you could have waited for the French *Malte* before giving the Polish text your final " imprint ". The French one is completely trustworthy and, with the unequivocalness and logic of the language, might perhaps have helped to clarify for you the meaning of certain still more doubtful passages and in particular the relationship between the words. In this text many things, I believe, that were dark to you in German could not now be misunderstood. I have great confidence in this French version which is to appear before Christmas. (In any case you will receive the volume as soon as it is ready.)

But now I must rush off to other things ! — Take kindly the hand which, in conclusion, I offer you in spirit, and always the best thanks for your faith and trouble, Your R. M. RILKE.

106. *To Witold von Hulewicz*

Postmark : SIERRE, 13.11.25

[This letter concerns the *Duino Elegies*, which Hulewicz was translating into Polish.]

Here, my friend, I myself hardly know what to say. Out of the poems themselves some attempt at elucidation might be made, but like this ? Where to begin ? And am *I* the one to give the Elegies their proper explanation ? They pass infinitely beyond me. I regard them as a further working out of those basic propositions already given in the *Stundenbuch*, propositions which, in the two parts of the *Neue Gedichte*, use the phenomenal world for play and experiment and finally, in *Malte*, drawn together as if in conflict, refer back to life again and almost lead to the conclusion that this life of ours, suspended as it is over a bottomless pit, is impossible. In the Elegies life, starting from the same data, becomes possible once more, indeed it experiences here that ultimate affirmation towards which the young Malte, although on the right and difficult road " *des longues études* ", could not yet guide it. *Affirmation of life as well as of death prove themselves* one *in the Elegies.* To admit the one without the other would, it is here realised with exultance, be a limitation which would ultimately exclude everything infinite. *Death is the side of life that is turned away from, and unillumined by, us:* we must try to achieve the greatest possible consciousness of our being, which is at home in *both* these immeasurable realms and is nourished inexhaustibly by both. The true pattern of life extends through both domains, the blood with the greatest circuit runs through both: there is neither a This-side nor a That-side, but a single great unity in which the beings who transcend us, the angels, have their habitation. And then there is the position of the love-problem in this world augmented by its greater half, this world now, at last, whole, holy.

I am astonished that the *Sonnets to Orpheus*, which are at least as "hard", filled with the same essence, are not more helpful to your understanding of the Elegies. The latter were begun in 1912 (at Duino), continued fragmentarily in Spain and Paris till 1914; the Great War completely interrupted this, my greatest work, and when I ventured to take it up again here in 1922, the new Elegies found their termination forestalled by the tempestuous imposition, within a few days, of the Sonnets (which were *not* in my plan). These, and it cannot be otherwise, are of the same "birth" as the Elegies, and the fact that they arose suddenly in connection with the premature death of a young girl brings them still nearer to their original fountain-head; for this connection is another point of contact with the centre of that kingdom whose depth and influence we share, boundlessly, with the dead and the unborn. We, the men of the present and today, we are not for one moment content in the world of time, nor are we fixed in it; we overflow continually towards the men of the Past, towards our origin and towards those who apparently come after us. In that most vast, *open* world all beings are — one cannot say "contemporaneous", for it is precisely the passage of Time which determines that they all *are*. This transitoriness rushes everywhere into a profound Being. And thus all the manifestations of the Actual are not to be used as mere time-bound things, rather are they to be embodied, as far as lies within our power, in that nobler significance which we, too, share. Not, however, in the Christian sense (from which I always passionately dissociate myself) ; but, with a consciousness that is purely, deeply, serenely *earthly*, it behoves us to bring the things we here behold and touch within the greater, the very greatest circumference. Not into a Beyond whose shadow obscures the Earth, but into a Whole, into *the* Whole. Nature, and the objects of our environment and usage, are but frail, ephemeral things ; yet, as long as we are here, they are *our* possession and our friendship, knowing our wretchedness and our joy, just as they were the familiars of our ancestors. Thus it is meet for us not only not to pollute and degrade the Actual, but, precisely because of the transitoriness which it shares with us, we should seize these things and appearances with the most fervent comprehension and transform them. Transform them ? Yes, for such is our task : to impress this fragile and transient earth so sufferingly, so passionately upon our hearts that its essence shall rise up again, invisible, in us. *We are the bees of the Invisible. Nous butinons éperdument le miel du visible, pour l'accumuler dans la grande ruche d'or de l'Invisible.* The Elegies shew us engaged on this work, the work of the perpetual transformation of beloved and tangible things into the invisible vibration and excitability of our nature, which introduces new " frequencies " into the pulsing fields of the universe. (Since the various materials in the Universe are only varying coefficients of vibration, we build in this way not only intensities of a spiritual kind, but, who knows ? new bodies, metals, nebulae and stars.) And this activity is sustained and accelerated by the increasingly rapid disappearance today of so much of the Visible which we cannot replace. Even for our grandfathers a house, a fountain, a familiar tower, their very clothes, their coat, was infinitely more, infinitely more intimate ; almost every object a vessel in which they found something human or added their morsel of humanity. Now, from America, empty indifferent things crowd over to us, counterfeit things, the veriest dummies. A house, in the American sense, an American apple or one of the vines of that country has *nothing* in common with the house, the fruit, the grape into which have entered the hope and meditation of our forefathers. The lived and living things, the things that share our thoughts, these are on the decline and can no more be replaced. *We are perhaps the last to have known such things.* The responsibility rests with us not only to keep remembrance of them (that would be but a trifle and unreliable), but also their human or " laric " value (" laric " in the sense of household gods). The earth has no alternative but to become invisible — IN us, who with a portion of our being have a share in the Invisible, or at least the appearance of sharing; we who can multiply our possessions of the Invisible during our earthly existence, in us *alone* can there be accomplished this intimate and continual transmutation of the Visible into the Invisible . . . just as our own destiny becomes unceasingly MORE PRESENT, AND AT THE SAME TIME INVISIBLE, in us.

The Elegies set up this norm of existence : they affirm, they glorify this consciousness. They place it carefully among its own traditions, claiming in support of this assumption immemorial customs and rumours of customs and even evoking, in the Egyptian cult of the Dead, a foreknowledge of such affinities. (At the same time the " Land of the Threnodies " through which the Threnody Elder conducts the young man who has just died, is not to be identified with Egypt, it is only the reflection, so to speak, of the Nile country in the desert-like clarity of the dead man's mind.) If one makes the mistake of applying Catholic conceptions of death, the Hereafter and Eternity to the Elegies or Sonnets, one isolates oneself completely from their conclusions and becomes involved in a fundamental misunderstanding. The angel of the Elegies has nothing to do with the angel of the Christian heaven (rather with the angelic figures of Islam. . . .) The angel of the Elegies is that Being in whom the transmutation of the Visible into the Invisible, which we seek to achieve, is consummated. For the angel of the Elegies all the towers and palaces of the Past are existent *because* they have long been invisible, and the still existing towers and bridges of our world *already* invisible, although still materially enduring for us. The angel of the Elegies is that Being who stands for the recognition in the Invisible of a higher degree of reality. That is why he is " terrible " for us, because we, its lovers and transmuters, still cling to the Visible. — All the worlds in the Universe rush into the Invisible as into their next-deeper reality ; a few stars undergo immediate sublimation and are lost in the infinite consciousness of the angels, — others are committed to beings who slowly and painfully transform them, beings in whose terror and rapture they attain their approaching consummation in the Invisible. We, let it be emphasised again, in the sense of the Elegies WE are the transmuters of the earth; our whole existence here, the flights and falls of our love, all strengthen us for this task (beside which there is really no other). (The Sonnets reveal single aspects of this activity, which is seen to take place under the name and guardianship of one dead, a young girl whose immaturity and innocence hold open the portals of the dead so that, departed from us, she now belongs to those powers which keep the one half of life fresh and open to that other half with its wide-open wound.) Elegies and Sonnets sustain one another at all points, — and I deem it an infinite grace that I have been able, with the same breath, to swell these two sails: the little rust-coloured sail of the Sonnets and the gigantic white canvas of the Elegies.

May you, dear friend, find here some counsel and instruction, and for the rest help yourself as best you may. For: I do not know whether I can ever say anything more.

107. *To Clara Rilke*

CHÂTEAU DE MUZOT SUR SIERRE, VALAIS
17 *November* 1925

MY DEAR CLARA,—*Where* is your birthday going to be celebrated? I am sending off these lines with something of a start in case they have to follow you about; and I almost wish they had to, preferably to Ruth and Christine who would bring your birthday home to you in the most natural and affectionate way.

From me, dear Clara, come all good wishes: it is lovely to feel that, with you, all wishes are received and used in a true sense: you are so resolved to see and confirm the good in everything that you cannot do otherwise than take good wishes as something very good indeed. Please do so with this impulse of mine; I hope it will come to you feelingly and fondly, despite my continuing silence.

Yes, I am silent, have been silent for long, in all directions;

Ruth too has felt this heavily enough in all conscience. It seems that one's fiftieth year does mark a sort of crisis after all ; for me at any rate it will have been one, the most fundamental of my life ; I don't yet see how I can get over it, and where I am going to. But as nothing stops still in its tracks a way will have to be found. I am quite unable to express my insurmountable weariness, it comes from my health which seems to be attacked more centrally than the doctors have hitherto wished to acknowledge. But probably I am meeting this growing fact with the falsest of attitudes : instead of seeing clearly as *you* have learnt to do, I see black, and this casts confusion and darkness over everything. But enough, enough of these outpourings in a birthday letter, they are altogether inappropriate and, after such a long silence on my part, not exactly understandable.

Ruth, for a moment, had the sudden sweet idea of paying me a visit whilst I was in Ragaz ; it was as you can imagine not easy for me to say No : but finally I had to : they were closing down in Ragaz, it was not comfortable in that completely empty hotel and besides, I want to be really happy and quite myself for Ruth : I'm working towards this and I hope that at a not too distant date I shall be able to ask the children over. I read with great regret that they are faced in all probability with a move to Liebau, how sad it is about the good old house in Alt-Jocketa behind its glorious chestnuts !

May you extract from all this my good thoughts and wishes and, disregarding the mood from which they go forth somewhat dismally, take them simply to your heart !—Rainer Maria.

112. *To Georg Reinhart*

Château de Muzot sur Sierre, Valais
19 *December* 1925

My dear Herr Georg Reinhart,—" Reality " has one formidable advantage over fiction and all its works — wherever Reality sends forth possibilities into an imaginary field, thereby challenging and to a certain extent training and exercising our imagination, this faculty, usually so stimulating, gives way, relaxes when faced with the proofs with which actuality out-trumps it, — and yet our imagination is not chagrined : for all the time it was taking part in that living achievement by which it appeared outdone — outdone by Life itself, sweeping our impulses on, confirming them, extending and multiplying them ! Yesterday evening I could conceive of no tale that could have affected me more closely and borne me along more delightedly than this story of the "House of Volkart" which, in the objective way you recounted it, actually contains only dates, simple statements of what has been done from the time of its foundation down to its present-day expansion.

What a document lies here in this book : what a model of co-operative labour, what an example of powers all uniting to one purpose ! From the very beginning and over and over again reality has always said "yes" to any genuine enterprise which occurred not for the sake of profit but which derived from the recognised need for commerce, for exchange, for the weighing of familiar things against strange ones. And when profit did come to reward the precise and seasonable shrewdness of those principles and procedures, how dextrously the early administrators of these ever-expanding businesses converted it into power again, so that it nowhere ran to seed but led on continually to the happiest and healthiest growth.

When I entered your business house in Winterthur for the first time I sensed clearly enough, but could little express, what now grips me anew with this book : the idea of trade in its *human* immediacy and purity. The language of the earth's quarters among themselves, a language whose bearers are the things of wont and worth ; the materials and what may with care be gained and derived from them. And how trade, despite its multitudinous usage and the inevitable complications brought about by time, has lost nothing of its "originality" and youthfulness : the fascination of the strange and far-distant is still operative, the eager curiosity and the joy of exchanging things and the inexhaustible wonder — at finding some product fetched from afar so different, so essentially precious, so flawless in its structure, so at one with its scent. And the joy, too, of trading away the things of your own country, chaste and modest in keeping with its climate, but along with them all the deft and subtle inventions and devices of the European spirit which in their turn will excite astonishment among peoples of different birth and creed, and satisfy or surpass their naïve curiosity. . . . All this, valued and striven for according to its true worth and always, all over the world, accompanied by phenomena which pass beyond the merely utilitarian, fulfilling or transforming our human lot ; and only at the very end the profit, and the profit never wantonly squandered but always directed inwards again and guided back into the ramifications of the work, there to generate prosperity in its own self, — until finally in its last workings, irresistible, it is acknowledged as the personal and peculiar possession of the stewards of so many things and destinies all linked to one common endeavour. . . . And here, in the realm of the personal, it is once more responsible, pressed into the service of great and known values and employed as only those can employ it who have trained themselves in their professions for the genuine, the true, for that which endures.

So you see, dear Reinhart, how your little book of facts invites all sorts of elaborations and interpretations ; I could fill more than these two pages with them. But may I, in conclusion, voice a request ? I assume, probably correctly, that your publication is reserved for friends and is not purchasable on the bookstalls. Now I would like so much to lay a copy of the memoirs before my publisher and friend Professor Kippenberg. This diligent and active proprietor and director of the Insel Verlag, famed besides (as you know) for his impressive Goethe Collection — the largest private collection of manuscripts and pictures from Goethe's life and times, — would (I am sure), being the great and fortunate merchant of spiritual values that he is, have the liveliest pleasure in owning a copy of your publication ; in his way he would have the finest sense for it and would appreciate the story of this traditionary rise, and for him (as for me) such a document would be very comforting in an age which values "novelty" at the expense of its continuity. How much old Goethe, who developed his mighty grasp of the Real and his reverence for tradition precisely through his concern with the structural world and through his need for universal relationships — how very much the older Goethe would have done honour to your memoirs — one can hear him saying a word to Eckermann about it!

So if it is not too brazen of me to make a suggestion of this sort, please would you have a copy of the book (with a notice that it was at my behest !) sent to Professor Kippenberg ?—With hearty thanks and Christmas greetings, Ever your devoted RILKE.

118. *To Lili Schalk*

VAL-MONT PAR GLION SUR TERRITET, VAUD
14 *March* 1926

LIEBE GNÄDIGSTE FRAU,—Could I have been mistaken when I thought I recognised *your* writing on that envelope, which I have to thank for Kassner's article on *The Wandering Jew* ? It would add a special flavour to the joy I had in coming across Rudolf Kassner again in this work (which once more radiates its sure and steadfast wholeness with, one thinks each time, even greater perfection and directness in every sentence) — if I knew YOU had thought of me and sent me this page of the *Frankfurter Zeitung*. The fact that your good memory found time for me would be the loveliest token of its continued existence, despite my having done nothing and again nothing all these many years for the continuance of a sympathy that has remained so valuable. But, frustrated on all hands and compelled to silence, I had to leave so much that was dear to me to those powers which vouch for the miraculous preservation and nourishment of the Unattended . . .

Kassner : though I may count myself among his old friends I am not among those who are still closer to him, enjoying the prerogative of seeing him again and again, which I so sensibly lack. If in his writings his habit of insistence and emphasis never becomes a weight that makes the words heavy, — so, too, friendship with him means nothing but this joyful sublimation of all strains and stresses into a soaring (and yet how precise) judgement ! I am going through a time when the influence of his sure and friendly being would have been an infinite help : and so I miss him more than ever !

But his oldest friends, — do they not admit as an elementary truth that, because they were able to accept so capaciously the bounds in which this dynamic spirit first appeared to them years ago, they have now made it feel at home with them, unrestricted in all its movements, belonging to them, to their sympathy and astonishment, like a true constant ? The stupendous demands which he now and then seemed to postulate right out of our reach become, in time, so purely and entirely filled with his own self that those who have remained at a sufficiently 'high tension' to receive the propositions of his world, feel themselves rising with him, like blood in the capillaries, into the next greater reality.

I am writing this, just extemporising my feelings, and I well know that I have made no reference to the strange and wonderful things in his essay about which so much could be said ; I write rather to feel my way into the Past and bridge over the river of time which you, in your kindness, have crossed in a single wing-beat, an action accompanied only by the light rustle of a written address.

Thank you ! And with all my old devotion.—Your RILKE.

122. *To Hans Ulbricht*

VAL-MONT PAR GLION SUR TERRITET
VAUD, 24 *March* 1926

Ever since your letter came I have often considered what friendly thing I could give you for your new journey : above all, what useful thing ? You have not made it easy for me. Although your letter, like one or two of your lyrical experiments (particularly the last ones) contains passages of a personal and individual stamp which reveal you more clearly, between these two forms of expression (that which is intended artistically and that which aims at being informative) there is too great a similarity.

It has now (once again) become clear to me what a wearisome and hopeless task the lyric must be at certain periods, simply because it works with the instruments of speech and does not entail sufficient *handwork* to enable you to develop it into an independent entity (this is meant not in the artistic, but in a purely vital, sense). The exhalations of life perpetually beat back again into life, — and an essence that seeks to discharge itself by its own means nevertheless charges itself with the intensified expression of its own unbearabilities, remains compassed about by the miseries it has overcome in apparently dispelling or transcending them, and yet is more abandoned to them than if it had never blossomed and condensed into lyrical consciousness. Even where an early talent benefits or possibly *forestalls* this struggle (Heym or Trakl) the result has had too little substance to do battle with to find any joy in the transubstantiation ; a Trakl (one thinks) who could have exercised his genius in painting or music instead of poetry, would not have perished under the too great weight of his creation and the darkness which it brought upon him.

Since life, as you tell me, will shortly require all sorts of alterations in you, it remains for me to wish that they may be such as will force something absolutely concrete, an occupation in the most *un*-figurative sense, between your hands. Even at the risk of your being deprived for a while of your attempts at poetry. But if you nevertheless find a pen in your head, you must forbid it to put down anything " impressionistic ", compel it to note the facts of your own life and, better still, of a life that is more foreign to you, and above all, you must fashion beside the pen intended to furnish your friends with the signs of your doing and striving, a second pen which you will treat like a tool : and do not let yourself be swayed by what comes from this second pen, be hard towards the least of its products. The workmanlike output which this other pen adumbrates should not work back into your own life, should be a design, an alchemy, a transmutation of which the " I " was only the first and last stimulus, but which from then on remains facing you, sprung from your own impulses yet instantly thrust out again so far upon the plane of artistic estrangement, of thing-like solitude, that you only feel yourself sharing in the completion of this mysterious object like some quiet deputy.

In any case this is important for you : to get away from the vicinity of your lyrics, not to start letters as though they were poems, and to accept life not merely as a fillip for the whims and ficklenesses of feeling. It is so much more. And it would be a pity if you, outdistanced by words, should in the end have suffered only the confusions of youth without knowing the triumph of youthfulness, which is nothing but being.—RAINER MARIA RILKE.

127. *To Beppy Veder*

RAGAZ, 23 *August* 1926

Now each one of the different people to whom you have been an ever certain joy, has had time to practise his loss : mine is of so special a kind that I was unable to write to you. Perhaps because I was so accustomed to your being there that it bewilders me to learn another set of bearings, less immediate ones, which use the scale of distance and separation. Perhaps also because I have somehow got stuck in our farewell : can you understand this ?

I think this letter has admitted something in advance, for it is only since the summer that the great blows of Fate have come upon our sunny family and in my being. Yet I am convinced that they have made us richer, if we have but the strength to accept them.

128. *To Rudolf Kassner*

Wednesday, 15 *December* 1926

My dear Kassner, so this it is about which my nature has urgently forewarned me these three years : I am fallen ill of a miserable and infinitely painful malady, a little-known mutation of the blood-corpuscles has become the cause of the most hideous processes dispersed over the whole of my body. And I, who have never wished to look it squarely in the face, am now learning to adapt myself to this immeasurable and anonymous pain. Learn it hard, with a hundred refusals, and so desolately dismayed. — I wanted you to know of my position, which will be no temporary one. Inform the dear Princess of it, as much as you think fit. I hear through the Princess Gargarine that the Princess Marie is going to settle in her beautiful flat in the Palazzo Borghese for the winter. And you, dear Kassner ? How did Paris strike you ? I was happy to find the *Eléments de la Grandeur humaine* in the *Commerce* !

All my affection, Kassner !—I think much, much of you. Your Rilke.

129. *To Supervielle*

Clinique de Val-Mont sur Territet par Glion
21 *December* 1926

Mon cher cher Supervielle,—Gravement malade, douloureusement, misérablement, humblement malade, je me retrouve un instant dans la douce conscience d'avoir pu être rejoint, même là, sur ce plan insituable et si peu humain, par votre envoi et par toutes les influences qu'il m'apporte.

Je pense à vous, poète, ami, et faisant cela je pense encore le monde, pauvre débris d'un vase qui se souvient d'être de la terre. (Mais cet abus de nos sens et de leur ' dictionnaire ' par la douleur qui le feuillette !)—R.

PART FOUR

LETTERS TO A YOUNG POET

INTRODUCTION BY THE YOUNG POET

It was in the late autumn of 1902 – I was sitting in the park of the Military Academy in Wiener-Neustadt, beneath some ancient chestnut trees, and was reading a book. I was so engrossed in reading that I hardly noticed how I was joined by the only non-officer among our professors, the learned and kind-hearted parson of the Academy, Horaček. He took the volume out of my hand, looked at the wrapper and shook his head. "Poems by Rainer Maria Rilke?" he asked meditatively. He turned over the leaves here and there, glanced through a few verses, gazed thoughtfully into the distance and finally nodded. "So then the pupil René Rilke has become a poet."

And I learnt about the thin, pale-faced boy whom his parents had sent to the Military *Unterrealschule* in Sankt-Pölten more than fifteen years previously, so that he might later become an officer. At that time Horaček had been employed there as chaplain, and he still remembered his former pupil distinctly. He depicted him as a quiet, solemn, highly capable boy who liked to keep himself apart, bore the restrictions of a boarder's life patiently, and after his fourth year moved on with the others to the Military *Oberrealschule* which was situated in Mährisch-Weisskirchen. There, however, his constitution proved insufficiently resilient, and so his parents removed him from the institution and let him continue his studies at home in Prague. Horaček could report no further on the course which his outward life had thereafter taken.

After all this it may be easily understood that I resolved in that very hour to send my poetical efforts to Rainer Maria Rilke and ask for his opinion. Being not yet twenty years old and barely on the threshold of a profession which I felt to be directly opposed to my inclinations, I hoped to find understanding, if anywhere at all, in the writer of the poems *To Celebrate Myself.* And without my actually having wished it, my verses came to be accompanied by a covering letter in which I revealed myself without reserve as I have never done before or since to another human being.

Many weeks went by before an answer came. The blue-sealed communication bore the post mark of Paris, weighed heavy in the hand and shewed on the envelope the same clear, beautiful and firm characters in which the text was set down from the first line to the last. With that began my regular correspondence with Rainer Maria Rilke, which lasted until 1908 and then gradually trickled into nothing, since life drove me off into regions against which the poet's warm, delicate and touching solicitude had really tried to guard me.

But that is not important. The only thing of importance is the ten letters which here follow, important for the appreciation of the world in which Rainer Maria Rilke lived and worked, and important too for many who are now growing up and developing, today and tomorrow. And where a great and unique man speaks, small men must keep silence.

Franz Xaver Kappus

Berlin, *June* 1929

THE LETTERS

1

PARIS, *February* 17*th* 1903

DEAR SIR,

Your letter reached me only a few days ago. I want to thank you for its great and welcome trust. I can hardly say more. I cannot go into the quality of your verses; for I am too far removed from every kind of critical intention. In making contact with a work of art nothing serves so ill as words of criticism: the invariable result is more or less happy misunderstandings. Things are not all so comprehensible and utterable as people would mostly have us believe; most events are unutterable, consummating themselves in a sphere where word has never trod, and more unutterable than them all are works of art, whose life endures by the side of our own that passes away.

Having written this note by way of introduction, may I just go on to tell you that your verses have no individual quality, but rather, quiet and hidden tendencies to something personal. I feel this most clearly in the last poem *My Soul*. And in the beautiful poem *To Leopardi* there is perhaps growing up a kind of relationship with that great and solitary man. All the same, the poems are not yet anything in themselves, nothing independent, not even the last one or the one to Leopardi. Your friendly letter which accompanied them did not fail to explain to me a number of deficiences which I felt in reading your verses, without however being able to give a name to them.

You ask if your verses are good. You ask me. You have previously asked others. You send them to journals. You compare them with other poems, and you are troubled when certain editors reject your efforts. Now (as you have permitted me to advise you) I beg you to give all that up. You are looking outwards, and of all things that is what you must now not do. Nobody can advise and help you, nobody. There is only one single means. Go inside yourself. Discover the motive that bids you write; examine whether it sends its roots down to the deepest places of your heart, confess to yourself whether you would have to die if writing were denied you. This before all: ask yourself in the quietest hour of your night: *must* I write? Dig down into yourself for a deep answer. And if this should be in the affirmative, if you may meet this solemn question with a strong and simple "*I must*", then build your life according to this necessity; your life must, right to its most unimportant and insignificant hour, become a token and a witness of this impulse. Then draw near to Nature. Then try, as if you were one of the first men, to say what you see and experience and love and lose. Do not write love poems; avoid at first those forms which are too familiar and usual: they are the most difficult, for great and fully matured strength is needed to make an individual contribution where good and in part brilliant traditions exist in plenty. Turn therefore from the common themes to those which your own everyday life affords; depict your sorrows and desires, your passing thoughts and belief in some kind of beauty – depict all that with heartfelt, quiet, humble sincerity and use to express yourself the things that surround you, the images of your dreams and the objects of your memory. If your everyday life seems poor to you, do not accuse it; accuse yourself, tell yourself you are not poet enough to summon up its riches; since for the creator there is no poverty and no poor or unimportant place. And even if you were in a prison whose walls allowed none of the sounds of the world to reach your senses – would you not still have always your childhood, that precious, royal richness, that treasure house of memories? Turn your attention there. Try to raise the submerged sensations of that distant past; your personality will grow stronger, your solitude will extend itself and will become a twilit dwelling which the noise of others passes by in the distance. – And if from this turning inwards, from this sinking into your private world, there come verses, you will not think to ask anyone whether they are good verses. You will not attempt, either, to interest journals in these works: for you will see in them your own dear genuine possession, a portion and a voice of your life. A work of art is good if it has grown out of necessity. In this manner of its origin lies its true estimate: there is no other. Therefore, my dear Sir, I could give you no advice but this: to go into yourself and to explore the depths whence your life wells forth; at its source you will find the answer to the question whether you *must* create. Accept it as it sounds, without enquiring too closely into every word. Perhaps it will turn out that you are called to be an artist. Then take your fate upon yourself and bear it, its burden and its greatness, without ever asking for that reward which might come from without. For the creator must be a world for himself, and find everything within himself, and in Nature to which he has attached himself.

Perhaps however, after this descent into yourself and into your aloneness, you will have to renounce your claim to become a poet; (it is sufficient, as I have said, to feel that one could live without writing, in order not to venture it at all.) But even then this introversion which I beg of you has not been in vain. Your life will at all events find thenceforward its individual paths; and that they may be good and rich and far reaching I wish for you more than I can say.

What more shall I say to you? Everything seems to me to have its proper emphasis; I would finally just like to advise you to grow through your development quietly and seriously; you can interrupt it in no more violent manner than by looking outwards, and expecting answer from outside to questions which perhaps only your innermost feeling in your most silent hour can answer.

It was a joy to me to find the name of Professor Horaček in your letter; I retain a great admiration for that dear and learned man, and a gratitude that persists through the years. Will you please tell him of this sentiment of mine; it is very good of him still to remember me, and I know how to appreciate it.

The verses which you kindly entrusted to me I am returning at the same time as this. And I thank you again for the magnitude and cordiality of your trust; in this answer, given with sincerity and to the best of my knowledge, I have sought to make myself a little worthier of it than, as a stranger, I actually am.

With every respect and sympathy:

RAINER MARIA RILKE.

2

VIAREGGIO near PISA (ITALY), *April 5th* 1903

You must forgive me, my dear and honoured Sir, for not gratefully remembering your letter of February 24th before today: I was suffering the whole time, not exactly from an illness, but oppressed by an influenza-like exhaustion which made me incapable of anything. And finally, when it would not improve, I came to this southerly sea, whose benefit has helped me before now. But I am not yet well, I find writing difficult, and so you must take these few lines in lieu of more.

You must of course know that you will always give me pleasure with every letter, and be only indulgent towards the answer, which will often perhaps leave you empty handed; for fundamentally, and precisely in the deepest and most important things, we are unspeakably alone, and a great deal must happen in order that one man may be able to advise or even help another – a great deal must succeed, a whole constellation of things must be realized for it once to prosper.

I wanted to say two further things to you today: irony:

Do not let yourself be governed by it, especially not in unproductive moments. In productive ones try to make use of it as one more means of seizing life. Used purely, it is itself pure, and one need not be ashamed of it; and when you feel too familiar with it, when you fear the growing intimacy with it, then turn towards great and serious subjects, before which it becomes small and helpless. Seek for the depth of things: there irony never descends – and when you have thus brought it to the edge of greatness, test at the same time whether this mode of perception springs from a necessity of your being. For under the influence of serious things it will either fall away from you (if it is something non-essential), or else it will (if it belongs to you innately) with gathering strength become a serious tool and be ranked among the means by which you will have to form your art.

And the second thing that I wanted to tell you today is this:

Only a few of all my books are indispensable to me, and two of these are actually always among my things wherever I am. Even here they are round me: the Bible, and the books of the great Danish writer Jens Peter Jacobsen. It occurs to me to wonder whether you know his works. You can easily procure them, for a part of them has appeared in Reclam's Universal Library in a very good translation. Get hold of the little volume called *Six Tales* by J.P. Jacobsen, and his novel *Niels Lyhne*, and start with the first story in the former book, which is called *Mogens*. A world will come over to you, the happiness, the wealth, the inconceivable greatness of a world. Live for a while in these books, learn from them what seems to you worth learning, but above all love them. Your love will be repaid a thousand thousandfold, and whatever your life may become – will, I am convinced, run through the texture of your growing as one of the most important threads among all the threads of your experiences, disappointments and joys.

If I am to say from whom I have learnt anything about the nature of creation, about its depth and everlastingness, there are only two names that I can mention: Jacobsen, that great, great writer, and Auguste Rodin, who has not his peer among all the artists who are alive today.

And may all success attend your ways!

Yours:

RAINER MARIA RILKE.

3

VIAREGGIO near PISA (ITALY), *April 23rd* 1903

You have given me much pleasure, my dear and honoured Sir, with your Easter letter; for it said much that was good of yourself, and the way in which you spoke of Jacobsen's great and beloved art shewed me that I was not mistaken when I led your life and its many questions to that abundant source.

Now *Niels Lyhne* will reveal itself to you, a book of splendours and of depths; the oftener one reads it: everything seems to be in it, from the gentlest possible scents of life to the full, large taste of its heaviest fruits. Nothing is there that had not been understood, conceived, experienced and recognized in the vibrating echo of memory; no experience has been too slight, and the smallest happening unfolds like a destiny, and the destiny itself is like a wonderful broad tapestry where every thread is inwoven by an infinitely delicate hand, laid next to its fellow, and held and supported by a hundred others. You will experience the great happiness of reading this book for the first time, and will go through its innumerable surprises as in a new dream. But I can tell you that later too one goes again and again through these books, marvelling in the same way, and that they lose nothing of the wonderful power, and surrender nothing of the fairy-tale quality with which they overwhelm the reader at the start.

One only enjoys them ever increasingly, becomes more grateful and somehow better and simpler in one's gazing, deeper in one's believing of life, and in life greater and more blessed.

And, later you must read the wonderful book of the destiny and longing of *Marie Grubbe* and Jacobsen's letters and diaries and fragments, and finally his verses, which (even though they are only moderately well translated) live in everlasting sound. (To that end I would advise you to buy, when you get the chance, the lovely complete edition of Jacobsen's works, which contains all the above. It appeared in three volumes, well translated, published by Eugen Dietrichs of Leipzig, and costs, I rather think, only five or six marks a volume.)

Your opinion of *There should have been roses there . . .* (that work of such incomparable delicacy and form) is of course, in contrast with that expressed in the introduction, quite, quite unimpeachably correct. And let me here at once request you: read as few aesthetic-critical things as possible – they are either partisan opinions, become hardened and meaningless in their lifeless petrification, or else they are a skilful play upon words, in which one view is uppermost today and its opposite tomorrow. Works of art are of an infinite solitariness, and nothing is less likely to bring us near to them than criticism. Only love can apprehend and hold them, and can be just towards them. – Decide each time according to *yourself* and your feelings in the face of every such declaration, discussion or introduction; if you should still be wrong, the natural growth of your inner life will lead you slowly in the course of time to other perceptions. Let your judgements have their own quiet, undisturbed development, which must, like all progress, come from deep within, and cannot in any way be pressed or hurried. It means everything to carry for the full time and then to bring forth. To allow every impression and every germ of a feeling to grow to completion wholly in yourself, in the darkness, in the unutterable, unconscious, inaccessible to your own understanding, and to await with deep humility and patience the hour of birth of a new clarity: that is alone what living as an artist means: in understanding as in creation.

There is no measuring by time there, a year there has no meaning, and ten years are nothing. To be an artist means: not to reckon and count; to ripen like the tree which does not force its sap and stands confident in the storms of Spring without fear lest no Summer might come after. It does come. But it comes only to the patient ones, who are there as if eternity lay in front of them, so unconcernedly still and far. I am learning it daily, learning it through pains to which I am grateful: patience is all!

Richard Dehmel: I feel about his books (and incidentally about the man too, whom I know slightly) that when I have found one of his lovely pages I am always afraid of the one that follows, which may ruin everything again and turn what is charming into something unworthy. You have characterized him quite well in the phrase "living and writing in heat". – And in point of fact artistic experience really lies so incredibly close to sexual, to its agony and its ecstasy, that both phenomena are actually only different forms of one and the same longing and felicity. And if instead of heat one might speak of – sex, sex in the large, wide, pure sense, without any slur of ecclesiastical error, his art would be very great and infinitely important. His poetic strength is great, and strong as a primitive impulse, it has its own uncompromising rhythms within itself, and gushes out as if from a mountain side.

But it seems that this strength is not always quite sincere and without pose. (But that is just one of the most difficult tests with a creator: he must always remain unconscious, unsuspecting of his best virtues, if he does not want to deprive them of their unselfconsciousness and integrity!) And then, when it comes rushing through his being into sexuality, it finds there a man not quite so pure as it required him to be. There it sees no entirely mature and unmixed sex world, but one which is not human enough, merely masculine, which is heat, intoxication and restlessness, and loaded with the old prejudices and arrogances with which men have disfigured and burdened love. Because he loves only as man, not as human being, there is in his sexual feelings something narrow, seemingly wild, malicious, temporal, finite, which weakens his art and makes it equivocal and dubious. It is not without blemish, it bears the imprint of time and of passion, and little of it will endure and persist. (But most art is like that!) But nevertheless we can deeply enjoy what is great in it, only we must not get lost over it and become adherents of that Dehmel world which is so infinitely frightening, full of adultery and confusion, far from the real destinies which make us suffer more than these temporal glooms, but also give us more opportunity for greatness and more courage for eternity.

Finally, as far as my books are concerned, I should like best to send you all that could give you any pleasure. But I am very poor, and my books, as soon as they have once appeared, belong no more to me. I cannot buy them myself – and, as I should so often like, give them to those who would be good to them.

Therefore I am writing out for you on a slip of paper the titles (and publishers) of my most recent books (the latest, I have published some twelve or thirteen in all), and must leave it to you, dear Sir, to procure some of them for yourself at your leisure.

I am glad to know that my books are in your hands.

Goodbye.

Yours:

RAINER MARIA RILKE.

4

Temporarily at WORPSWEDE near BREMEN,
July 16th 1903

I left Paris about ten days ago, badly ailing and tired, and came to a great northern plain, whose remoteness and silence and sky are to make me well again. But I ran into a long spell of rain, which has only today begun to clear a little over the restlessly waving land; and I am using this first moment of brightness to send you, dear Sir, my greetings.

My dear Herr Kappus: I have left a letter of yours long unanswered, not that I had forgotten it – on the contrary: it was of the kind that one reads again when one finds it among other letters, and I recognized you in it as if you were close at hand. It was the letter of May 2nd, and you doubtless remember it. When I read it, as I do now, in the great stillness of this faraway place, your beautiful concern for life moves me even more than I experienced it in Paris, where everything has a different ring and dies away by reason of the monstrous noise that makes all things tremble. Here, where a vast countryside is around me, over which the winds come in from the seas, here I feel that there is nowhere a human being who can answer you those questions and feelings which have a life of their own within their depths; for even the best men go astray with words, when these are to express something very gentle and almost unutterable. But I believe nevertheless that you need not be left without some solution, if you hold to things similar to those on which my eyes now take their recreation. If you hold to Nature, to the simplicity that is in her, to the small detail that scarcely one man sees, which can so unexpectedly grow into something great and boundless; if you have this love for insignificant things and seek, simply as one who serves, to win the confidence of what seems to be poor: then everything will become easier for you, more coherent and somehow more conciliatory, not perhaps in the understanding, which lags wondering behind, but in your innermost consciousness, wakefulness and knowing. You are so young, you have not even begun, and I would like to beg you, dear Sir, as well as I can, to have patience with everything that is unsolved in your heart and to try to cherish the questions themselves, like closed rooms and like books written in a very strange tongue. Do not search now for the answers which cannot be given you because you could not live them. It is a matter of living everything. Live the questions now. Perhaps you will then gradually, without noticing it, one distant day live right into the answer. Perhaps indeed you carry within yourself the possibility of shaping and forming, as a particularly pure and blessed kind of life; train yourself for it – but take what comes in complete trust, if only it comes from your will, from some inner need of yours, take it to yourself and do not hate anything. Sex is difficult; yes. But it is the difficult that is enjoined upon us, almost everything serious is difficult, and everything is serious. If you only recognize that and contrive, yourself, out of your own disposition and nature, out of your experience and childhood and strength to achieve an entirely individual relationship to sex (not influenced by convention and custom), then you need no longer fear to lose yourself and become unworthy of your best possession.

Bodily delight is a sense of experience, just like pure seeing or the pure feeling with which a lovely fruit fills the tongue; it is a great boundless experience which is given us, a knowing of the world, the fullness and the splendour of all knowing. Our acceptance of it is not bad; what is bad is that almost all men misuse and squander this experience, and apply it as a stimulus to the weary places of their life, a dissipation instead of a rallying for the heights. Mankind have turned eating, too, into something else: want on the one hand, and superfluity on the other, have dulled the clarity of this need, and all those deep, simple necessities by which life renews itself have become similarly dull. But the individual can clarify them for himself and live clearly, (or if not the individual, who is too dependent, then at any rate the solitary man.) He can remember that all beauty in animals and plants is a quiet enduring form of love and longing, and he can see the animal, as he sees the plant, patiently and willingly uniting and propagating itself and growing, not from physical lust, not from physical pain, but bowing to necessities which are greater than lust and pain and more powerful than will and opposition. O that man might be more humble in accepting this secret of which the earth is full even in its tiniest creatures, and more sincere in bearing, enduring and feeling how frightfully serious it is, instead of taking it lightly. That he might be reverent towards his fertility, which is all one whether it be intellectual or physical; for intellectual creation too derives from the physical, is of one substance with it, it is only like a gentler, more enraptured and everlasting repetition of bodily delight. "The thought of being a creator, of begetting and forming" is nothing without its continual great confirmation and realization in the world, nothing without the thousandfold assent from things and animals – and its enjoyment is so indescribably beautiful and rich only because it is full of inherited memories of the begetting and bearing of millions. In one creator's thought a thousand forgotten nights of love revive again and fill it full of loftiness and grandeur. Those who come together in the night time and entwine in swaying delight perform a serious work and gather up sweetness, depth and strength for the song of some poet that is to be, who will rise to tell of unspeakable bliss. And they summon the future; and even though they go astray and embrace blindly, yet the future comes, a new human being arises, and on the basis of the chance occurrence which here seems consummated, awakens the law by which a resistant vigorous seed forces its way to the egg-cell that advances openly to meet it. Do not let yourself be misled by outward appearances; in the depths everything becomes law. And those who live the secret falsely and badly (and they are very many) only lose it for themselves and yet hand it on like a sealed letter, without knowing it. And do not be confused by the multiplicity of names and the complexity of instances. Perhaps there is over everything a great motherhood, as a common longing. The loveliness of the virgin, a being that (as you so beautifully say) "has not yet accomplished anything", is motherhood foreboding and preparing itself, uneasy and yearning. And the mother's beauty is serving motherhood, and in the old woman there is a great memory. And in the man too there is motherhood, it seems to me, physical and spiritual; his begetting is also a kind of birth-giving, and it is birth-giving when he creates out of his innermost fullness. And perhaps the sexes are more akin than we suppose, and the great renewal of the world will perhaps consist in this, that man and maiden, freed from all false feelings and perversions, will seek each other not as opposites but as brother and sister, as neighbours, and will unite as human beings to bear in common, simply, seriously and patiently, the heavy sex that has been laid upon them.

But everything that once perhaps will be possible to many, the solitary man can already prepare for and build now with his hands, which go less astray. Therefore, dear Sir, love your solitude and bear the pain which it has caused you with fair-sounding lament. For those that are near you are far, you say, and this shews that distance begins to grow round you. And when your nearness is far, then your distance is already among the stars and very great; be glad of your growing, into which you can take no one else with you, and be good to those that remain behind, and be self-possessed and quiet with them and do not torment them with your doubts and do not frighten them with your confidence or joy, which they could not comprehend. Seek some unpretending and honest communication with them, which you are under no necessity to alter when you yourself become more and more different; love life in a strange guise in them, and make allowance for those ageing people who fear the solitude in which you trust. Avoid furnishing material for a drama which is always impending between parents and children; it uses up much of the children's strength and wastes away the love of their elders, which is operative and warm even when it does not comprehend. Demand no advice from them and reckon with no understanding; but believe in a love that is preserved for you like a heritage, and trust that in this love there is a strength and a blessing which you are not bound to leave behind you though you may travel far!

It is good that you are entering first of all upon a profession which makes you independent and places you on your own in every sense. Wait patiently to see whether your innermost life feels constrained by the form of this profession. I consider it a very difficult one and a hard taskmaster, as it is burdened with much convention and gives hardly any scope to a personal interpretation of its tasks. But your solitude will be your home and haven even in the midst of very strange conditions, and from there you will discover all your paths. All my wishes are ready to accompany you, and my trust is with you.

Yours:

RAINER MARIA RILKE.

5

ROME, *October 29th* 1903

DEAR AND HONOURED SIR,

I received your letter of August 29th in Florence, and now – a whole two months later – I am telling you of it. Do forgive this dilatoriness – but I do not like writing letters while I am on the move, because I need more for letter writing than the absolutely necessary implements: some quiet and solitude and an hour that is not too strange.

We arrived in Rome about six weeks ago, at a time when it was still empty, the hot, the fever-discredited Rome, and this circumstance, together with other practical difficulties of settling in, helped to perpetuate the unrest about us, so that the foreigness lay upon us with the weight of homelessness. Add to this that Rome (when you do not yet know it) has a stifling, saddening effect upon you during the first few days: through the inanimate and dismal museum feeling which it exhales, through the multiplicity of its pasts, dragged into view and laboriously maintained parts (on which a small present supports itself), through the unspeakable over-estimation of all these defaced and dilapidated things, fostered by savants and philologists and imitated by the ordinary tourist to Italy, which are yet fundamentally no more than fortuitous remains of another time and a life that is not ours and should not be ours. Finally after weeks of daily resistance you find your bearings again, although still a little bewildered, and you reflect: no, there is not more beauty here than elsewhere, and all these objects which have been continuously admired for generations, which workmen's hands have mended and restored, signify nothing, are nothing and have no heart and no worth – but there is much beauty here, because there is much beauty everywhere. Eternally living waters move along the old aqueducts into the great town and dance in the numerous squares over white stone bowls and display themselves in broad capacious basins and murmur by day and increase their murmuring in the night, which here is great and starry and soft with winds. And gardens are here, unforgettable avenues and flights of stairs, stairs devised by Michelangelo, stairs which are built after the pattern of downward gliding waters – broad in their descent, bringing forth step from step as if they were waves. Through impressions like these you come to yourself, win your way back from the pretentious manifold which talks and chatters there (and how talkative it is!), and you learn slowly to recognize the very few things in which something eternal endures that you can love, and something solitary in which you can gently share.

I am still living in the town, on the capitol, not far from the loveliest equestrian statue that has been preserved to us from Roman art – that of Marcus Aurelius; but in a few weeks I shall be moving to a quiet unpretentious room, an old pavilion that lies quite deep within a large park, hidden from the town, its bustle and hazard. There I shall live the whole winter and rejoice in the great stillness, from which I expect the gift of good and effective hours . . .

From there, where I shall be more at home, I will write you a longer letter, in which I will also deal with what you wrote to me. Today I must only tell you (and perhaps it is wrong of me not to have done this before) that the book announced in your letter (which was to contain works of your own) has not turned up here. Has it been returned to you, perhaps from Worpswede? (Because parcels may not be forwarded abroad.) That is the happiest possibility, and I should be glad to have it confirmed. I hope there is no question of its loss – but indeed in the conditions of the Italian postal system that would be no exceptional occurrence – unfortunately.

I should have been glad to receive this book (as I should any token from you); any verses which have come into existence meanwhile (if you will entrust them to me) I will always read and re-read and experience as well and as cordially as I can. With good wishes and greetings.

Yours:

RAINER MARIA RILKE.

6

ROME, *December 23rd* 1903

MY DEAR HERR KAPPUS,

You shall not go without a greeting from me now that Christmas is approaching and you are bearing your solitude, in the midst of the festival, more heavily than usual. But when you notice that it is great, be glad of that; for what (you must ask yourself) would solitude be that had not greatness; there is only one solitude, and it is great and is not easy to bear, and to almost everyone there come hours when they would gladly exchange it for some kind of communion, however banal and cheap, for the appearance of some slight harmony with the most easily available, with the most undeserving . . . But perhaps those are just the hours when solitude grows; for its growing is painful like the growing of boys and sad like the beginning of Spring. But that must not mislead you. What is needed is, in the end, simply this: solitude, great inner solitude. Going into yourself and meeting no one for hours on end – that is what you must be able to attain. To be alone, as you were alone in childhood, when the grown-ups were going about, involved with things which seemed important and great, because the great ones looked so busy and because you grasped nothing of their business.

And when one day you perceive that their pursuits are paltry, their professions torpid and no longer connected with life, why not proceed like a child to look upon them as something alien, from out of the depth of your own world, out of the spaciousness of your own solitude, which is itself work and status and profession? Why want to exchange a child's wise non-understanding for defensiveness and disdain, when surely non-understanding is aloneness, but defensiveness and disdain are participation in what you want by these means to avoid.

Think, dear Sir, of the world which you carry within yorself, and call this thinking what you like; let it be memory of your own childhood or longing for your own future – only pay attention to what arises within you, and set it above everything that you notice about you. Your inmost happening is worth your whole love, that is what you must somehow work at, and not lose too much time and too much courage in explaining your attitude to people. Who tells you, anyhow, that you have such a thing at all? – I know your profession is hard and filled with contradiction of yourself, and I anticipated your lament and knew that it would come. Now it has come I cannot appease it, I can only advise you to consider whether all professions are not like that, full of demands, full of hostility against the individual, saturated so to say with the hatred of those who have reconciled themselves mutely and morosely to their own insipid duty. The situation in which you now have to live is no more heavily burdened with convention, prejudice and error than all the other situations, and if there are some which make parade of a greater freedom, there is certainly none which is in itself wide and spacious and related to the great things of which real life consists. Only the individual who is solitary is brought like a thing under the deep laws, and when a man steps out into the morning that is just beginning, or looks out into the evening that is full of happenings, and when he feels what is coming to pass there, then all rank drops from him as from a dead man, although he is standing in the midst of sheer life. What you now, dear Herr Kappus, have to experience as an officer, you would have felt similarly in every profession that exists, even if you had sought only easy and independent contacts in society, apart from any occupation, this oppressive feeling would not have been spared you. It is the same everywhere; but that is no reason for anxiety or depression; if there is no communion between other people and yourself, try to be near things, which will not desert you; the nights are still there, and the winds that go through the trees and over many lands; among things and with the animals everything is still full of happening, in which you may take a part; and the children are still as you were in childhood, as sad and happy – and when you think of your childhood you are living among the solitary children, and the grown-ups are nothing, and their dignity has no worth.

And if it dismays and torments you to think of childhood and of the simplicity and stillness that goes with it, because you can no longer believe in God who is to be met with everywhere there, ask yourself, dear Herr Kappus, whether you have after all really lost God? Is it not much rather the case that you have never yet possessed him? For when might that have been? Do you believe a child can hold him, him whom men bear only with difficulty, whose weight bows down the aged? Do you believe that one who really has him could lose him like a little stone, or do you not also feel that one who had him could but be lost by him? – But when you realize that he was not in your childhood, and not beforehand, when you surmise that Christ was deluded by his longing and Mahomet betrayed by his pride – and when you feel with horror that he does not exist now either, in this hour when we are speaking of him – what entitles you then to miss, as if he had passed away, and to seek, as if he were lost, someone who has never been?

Why do you not think that he who draws near from all eternity is still to come, that he is in the future, the final fruit of a tree whose leaves we are? What prevents you from throwing forward his truth into times yet to be, and living your life as a painful and beautiful day in the history of a great gestation? Do you not see, then, how everything that happens is for ever a beginning, and might it not be His beginning, since beginning is in itself always so beautiful? If he is the most perfect, must not the inferior precede him, that he may choose himself out of abundance and profusion? – Must he not be the last, in order to embrace everything within himself, and what sense should we have if he for whom we crave had already been?

As bees collect honey, so we take what is sweetest out of everything and build Him. We start actually with the slight, with the unpretentious (if only it is done with love), with work and with resting after it, with a silence or with a little solitary joy, with everything that we do alone, without helpers or adherents, we begin him whom we shall not experience any more than our forefathers could experience us. And yet they are in us, those who have long since passed away, as natural disposition, as burden on our destiny, as blood that throbs, and as gesture that rises up out of the depths of time.

Is there anything which can take from you the hope of thus being hereafter in him, in the most distant, the uttermost?

Celebrate Christmas, dear Herr Kappus, in this pious feeling, that He perhaps needs just this fear of life from you in order to begin; these very days of your transition are perhaps the time when everything in you is working upon him, as once before in childhood you worked upon him breathlessly. Be patient and without resentment, and reflect that the least we can do is, not to make his becoming more difficult for him than the earth makes it for the Spring that wants to come.

And be glad and comforted.

Yours:

RAINER MARIA RILKE.

7

ROME, *May 14th* 1904

MY DEAR HERR KAPPUS,

Much time has passed since I received your last letter. Do not take it ill of me; it was first of all work, then interruption, and finally weakness of health that continuously held me back from this answer, which (so I intended) was to come to you from good and quiet days. Now I feel somewhat better again (the beginning of Spring with its wicked wayward changes touched us badly even here) and find the time, dear Herr Kappus, to greet you and (as I am glad with all my heart to do) to answer this and that point in your letter to the best of my knowledge.

You see: I have copied out your sonnet, because I found it beautiful and simple, and born in the form which it wears with such quiet grace. Those are the best of the verses which you have permitted me to read. And now I am giving you that copy, because I know that it is important and full of new experience to find one's own work again in a strange handwriting. Read the verses as though they were strange, and you will feel in your innermost self how very much they are yours. – It has been a joy for me to read this sonnet and your letter many times; I thank you for them both.

And you must not let yourself be misled, in your solitude, by the fact that there is something in you which wants to escape from it. This very wish will, if you use it quietly and pre-eminently and like a tool, help to spread your solitude over wide country. People have (with the help of convention) found the solution of everything in ease and the easiest side of ease; but it is clear that we must hold to the difficult; everything living holds to it, everything in Nature grows and defends itself according to its own character and is an individual in its own right, strives to be so at any cost and against all opposition. We know little, but that we must hold to the difficult is a certainty that will not leave us; it is good to be solitary, for solitude is difficult; the fact that a thing is difficult must be one more reason for our doing it.

To love is also good: for love is difficult. Fondness between human beings: that is perhaps the most difficult task that is set us, the ultimate thing, the final trial and test, the work for which all other work is only preparation. Therefore young people, who are beginners in everything, *cannot* know love yet: they have to learn it. With their whole being, with all their strength gathered about their lonely, fearful, upward beating heart, they must learn to love. But apprenticeship is always a long, secluded time, and therefore loving is for a long while, far into life – : solitude, heightened and deepened aloneness for him who loves. Loving in the first instance is nothing that can be called losing, surrendering and uniting oneself to another (for what would a union be, of something unclarified and unready, still inferior – ?), it is a sublime occasion for the individual to mature, to grow into something in himself, to become world for himself for another's sake, it is a great exacting claim upon him, something that chooses him and summons him to a distant goal. Only in this sense, as a task to work upon themselves ("to hearken and to hammer day and night") might young people use the love that is given them. The self-losing and the surrender and all manner of communion is not for them (they must save and treasure for a long, long while yet), it is the ultimate thing, it is perhaps something for which human lives are so far hardly adequate.

But that is where young people so often and so grievously go wrong: that they (whose nature it is to have no patience) throw themselves at each other when love comes over them, scatter themselves abroad, just as they are in all their untidiness, disorder and confusion . . . : But what is to be done then? How is life to act upon this heap of half crushed matter which they call their communion and which they would dearly like to style their happiness, if that were possible, and their future? So each one loses himself for the other's sake, and loses the other and many others who wanted still to come. And loses the expanses and possibilities, exchanges the drawing near and fleeting away of gentle, presageful things for a sterile helplessness out of which nothing more can come; nothing but a little disgust, disillusion and poverty and deliverance into one of the many conventions which are set up in large numbers as public refuges along this most dangerous of roads. No region of human experience is so well supplied with conventions as this; life-belts of the most varied invention, boats and swimming-bladders are there; social perception has contrived to create shelters of every description, for as it was disposed to take love-life as a pleasure, it had to mould it into something easy, cheap, innocuous and safe, as public pleasures are.

Many young people, to be sure, who love falsely, that is simply surrendering, letting solitude go (the average person will always persist in that way), feel the oppression of failure and want to make the situation in which they find themselves full of vitality and fruitful in their own personal fashion – ; for their nature tells them that even less than anything else of importance can the questions of love be resolved publicly and by this or that compromise; that they are questions, intimate questions from one human being to another, which need in every instance a new, particular, purely personal answer – : but how should those who have already confounded themselves and are no longer bounded or separate, who therefore no longer possess anything individual, be able to find a way out of themselves, out of the depth of their already shattered solitude?

They act out of mutual helplessness, and if then they want, with the best of intentions, to avoid the convention that catches their eye (say that of marriage), they end up in the clutches of a less clamorous but equally deadly conventional solution; for there everything all round them is – convention; where it is a question of a hastily fused, turbid communion, every possible action must be conventional; every relationship to which such entanglement leads has its convention, be it as unusual as it may (that is, in the ordinary sense immoral); why, even separation would in such a case be a conventional step, an impersonal random decision without strength and without effect.

Anyone who considers it seriously will find that for difficult love, as for death, which is difficult, no explanation, no solution, neither sign nor path has yet been made known; and for both these tasks which we carry secretly and hand on without uncovering them, no universal rule based on agreed principles can be discovered. But in proportion as we begin to make individual trial of life, these great things will meet us as individuals at closer quarters. The claims which the difficult work of love lays upon our development are more than life-sized, and as beginners we are not equal to them. But if we continue to hold out and take this love upon ourselves as a burden and apprenticeship, instead of losing ourselves in all the light and frivolous play behind which mankind have concealed themselves from the most serious gravity of their existence – then perhaps some small progress and some alleviation will become perceptible to those who come long after us; that would be much.

We are really only just beginning to regard the relationship of a human individual to another individual dispassionately and objectively, and our attempts to live such a relationship have no pattern before them. And yet in the passage of time there are now several things that are ready to help our shy novitiate.

The girl and the woman in their new, individual unfolding will be only transient imitators of bad or good masculine behaviour, and repeaters of masculine professions. After the uncertainty of such transitions it will be seen that women have passed through the exuberance and vicissitudes of those (often ridiculous) disguises, only in order to purify their most essential being from the distorting influences of the other sex. Surely women, in whom life tarries and dwells more immediately, fruitfully and confidently, must have become fundamentally more mature human beings, more *human* human beings, than light man, whom the weight of no body's fruit pulls down beneath the surface of life, who, conceited and rash as he is, underrates what he thinks he loves. This humanity of woman, brought forth in pains and degradations, will come to light when she has shed the conventions of mere femininity in the alterations of her outward station, and the men who today do not feel it coming will be surprised and struck by it. One day (for this there are already reliable signs speaking and shining, especially in the northern countries), one day the girl will be here and the woman whose name will no longer signify merely the opposite of masculinity, but something in itself, something which makes us think of no complement or limitation, but only of life and existence – : the feminine human being.

This step forward will (very much against the wishes of outstripped man to begin with) change the love experience that now is full of error, alter it fundamentally, refashion it into a relationship meant to be between one human being and another, no longer between man and wife. And this more human love (which will consummate itself infinitely thoughtfully and gently, and well and clearly in binding and loosing) will be something like that which we are preparing with struggle and toil, the love which consists in the mutual guarding, bordering and saluting of two solitudes.

And one thing more: do not think that the great love which was once enjoined upon you as a boy, became lost; can you say whether great and good wishes were not then ripening within you, and resolutions by which you live to this day? I believe that this love remains so strong and powerful in your memory because it was your first deep aloneness and the first inner work which you did upon your life. – All good wishes for you, dear Herr Kappus!

Yours:

RAINER MARIA RILKE.

8

BORGEBY GÅRD, FLÃDIE, SWEDEN, *August 12th 1904*

I want to talk to you again for a while, dear Herr Kappus, although I can say almost nothing that is helpful, hardly anything profitable. You have had many great sorrows, which have passed away. And you say that even this passing was difficult and jarring for you. But please consider whether these great sorrows have not rather passed through the midst of yourself? Whether much in you has not altered, whether you have not somehow changed in some part of your being, while you were sorrowful? Only those sorrows are dangerous and bad which we carry about among our fellows in order to drown them; like diseases which are superficially and foolishly treated, they only recede and break out after a short interval all the more frightfully; and gather themselves in our inwards, and are life, are unlived, disdained, lost life, of which one can die. If it were possible for us to see further than our knowledge extends and out a little over the outworks of our surmising, perhaps we should then bear our sorrows with greater confidence than our joys. For they are the moments when something new, something unknown, has entered into us; our feelings grow dumb with shy confusion, everything in us retires, a stillness supervenes, and the new thing that no one knows stands silent there in the midst.

I believe that almost all our sorrows are moments of tension which we experience as paralysis, because we no longer hear our estranged feelings living. Because we are alone with the strange thing that has entered into us; because for a moment everything familiar and customary has been taken from us; because we stand in the middle of a crossing where we cannot remain standing. Therefore it is, also, that the sorrow passes by us: the new thing in us, that has been added to us, has entered into our heart, has gone into its innermost chamber, and is no more even there – is already in the blood. And we do not realize what it was. We could easily be made to believe that nothing had happened, and yet we have been changed, as a house is changed into which a guest has entered. We cannot say who has come, perhaps we shall never know, but there are many indications to suggest that the future is entering into us in this manner in order to transform itself within us long before it happens. And therefore it is so important to be solitary and heedful when we are sad: because the seemingly uneventful and inflexible moment when our future sets foot in us stands so much nearer to life than that other noisy and fortuitous instant when it happens to us as if from without. The more patient, quiet and open we are in our sorrowing, the more deeply and the more unhesitatingly will the new thing enter us, the better shall we deserve it, the more will it be our own destiny, and when one day later it "happens" (that is, goes forth from us to others) we shall feel in our inmost selves that we are akin and close to it. And that is necessary. It is necessary – and in that direction our development will gradually move – that nothing alien shall befall us, but only what has long been part of us. We have already had to think anew so many concepts of motion, we shall also learn gradually to realize that it is out of mankind that what we call destiny proceeds, not into them from without. Only because so many did not absorb their destinies and transform these within themselves as long as they lived in them, they did not recognize what went forth from them; it was so alien to them that they believed, in their bewildered terror, it must have just entered into them, for they swore that they had never before found anything similar in themselves. As we have long deceived ourselves about the motion of the sun, so we still continue to deceive ourselves about the motion of that which is to come. The future stands firm, dear Herr Kappus, but we move about in infinite space.

How should we not find it difficult?

And, to speak again of solitude, it becomes increasingly clear that this is fundamentally not something that we can choose or reject. We *are* solitary. We can delude ourselves about it, and pretend that it is not so. That is all. But how much better it is to realize that we are thus, to start directly from that very point. Then, to be sure, it will come about that we grow dizzy; for all the points upon which our eyes have been accustomed to rest will be taken away from us, there is no longer any nearness, and all distance is infinitely far. A man who was taken from his study, almost without preparation and transition, and placed upon the height of a great mountain range, would be bound to feel something similar: an uncertainty without parallel, an abandonment to the unutterable would almost annihilate him. He would imagine himself to be falling or fancy himself flung outwards into space or exploded into a thousand pieces: what a monstrous lie his brain would have to invent in order to retrieve and explain the condition of his senses. So all distances, all measures are changed for the man who becomes solitary; many of these changes take effect suddenly, and, as with the man on the mountain top, there arise singular fantasies and strange sensations which seem to grow out beyond all endurance. But it is necessary for us to experience that too. We must accept our existence as far as ever it is possible; everything, even the unheard of, must be possible there. That is fundamentally the only courage which is demanded of us: to be brave in the face of the strangest, most singular and most inexplicable things that can befall us. The fact that human beings have been cowardly in this sense has done endless harm to life; the experiences that are called "apparitions", the whole of the so-called "spirit world", death, all these things that are so closely related to us, have been so crowded out of life by our daily warding them off, that the senses by which we might apprehend them are stunted. To say nothing of God. But fear of the inexplicable has not only impoverished the existence of the solitary man, it has also circumscribed the relationships between human beings, as it were lifted them up from the river bed of infinite possibilities to a fallow spot on the bank, to which nothing happens. For it is not only indolence which causes human relationships to repeat themselves with such unspeakable monotony, unrenewed from one occasion to another, it is the shyness of any new, incalculable experience which we do not feel ourselves equal to facing. But only the man who is prepared for everything, who excludes nothing, not even the most unintelligible, will live the relationship with another as something vital, and will himself exhaust his own existence. For if we think of this existence of the individual as a larger or smaller room, it becomes clear that most people get to know only one corner of their room, a window seat, a strip of floor which they pace up and down. In that way they have a certain security. And yet how much more human is that insecurity, so fraught with danger, which compels the prisoners in Poe's Tales to grope for the shapes of their ghastly prisons and not to remain unaware of the unspeakable horrors of their dwelling. But we are not prisoners. No snares and springes are laid for us, and there is nothing that should alarm or torment us. We are set in life as in the element with which we are most in keeping, and we have moreover, through thousands of years of adaptation, become so similar to this life that when we stay still we are, by a happy mimicry, hardly to be distinguished from our surroundings. We have no cause to be mistrustful of our world, for it is not against us. If it has terrors they are our terrors; if it has abysses those abysses belong to us, if dangers are there we must strive to love them. And if only we regulate our life according to that principle which advises us always to hold to the difficult, what even now appears most alien to us will become most familiar and loyal. How could we forget those old myths which are to be found in the beginnings of every people; the myths of the dragons which are transformed, at the last moment, into princesses; perhaps all the dragons of our life are princesses, who are only waiting to see us once beautiful and brave. Perhaps everything terrifying is at bottom the helplessness that seeks our help.

So you must not be frightened, dear Herr Kappus, when a sorrow rises up before you, greater than you have ever seen before; when a restlessness like light and cloud shadows passes over your hands and over all your doing. You must think that something is happening upon you, that life has not forgotten you, that it holds you in its hand; it will not let you fall. Why do you want to exclude any disturbance, any pain, any melancholy from your life, since you do not know what these conditions are working upon you? Why do you want to plague yourself with the question where it has all come from and whither it is tending? Since you know that you are in a state of transition and would wish nothing so dearly as to transform yourself. If something in your proceedings is diseased, do reflect that disease is the means by which an organism rids itself of a foreign body; you must then simply help it to be ill, to have its full disease and to let it break out, for that is its development. In you, dear Herr Kappus, so much is happening now; you must be patient like a sick man and sanguine like a convalescent; for perhaps you are both. And more than that: you are also the doctor who has to superintend yourself. But in every illness there are many days when the doctor can do nothing but wait. And that is what you, in so far as you are your own doctor, must now above all things do.

Do not observe yourself too closely. Do not draw too rapid conclusions from what happens to you; let it simply happen to you. Otherwise you will too easily reach the point of looking reproachfully (that is morally) at your past, which is naturally concerned with everything that is now occurring to you. But what is taking effect in you from the mistakes, desires and longings of your boyhood is not what you recall and condemn. The extraordinary circumstances of a solitary and helpless childhood are so difficult, so complicated, exposed to so many influences and at the same time so untrammelled by all real connection with life, that where a vice appears in it we must not call it a vice and leave it at that. One must in general be so careful with names; it is so often the name of a misdeed upon which a life is shattered, not the nameless and personal action itself, which was perhaps a quite definite necessity of that life and could be taken on by it without trouble. And the expense of energy seems to you so great only because you overrate the victory; this latter is not the "great thing" that you think you have achieved, although you are right about your feelings; the great thing is that something was already there which you could set in place of that betrayal, something true and genuine. Apart from this even your victory would have been only a moral reaction without great significance, but thus it has become a chapter of your life. Of your life, dear Herr Kappus, about which I am thinking with so many wishes. Do you remember how this life has longed ever since childhood for the "great"? I see how it is now longing to leave the great for greater. Therefore it does not cease to be difficult, but therefore it will not cease, either, to grow.

And if I may say one thing more to you, it is this: do not think that the man who seeks to comfort you lives untroubled among the simple and quiet words which sometimes do you good. His life has much hardship and sadness and lags far behind them. If it were otherwise, he could never have found those words.

Yours:

RAINER MARIA RILKE.

9

FURUBORG, JONSERED, SWEDENXS, *November 4th* 1904

MY DEAR HERR KAPPUS,

During the time which has passed without a letter I have been partly on the move, partly so busy that I could not write. And even today I find writing difficult, because I have already had to write a number of letters, so that my hand is tired. If I could dictate, I would say much to you, but as it is you must accept only a few words in answer to your long letter.

I think of you often, dear Herr Kappus, and with such concentrated wishes that it really must help you in some way. Whether my letters could be truly a help, I often doubt. Do not say: yes, they are. Accept them quietly and without many thanks, and let us wait to see what will come.

It is perhaps no use now to reply to your actual words; for what I could say about your dispostion to doubt or about your inability to bring your outer and inner life into harmony, or about anything else that oppresses you – : it is always what I have said before: always the wish that you might be able to find patience enough in yourself to endure, and single-heartedness enough to believe; that you might win increasing trust in what is difficult, and in your solitude among other people. And for the rest, let life happen to you. Believe me: life is right, at all events.

And about feelings: all feelings are pure which gather you and lift you up; a feeling is impure which takes hold of only one side of your being and so distorts you. Everything that you could think in the light of your childhood is good. Everything which makes more of you than you have previously been in your best hours, is right. Every exaltation is good if it is in your whole blood, if it is not intoxication or turbidness, but joy into whose depths you can see. Do you understand what I mean?

And your doubt can become a good quality if you train it. It must become *aware*, it must become criticism. Ask it, whenever it wants to spoil something for you, *why* something is ugly, demand proofs from it, test it, and you will perhaps find it helpless and nonplussed, perhaps also aggressive. But do not give way, demand arguments and conduct yourself thus carefully and consistently every single time, and the day will dawn when it will become, instead of a subverter, one of your best workmen – perhaps the cleverest of all who are building at your life.

That is all, dear Herr Kappus, that I am able to say to you today. But I am sending you by the same post the off-print of a little composition which has just appeared in the Prague *Deutsche Arbeit*. There I speak to you further of life and of death, and of the greatness and splendour of both.

Yours:

RAINER MARIA RILKE.

10

PARIS, *the second day of Christmas* 1908

You must know, dear Herr Kappus, how glad I was to have that beautiful letter from you. The news which you give me, real and expressible as it now again is, seems to me good, and the longer I have considered it, the more I have felt that it is in actual fact good. I really wanted to write this to you for Christmas Eve; but with all the work in which I have been variously and unremittingly living this winter, the festival has come upon me so quickly that I have hardly had any time over to see to my most necessary business, much less to write.

But I have thought of you often during these festival days, and imagined how quiet you must be in your lonely fort among the empty mountains, over which those great southerly winds are pouring themselves as if they wanted to devour them in great lumps.

The stillness must be immense in which such sounds and movements have room, and when one considers that to all these is added at the same time the resounding presence of the distant sea, perhaps as the innermost voice in this prehistoric harmony, one can only wish for you that you may confidently and patiently let that sublime solitude work upon you, which can no more be expunged from your life; which will work continuously and with gentle decision as an anonymous influence in everything that lies before you, somewhat as ancestral blood moves incessantly within us and mingles with our own to form that unique and unrepeatable compound that we are at every turning of our life.

Yes: I am glad that you have this steady expressible existence with you, this title, this uniform, this duty, all this which is palpable and defined, which in such surroundings with a similarly isolated, not numerous body of men assumes gravity and necessity, betokens a vigilant employment over and above that element of playing and passing the time in the military profession, and not only admits but positively trains an independent alertness. And that we are in circumstances which work upon us, which set us free from time to time to face things that are great and natural, is all that is necessary.

Art too is only a way of living, and one can prepare for it, living somehow, without knowing it; in everything real one is a closer, nearer neighbour to it than in the unreal semi-artistic professions which, while they make show of a relatedness to art, in practice deny and attack the existence of all art, as for instance the whole of journalism does, and almost all criticism and three-quarters of what calls itself and likes to be called literature. I am glad, in a word, that you have overcome the danger of ending up there, and remain solitary and courageous somewhere in a raw reality. May the year that lies before you preserve and strengthen you in that.

Ever yours;

R. M. Rilke.

APPENDIX

DEATH AND BURIAL

(From *Rainer Maria Rilkes Schweizer Jahre*, by J. R. von Salis : Verlag von Hubert & Co., 1936)

DURING the first days in Valmont Rilke was treated by a different doctor from his usual one (Dr. Hämmerli), who was only able to get back from a medical conference abroad on the 9th December. Rilke wished to suffer his illness in complete seclusion. The only thing the public heard about him before the news of his death was a short notice in the papers saying that Rilke had declined his election to the German Academy. He remained true to his freedom to the last. — On the 8th December he wrote a letter in pencil to Frau Wunderly ; the writing is extremely laboured and very uneven, almost unrecognisable. The recipient hastened to Valmont immediately. Rilke had written :

". . . Jour et nuit, jour et nuit : l'Enfer ! on l'aura connu !

" Merci que de tout votre être (je le sens) vous m'accompagnez dans ces régions anonymes.

" Le plus grave, le plus long : c'est d'abdiquer : devenir ' le malade '. Le chien malade est encore chien, toujours. Nous à partir d'un certain degré de souffrances insensées, sommes-nous encore nous ? Il faut devenir le malade, apprendre ce métier absurde sous l'œil des médecins. C'est long. Et je ne serai jamais assez rusé pour ' en tirer profit '. Dans cette affaire je perds. . . ."

In Valmont the doctors, the nurse and Frau Wunderly were the sole witnesses of his long, hard death. Visits, no matter from whom, even from those who had once stood closest to him in life, the sick man forbad repeatedly, almost imploringly. The idea that people might come to view him and pity him in this state was quite insupportable. Also, he voiced anew his wish not to see a priest. In the midst of his dreadful sufferings the thought of his trip to the south of France, to the sea, occupied him continuously. With his usual precision he dictated all orders to his housekeeper in Muzot : more than anything else he desired clean linen and a quantity of books for the journey, which it was his wish to begin as soon as possible.

His words to the last friends who surrounded him changed with the situation and with the state of his sufferings. With the joyful cry " You bring me life ! " he received his ministering friend on her arrival at Valmont. But another time it was: "Help me towards my death." And in the hell of illness he found strength to say: "Never forget, dear one, life is magnificent!" With the approach of Christmas he demanded a writing-pad and pencil so as to send word to his friends; not one of these pages toilsomely written with an aching and bandaged arm is a farewell letter in the literal sense; and yet these last lines of faithful, unspeakably sad remembrance could hardly be misinterpreted. . . . Reports of his illness might only be sent to Lou Andreas-Salomé, whom Rilke credited with an almost supernatural power of understanding the processes in his body and the nature of his malady; three letters came from her, but none contained the solution of the riddle that engrossed him — and a mournful shake of the head was the only sign he gave when he held the letter of his old friend in his hand. No, people could not help him any more.

Whereas in his previous illnesses no pathological symptoms could be established in his blood, after Rilke's arrival in Valmont an acute leucaemia was diagnosed — a rare and incurable disease which, in him, had assumed a particularly grave form unknown to the ordinary medical picture. Yet the inception of the disease was the same as in most cases of acute leucaemia — a septic infection of the skin setting in at the outward point of some slight wound. Rilke was comforted that his sufferings had their cause in a wound given him by the thorn of a rose-tree. During the course of the sickness black ulcers formed on various parts of his body, which burst and bled; the mucous membranes of the nose and mouth were covered with similar little ulcers as far back as the oesophagus, so that it became difficult to slake the sick man's terrible thirst. (They tried giving him liquids through little glass tubes.) According to the testimony of the doctor attending he underwent appalling pain. — The black abscesses were dressed daily and the field of ulceration lightly treated with cocaine (including the inside of the mouth). He had twice wanted to be shaved, and this took place under great difficulties. Also his wish to be looked after by a simple nurse who did not know he was a writer, was granted him. Even during his worst periods he made the nurse read the *Chronique mondaine* from *Figaro* aloud to him every morning; evidently he wished to hear no more than this distant patter of external life, whilst being spared the more important news of the world. In the afternoons Frau Wunderly read to him, often for hours on end, from a volume of the *Cahiers verts*; if she fancied the invalid asleep and broke off her reading, he would call out in an almost commanding voice: "Continuez!"

He welcomed Dr. Hämmerli on his return with the words:

" Dear friend, how good it is you are here, that you know what's wrong, and I am sure you will not tell me." And another time: " It is a comfort to me that you know what surpassing torments I suffer." He refused all words of consolation, absolutely, he only wanted people to *know* of his sufferings. Rilke did not judge his malady by medical and physiological standards. He believed that tremendous happenings had been dammed up in him which were using this physical outburst as an excuse to manifest themselves: " We were such wonderfully good friends, my body and I; I do not know how it is that we have separated and become strangers to one another. For two years I have had the feeling and the absolute certainty that something was piling itself up and up in me, and now the collapse has come." — The appearance of the abscesses had shocked him, but also strengthened him in his idea that there was a special and individual illness for each person. He did not want to know what illness he was suffering from. He did not believe in bacterial causes; he sublimated even this crowning terror as he had sublimated everything else in his life, transferring it into the workings of some metaphysical process. He did not wish to be told of any deteriorations, nor be given medicines or anodynes. (During the treatment care was taken that the necessary alleviation of pain through narcotics should not overstep the limits of merely clouding the consciousness.) Only with difficulty could he be persuaded to accept the visit of a consultant; Dr. Hämmerli had to promise him that it was a doctor who had no thought of tabulating his illness like a schoolmaster: " If you wish," replied Rilke, " but he is only to examine the blood for its own sake and not, in Heaven's name, try to give a professional explanation. Think how terrible it would be if some wretched pedant came and destroyed all this with the banal consolations of a physician's visit."— And indeed two professors did come, from Zürich and Leipzig, the latter on the instructions of the Insel Verlag, to consult by the sick-bed of the poet. — Medical examinations caused him the greatest pain. He was literally like one flayed alive.

In Rilke's talks with his doctor there was a constant recurrence of the fear that this was *nobody's* illness. His old notions of death and sickness as being vast, mysterious occurrences which somewhere have their profound cause and meaning, and therefore cannot be simply reproduced on different people,[1] seem to have engaged his spirit incessantly to the last. Dr. Hämmerli tells how remarkable these conversations were, which always went up to the furthest point where the sick man would have had to utter the word " Death ", but suddenly broke off cautiously, — fearing, perhaps, lest the unseizable be

1 See *Malte Laurids Brigge* (*Collected Works*, vol. v. pp. 13-22).

seized by some medical expression or shattered by a word of comfort. Each time it was wonderful and affecting how, on the doctor's entry into his room, Rilke said to him: "So you're there, dear friend. Somehow you keep everything away."

The witnesses of these events are convinced that for a long time Rilke had no thought of dying. Only three days before his death, thinks the doctor, did he know in his deepest heart that he must die. "Don't tell me how things are going with me," he begged. "If you come in and I am asleep, do not speak to me. But press my hand so that I shall know you are there, and I'll press yours — like this — then you will know I am awake. If I do not press your hand, promise me to prop me up and do something to get me back to my limits again." — Several times during the last two days he said: "Perhaps Lou will understand, after all, what the reason was. . . ."

Parched by raging fevers, with face completely emaciated, the dying man lay in his pillows. On the last night he was quite clear for some time. Then suddenly the swellings in the mouth and on the tongue became so fierce that appalling pains racked him. Afterwards he slept for hours, moaning softly every now and then. The doctor supported him in an upright position with the help of the nurse. To lessen his pain he gave him an injection. — An hour before his death he pressed Dr. Hämmerli's hand with the agreed sign. — Suddenly he looked up with wide-open blue eyes, like a healthy man, gazed for a long time straight in front of him, as though he were seeing someone, clutched convulsively the hands that held him. In this visionary attitude it was not possible to tell that he was dead. — On the 29th December 1926, in the morning at five o'clock, Rilke had passed away. As one of those present opened the window, a cold morning wind blew across from the sea.

On those who saw it the body of the poet left behind a deep impression — the lean, almost brown face, the wonderful brow, whose noble contours still seemed to portray the departed spirit, the fresh beard black on the chin, and the heavy lids sunk over the great mystery — an hieratic head as though of some distinguished Persian or Indian, of a sage who had come from afar off for a brief life and who now, triumphant over martyrdom, lay remote and lifeless on his death-bed. A small Russian cross of silver which he had always worn in life, decked the breast of the dead. Sprays of laurel, which bloomed at that time amid the snow of Valmont, surrounded his face.

In a raw winter's night the coffin was borne out of the clinic and lifted on to a sleigh. The three people who had been round him and tended him to his last breath with sacrificial faithfulness, accompanied the dead poet to a chapel where he was laid on a bier. The old year passed, a new year came in before he left this spot. In a hearse he was led to his last resting-place.

Following Rilke's wish and will his Zürich friends had reserved a grave for him at the foot of the church at Raron "for all time". Though he had entrusted them in his testament with the preparation of his burial-ground and the disposal of his possessions in Muzot, he had stipulated nothing definite concerning the form of his sepulture. That it would be Catholic was made evident by the position of the grave beside the old church at Raron and by the inherited religion of the poet. How eloquently and movingly had he, the God-seeker, described in his "worker-letter" [1] the presence of God in old churches. . . . This high mountain church and its peaceful graveyard, from which Rilke used to gaze out wonderingly and with full heart over the broad valley and the silver Rhone, came to him as the resting-place to which he could bequeath his tired body as to a native soil.

On Sunday, the 2nd January 1927, those of the poet's friends who had not fought shy of the journey and who had to represent a mourning world, were gathered together in the little mountain village in Valais. Without pomp, without official honours, as was meet for the dead who had lived his life far from all worldly vanities, Rainer Maria Rilke was laid in earth. . . . During the quiet mass the coffin was set on a bier in the church. Organ and violin filled the air with the music of Johann Sebastian Bach. With difficulty the sturdy grave-diggers had broken open the frozen earth for the coffin. According to peasant custom, children formed a circle round the open grave. "Without pity the stony clods beat and thudded on the sunken coffin. But those who trembled at the hardness of this moment might have found comfort in the spectacle of the children who, with touching constancy all through the stranger's interment, held the heavy wreaths so high with their frost-blue hands that they did not touch the earth till we lowered the wreaths into the grave, not to overburden it, but to fill it with green. . . ."

Thus the rough winter earth of a humble country churchyard closed over this darling of men, and now that he was given back to his greatest solitude, there remains what the lament of a woman [2] expresses so movingly :

"Rilke is not dead : from Muzot to Raron the way is not long. He lived in a tower on a hill, and the whole land belonged to him. Now he rests at the foot of a church, alone as in Muzot. The church

[1] See p. 342.

[2] Monique Saint-Hélier : "*A Rilke pour Noël*". Berne 1927.

gives him its peace, the angelus in the morning, the angelus in the evening, and the mighty landscape is his. Every cloud, every peak — his ; the roar from the valley, the song of the Rhône rise up to him. When a jackdaw wheels in the sky — it does it for him ; the first snowdrop blossoms for him ; and when the earth under its light burden of snow becomes soft and the scent seeps through and fills the whole region with living life — this scent, too, will be for him. Spring will thaw away the last snows and strain towards him with its great surge."

" And at last they need us no longer who early were ravished away.
Gently we're weaned from the earth, as we mildly outgrow
the breasts of our mother. But we, who have need of such great
secrets, for whom out of sorrow so often arises
blessed advancing : could we have being without them ?
Is the legend in vain how once in the weeping for Linus
a bold first harmony burst the inflexible starkness,
whereupon the tumultuous void, which an all-but divine youth
stepped suddenly out of forever, fell into that timeless
pulsing which now transports us and comforts and helps."

INDEX

(N.B. – Persons listed under "Index of Recipients" on p. xix do not reappear below unless specifically referred to in the text.)

QUARTET ENCOUNTERS

The purpose of this paperback series is to bring together influential and outstanding works of twentieth-century European literature in translation. Each title has an introduction by a distinguished contemporary writer, describing a personal or cultural 'encounter' with the text, as well as placing it within its literary and historical perspective.

Quartet Encounters will concentrate on fiction, although the overall emphasis is upon works of enduring literary merit, whether biography, travel, history or politics. The series will also preserve a balance between new and older works, between new translations and reprints of notable existing translations. Quartet Encounters provides a much-needed forum for prose translation, and makes accessible to a wide readership some of the more unjustly neglected classics of modern European literature.

Aharon Appelfeld · *The Retreat*

Gaston Bachelard · *The Psychoanalysis of Fire*

Robert Bresson · *Notes on the Cinematographer*

Hermann Broch · *The Sleepwalkers*

E.M. Cioran · *The Temptation to Exist*

Stig Dagerman · *The Games of Night*

Grazia Deledda · *After the Divorce*

Marcellus Emants · *A Posthumous Confession*

Carlo Emilio Gadda · *That Awful Mess on Via Merulana*

Andrea Giovene · *Sansevero*

Martin A. Hansen · *The Liar*

Eugene Ionesco · *Fragments of a Journal*

Gustav Janouch · *Conversations with Kafka*

Ismaïl Kadaré · *The General of the Dead Army*

Miroslav Krleža · *On the Edge of Reason*

Pär Lagerkvist · *The Dwarf*

Osip Mandelstam · *The Noise of Time*

Henry de Montherlant · *The Bachelors*

Stratis Myrivilis · *Life in the Tomb*

Luigi Pirandello · *Short Stories*

D.R. Popescu · *The Royal Hunt*

Rainer Maria Rilke · *Rodin and other Prose Pieces*

Rainer Maria Rilke · *Selected Letters*

Lou Andreas-Salomé · *The Freud Journal*

Stanislaw Ignacy Witkiewicz · *Insatiability*